The Complete Books of Enoch, Jasher and Jubilees

A Detailed Collection of the Hidden Scriptures of the Bible

Judah Publishing

Copyright © 2024 Judah Publishing

All rights reserved.

No part of this book may be reproduced, distributed, or transmitted in any form or by any means, including photocopying, recording, or other electronic or mechanical methods, without the prior written permission of the publisher, except in the case of brief quotations embodied in critical reviews and certain other noncommercial uses permitted by copyright law.

Table of Contents

Introduction iv
The Books of Enoch 1
   The Book of Watchers – Enoch's Ethiopic Book 1..1
   The Book of Parables - Enoch's Ethiopic Book 2 15
   The Book of The Luminaries of The Heaven – Enoch's Ethiopic Book 3.................... 32
   The Book of Dream and Vision – Enoch's Ethiopic Book 4 40
   The Epistle of Enoch – Enoch's Ethiopic Book 5 49
The Book of Jasher..59
Book of Jubilees 252

Introduction

Throughout human history, religious and spiritual writings have provided profound insight into the beliefs, values, and worldviews of ancient civilizations. Some texts, preserved outside the official canon, reveal equally powerful narratives and teachings, offering alternate perspectives and historical depth to canonical scriptures. Among these apocryphal works, the Books of Enoch, Jasher, and Jubilees stand out as essential writings that span generations, interweave myth and morality, and provide context to the sacred traditions of ancient Judaism and early Christianity. This compilation of the Books of Enoch, Jasher, and Jubilees seeks to honor these texts, recognizing their role in shaping religious thought and spiritual imagination.

The Books of Enoch, Jasher, and Jubilees have a complex relationship with canonical scriptures. All three originated in the Jewish tradition and were initially circulated alongside other influential texts. Despite their early prominence, they were eventually excluded from the Hebrew Bible's official canon. However, each text continued to influence religious thought, gaining adherents in different sects and cultural traditions, especially in the Ethiopian Orthodox Church, which canonizes both Enoch and Jubilees. Over time, they came to be respected as apocryphal or pseudepigraphal works, providing alternative perspectives on biblical events and doctrines.

The status of these books as "extra-biblical" has led to divergent interpretations. Some communities view them as valuable supplements to the canonical texts, while others interpret them as symbolic or legendary narratives. This complex reception history reflects the theological diversity of ancient Judaism and early Christianity, as well as the role of sacred texts in shaping community identity and belief systems. Whether regarded as historical, allegorical, or theological, the Books of Enoch, Jasher, and Jubilees continue to captivate readers, illuminating ancient perceptions of the divine and humanity's place within the cosmos.

The Books of Enoch

The Books of Enoch, encompassing several ancient Jewish texts, are attributed to the prophet Enoch, the great-grandfather of Noah. These texts hold particular significance within the Ethiopian Orthodox Church, where they are fully recognized and preserved within the biblical canon, in contrast to many other branches of Christianity—such as Protestant, Roman Catholic, and Eastern Orthodox traditions—where they are often categorized as apocryphal or pseudepigraphal. Similarly, mainstream Judaism does not regard these books as canonical, though fragments have been found among the Dead Sea Scrolls, indicating their historical influence.

Scholars believe that the Books of Enoch were written between the 3rd century BCE and the 1st century CE. They are composed of five distinct sections: *The Book of the Watchers*, *The Book of Parables*, *The Astronomical Book*, *The Dream Visions*, and *The Epistle of Enoch*. Together, these texts explore a range of topics from Enoch's visions of heaven, the fall of the angels (or Watchers) who transgressed divine law, to apocalyptic prophecies and detailed descriptions of celestial mechanics.

The Books of Enoch are particularly notable for their rich angelology and cosmology, providing one of the earliest accounts of fallen angels and the moral consequences of their actions on humanity. They also introduce the concept of divine judgment, with vivid imagery depicting the rewards for the righteous and punishment for the wicked. The texts emphasize the importance of moral purity and divine law and offer a complex portrayal of the heavens, contributing substantially to early Jewish and Christian apocalyptic literature.

"BEHOLD, THE BOOK OF THE WORDS OF RIGHTEOUSNESS, THE WORDS OF THE VISION OF ENOCH, TO BLESS THE RIGHTEOUS AND THE CHOSEN WHO WILL BE PRESENT ON THE DAY OF TRIBULATION, TO REMOVE ALL ENEMIES."

The Book of Watchers – Enoch's Ethiopic Book 1

Chapter 1

1. Who will be alive during the time of tribulation, when the wicked and godless are removed?
2. And Enoch, a righteous man, blessed with sight by God, began his vision. He saw the Holy One in the heavens, as shown by the angels, hearing and understanding all that they revealed—not for his own generation, but for a distant one that is to come.
3. He spoke of the chosen and took up his parable concerning them: The Holy Great One will come forth from His dwelling.
4. The eternal God will step upon the earth, even on Mount Sinai, and will reveal His strength, appearing from the heavens.

5. All will be struck with fear, and the watchers shall tremble. A great fear will spread across the earth.
6. High mountains will shake, and towering hills will be made low, melting like wax before the fire.
7. The earth will split apart, and everything on it will perish, for judgment will fall upon all humanity.
8. But with the righteous, He will make peace, protecting the elect with mercy. They shall belong to God, prosper, be blessed, and find His help, and light will shine upon them as He brings peace to them.
9. Behold! He comes with ten thousand of His holy ones to execute judgment upon all, to destroy the ungodly, and to convict all flesh of the works of their ungodliness and of the harsh words spoken against Him.

Chapter 2

1. Look at everything in the heavens; observe how they do not stray from their paths, and see how the celestial bodies rise and set each in its appointed season.
2. Do not transgress against their order. Look at the earth and see all that occurs upon it, from first to last, remaining steadfast without change.
3. Witness the works of God displayed for you. Behold how the earth is filled with water in summer and winter, with clouds, dew, and rain covering it.

Chapter 3

1. Notice how, in winter, all the trees appear withered, shedding their leaves—except for fourteen trees that retain their leaves for two to three years until new leaves grow.

Chapter 4

1. Observe the summer days when the sun is above the earth

2. And people seek shade from its intense heat. The earth itself becomes so hot that one cannot step upon it or a rock due to the heat.

Chapter 5

1. See how the trees cover themselves in green leaves and bear fruit. Take note of all His works, and recognize that the Eternal One has made them this way.
2. All His creations continue their tasks year after year without change, fulfilling what God has ordained.
3. The sea and rivers perform their duties and do not stray from His commands.
4. Yet, you have not been steadfast, nor followed the Lord's commands. Instead, you have turned

away, speaking proud and hard words with impure mouths against His greatness.

5. Hard-hearted ones, you will find no peace. You will curse your days, and the years of your life will vanish, multiplying in eternal condemnation with no mercy for you.

7. In that time, your name will become an everlasting curse to the righteous. Through you, all who curse will curse, and the godless will be cursed because of you.

8. Joy and forgiveness of sins will come to the righteous, with mercy, peace, and patience. Salvation will come to them, a beautiful light.

9. But for all sinners, there will be no salvation; instead, a curse will remain upon you.

10. For the chosen, there will be light, joy, and peace, and they will inherit the earth.

11. Wisdom will be granted to the elect, and they will live without sin, neither through ungodliness nor pride; the wise will remain humble.

12. They will not sin again, nor transgress all their days, nor die from divine anger or wrath. They will complete their allotted days in peace,

13. And their lives will lengthen in joy, with their years multiplying in eternal gladness and peace, all their days.

Chapter 6

1. As humanity grew in numbers, in those days, beautiful daughters were born to them.

2. The angels, sons of heaven, saw these daughters and felt desire, saying to one another, "Let us choose wives from among the children of men,

3. And have children by them." Then Semjaza, their leader, said,

4. "I fear you will not truly agree to do this deed, and I alone will bear the punishment for a great sin."

5. But they all responded, "Let us swear an oath and bind ourselves by a mutual curse,

6. Not to abandon this plan but to fulfill it." They all swore together, binding themselves by a mutual oath.

7. Altogether, they were two hundred who descended in the days of Jared to the summit of Mount Hermon, named so because they had sworn

8. And bound themselves there by a mutual curse.

9. Their leaders were: Samlazaz, their chief, along with Araklba, Rameel, Kokabel, Tamlel, Ramlel, Danel, Ezeqeel, Baraqijal,

10. Asael, Armaros, Batarel, Ananel, Zaqiel, Samsapeel, Satarel, Turel, Jomjael, and Sariel. These were chiefs of tens.

Chapter 7

1. Then, all the others with them took wives, each choosing one, and they began to live with them, defiling themselves and teaching them charms,

2. Enchantments, root-cutting, and made them familiar with plants.

3. The women conceived and bore great giants, whose height was three thousand cubits.
4. These giants consumed all of humanity's provisions, and when men could no longer sustain them, they turned against them
5. And began devouring humanity.
6. They began to sin against birds, beasts, reptiles,
7. And fish, devouring each other's flesh and drinking blood. Then the earth brought accusation against the lawless ones.

Chapter 8

1. Azazel taught humanity to make swords, knives, shields, breastplates, and revealed metals and how to work them, as well as bracelets, ornaments, and the use of antimony. He showed them how to beautify the eyelids, use precious stones,
2. And coloring tinctures. Great wickedness arose, and people engaged in fornication,
3. Becoming corrupt in all their ways. Semjaza taught enchantments and root-cutting; Armaros taught the resolution of enchantments; Baraqijal taught astrology; Kokabel taught the constellations; Ezeqeel taught cloud lore; Araqiel taught earth signs; Shamsiel taught sun signs; and Sariel taught the course of the moon. As people perished, they cried out, and their cry reached the heavens.

Chapter 9

1. Michael, Uriel, Raphael, and Gabriel looked down from heaven
2. And saw much bloodshed on the earth and the widespread lawlessness. They spoke to one another, saying, "The earth, without inhabitants, cries out, raising its voice to the gates of heaven.
3. And now, holy ones in heaven, the souls of men bring their petition, saying, 'Present our case before the Most High.'"
4. They said to the Lord of ages, "Lord of lords, God of gods, King of kings, and God of the ages, the throne of Your glory stands for all generations,
5. And Your name is holy, glorious, and blessed through all ages! You have created all things and hold authority over them. All is exposed before You, and You see everything;
6. Nothing is hidden from You. You see what Azazel has done, teaching all unrighteousness on earth and revealing eternal secrets preserved in heaven,
7. Which humanity has sought to know. And Semjaza, who You appointed to lead his associates,
8. Has gone to the daughters of men, defiling himself and revealing to them all kinds of sin. The women have borne giants,
9. And the earth is now filled with blood and unrighteousness.
10. Now, the souls of the dead cry out, their cries reaching heaven and unable to cease because of the lawlessness on earth.
11. You know all things before they happen, and You see these deeds and let them continue. You do not tell us what we are to do concerning these matters."

Chapter 10

1. Then the Most High, the Holy and Great One, spoke and sent Uriel to the son of Lamech,
2. Saying, "Go to Noah and tell him in My name, 'Hide yourself!' and reveal to him the approaching end: the earth will be destroyed, and a deluge will cover it,
3. Destroying all upon it. Instruct him to escape
4. So that his descendants may continue for future generations." Then the Lord spoke to Raphael, saying, "Bind Azazel, hand and foot, and cast him into the darkness. Create an opening in the desert,
5. In Dudael, and throw him there. Cover him with jagged rocks and darkness, leaving him there forever, blocking his view from any light.
6. On the day of great judgment, he will be thrown into the fire.
7. Heal the earth, which the angels have corrupted, and proclaim its healing so the plague may cease, ensuring humanity does not perish because of the secrets the Watchers disclosed and taught to their children.
8. All sin shall be attributed to Azazel.
9. To Gabriel, the Lord said, "Proceed against the offspring and the godless, the children born of sin. Destroy them, sending them to battle one another.
10. They will not live long. No request made for them by their fathers shall be granted, for they hope for eternal life,
11. Expecting each to live five hundred years." Then the Lord spoke to Michael, "Go, bind Semjaza and his companions who defiled themselves with women,
12. Alongside them in all their impurity. When their children have killed one another, and they witness the ruin of their beloved, bind them for seventy generations in the valleys of the earth, till the day of judgment and eternal condemnation.
13. They will be taken to the abyss of fire,
14. To torment and imprisonment, confined forever. Anyone condemned with them will be bound till the end of all generations.
15. Destroy the spirits of the godless and the offspring of the Watchers,
16. For they have wronged humanity. Let every evil deed cease from the earth, allowing righteousness and truth to flourish in blessing; the works of righteousness shall bring lasting joy and peace.
17. Then the righteous will escape, living to beget thousands, completing their days in peace in youth and old age.
18. The entire earth shall be cultivated in righteousness, filled with trees and blessings.
19. Desirable trees shall be planted, vines yielding abundant wine, and seeds sown will produce a thousandfold, with each olive measure yielding ten presses of oil.
20. Cleanse the earth from oppression, sin, and godlessness, removing all impurities. Humanity will become righteous,
21. All nations will worship and praise Me. The earth shall be cleansed of all defilement, sin,

punishment, and torment, and I will never again bring such things upon it from generation to generation, forever."

Chapter 11

1. In those days, I will open the storehouses of blessings in the heavens
2. To pour them out upon the earth, for the work and labor of humanity. Truth and peace will unite, enduring through all generations.

Chapter 12

1. Before these events, Enoch was hidden, and none among humankind knew his whereabouts—
2. Where he dwelled or what became of him. His tasks involved the Watchers, and his days were spent with the holy ones.
3. And I, Enoch, blessed the Lord of majesty and the King of all ages. Suddenly,
4. The Watchers called me—Enoch, the scribe—and said, "Enoch, scribe of righteousness, go and tell the Watchers of heaven who left the holy, eternal place, defiling themselves with women and acting like earthly beings,
5. Taking wives for themselves. 'You have caused great destruction on the earth, and for you, there will be no peace or forgiveness of sin.
6. Though you delight in your children, you will witness their destruction and weep over them. You will make pleas for eternity, but mercy and peace shall not be yours.'"

Chapter 13

1. Enoch went and declared, "Azazel, you will have no peace. A severe judgment has been issued,
2. Against you to bind you in chains. You will receive no tolerance nor any granted requests because of the unrighteousness you have taught and the works of godlessness,
3. Sin, and iniquity that you have shown to men." Then I went and spoke to all of them together,
4. And they were filled with fear; trembling and dread overtook them. They pleaded with me to draft a petition on their behalf, seeking forgiveness, and to read their appeal before the Lord of heaven.
5. For from that point on, they were unable to speak to Him or lift their eyes to heaven, ashamed of their sins and the condemnation they had received. I wrote down their request, including prayers concerning their spirits and deeds, each request recorded individually, seeking forgiveness and length of days.
6. Then I went and sat by the waters of Dan, in the land of Dan, to the south and west of Mount Hermon, reading their petition until I fell asleep.
7. And as I slept, a dream came to me, visions descended upon me, and I saw scenes of judgment. A voice called, instructing me to tell these visions to the sons of heaven and to reprimand them.

8. When I awoke, I went to them, and there they were, all gathered together, weeping at Abelsjail,
9. Between Lebanon and Seneser, their faces covered. I recounted to them all the visions I had seen in my sleep, and I began to speak the words of righteousness, reprimanding the heavenly Watchers.

Chapter 14

1. This is the book of the words of righteousness and the reprimand of the eternal Watchers,
2. According to the command of the Holy Great One, as revealed in the vision. In my dream, I saw with human understanding—granted by the Great One to express and comprehend wisdom.
3. Just as He granted wisdom to humanity, so He empowered me to reprimand the Watchers,
4. The sons of heaven. I wrote your petition, and in my vision, I saw that it would not be granted;
5. Judgment had been pronounced, and you would not be allowed to return to heaven for eternity. You are bound on earth by this decree.
6. Before then, you will witness the destruction of your beloved sons and find no joy in them, for they shall fall by the sword.
7. Your petition for them will not be granted, nor will your own, even if you plead, pray, and speak all that I have written.
8. In my vision, clouds surrounded me, mist drew me in, and stars and lightning rushed me forward.
9. Winds lifted me up, and I was carried into heaven. I reached a wall built of crystal, surrounded by tongues of fire, which filled me with fear.
10. Passing through the fire, I drew near to a great house of crystal, with walls like a mosaic of crystals and a foundation of crystal.
11. The ceiling was as the path of stars and lightning, with fiery cherubim, and the sky was as clear as water. A blazing fire surrounded the walls, and its doors blazed with flames.
12. I entered the house, feeling heat like fire and cold like ice.
13. There were no pleasures within, only fear and trembling seized me.
14. Shaking, I fell on my face.
15. I saw another house, larger than the first,
16. With an open portal before me, made of flaming fire. Its grandeur and extent exceeded all description.
17. Its floor was of fire, with lightning and stars above,
18. And a ceiling also of flaming fire. There was a high throne within, like crystal, with wheels shining like the sun and cherubim visions surrounding it.
19. From beneath the throne flowed streams of flaming fire, making it impossible to gaze upon.
20. The Great Glory sat upon it, His robe shining brighter than the sun, whiter than any snow.
21. No angel could enter, nor could anyone behold His face, because of the magnificence and glory.
22. Flames surrounded Him, with a great fire before Him, and no one could approach. Ten

thousand times ten thousand stood before Him,
23. Yet He needed no advisor. The most holy ones remained by His side, never departing.
24. Lying prostrate, trembling, I heard the Lord call to me with His voice, saying, "Come near,
25. Enoch, and listen to My word." One of the holy ones helped me up, bringing me near to the door, and I bowed my face down.

Chapter 15

1. He spoke, and I heard His voice, "Fear not, Enoch, righteous man and scribe of righteousness.
2. Approach and hear My voice. Go, tell the Watchers of heaven, who sent you to plead for them: 'You should intercede for humanity, not humanity for you.
3. Why did you leave the high, holy, and eternal heaven, lying with women, defiling yourselves with the daughters of men,
4. And taking wives, behaving like the children of earth and begetting giants as sons? Though you were holy, spiritual, living an eternal life, you have defiled yourselves with the blood of women, lusting after flesh and blood, like those who perish.
5. I gave humanity wives so they might bear children,
6. Ensuring nothing would be lacking on earth. But you were spiritual,
7. Living the eternal life, immortal throughout all generations. Therefore, I did not appoint wives for you, for the spiritual beings of heaven have their dwelling in heaven.
8. Now, the giants born from spirits and flesh shall be called evil spirits upon the earth,
9. And they will dwell on earth. Evil spirits come forth from their bodies because they are born of humans and the holy Watchers,
10. Making them evil spirits on earth. Heaven is the home for heavenly spirits, but spirits born on earth will remain on earth.
11. The spirits of the giants afflict, oppress, destroy, and fight, bringing destruction and trouble; they hunger and thirst,
12. Though they take no food, and cause offense. These spirits will rise against humanity and the women from whom they came.

Chapter 16

1. From the days of the giants' slaughter and death, as their flesh decayed, the spirits emerged, wreaking destruction without judgment. They will continue until the day of completion, the great judgment ending the age,
2. Consummating judgment over the Watchers and the godless forever." To the Watchers who sent you to intercede, say,
3. "Though you were in heaven, you did not know all mysteries. The insignificant secrets you learned, you revealed to women, leading to great evil on earth."
4. Say to them, "You shall have no peace."

Chapter 17

1. They brought me to a place where those present appeared as flames of fire,
2. Yet could take on human form when they desired. They guided me to a place of darkness and a mountain whose summit touched the heavens.
3. I saw the realms of the luminaries and the storehouses of the stars and thunder, in the deepest depths,
4. Where there was a fiery bow, arrows, a quiver, a fiery sword, and flashes of lightning. They led me to the waters of life,
5. And to the western fire, which receives the setting of the sun.
6. I came to a river of fire, where flames flowed like water, emptying into the vast sea toward the west. I saw mighty rivers and came to a great river and a place of deep darkness,
7. Reaching the region where no living being treads. I beheld the mountains of winter's darkness and the source
8. From which all the waters of the abyss flow. I saw the mouths of every earthly river and the mouth of the abyss.

Chapter 18

1. I observed the storehouses of all the winds, seeing how He furnished creation with them
2. And laid the earth's foundations. I saw the cornerstone of the earth and the four winds
3. That bear up the earth and the firmament of heaven. I saw the winds that expand the heavenly vault, stationed between heaven and earth as the pillars of the heavens.
4. I witnessed the winds of heaven turning to guide the sun
5. And all the stars to their settings. I saw the earthbound winds that carry clouds, and I saw the paths of the angels.
6. At the earth's edge, I saw the firmament of heaven above. Moving forward, I saw a place burning both day and night, where seven mountains stood made of beautiful stones,
7. Three towards the east and three towards the south. The eastern mountains were of varied colors—one of colored stone, one of pearl, and one of jacinth—while the southern mountains were of red stone.
8. The central mountain rose to heaven, resembling God's throne, made of alabaster, with a sapphire peak.
9. And I saw a blazing fire.
10. Beyond these mountains lay the realm where earth comes to an end; there, the heavens were completed.
11. I saw a deep abyss with columns of heavenly fire, and within them, pillars of fire fell, beyond measure in height and depth.
12. Beyond that abyss, I found a place without the heavens above or the solid ground beneath; no

water
13. Or birds, only a vast, desolate, and dreadful place. I saw seven stars like burning mountains,
14. And when I inquired about them, the angel told me, "This is the end of heaven and earth; it has become a prison for the stars and the hosts of heaven.
15. These stars that roll over the fire transgressed the Lord's command from the beginning of their rising,
16. For they failed to appear at their appointed times. In His anger, He bound them until their sins are fulfilled after ten thousand years."

Chapter 19

1. Uriel said to me, "Here stand the angels who united with women, and their spirits, assuming various forms, defiled humankind, leading them astray to worship demons as gods. Here they shall stand until the day of great judgment,
2. When they will be condemned until their end. The women of the angels,
3. Who went astray, will become sirens." I, Enoch, alone saw this vision of the end of all things, and no one shall see as I have seen.

Chapter 20

1. Here are the names of the holy angels who keep watch.
2. Uriel, one of the holy angels, presides over the world and Tartarus.
3. Raphael, one of the holy angels, presides over the spirits of men.
4. Raguel, one of the holy angels, takes vengeance upon the world of the luminaries.
5. Michael, one of the holy angels, is set over the best of humankind and over chaos.
6. Saraqael, one of the holy angels, is set over the spirits who sin in the spirit.
7. Gabriel, one of the holy angels, presides over Paradise, the serpents, and the cherubim.
8. Remiel, one of the holy angels, is appointed by God over those who rise.

Chapter 21

1. I proceeded to a place of chaos,
2. Where I saw something terrible: there was neither a heaven above nor a firmly founded earth, only a chaotic and dreadful place.
3. There I saw seven stars of heaven bound together, like great mountains ablaze with fire.
4. I asked, "For what sin are they bound, and why have they been cast here?"
5. Uriel, one of the holy angels with me, and chief over them, replied, "Enoch, why do you ask, and why seek the truth?
6. These are the stars of heaven that transgressed the Lord's command and are bound here until their sins are fulfilled after ten thousand years."
7. From there, I went to another place, even more dreadful than the last, where I saw an alarming sight: a great fire blazing and cleaving down to the abyss, filled with immense descending

columns of fire. Its extent was beyond measure or imagination.
8. I said, "How terrifying this place is, and how dreadful to behold!"
9. Uriel, one of the holy angels with me, answered, "Enoch, why are you so fearful?"
10. I replied, "Because of this frightening place and the sight of this suffering." Uriel said to me, "This place is the prison of the angels, where they will be confined forever."

Chapter 22

1. From there, I went to another place, where I was shown a high mountain in the west made of solid rock.
2. This mountain contained four deep, wide, and incredibly smooth hollow places, which were dark and profound to gaze upon.
3. Then Raphael, one of the holy angels with me, said, "These hollow places were created to gather the spirits of the dead,
4. So that all the souls of humankind may assemble here. These places have been prepared to hold them until the day of their judgment, the time set for the great judgment."
5. I saw the spirits of dead people, and their voices rose to heaven, pleading.
6. Then I asked Raphael, the angel who was with me, "Whose spirit is this that makes such pleas and sends its voice to heaven?"
7. He answered, "This is the spirit of Abel, slain by his brother Cain. It cries out against him until Cain's descendants are removed from the earth and his line is cut off from humankind."
8. I then asked about these hollow places and why they were separated.
9. He explained, "These three places were made to separate the spirits of the dead. One division is for the righteous, where there is a bright spring of water.
10. Another is for sinners who died and were buried without judgment during their lifetimes.

11. Here they suffer great pain until the day of judgment and punishment when those who cursed will face eternal retribution.
12. There, they will be bound forever. Another division is for the spirits of those who plead for justice, revealing their destruction from the days of sinners.
13. The last is for those who were not righteous but were sinners, completely immersed in transgression. Their spirits are placed here as companions to other transgressors, but they will not die on judgment day nor be raised from this place."
14. Then I praised the Lord of glory, saying, "Blessed is the Lord, the righteous ruler forever."

Chapter 23

1. From there, I traveled to a place at the western edge of the earth.
2. I saw an unceasingly burning fire that ran its course without pause, day or night.
3. I asked, "What is this fire that never rests?"

4. Raguel, one of the holy angels with me, answered, "This continuous fire is the flame of the west, which pursues all the heavenly lights."

Chapter 24

1. From there, I went to another place on earth, where I was shown a range of mountains burning with fire, day and night.
2. Beyond it, I saw seven splendid mountains, each unique in appearance. Their stones were magnificent and beautiful, forming a glorious and remarkable sight. Three mountains stood toward the east, each set upon the other, and three toward the south, also placed one upon the other. The mountains were separated by deep, rugged ravines that did not intersect.
3. The seventh mountain, standing in the middle, surpassed the others in height, resembling a throne. Fragrant trees surrounded it.
4. Among these trees, I found one unlike any I had ever seen, with a fragrance surpassing all others. Its leaves, blossoms, and wood never wither,
5. And its fruit, beautiful in appearance, resembled the dates of a palm. I said, "How beautiful and fragrant this tree is, with its lovely leaves and delightful blossoms."
6. Then Michael, one of the holy and honored angels with me, and their leader, responded.

Chapter 25

1. He said to me, "Enoch, why do you inquire about the fragrance of this tree and desire to learn its significance?"
2. I replied, "I wish to know everything, especially about this tree."
3. He answered, "This high mountain you see, whose summit resembles God's throne, is indeed His throne, where the Holy Great One, the Lord of Glory, the Eternal King, will sit when He visits the earth in goodness.
4. Regarding this fragrant tree, no mortal may touch it until the day of great judgment when He will exact vengeance and bring all to completion forever. Then, it shall be given to the righteous and holy.
5. Its fruit will be food for the chosen, and it will be transplanted to the holy place, the Lord's eternal temple.
6. They will rejoice with joy, entering the holy place, and its fragrance will be within their bones. They shall live long lives on earth, as did their ancestors, free from sorrow, plague, torment, or calamity."
7. Then I blessed the God of Glory, the Eternal King, who has prepared such blessings for the righteous, creating and promising them as gifts.

Chapter 26

1. From there, I traveled to the earth's center, where I saw a blessed place filled with trees bearing ever-blooming branches from a single tree.

2. I saw a holy mountain, and beneath it, on the eastern side, a stream flowed toward the south.
3. To the east, I saw another mountain higher than the first, with a deep and narrow ravine between them, in which a stream ran beneath the mountain.
4. To the west of these was another, lower mountain of slight elevation, with a deep, dry ravine between them. Another deep, dry ravine was at the ends of the three mountains.
5. The ravines were all deep and narrow, formed of solid rock, with no trees upon them. I marveled at the rocks and the ravine, astonished by its depth and ruggedness.

Chapter 27

1. Then I asked, "What purpose does this blessed land serve, filled entirely with trees, and the accursed valley beside it?"
2. Uriel, one of the holy angels with me, answered, "This valley of curse is for those who are cursed forever. Here, all who speak against the Lord, uttering harsh words and defaming His glory, will be gathered. This will be their place of judgment.
3. In the last days, the righteous will witness the spectacle of judgment upon them, in the presence of the righteous, forever. Here, the merciful will bless the Lord of Glory, the Eternal King.
4. During the days of judgment upon the former, they will bless Him for the mercy He has shown, in assigning them their fate."
5. Then I praised the Lord of Glory, proclaiming His glory and praising Him magnificently.

Chapter 28

1. From there, I traveled east, entering a mountainous region of the desert, and I saw a solitary wilderness filled with trees and plants.
2. Water flowed from above,
3. Rushing like a mighty river toward the northwest, causing clouds and dew to rise on all sides.

Chapter 29

1. Then I went to another place in the desert, approaching the eastern side of this mountain range.
2. There, I found aromatic trees, exuding the fragrances of frankincense and myrrh. The trees resembled almond trees.

Chapter 30

1. Beyond these, I traveled further east and saw another place, a valley filled with water.
2. Within this valley was a tree with a color similar to fragrant trees, like the mastic.
3. On the sides of the valley, I saw fragrant cinnamon, and beyond this, I continued eastward.

Chapter 31

1. I came upon other mountains, where groves of trees flourished, and nectar called Sarara and Galbanum flowed from them.
2. Beyond these mountains, to the easternmost part of the earth, I saw another mountain covered with aloe trees, each filled with stacte, resembling almond trees.
3. When burned, the aroma was sweeter than any fragrant smell.

Chapter 32

1. After experiencing these fragrances, I looked north over the mountains and saw seven mountains full of choice nard, fragrant trees, cinnamon, and pepper.
2. Then I traveled over the peaks of these mountains far to the east, passed above the Erythraean Sea, and went beyond it, passing over the angel Zotiel.
3. I arrived at the Garden of Righteousness, and from a distance, I saw trees more numerous and greater than any others. Two trees stood out, beautiful, glorious, and magnificent—the Tree of Knowledge, whose holy fruit bestows great wisdom.
4. This tree was as tall as a fir, with leaves like those of the carob tree, and its fruit clustered like grapes on a vine, exceptionally beautiful. The fragrance of this tree extended far.
5. I said, "How beautiful is this tree, and how pleasing to behold!"
6. Then Raphael, the holy angel with me, responded, "This is the Tree of Wisdom. Your forefathers, old in age, ate from it, and upon eating, they gained wisdom. Their eyes were opened, they realized their nakedness, and they were expelled from the garden."

Chapter 33

1. From there, I traveled to the ends of the earth, where I saw great beasts, each distinct from the other, and birds that varied in appearance, beauty, and voice, each different from the next.
2. To the east of these creatures, I saw the edge of the earth, where the heavens rest, and where the portals of heaven open.
3. I observed how the stars of heaven emerge and counted the portals from which they proceed. I recorded the paths of each star, noting their numbers, names, courses, positions, times, and months, as Uriel, the holy angel with me, explained.
4. He revealed all these things to me, writing down their names, laws, and groupings for me.

Chapter 34

1. Then I traveled north to the ends of the earth, where I saw an extraordinary and magnificent structure at the earth's boundary. There, I saw three portals of heaven open in the sky, through which north winds blow, bringing cold, hail, frost, snow, dew, and rain.
3. One portal allows the winds to blow favorably, but the other two portals release winds with force and hardship upon the earth, blowing violently.

Chapter 35

1. From there, I went west to the ends of the earth and saw three heavenly portals open, identical to those I had seen in the east, with the same number of portals and outlets.

Chapter 36

1. Then I traveled south to the ends of the earth and saw three open portals in the heavens there.
2. Through these portals come dew, rain, and wind. From there, I returned east to the edge of the heavens, where I saw three eastern portals open, with smaller portals above them.
3. Through these small portals, the stars of heaven pass, following their course to the west along the paths shown to them. Each time I observed these wonders, I blessed the Lord of Glory, continually offering praise to the Lord of Glory, who has created such great and wondrous works. He has revealed the splendor of His creation to angels, spirits, and humankind so that they might witness and praise His might, marvel at the works of His hands, and bless Him forever.

The Book of Parables - Enoch's Ethiopic Book 2

Chapter 37

1. This is the second vision that Enoch, the son of Jared, son of Mahalalel, son of Cainan, son of Enos, son of Seth, son of Adam, received—a vision of wisdom.
2. And these are the initial words of wisdom that I raised my voice to proclaim to those on earth: "Listen, you who lived in ancient times, and you who come later, to the words of the Holy One, which I will speak before the Lord of Spirits.
3. It might have been fitting to share this only with the people of old, but we will not withhold the beginning of wisdom even from those who come after.
4. Until now, such wisdom has not been given by the Lord of Spirits as I have received according to my understanding, by the good will of the Lord of Spirits, who has granted me the gift of eternal life.
5. Three parables were given to me, and I raised my voice to tell them to those who dwell on earth."

Chapter 38

1. The first parable: When the assembly of the righteous appears, and sinners are judged for their deeds, they will be banished from the face of the earth.
2. When the Righteous One is revealed before the eyes of the just, whose chosen works are upheld by the Lord of Spirits, light will appear for the righteous and the elect who live on earth. Where then will sinners dwell, and where will those who denied the Lord of Spirits find rest? It

would have been better if they had never been born.
3. When the secrets of the righteous are unveiled and the sinners judged, the ungodly will be driven away from the presence of the righteous and the chosen.
4. From that time, those who possess the earth will no longer be mighty or exalted, and they will not be able to look upon the face of the holy, for the Lord of Spirits has made His light shine upon the faces of the holy, righteous, and chosen.
5. Then, the kings and the powerful will perish and be handed over to the righteous and holy.
6. And from that time, none will seek mercy from the Lord of Spirits, for their lives will have come to an end.

Chapter 39

1. In those days, the chosen and holy children will descend from heaven,
2. And their offspring will be united with the children of men. During those times, Enoch received books of zeal and wrath, as well as books of unrest and banishment. And the Lord of Spirits declared that they would receive no mercy.
3. In those days, a whirlwind carried me from the earth and set me down at the ends of the heavens.
4. There, I saw another vision—dwellings for the holy and resting places for the righteous.
5. My eyes saw their homes with the righteous angels, and their resting places with the holy. They offered prayers, intercessions, and pleas for humanity, and righteousness flowed before them like water, while mercy descended like dew upon the earth. Such will be their state forever.
6. In that place, I saw the Chosen One of righteousness and faith, dwelling beneath the wings of the Lord of Spirits. Righteousness will flourish during His time, and the number of the righteous and chosen will be without end before Him for all eternity.
7. All the righteous and chosen will be as bright as fiery lights before Him, their mouths full of blessings, and their lips will praise the name of the Lord of Spirits. Righteousness will never fail before Him, and uprightness will never falter.
8. I desired to dwell there, and my spirit longed for that place. That has been my appointed portion, as it was decreed for me before the Lord of Spirits.
9. During those days, I praised and exalted the name of the Lord of Spirits with blessings and songs, for He has destined me for blessings and glory according to His good pleasure.
10. For a long time, my eyes observed that place, and I continued to bless and praise, saying, "Blessed is He, and may He be praised from the beginning and forevermore." There is no end to His existence; He knew all things before the creation of the world and knows what will happen from generation to generation.
11. Those who do not sleep bless You; they stand before Your glory, offering praise, and proclaiming, "Holy, holy, holy is the Lord of Spirits; He fills the earth with spirits."
12. There, I saw all those who do not sleep; they stand before Him, praising and declaring, "Blessed are You, and blessed is Your name, O Lord, forever and ever."

Chapter 40

1. After this, I saw a multitude—thousands upon thousands and myriads upon myriads—standing before the Lord of Spirits.
2. I noticed four distinct figures among them, who approached the Lord of Spirits. I recognized their appearance; they neither rested nor slumbered but stood before the Lord in continual praise.
3. I heard the voices of the four beings as they offered praise before the Lord of Glory.
4. The first voice blessed the Lord of Spirits forever.
5. The second voice blessed the Chosen One and the chosen ones who rely on the Lord of Spirits.
6. The third voice praised the holy ones and the spirits of the righteous.
7. The fourth voice removed wicked spirits, preventing them from standing before the Lord of Spirits and accusing the saints of the earth.
8. I then asked the angel who was with me, "Who are these four figures whose voices I have noted and whose praises I have written down?"
9. He replied, "The first is Michael, full of mercy and long-suffering; the second, who watches over the wounds and sufferings of humanity, is Raphael; The third, who holds power over all, is Gabriel; and the fourth, who is responsible for repentance and the hope of those who will inherit eternal life, is Phanuel."
10. These are the four angels of the Lord of Spirits, and these are the four voices I heard during my vision.

Chapter 41

1. After this, I was shown all the secrets of the heavens, the ways in which the kingdom is divided, and how the actions of men are measured on the scales.
2. I saw the dwellings of the elect and the holy, protected under the wings of the Lord of Spirits.
3. All the righteous and chosen ones appeared as radiant lights, their mouths full of blessings as they praised the name of the Lord of Spirits forever.
4. There, I also saw the mysteries of lightning and thunder—how they are set apart and how they return to their places at appointed times.
5. I saw the storehouses of the wind and the way they are divided.
6. I saw the storehouses of the rain and dew, separated by the clouds that carry them over the earth.
7. I observed the chambers of the sun and moon, noting where they come from, where they return, and how one surpasses the other in brilliance.
8. I watched their grand rotation, creating day and night in perfect order, never deviating or ceasing.
9. I saw the radiant mysteries of the stars, arranged by divine order, each called by name and fulfilling its unique station.

Chapter 42

1. Wisdom searched for a place to dwell but found none. Although she desired a home, she found no place.
2. So Wisdom returned to her origin, taking her place among the angels.
3. Meanwhile, iniquity emerged from its dwelling, seeking the children of men. It established its foundation upon the earth, bringing wrongs continuously in its path.

Chapter 43

1. I saw another spectacle among the stars of heaven, and observed that each was called by name.
2. I watched the paths of light as they moved through the heavens. I measured their distances and calculated the balance of their orbits.
3. I saw how their rotations produced radiant flames, each unique in brilliance, with one flame surpassing another in brightness.

Chapter 44

1. Again, I saw another wonder regarding the stars: they moved like blazing fire but maintained their designated paths.

Chapter 45

1. This is the second parable, concerning those who deny the name of the Lord of Spirits. They will not ascend to heaven, nor will they walk upon the earth.
2. This is the destiny of the sinners who deny the name of the Lord of Spirits. They will be preserved for a day of torment and suffering.
3. On that day, the Elect One will sit on the throne of glory, and His deeds will go forth before Him. The scales of justice will weigh the deeds of sinners, and their works will be measured.
4. Heaven and earth will rejoice, and the chosen ones from heaven will reside among them.
5. On that day, the Elect One will dwell among the righteous, and the chosen will walk beside Him. All will behold His glory.
6. Sin will disappear from the earth, and righteousness will flourish. The righteous will inherit eternal life, and the Lord of Spirits will dwell among them forever.

Chapter 46

1. I saw the Elect One seated on the throne of glory, appearing like a man but filled with majesty and splendor.
2. All the kings, the mighty, and the exalted of the earth stood before Him, lowering their faces in reverence.
3. They trembled, overwhelmed by fear, unable to lift their eyes to gaze upon Him.

4. The powerful ones of the earth attempted to speak but were silenced, their thoughts vanishing, and they were seized by terror.
5. I saw the angels of punishment preparing chains and weapons to bring justice to the kings and mighty ones of the earth.
6. They will be delivered into the hands of the righteous and the chosen, unable to elevate themselves above the chosen, for judgment will be swift, and they will fall from their positions of power.
7. The Elect One will judge them with righteousness and truth, for He is the appointed ruler over all.

Chapter 47

1. In those days, the prayers of the righteous and the blood of the just will rise up to the Lord of Spirits.
2. During that time, the holy ones who dwell above in the heavens will unite in one voice, offering praise and thanks to the Lord of Spirits on behalf of the righteous who endure hardship. They will call upon the Lord of Spirits, acknowledging the spilled blood of the just, and pray that their pleas and cries be heard so they may receive justice for their suffering.
3. Then, the Holy One will hear them and respond with judgment. The days of sinners will come to an end, and all forms of oppression will cease.
4. The earth will be cleansed of all injustice, and wrongdoers will be removed from its face. The righteous will live in peace, and their prayers will be answered.

Chapter 48

1. In that place, I saw a fountain of righteousness that was endless, surrounded by springs of wisdom. All who were thirsty came to drink and were filled with wisdom.
2. At that moment, the Son of Man was named in the presence of the Lord of Spirits,
3. Before the stars of heaven were created and before the foundations of the earth were laid.
4. He was named and chosen to be the light of the righteous, to reign over them and give them strength and hope.
5. Through His name, they will find salvation, and all nations of the earth will bow down to Him in homage.
6. He will be a light to the nations, and His presence will bring peace.
7. The kings and mighty ones of the earth will fall before Him, and none will be able to stand against Him.
8. He will fill the chosen with wisdom and righteousness, and they will rejoice in His presence forever.
9. The righteous and the elect will be saved through His name, and their inheritance will be eternal life.

Chapter 49

1. The Lord of Spirits has poured out wisdom like water upon the righteous, with no need to conceal it.
2. Wisdom serves as their light and the source of their glory.
3. The wisdom of the Lord of Spirits has filled the righteous and the elect, enabling them to live in peace forever. The power of the Lord of Spirits will dwell with them, and they will be with the Son of Man, in eternal glory and righteousness.
4. The Lord of Spirits will fill the chosen ones with the spirit of wisdom, so they will live in peace and righteousness for all time.

Chapter 50

1. In those days, a transformation will occur for the holy and the chosen. They will experience an enduring light upon them, and honor and glory will be granted to the holy.
2. This will take place on the day of affliction, when the stored-up evil is unleashed upon sinners. The righteous will emerge victorious in the name of the Lord of Spirits. God will cause sinners to witness the triumph of the righteous, giving them a chance to repent and turn from their wickedness.
3. Yet, they will not gain honor by the name of the Lord of Spirits. Even so, through His name, they may find salvation, for the Lord of Spirits is merciful.
4. The Lord is just in His judgments, and unrighteousness cannot remain in His presence. Those who refuse to repent will perish before Him.
5. From this time forward, the Lord of Spirits declares that there will be no more mercy for those who remain unrepentant.

Chapter 51

1. In those days, the earth will return everything that has been entrusted to it. Sheol will give back what it has received, and the underworld will release what it owes,
2. For in those days, the Elect One will arise. The Elect One will choose the righteous and the holy among them, for the day of their salvation is near.
3. The Elect One will sit on God's throne, and from His mouth will flow all the secrets of wisdom and counsel, given to Him by the Lord of Spirits, who has glorified Him.
4. In those days, the mountains will leap like rams, and the hills will skip like lambs, filled with joy.
5. All the angels in heaven will shine with happiness, and the earth will rejoice. The righteous will dwell upon it, and the chosen will walk upon the land.

Chapter 52

1. After those days, I was taken to the place where I had seen hidden things in my visions. I was carried by a whirlwind toward the west.
2. There, I saw mountains made of iron, copper, silver, gold, soft metal, and lead.
3. I asked the angel with me, "What are these things that I have seen in secret?"
4. He answered, "These things are for the dominion of the Anointed One, to make Him powerful upon the earth."
5. Then the angel of peace said, "Wait a little, and all the hidden things surrounding the Lord of Spirits will be revealed to you."
6. He continued, "These mountains of iron, copper, silver, gold, soft metal, and lead will all melt before the Elect One, like wax before fire or like water flowing down. They will be powerless before His feet."
7. In those days, wealth will not save anyone—neither gold nor silver—and no one will escape judgment.
8. Iron will no longer be used in war, and armor will be of no value. Bronze will serve no purpose, tin will hold no worth, and lead will no longer be sought.
9. All these things will be removed from the earth when the Elect One appears before the Lord of Spirits.

Chapter 53

1. My eyes saw a deep valley with open mouths. All the inhabitants of the earth, sea, and islands will bring gifts, offerings, and homage to Him, yet the valley will never be filled.
2. Their hands commit lawless deeds, and sinners devour those they oppress. Yet, they will be destroyed before the face of the Lord of Spirits and removed from His earth. They will perish forever.
3. I saw all the angels of punishment residing there, preparing instruments of destruction for Satan.
4. I asked the angel of peace, "For whom are these instruments being prepared?"
5. He replied, "They are prepared for the kings and the mighty of the earth, so that they may be destroyed by them."
6. After this, the Righteous and Elect One will reveal the house of His congregation. From that moment, they will no longer be hindered in the name of the Lord of Spirits.
7. These mountains will no longer stand firm but will flow like water, and the righteous will find rest from the oppression of the sinners.

Chapter 54

1. I looked and turned to another part of the earth, where I saw a deep valley filled with burning fire.
2. The kings and the mighty were brought there and cast into this deep valley.
3. In that place, I saw how they were bound with iron chains of immeasurable weight.
4. I asked the angel of peace, "For whom are these chains prepared?"
5. He replied, "These chains are prepared for the hosts of Azazel, to bind them and cast them into the abyss of complete condemnation. Rough stones will cover their jaws, as the Lord of Spirits has decreed."
6. On that great day, Michael, Gabriel, Raphael, and Phanuel will seize them and cast them into the burning furnace, where the Lord of Spirits will bring vengeance upon them for their sins. They had submitted to Satan and led humanity astray.
7. In those days, punishment will come from the Lord of Spirits, and He will open all the chambers of waters above the heavens and the fountains beneath the earth.
8. All the waters will join together—the masculine waters above the heavens and the feminine waters beneath the earth.
9. These waters will destroy all who dwell on the earth and those who live under the heavens.
10. When the sinners realize the wrongs they have committed on the earth, they will perish by these waters.

Chapter 55

1. Afterward, the Ancient of Days repented, saying, "In vain have I destroyed all who dwell on the earth."
2. He swore by His great name, "From now on, I will not do so to those who live on the earth. I will set a sign in the heavens as a pledge of faith between Me and them, lasting as long as the heavens remain above the earth. This is in accordance with My command."
3. When I choose to take hold of them by the hand of the angels during the day of tribulation and affliction, My chastisement and wrath will remain upon them, says the Lord of Spirits.
4. "You mighty kings who dwell on the earth will see My Elect One. He will sit upon the throne of glory and judge Azazel, all his followers, and his entire host, in the name of the Lord of Spirits."

Chapter 56

1. And I saw the hosts of the angels of punishment advancing, holding scourges and chains of iron and bronze.
2. I asked the angel of peace who was with me, "Where are those holding the scourges going?"
3. He answered, "They are going to their chosen and beloved ones, to cast them into the abyss of the valley."
4. Then that valley will be filled with their chosen and beloved, and the days of their lives will end. Their days of leading others astray will no longer be counted.

5. In those days, the angels will return and descend upon the Parthians and Medes, stirring up the kings so that a spirit of unrest comes upon them. They will rise from their thrones, breaking out like lions from their dens and like hungry wolves among their flocks.

6. They will tread upon the land of the Elect, turning it into a threshing-floor and a highway.

7. However, the city of the righteous will hinder their horses. They will begin to fight among themselves, and one hand will rise against the other. A man will not recognize his brother, nor a son his father or mother, until countless corpses lie from the slaughter, and their punishment is not in vain.

8. In those days, Sheol will open its jaws, and they will be swallowed up within it. Their destruction will be complete, and Sheol will consume the sinners in the presence of the Elect.

Chapter 57

1. After this, I saw another host of wagons and riders coming on the winds from the east, west, and south.

2. The noise of their wagons echoed, and when this commotion occurred, the holy ones in heaven remarked upon it, and the pillars of the earth trembled. The sound was heard from one end of heaven to the other, in a single day.

3. They shall all fall down and worship the Lord of Spirits. This marks the end of the second Parable.

Chapter 58

1. I began to speak the third Parable concerning the righteous and the elect.

2. "Blessed are you, righteous and elect, for glorious shall be your inheritance.

3. The righteous will dwell in the light of the sun, and the elect in the light of eternal life. Their days shall be endless, and the days of the holy will be without number.

4. They shall seek the light and find righteousness with the Lord of Spirits. There will be peace for the righteous in the name of the Eternal Lord.

5. After this, it will be said to the holy ones in heaven that they should seek out the mysteries of righteousness, the heritage of faith. For it has shone upon the earth like the sun, and the darkness has passed away.

6. There will be a light that never fades, with days that know no end, for darkness will have been destroyed, and the light established before the Lord of Spirits. The light of uprightness will be fixed forever before the Lord of Spirits.

Chapter 59

1. In those days, my eyes saw the mysteries of the lightning, the lights, and the judgments they execute. They flash forth for either a blessing or a curse, as the Lord of Spirits wills.

2. There, I saw the secrets of thunder and how its sound is heard in heaven above. He allowed me to witness the judgments executed upon the earth, whether for well-being and blessing or for a

curse, according to the word of the Lord of Spirits.
3. Afterward, all the mysteries of the lights and lightnings were shown to me. They shine forth for blessing and satisfaction.

The Book Of Noah – Apocryphal Part Of Noah's Book Excluded From Canonical Bible

Chapter 60

1. In the year five hundred, in the seventh month, on the fourteenth day of Enoch's life, I saw a vision. A mighty shaking caused the heavens to tremble, and the heavenly host, a multitude of thousands upon thousands of angels,
2. Were disturbed with a great disquiet. The Head of Days was seated on His throne of glory, and the angels and the righteous stood around Him.
3. A powerful trembling overtook me; fear seized me, and I felt weak, my strength failing, so I fell upon my face.
4. Michael sent another angel from among the holy ones to raise me up, and when he had lifted me, my spirit returned, for I could not endure the sight of that host and the shaking of the heavens.
5. Michael said to me, "Why are you troubled by such a vision? Until today, His mercy has lasted, and He has been patient and long-suffering with those on earth.
6. But when the day, the power, the punishment, and the judgment arrive—which the Lord of Spirits has prepared for those who do not follow the righteous law, those who deny His judgment, and those who profane His name—that day is prepared: for the elect, a covenant; for sinners, an inquisition.
7. On that day, two monsters will be separated: a female monster, Leviathan, to dwell in the abyss of the ocean over the fountains of the waters;
8. And a male, named Behemoth, who will reside in a desolate wilderness called Duidain, east of the garden where the elect and righteous dwell, where my forefather, the seventh from Adam, was taken up.
9. I asked the other angel to show me the might of these monsters, how they were separated in a single day, with one cast into the sea's depths and the other to the dry land of the wilderness.
10. He said to me, "You, son of man, seek to understand mysteries that are hidden."
11. The other angel with me revealed secrets of the heavens above, the depths of the earth below, and the ends of the heavens and their foundation.
12. He showed me the storehouses of the winds, how they are divided, weighed, and measured according to their power.
13. He showed me the light of the moon, which is righteous, led by the angels of heaven. He also revealed the laws governing the stars and lights, and how they all obey Him.
14. Thunder has resting places assigned to it while awaiting its sound. Thunder and lightning move together, guided by the spirit, yet they are distinct; they follow in harmony and do not separate.

15. When lightning flashes, thunder follows with its voice, and the spirit pauses, dividing the sound equally. The treasury of their peals is vast, like the sand, and each peal is restrained by a bridle, controlled by the spirit and directed across the earth.

16. The spirit of the sea is powerful, holding it back with a rein and then releasing it, dispersing its waters among the mountains.

17. The spirit of frost has its own angel, and the spirit of hail is under the care of a good angel.

18. The spirit of snow, in its strength, emerges from its chambers with a unique spirit, and what ascends from it is like smoke, called frost.

19. The spirit of mist is separate from other elements, residing in its own chamber. Its journey is magnificent, moving in both light and darkness, winter and summer, under the guidance of an angel.

20. The spirit of dew dwells at the ends of the heavens, connected to the rain chambers. Its course continues through winter and summer, as the clouds of dew and mist are interconnected.

21. When the spirit of rain leaves its chamber, angels open it and lead it out. As it spreads over the earth, it unites with the waters below, nourishing those who dwell upon it.

22. The waters sustain the earth, provided by the Most High. The rain has its measure, and angels distribute it. These things I saw near the Garden of the Righteous.

23. The angel of peace with me said, "These two monsters, created by God's greatness, will be preserved."

Chapter 61

1. I saw in those days how long cords were given to certain angels, and they took flight towards the north.

2. I asked the angel with me, "Why have those angels taken these cords and flown away?" He replied, "They have gone to measure."

3. The angel said, "These angels will bring measures for the righteous and the cords of the righteous, that they may rest upon the name of the Lord of Spirits forever."

4. The elect will begin to dwell with the elect, and these measures will bring strength to righteousness.

5. These measures will reveal all the mysteries of the earth—the remains of those lost in deserts, those devoured by beasts, and those taken by the sea, so they may return and rest on the day of the Elect One. For none shall perish utterly before the Lord of Spirits.

6. All who dwell above in heaven received a command and power, and with one voice and a fiery light, they blessed.

7. With their first words, they praised, extolled, and honored with wisdom, being wise in word and spirit.

8. The Lord of Spirits placed the Elect One upon the throne of glory, where He will judge the deeds of the holy ones above in heaven, weighing their actions in balance.

Chapter 62

1. The Lord commanded the kings, the mighty, the exalted, and those on earth, saying, "Open your eyes and lift up your heads if you can recognize the Elect One."
2. The Lord of Spirits seated Him on the throne of glory, and the spirit of righteousness was poured out upon Him.
3. By the word of His mouth, sinners will be slain, and the unrighteous will be destroyed from before Him.
4. On that day, all the kings, the mighty, the exalted, and those who rule the earth will see and recognize how He sits on the throne of glory, judging with righteousness, and no false word is spoken before Him.
5. Then pain will come upon them, like a woman in labor, as she feels the pain of bringing forth a child.
6. They will look at one another, filled with terror, downcast and in anguish when they see the Son of Man on the throne of glory. The kings, mighty ones, and all who hold power will bless, glorify, and extol Him who rules over all and who was once hidden.
7. From the beginning, the Son of Man was hidden, preserved by the Most High in His presence and revealed to the elect.
8. The congregation of the elect and holy shall flourish, standing before Him on that day.
9. All the kings, mighty, and exalted of the earth will fall before Him, worshiping and placing their hope upon the Son of Man, pleading for mercy.
10. Yet the Lord of Spirits will press them to leave His presence, their faces filled with shame, darkness deepening upon them.
11. He will deliver them to the angels for punishment, to exact vengeance for the oppression of His children and His chosen.
12. They will become a spectacle for the righteous and the elect, who will rejoice over them as the wrath of the Lord of Spirits rests upon them, and His sword is drenched in their blood.
13. On that day, the righteous and elect will be saved, never again to see the face of sinners and the unrighteous.
14. The Lord of Spirits will dwell over them, and with the Son of Man, they will eat, rest, and rise forever.
15. The righteous and elect, having risen from the earth, will no longer be downcast, but clothed in garments of glory.
16. These are the garments of life from the Lord of Spirits, and their garments will not age, nor will their glory fade before the Lord of Spirits.

Chapter 63

1. In those days, the mighty and the kings who possess the earth will plead with Him to grant them a brief respite from His angels of punishment, to whom they have been delivered, so they may fall down and worship before the Lord of Spirits and confess their sins before Him.
2. They will bless and glorify the Lord of Spirits, saying, "Blessed is the Lord of Spirits, the Lord of kings, the Lord of the mighty, the Lord of the rich, the Lord of glory, and the Lord of

wisdom."

3. "Splendid in all hidden things is Your power from generation to generation, and Your glory endures forever. Deep and innumerable are Your secrets, and Your righteousness cannot be measured."

4. "Now we have learned that we should glorify and bless the Lord of kings, the King over all kings."

5. They will say, "If only we had rest to glorify and give thanks and confess our faith before His glory!

6. But now we long for a little rest and do not find it. We seek it but cannot obtain it. Light has vanished from us, and darkness is now our eternal dwelling place."

7. "We did not believe in Him or glorify the name of the Lord of Spirits, nor did we honor our Lord. Instead, we placed our hope in the scepter of our kingdom and our own glory."

8. "In the day of our suffering and distress, He does not save us, and we find no relief in confessing that our Lord is true in all His works and judgments. His justice is without partiality."

9. "We pass away from His presence because of our deeds, and all our sins are accounted for in righteousness."

10. Then they will say to themselves, "Our souls are filled with unrighteous gain, but it does not save us from descending into the burden of Sheol."

11. After this, their faces will be filled with darkness and shame before the Son of Man, and they will be driven from His presence, with the sword set before His face in their midst.

12. Thus says the Lord of Spirits: "This is the ordinance and judgment concerning the mighty, the kings, the exalted, and those who possess the earth, before the Lord of Spirits."

Chapter 64

1. And I saw other forms hidden in that place.
2. I heard the voice of the angel saying, "These are the angels who descended to the earth and revealed hidden things to the children of men, leading them into sin."

Chapter 65

1. In those days, Noah saw that the earth had sunk down and that its destruction was near.
2. He arose and went to the ends of the earth, crying out to his grandfather Enoch. Noah spoke with a sorrowful voice, "Hear me, hear me, hear me!"
3. I said to him, "Tell me what is falling upon the earth that it is in such a dire state and shaken, so that I may not perish with it."
4. Then there was a great commotion on the earth, and a voice was heard from heaven, causing me to fall upon my face.
5. My grandfather Enoch came and stood beside me, saying, "Why have you cried out to me with such a bitter voice?"
6. "A command has gone out from the presence of the Lord concerning those who dwell on the

earth: their ruin is decreed because they have learned all the secrets of the angels, all the violence of the Satans, and the powers of the most hidden ones." "They have acquired the powers of sorcery, witchcraft, and the making of molten images for the entire earth, along with knowledge of how silver is produced from the dust of the earth, and the origin of soft metals within it."
9. "For lead and tin do not come from the earth like other metals; a fountain produces them, and an angel presides over it."
10. After that, my grandfather Enoch took me by the hand and raised me up, saying, "Go, for I have asked the Lord of Spirits about this commotion on the earth."
11. He replied, 'Because of their unrighteousness, their judgment has been determined and will not be withheld by Me forever.
12. Because of the sorceries they have sought and learned, the earth and all its inhabitants will be destroyed.'"
13. "They have no place of repentance forever because they revealed what was hidden, and they are condemned. But as for you, my son, the Lord of Spirits knows you are pure and free from this reproach regarding the secrets."
14. "He has destined your name to be among the holy, to preserve you among those who dwell on earth. Your righteous descendants are destined for kingship and great honors, and from your lineage will arise a fountain of the righteous and holy, without number forever."

Chapter 66

1. After that, He showed me the angels of punishment, who are prepared to unleash all the powers of the waters beneath the earth to bring judgment and destruction upon those who dwell on the earth.
2. The Lord of Spirits gave a command to the angels, instructing them not to let the waters rise but to hold them back, for these angels oversee the powers of the waters.
3. I then departed from the presence of Enoch.

Chapter 67

1. In those days, the word of God came to me, saying, "Noah, your lot has been chosen before Me—a lot of blamelessness, love, and uprightness."
2. "Now, the angels are constructing a wooden structure, and when they complete their task, I will place My hand upon it to preserve it. From it shall come the seed of life, and a change will come, so the earth will not remain uninhabited."
3. "I will establish your descendants before Me forever, and I will spread those who dwell with you. They shall not be barren upon the earth, but they will be blessed and multiply in the name of the Lord."
4. "He will imprison those angels who have acted unrighteously in that burning valley, which my

grandfather Enoch showed me in the west, among mountains of gold, silver, iron, soft metal, and tin."

5. I saw that valley where a great commotion and upheaval of the waters took place.

6. When all of this happened, from the molten metals and the upheaval in that place, a smell of sulfur was produced, which mixed with the waters. The valley of the angels who led humanity astray burned beneath that land.

7. Through its valleys flow streams of fire where the angels who led humanity astray are punished.

8. But those waters will, in those days, serve for the kings, the mighty, the exalted, and those who dwell on earth. They will heal the body but punish the spirit; for their spirits are filled with lust, and they will be punished in their bodies for denying the Lord of Spirits.

9. As the burning of their bodies intensifies, a corresponding change will occur in their spirits forever, for no one can utter an idle word before the Lord of Spirits.

10. Judgment will come upon them because they believed in the lust of their bodies and denied the spirit of the Lord.

11. In those days, these waters of judgment will change; when the angels are punished in them, the springs will alter their temperature. When the angels ascend, the waters of the springs will change again and become cold.

12. I heard Michael respond, saying, "This judgment of the angels serves as a testimony to the kings and mighty ones who possess the earth."

13. "For these waters of judgment provide healing for the bodies of the kings and satisfy the lust of their bodies, yet they will not see or believe that these waters will become a fire that burns forever."

Chapter 68

1. After that, my grandfather Enoch taught me all the secrets contained in the book of the Parables, which had been given to him. He assembled these teachings for me in the words of the book of the Parables.

2. On that day, Michael spoke to Raphael, saying, "The power of the spirit brings me trembling because of the severity of the judgment, the judgment of the secrets, and the judgment of the angels. Who can endure this harsh judgment that causes them to dissolve?"

3. Michael spoke again to Raphael, "Who among us does not feel his heart softened by it, and whose inner parts are not troubled by the judgment that has come upon them, for leading others astray?"

4. When he stood before the Lord of Spirits, Michael said to Raphael, "I will not defend them in the Lord's presence, for the Lord of Spirits is angry with them for acting as though they were the Lord."

5. Because of this, all hidden things shall come upon them forever. No angel or human will share in this; they alone will receive their judgment forever.

Chapter 69

1. After this judgment, they will tremble and be terrified because they revealed these secrets to those on earth.
2. Here are the names of those angels: the first is Samjaza, the second is Artaqifa, the third is Armen, the fourth is Kokabel, the fifth is Turael, the sixth is Rumjal, the seventh is Danjal, the eighth is Neqael, the ninth is Baraqel, the tenth is Azazel, the eleventh is Armaros, the twelfth is Batarjal, the thirteenth is Busasejal, the fourteenth is Hananel, the fifteenth is Turel, the sixteenth is Simapesiel, the seventeenth is Jetrel, the eighteenth is Tumael, the nineteenth is Turel, and the twentieth is Rumael.
3. These are the leaders of their angels, ruling over groups of hundreds, fifties, and tens.
4. The name of the first, Jeqon, is the one who led astray all the sons of God and brought them down to the earth, misleading them through the daughters of men.
5. The second, Asbeel, gave evil counsel to the holy sons of God, leading them to defile themselves with the daughters of men.
6. The third, Gadreel, showed humanity the ways of death, misled Eve, and introduced mankind to weapons—the shield, coat of mail, sword for battle, and all instruments of death.
7. From his hand, these weapons came forth against those who dwell on earth, from that day and onward.
8. The fourth, Penemue, taught humanity the difference between bitter and sweet, revealing the secrets of wisdom.
9. He taught people to write with ink and paper, leading many to sin through this knowledge from eternity to eternity.
10. Humans were not created for this purpose, to secure their faith with ink and pen.
11. Humans were meant to be like the angels—pure and righteous—and death would not have taken hold of them. But through this knowledge, they perish, and it consumes me.
12. The fifth, Kasdeja, showed humanity the evil smitings of spirits and demons, the strikes to the embryo in the womb, and the blows of the soul. He revealed serpent bites and the afflictions from noon heat—the son of the serpent, named Tabaet.
13. This was the task of Kasbeel, chief of the oath, who revealed it to the holy ones when he was in glory, and its name is Biqa.
14. This angel asked Michael to show him the hidden name so he might pronounce it in the oath, making all who revealed secrets to humanity tremble.
15. This is the power of the oath—it is mighty and strong. Michael placed this oath, Akae, in his hand.
16. These are the secrets of the oath, and through it, they are strong: the heavens were suspended before creation, and they remain forever.
17. Through it, the earth was set upon the waters, and the waters flow from the hidden places of the mountains from creation to eternity.
18. By this oath, the sea was formed, with sand as its boundary, to contain its wrath, never to cross its limit from creation to eternity.

19. The abyss was established by this oath and remains unmoved from eternity to eternity.
20. Through it, the sun and moon complete their courses without deviation, from eternity to eternity.
21. Through it, the stars complete their paths, and He calls them by name, and they respond from eternity to eternity.
22. So, too, are the spirits of the waters, winds, and all breezes, each following their designated paths.
23. The voices of thunder and the light of lightning are stored there, along with the chambers of hail, frost, mist, rain, and dew.
24. All these elements give thanks and glorify the Lord of Spirits, praising His name with all their might. Their food is thanksgiving, and they honor the Lord of Spirits forever.
25. This oath is powerful over them; by it, they are preserved, and their courses are maintained.
26. They rejoiced greatly, blessing, glorifying, and extolling, for the name of the Son of Man was revealed to them.
27. He sat upon His throne of glory, and judgment was given to the Son of Man. He caused sinners to perish and removed those who led the world astray.
28. With chains, they were bound, and in the assembly of their destruction, they were imprisoned, and all their deeds vanished from the earth.
29. From now on, nothing corruptible shall remain, for the Son of Man has taken His seat on His throne of glory. All wickedness will vanish from His presence, and the word of the Son of Man will prevail before the Lord of Spirits.

Chapter 70

1. After this, during Enoch's lifetime, his name was elevated to that of the Son of Man and the Lord of Spirits among those on earth.
2. Enoch was raised on the chariots of the spirit, and his name disappeared among them. From that day, I was no longer counted among them, and He placed me between the two winds, the North and the West.
3. There, the angels took cords to measure the place prepared for the elect and righteous.
4. I saw the ancient fathers and the righteous who have dwelt there from the beginning.

Chapter 71

1. After this, my spirit was taken up, and I ascended into the heavens. I saw the holy sons of God walking on flames of fire. Their garments were white, and their faces shone like snow.
2. I saw two streams of fire, with the light of that fire glowing like hyacinth. I fell upon my face before the Lord of Spirits.
3. Then Michael, one of the archangels, took my right hand, raised me up, and led me into all the secrets, revealing the mysteries of righteousness.
4. He showed me the ends of the heavens, all the chambers of the stars, and the luminaries from

where they proceed before the holy ones.

5. My spirit was transported into the highest heaven, where I saw a structure made of crystals, with tongues of living fire between them.

6. My spirit saw the girdle encircling that house of fire, and on its four sides were streams of living fire, surrounding that house.

7. Around it were Seraphim, Cherubim, and Ophanim—those who do not sleep but guard the throne of His glory.

8. I saw countless angels, a thousand thousands and ten thousand times ten thousand, encircling that house.

9. Michael, Raphael, Gabriel, Phanuel, and the holy angels who are above the heavens entered and exited that house.

10. The Head of Days came forth, His head as white as wool, and His garment beyond description.

11. I fell upon my face, and my whole body became weak, while my spirit was transformed. I cried out, blessing and glorifying the Lord of Spirits.

12. The blessings from my mouth were pleasing to the Head of Days, who came with Michael, Gabriel, Raphael, Phanuel, and countless angels.

13. Here, a portion is lost that described the Son of Man accompanying the Head of Days. Enoch asked an angel about the identity of the Son of Man.

14. The angel greeted me, saying, "This is the Son of Man born to righteousness, with righteousness upon Him. The righteousness of the Head of Days never leaves Him."

15. "He brings peace in the name of the coming world, for peace has existed since creation and will endure for you forever."

16. "All will follow His ways, for righteousness will never depart from Him. With Him will be their dwellings and inheritance, never separated from Him." "Length of days shall be with the Son of Man, and the righteous shall have peace and walk uprightly before the Lord of Spirits forever."

The Book of The Luminaries of The Heaven – Enoch's Ethiopic Book 3

Chapter 72

1. The book of the courses of the heavenly luminaries describes the paths of each, according to their classifications, rule, and seasons, along with their names and places of origin, and also by their months. Uriel, the holy angel, who is their guide, showed me everything about them. He revealed all their laws exactly as they are, relating to all the years of the world and into eternity, until the new creation will be established, which will last forever.

2. This is the first law of the luminaries: the great luminary, the sun, rises in the eastern portals of heaven and sets in the western portals.

3. I saw six portals from which the sun rises and six portals where it sets, as well as the moon rising and setting through these same portals, with the stars and their followers arranged in six portals in the east and six in the west. They all follow each other in exact order.

4. Along with these portals, there are many windows to the right and left of each one.

5. First, there is the great luminary, the sun, whose circumference is like the circumference of heaven, and it is filled with illuminating and heating fire.

6. The chariot on which the sun ascends is driven by the wind. The sun descends from the heaven and moves through the north to reach the east, where it is guided to its appropriate portal and shines across the sky.

7. In the first month, the sun rises in the fourth of the six portals in the east. There are twelve windows in this portal, from which a flame proceeds at their designated season.

8. As the sun rises through this fourth portal in the first month, it continues for thirty mornings and sets accurately in the fourth portal in the west of heaven.

9. During this period, the day lengthens, and the night shortens, with the day being longer than the night by one-ninth. The day becomes ten parts, and the night eight parts.

10. After this, the sun rises and sets in the fifth portal of the east for thirty mornings.

11. The day increases by two parts, reaching eleven parts, while the night decreases to seven parts.

12. The sun then rises from the sixth portal and sets there for thirty-one mornings, following its sign.

13. On that day, the day becomes twice as long as the night, with the day totaling twelve parts and the night six parts.

14. The sun then begins to shorten the day, while the night lengthens. It rises and sets in the sixth portal for thirty more mornings.

15. At the end of this period, the day decreases by one part to total eleven parts, while the night increases to seven parts.

16. Afterward, the sun rises and sets in the fifth portal for thirty more mornings.

17. The day decreases again by two parts to ten parts, and the night increases to eight parts.

18. The sun continues this cycle, rising from the fourth portal for thirty-one mornings and setting in the west.

19. On this day, the day and night become equal in length, each with nine parts.

20. The sun then rises and sets from the third portal for thirty mornings, and as the cycle progresses, the night becomes longer than the day, reaching ten parts, while the day decreases to eight.

21. The sun rises in the second portal and sets there for thirty mornings.

22. The night continues to grow, reaching eleven parts, and the day decreases to seven parts.

23. The sun rises from the second portal and sets, then moves to the first portal for thirty-one mornings.

24. On that day, the night becomes twice as long as the day, totaling twelve parts, while the day totals six parts.

25. The sun then completes its circuit and begins again, rising from the first portal for thirty mornings.
26. By this time, the night decreases by one part, becoming eleven parts, and the day increases to seven parts.
27. The sun moves to the second portal and follows its path for thirty mornings.
28. On that day, the night decreases further to ten parts, and the day increases to eight parts.
29. The sun rises from the second portal and sets, then shifts to the third portal for thirty-one mornings.
30. On that day, the night decreases to nine parts, and the day increases to nine parts, making the year exactly 364 days.
31. The length of the day and night, as well as their shortening, is determined by the course of the sun.
32. The sun's course lengthens the day and shortens the night.
33. This is the law of the sun, as it completes its circuit sixty times, rising and setting. The sun, the great luminary, is named according to its appearance, as commanded by the Lord.
34. As the sun rises and sets, it does not rest nor diminish but continues to run both day and night. Its light is seven times brighter than the moon, yet in size, they are equal.

Chapter 73

1. After observing the law governing the sun, I noticed another law regarding the smaller luminary, which is called the moon.
2. Its circumference is like the heavens, and its chariot is driven by the wind. The moon receives light in exact portions, and its rising and setting vary each month.
3. Its days are like the sun's days, and when its light is complete, it is one-seventh of the sun's light.
4. On the thirtieth morning, the moon begins its first phase in the east, becoming visible and marking its first phase on that day, rising in the same portal as the sun.
5. One-seventh of its light appears, with the remainder of its circumference dark.
6. It gradually increases in light by one-seventh with each day.
7. And as the sun rises, the moon rises with it, gaining part of the sun's light.
8. Through the moon's phases each night, it continues to increase in light until it becomes full in thirteen parts.

Chapter 74

1. I observed yet another law regarding the moon's monthly revolution.
2. Uriel, the holy angel, showed me its movements and cycles, and I recorded everything according to how he revealed it, including its months and appearance until the fifteenth day.
3. The moon completes its light in the east and becomes dark in the west, all divided in single seventh parts.

4. In certain months, the moon alters its settings, while in others, it follows a unique course.
5. In two months, the moon sets with the sun through the third and fourth portals in the east.
6. The moon advances for seven days, then turns back and enters through the sixth portal, completing its light as it moves away from the sun.
7. The moon then returns to the fourth portal, turning back after seven days and retaining its light.
8. Afterward, it retreats to the first portal.
9. The moon's movements are in harmony with the sun's settings, and their orbits remain in alignment.
10. Every five years, an additional thirty days are added to the year, totaling 364 days.
11. The extra days from the sun and the stars add six days per year, resulting in thirty extra days over five years.
12. The moon lags behind the sun and stars by thirty days over these five years, balancing out the year.
13. In eight years, the moon falls behind by eighty days, completing its cycle alongside the sun and stars.

Chapter 75

1. The leaders of the heavenly hosts who oversee creation and the stars also control the four intercalary days that are not counted within the year.
2. People often make errors because they do not understand that these luminaries are correctly stationed—one in the first portal, one in the third, one in the fourth, and one in the sixth portal. The year is accurately completed with 364 days.
3. Uriel, the angel appointed by the Lord of glory, governs these luminaries. He revealed the signs, times, years, and days to me.
4. Uriel showed me twelve portals in the heavens from which the sun's rays break forth and from which warmth spreads across the earth.
5. These portals are situated at the ends of the heavens, allowing the sun, moon, stars, and all the workings of heaven to emerge from both the east and the west.
6. There are many windows to the right and left of each portal, each producing its own warmth at its appointed time. I saw chariots moving in the heavens above these portals, carrying the stars that never set. Among them is a larger chariot that travels across the entire world.

Chapter 76

1. At the ends of the earth, I observed twelve portals that open to all directions of the heavens, from which the winds blow over the earth.
2. Three portals face the east, three face the west, three are on the north, and three are on the south.
3. The first three portals belong to the east, the next three to the north, followed by those on the

south, and lastly, those facing the west.
4. Four of these winds bring blessings and prosperity, but the other eight bring destruction upon the earth and its inhabitants.
5. The east wind, blowing from the first eastern portal, brings desolation, drought, heat, and ruin.
6. The second eastern portal brings rain, fruitfulness, prosperity, and dew.
7. The third eastern portal brings cold and drought.
8. Through the portal next to it, fragrant smells emerge.
9. The southern winds bring heat from the first portal, and from the middle portal, they bring prosperity, health, and rain. The third portal brings dew, rain, and destruction.
10. The northern winds bring cold and rain from the first portal, while the middle portal brings health, dew, and prosperity. The third portal brings frost, snow, and locusts.
11. The western winds bring frost, dew, and rain from the first portal. The middle portal brings prosperity and blessings, and the third portal brings drought and devastation.
12. These twelve portals regulate the winds and all their laws, bringing either blessings or destruction upon the earth.

Chapter 77

1. The first quarter is called the east because it is the primary direction. The second quarter is the south, where the Most High will descend, a place uniquely blessed for His arrival.
2. The west is named the diminished quarter because all the luminaries in heaven wane and set there.
3. The north quarter is divided into three parts: the first part is for human habitation, the second contains seas, abysses, rivers, forests, and clouds, and the third part holds the garden of righteousness.
4. I saw seven high mountains, higher than any others on earth, from which frost originates.
5. The progression of days, seasons, and years arises from these mountains.
6. I also saw seven great rivers, larger than any on earth. One flows from the west into the Great Sea.
7. Two rivers come from the north and flow into the Erythraean Sea to the east. Four other rivers flow toward separate seas; two enter the Erythraean Sea, and two enter the Great Sea, though some say they empty into the desert.
8. I saw seven great islands, two on the mainland and five in the Great Sea.

Chapter 78

1. The sun has two names: the first is Orjares, and the second is Tomas.
2. The moon has four names: the first is Asonja, the second is Ebla, the third is Benase, and the fourth is Erae.
3. These are the two great luminaries. Their circumferences are like the heavens, and their circumferences are equal in size.

4. The sun's circumference has seven more portions of light than the moon, and its light is transferred in measured portions until the sun's seventh part is depleted.
5. They set and enter the western portals, turn to the north, and emerge through the eastern portals across the heavens.
6. When the moon rises, one-fourteenth of it becomes visible in the sky.
7. The moon's light becomes fully visible on the fourteenth day, reaching its full brightness.
8. On the fifteenth day, the moon reaches its fullest light and continues to grow, adding fourteenth parts. In its waning, the moon reduces daily from fourteen parts until none remain

9. Vanishing completely by the fifteenth day.
10. Some months contain twenty-nine days, and others contain twenty-eight.
11. Uriel showed me another law: the sun transfers its light to the moon, and during the moon's waxing, it gathers light over fourteen days until fully illuminated.
12. The new moon appears on the day it receives its first light.
13. The moon becomes fully illuminated on the fifteenth day when it rises opposite the setting sun.
14. The moon shines throughout the night until the sun rises, then wanes until its light disappears and the month ends.
15. The moon completes three months of thirty days and three months of twenty-nine days, during which it completes its waning.
16. The moon's cycle is precisely timed, alternating between periods of visibility lasting twenty days per month, appearing by night and resembling the heavens by day, except in its light.

Chapter 79

1. "Now, my son, I have shown you everything, and the laws of the stars are complete."
2. "I have been shown every law governing the stars for each day, season, year, month, and week."
3. "The moon's waning occurs in the sixth portal, where its light finishes

4. And begins to fade."
5. "The moon continues its cycle through the portals until it completes 177 days, totaling twenty-five weeks and two days."
6. "In each cycle, the moon lags behind the sun by five days, as directed by Uriel, the archangel in charge of the stars."

Chapter 80

1. "The angel Uriel said to me, 'Behold, Enoch, I have shown you everything—the sun, the moon, the leaders of the stars, their tasks, timings, and departures.'"
2. "'In the days of sinners, the years will shorten, and their crops and lands will no longer yield as they once did.' 'All things on earth will change, appearing out of their proper seasons. Rain will cease, and the skies will no longer send it forth.'"
3. "'The fruits of the earth will be delayed, not growing in their proper seasons, and the fruit of the trees will be withheld as well.'"
4. "'The moon will alter its course and will not appear as expected.'"
5. "'The sun will set in the west yet shine brighter than anticipated, disrupting the established order of light.'"
6. "'Many stars will stray from their designated paths, altering their orbits and failing to appear as commanded.'"
7. "'The stars' order will be hidden from sinners, causing those on earth to mistake them for gods.'"
8. "'Evil will increase upon them, and punishment will come to destroy them.'"

Chapter 81

1. "'Observe, Enoch, these heavenly tablets and read what is written on them. Take note of every individual detail.'"
2. "I looked at the heavenly tablets and read everything written on them. I understood all that was written, covering the deeds of humankind and the future of all generations."
3. "Immediately, I blessed the great Lord, the King of Glory, forever, for He created all the works of the world. I praised the Lord for His patience and blessed Him for the children of men."
4. "I then declared, 'Blessed is the one who dies in righteousness and goodness, for no book of unrighteousness is written against him, and no judgment awaits him.'"
5. "Then, seven holy ones brought me back to the earth, placing me at the door of my house. They instructed me, 'Tell all these things to your son Methuselah, and show all your children that no flesh is righteous in the sight of the Lord, for He is their Creator.'"
6. "'You will have one more year with your son Methuselah, during which you shall give him your final instructions. Record everything for him and testify to all your offspring. In the following year, we shall take you from among them.'"
7. "They encouraged me, saying, 'Let your heart be strong, for the righteous shall declare righteousness to one another. They will rejoice together and congratulate one another.'"
8. "'However,' they warned, 'the sinners will perish with the sinners, and apostates will descend with other apostates.'"
9. "'Those who practice righteousness will die due to human actions, and they will be taken away because of the godless.'"
10. "After they finished speaking, they departed from me. I returned to my people, blessing the Lord of the world."

Chapter 82

1. "'Now, my son Methuselah, I recount everything to you and have written it all down for you. I have revealed all these things and given you these writings. Make sure to preserve them and pass them down to future generations.'"

2. "'I have imparted wisdom to you and your descendants, and they should pass it on to their children for generations. This wisdom surpasses ordinary understanding.'"

3. "'Those who understand will not grow weary; they will eagerly listen and learn. This wisdom will satisfy them more than the finest of foods.'"

4. "'Blessed are the righteous, and blessed are all who walk in the ways of righteousness, for they will not fall into sin as others do during their days. The sun travels across the heavens, entering and departing through its portals for thirty days, along with the leaders of thousands of stars, accompanied by the four that divide the year.'"

5. "'Due to these, people will miscalculate the year, though these luminaries serve as accurate markers for the year's progression, precisely calculated to be 364 days.'"

6. "'People will err and fail to recognize the correct calculation, yet these luminaries are accurately documented for all time, with markers at the first, third, fourth, and sixth portals to divide the year into its four sections.'"

7. "'The year is exactly 364 days, and this calculation is exact. The sun, moon, stars, months, festivals, and days are revealed to me by Uriel, who is in charge of all the heavenly luminaries.'"

8. "'Uriel has authority over night and day, ensuring the sun, moon, and stars provide light for the world. They each follow their designated paths through the heavens.'"

9. "'These are the orders of the stars, each following its specific paths, seasons, and cycles. Their leaders guide them through their monthly and seasonal dominions.'"

10. "'Four leaders divide the year's four seasons, with twelve others guiding the months. There are also leaders over the thousands of days, and the four intercalary days have their own leaders, ensuring the year's exact division.'"

11. "'The leaders of the thousands are interspersed among the others to maintain these divisions. These are the names of the leaders who divide the four parts of the year: Milkiel, Helemmelek, Melejal, and Narel.'"

12. "'The names of the additional leaders are: Adnarel, Ijasusael, and Elomeel.

13. These three follow the main leaders and maintain the stations of the year.'"

14. "'The leader Melkejal rises first at the beginning of the year, also known as Tamaini, or the sun, ruling for ninety-one days.'"

15. "'During his reign, signs appear on the earth: warmth, calm winds, and growth. Trees bear fruit, leaves appear, and wheat ripens.

16. Flowers bloom, and fields thrive with vegetation, but winter trees wither away.'"

17. "'The leaders serving under him are Berkael, Zelebsel, and Hilujaseph, another head of a thousand. The rule of this leader ends when the next leader takes over.'"

18. "'Helemmelek, also known as the 'shining sun,' follows, ruling for ninety-one days.'"
19. "'Under his rule, signs appear: intense heat and dryness. Trees ripen with fruit, sheep conceive, and the earth yields its harvest. All produce is gathered, and the winepress is used.'"
20. "'Gidaljal, Keel, and Heel serve under Helemmelek, along with an additional head of a thousand, Asfael. His rule concludes as his days end.'"

The Book of Dream and Vision – Enoch's Ethiopic Book 4

Chapter 83

1. "Now, my son Methuselah, I will share with you all the visions I have seen, recounting each before you."
2. "I had two visions before taking a wife; each was distinct from the other. The first came as I was learning to write, and the second was before I married your mother, a vision filled with dread."
3. "Concerning these visions, I prayed to the Lord. As I lay in my grandfather Mahalalel's house, I saw in a vision how the heavens collapsed and fell to earth."
4. "The earth opened into a great abyss, mountains suspended on mountains, hills collapsed upon hills, and towering trees were uprooted and hurled down."
5. "A word entered my mouth, and I cried aloud, 'The earth is destroyed!'"
6. "My grandfather Mahalalel woke me from where I lay beside him, asking, 'Why do you cry out so, my son? What has caused such lament?'"
7. "I recounted to him the vision I had seen, and he said, 'You have witnessed something grave. This dream speaks of the sins of the earth. It will sink into the abyss, consumed by great destruction.'"
8. "He urged, 'Rise, my son, and make petition to the Lord of Glory, for you have faith. Pray that a remnant may be spared, that He may not destroy the entire earth.'"
9. "'For all this shall come upon the earth from heaven, and immense destruction will cover it.'"
10. "Following this, I arose, prayed, and wrote down my petition for the generations to come. I shall reveal everything to you, my son Methuselah." "As I went out, I saw the heavens, the sun rising in the east, the moon setting in the west, a few stars, and the earth in its fullness, just as it had been from the beginning. I blessed the Lord of Judgment and praised Him." "He brought forth the sun from the eastern windows, where it rose, traversed its appointed path, and ascended in the heavens."

Chapter 84

1. "I lifted my hands in righteousness, blessing the Holy and Great One. With the breath of my mouth and the tongue given by God to the children of men, I spoke."
2. "He has given us breath, a tongue, and a mouth to speak with, saying, 'Blessed are You, O Lord, King, Great and Mighty in Your greatness, Lord of all creation of the heavens, King of kings, and God of the entire world.'"
3. "Your power, kingship, and greatness endure forever, spanning all generations. The heavens are Your throne, and the earth Your footstool, forever and ever." "You made and rule all things; nothing is beyond Your power. Wisdom never departs from Your throne, nor does it turn away from Your presence." "You know, see, and hear all; nothing is hidden from You, for You behold everything."
4. "Now, the angels of Your heavens are guilty of transgression, and Your wrath rests upon humankind until the great day of judgment."
5. "O Great King, Lord God, I implore You to fulfill my prayer. Leave a remnant on the earth; do not destroy all humankind, lest the earth be left desolate and without inhabitants."
6. "Remove from the earth the flesh that has aroused Your wrath. But the flesh of righteousness and uprightness, establish as an eternal seed. Hide not Your face from Your servant's prayer, O Lord."

Chapter 85

1. "After this, I had another dream, which I will recount fully to you, my son."
2. "Enoch lifted his voice and spoke to Methuselah, 'Listen, my son, to the words of your father's dream vision.'"
3. "Before I married your mother, Edna, I saw a vision as I lay on my bed. A bull came forth from the earth, and that bull was white." "A heifer followed, accompanied by two bulls, one black and one red."
4. "The black bull attacked the red one, chasing him across the earth until he disappeared from view."
5. "The black bull grew, and the heifer stayed with him. I saw many oxen coming from him, resembling and following him."
6. "The first cow departed from the first bull to search for the red one but could not find him. She cried out in sorrow, seeking him."
7. "At length, the first bull returned to her and comforted her, and she ceased her lamenting."
8. "She then bore another white bull, followed by numerous bulls and black cows."
9. "In my sleep, I saw the white bull grow and become a mighty white bull. From him proceeded many white bulls, each resembling the others, following in a great procession."

Chapter 86

1. "Again, as I slept, I looked to the heavens and saw a star fall from above, rising and feeding among the oxen."
2. "Then I observed large black oxen, and they all altered their dwelling places, pastures, and companions, mingling with one another."
3. "I looked once more toward the heavens and saw many stars descending, casting themselves down to the first star. They transformed into bulls and pastured among the cattle."
4. "I watched them as they revealed their private members like horses, covering the cows of the oxen, causing them to conceive."
5. "They bore elephants, camels, and asses, terrifying the oxen, who began to devour and gore each other."
6. "Fear gripped the children of the earth, and they fled before them, trembling and quaking."

Chapter 87

1. "I saw how the creatures began to fight and devour one another, and the earth cried out."
2. "Lifting my eyes again to heaven, I saw in a vision beings descending, looking like white men. Four of them emerged, followed by three others."
3. "The last three took me by the hand, lifting me high above the earth to a vantage point where I saw a towering structure, elevated above all hills."
4. "One said to me, 'Remain here until you witness everything that happens to the elephants, camels, asses, stars, and oxen.'"

Chapter 88

1. "Then I saw one of the first four beings seize the fallen star, binding it hand and foot and casting it into the abyss. The abyss was narrow, deep, and filled with darkness and dread."
2. "One of them drew a sword, giving it to the elephants, camels, and asses, who began to attack one another. The earth shook as they fought."
3. "As I watched the vision, one of those four beings hurled stones from the heavens at the elephants, camels, and asses, gathering and binding the large stars whose private members resembled horses, casting them into the abyss of the earth."

Chapter 89

1. One of the four beings approached the white bull and, without frightening him, revealed a secret to him.

2. The bull transformed into a man and constructed a large vessel, in which he lived.

3. Three bulls joined him in the vessel, and they were covered within.

4. Then I looked to the heavens and saw a high roof, with seven torrents of water flowing upon it.

5. The torrents poured down heavily, filling an enclosure with water.

6. Fountains opened upon the surface of the enclosure, and the water began to rise.

7. Soon, the entire enclosure was covered with water, darkness, and mist.

8. The water continued to rise above the enclosure, spilling over and standing upon the earth.

9. All the cattle within the enclosure were gathered together, and I watched as they sank, swallowed by the water.

10. The vessel, however, floated upon the water, while the oxen, elephants, camels, and asses sank to the bottom with the other animals.

11. They could not escape, and all perished, sinking into the depths.

12. Then I saw that the torrents ceased to flow from the roof, and the chasms of the earth were leveled.

13. New abysses opened up, and the water began to drain, allowing the earth to become visible again.

14. The vessel settled upon the ground, and light replaced the darkness.

15. The white bull, who had become a man, emerged from the vessel along with the three bulls.

16. One bull was white, another was red like blood, and the third was black. The white bull departed from them.

17. Different animals of various kinds began to appear, such as lions, tigers, wolves, dogs, and other wild beasts.

18. Among them, a white bull was born, and the animals started to bite one another.

19. This white bull gave birth to a wild ass and another white bull.

20. The wild asses multiplied, while the white bull had a black wild boar and a white sheep.

21. The boar multiplied, and the sheep had twelve sheep.

22. As the twelve sheep matured, one was given to the asses, who then handed it over to the wolves.

23. This sheep grew among the wolves, and the Lord sent eleven more sheep to live with it.

24. They multiplied into large flocks, but the wolves oppressed and harmed them.

25. The wolves began to fear the sheep, and the sheep cried out in distress because of the wolves.

26. One sheep managed to escape to the wild asses, while the others cried out to their Lord with all their might.

27. Hearing their cries, the Lord descended from His high place and came to tend to them.

28. He called the sheep who had escaped and instructed it to warn the wolves not to harm the sheep.

29. The sheep went to the wolves with another sheep, and they spoke to the wolves as the Lord had commanded.

30. The wolves, however, continued to oppress the sheep, who cried out louder in anguish.

31. Then the Lord arrived and struck down the wolves, causing them to wail in pain.

32. The sheep quieted and stopped crying as the wolves began to flee.

33. The sheep moved away from the wolves, but the wolves pursued them relentlessly.

34. The Lord led His flock, and His face shone with a terrible and glorious brightness.

35. The wolves chased the sheep until they reached the edge of a vast sea.

36. The sea divided, and the water stood like walls on both sides as the Lord led the sheep forward.

37. The wolves, seeing the Lord, stopped in fear, but the sea closed upon them and drowned them.

38. The sheep escaped, crossing into a barren wilderness without food or water.

39. The Lord provided for them, giving them water and leading them to pastures.

40. The sheep that had previously led them ascended a high rock, and the Lord sent it back to guide them.

41. The sheep saw the Lord's majesty and trembled, for His appearance was great and terrifying.

42. They cried out, saying they could not bear to stand before the Lord.

43. The leading sheep ascended the rock again, while the rest began to stray from the path.

44. The Lord grew angry with the straying sheep, and the leading sheep descended from the rock.

45. This sheep found many others blind and lost and began to bring them back to the fold.

46. Those that had gone astray feared its presence and returned to their places.

47. This sheep then transformed into a man and built a house for the Lord of the sheep.

48. He placed all the sheep in the house, and they settled there in peace.

49. The sheep that had once led them died, and the flock mourned for it.

50. They crossed a stream, and two new leaders arose to guide them.

51. They brought the sheep to a pleasant land, and the house stood among them.

52. The sheep's eyes were sometimes opened and sometimes blind, but another leader rose to bring them back.

53. Wild beasts began to attack the sheep, but the Lord raised up a ram to defend them.

54. The ram fought off the wild beasts but later grew proud and oppressive.

55. The Lord sent another lamb to replace the first ram, giving it leadership over the flock.

56. The first ram chased the new leader, but the new leader escaped.

57. The dogs tore down the first ram, and the new leader led the flock in peace.

58. The flock grew and multiplied, while the wild beasts retreated in fear.

59. This leader built a house and a high tower, which pleased the Lord.

60. The flock strayed again, and the Lord sent messengers to bring them back.

61. The sheep killed many of these messengers, but one escaped and cried out.

62. The Lord of the sheep intervened, saving this messenger and bringing it up.

63. Other messengers were sent, but they, too, were slain by the rebellious sheep.

64. The flock fell into blindness and forsook the house and tower of the Lord.

65. The Lord allowed lions, tigers, wolves, and foxes to attack and scatter them.

66. The wild beasts tore them apart as punishment for their rebellion.

67. I cried out in anguish for the sheep, but the Lord was unmoved.

68. Seventy shepherds were appointed to lead the sheep, and each had a set number to destroy.

69. The Lord gave instructions to each shepherd, commanding them to pasture the sheep according to His will.

70. He instructed them to destroy those sheep He designated, sparing none.

71. An angel was appointed to observe the shepherds and record every act of destruction.

72. The shepherds began their duties, but they exceeded their commands, destroying more sheep than instructed.

73. Wild beasts joined in the destruction, and the sheep's house and tower were burned.

74. The shepherds handed the sheep over to wild beasts, and their destruction was recorded.

75. The angel brought the record before the Lord, who read and sealed it.

76. The Lord looked upon His flock with sorrow, as they had gone astray, and He promised that their faithful would be restored.

Chapter 90

1. And I saw until thirty-five shepherds had undertaken the task of pasturing the sheep, each completing their assigned period, just as the first shepherds did.

2. Then other shepherds received them into their hands, each one pasturing them in their own time.

3. Afterward, I saw in my vision all the birds of heaven coming—eagles, vultures, kites, and ravens—with the eagles leading them all.

4. They began to devour the sheep, picking out their eyes and consuming their flesh.

5. The sheep cried out as their flesh was devoured by the birds.

6. As for me, I lamented in my sleep over the shepherd who was supposed to care for the sheep.

7. I saw that the sheep were being devoured by dogs, eagles, and kites, leaving neither flesh, skin, nor sinew; only their bones remained.

8. Their bones also fell to the earth, and the sheep became few in number.

9. I saw that twenty-three more shepherds took up the task of pasturing, each completing their periods fifty-eight times.

10. Yet, behold, lambs were born among the white sheep, and they began to open their eyes and see.

11. They cried out to the sheep, but the others did not listen.

12. The older sheep were exceedingly deaf, and their eyes were severely blinded.

13. In the vision, I saw ravens fly upon the lambs, seize one, and dash it to pieces, devouring it.

14. Then horns began to grow on the lambs, but the ravens cast down these horns.

15. A great horn sprouted from one of the sheep, and its eyes were opened.

16. It looked at the sheep, and its eyes were fully opened, crying out to them.

17. The rams saw this and ran toward it.

18. Despite this, the eagles, vultures, ravens, and kites continued to swoop down upon the sheep, tearing at them.

19. The sheep remained silent, but the rams lamented and cried out.

20. The ravens fought against the ram, attempting to break its horn, but they could not overpower it.

21. All the eagles, vultures, ravens, and kites gathered together.

22. They brought with them all the sheep of the field, coming together to break the ram's horn.

23. I saw until a great sword was given to the sheep, and they rose against the beasts of the field to slay them.

24. All the beasts and birds fled from before the sheep.

25. Then the man who wrote the book at the Lord's command opened it, revealing the destruction wrought by the last twelve shepherds.

26. He showed how they had destroyed much more than their predecessors before the Lord of the sheep.

27. I saw until the Lord of the sheep came and took in His hand the staff of His wrath, striking the earth.

28. The earth split apart, and all the beasts and birds of the heaven fell among the sheep and were swallowed up by the earth, which covered them.

29. I saw until a throne was set in the pleasant land, and the Lord of the sheep sat upon it.

30. The man brought the sealed books and opened them before the Lord of the sheep.

31. The Lord called forth the seven first white ones and commanded them to bring the stars whose hidden parts were like horses.

32. They brought these stars before Him.

33. He spoke to the man who wrote before Him, one of the seven white ones, instructing him to bring the seventy shepherds who had slain more sheep than commanded.

34. The shepherds were bound and stood before Him.

35. First, judgment was held over the stars, finding them guilty, and they were cast into an abyss of flaming fire.

36. The seventy shepherds were judged, found guilty, and also cast into the fiery abyss.

37. At that time, a similar abyss opened in the earth, filled with fire.

38. The blinded sheep were brought forth, judged, found guilty, and cast into this fiery abyss to burn.

39. This abyss lay to the right of the house, and I saw the sheep and their bones burning.

40. I stood up and watched until they folded up the old house, carrying off its pillars, beams, and ornaments.

41. These were taken to a place in the southern land.

42. Then the Lord of the sheep brought forth a new house, greater and loftier than the first, setting it up in the place of the old one, and all the sheep were gathered within it.

The Epistle of Enoch – Enoch's Ethiopic Book 5

Chapter 91

1. "Now, Methuselah, gather your brothers and summon all your kin, for I have a message to share, and the Spirit has filled me to reveal what lies ahead."
2. "Methuselah went out and brought his brothers and relatives together."
3. "Enoch spoke to them, saying, 'Listen to the words of your father, and take heed to the guidance I give. I implore you to love righteousness and follow it.'"
4. "Approach righteousness with sincerity, and do not align yourselves with those who are divided in heart. Walk in righteousness, which will lead you along a safe path, and it will remain your true companion."
5. "I foresee a rise in violence on earth, and a severe judgment will come. Unrighteousness will be rooted out, and every part of it will be dismantled."
6. "Evil will increase again, with violence, sin, and blasphemy doubling on earth, bringing an end to peace."
7. "When this evil reaches its peak, judgment from heaven will fall. The Holy One will descend in wrath to judge the world."
8. "In that time, violence will be uprooted, and all evil deeds will be removed from under the heavens."
9. "Idols and false worship will be abandoned, and temples dedicated to false gods will be consumed by fire."
10. "Nations will face fiery judgment, enduring divine wrath forever."
11. "The righteous will awaken, gaining wisdom and clarity."
12. "The roots of wrongdoing will be pulled up, and those who blaspheme will fall to the sword. Those who defy will be removed entirely."
13. "I urge you to recognize the paths of righteousness and violence, so you understand the consequences."
14. "Follow the path of righteousness, for those who choose evil will face destruction forever."

Chapter 92

1. "Enoch's teachings encompass a complete wisdom, cherished and passed on to future generations who walk in peace and righteousness."
2. "Do not let your spirit be troubled by the times, for the Great One has set each day for its purpose."
3. "The righteous will awaken and walk in righteousness, and their ways will be filled with goodness and grace."
4. "The Holy One will grant them endless light and favor, guiding them with eternal grace."
5. "Sin will disappear into darkness forever, never to return."

Chapter 93

1. "Enoch began to recite from his writings, saying, 'I will speak of the children of righteousness, the chosen of the world, and the plant of righteousness.'"
2. "'I was born in the seventh generation during a time when righteousness and justice still endured.'"
3. "'In the second era, deceit arose, leading to the first judgment, but a single righteous one was saved.'"
4. "'In the third era, a righteous person was chosen, whose descendants would carry righteousness forever.'"
5. "'In the fourth, visions were given to the holy ones, and a law was established for all generations.'"
6. "'In the fifth era, an eternal house of glory was built.'"
7. "'During the sixth, people lost sight of wisdom and became blind.'"
8. "'In the seventh, an apostate generation appeared, practicing great unrighteousness.'"
9. "'At its end, the chosen righteous ones will receive sevenfold knowledge about creation.'"

Chapter 94

1. "'Love righteousness, my children, and follow it, for the ways of righteousness are worth accepting, but the paths of wickedness will lead to swift ruin.'"
2. "'Some will teach the ways of death and destruction, but the righteous will separate themselves from these.'"
3. "'Do not choose the ways of wickedness, for ruin awaits those who do.'"
4. "'Instead, pursue righteousness and a chosen life of peace, so that you may prosper.'"
5. "'Hold fast to my teachings and let them remain in your hearts, for I know that sinners will attempt to lead you away from wisdom.'"
6. "'Woe to those who build deceitful schemes, for they will collapse without peace.'"
7. "'Woe to those who establish their lives on wrongdoing, for they will fall by the sword.'"
8. "'Woe to the wealthy who trust in their riches and have forgotten the Most High.'"
9. "'Because of their wickedness, they prepare for the day of slaughter and ultimate judgment.'"
10. "I tell you: The One who made you will overthrow you, with no mercy for your downfall, and your Creator will find no pity in your ruin."
11. "'In that time, the righteous will be a reproach to the sinners and the ungodly.'"

Chapter 95

1. "'Oh, that my eyes were like rainclouds so I could weep for you, pouring my sorrow in tears to relieve my troubled heart!'"
2. "'Who allowed you to practice such reproach and wickedness? Judgment will soon be upon you.'"

3. "'Do not fear sinners, O righteous ones, for the Lord will deliver them into your hands for judgment.'"
4. "'Woe to those who utter curses that cannot be taken back; healing will be far from you because of your sins.'"
5. "'Woe to you who repay good with evil, for you will be repaid for your deeds.'"
6. "'Woe to false witnesses and those who act unjustly, for your end will come swiftly.'"
7. "'Woe to you, sinners, for you will be persecuted for your wrongs, and the weight of it will be heavy on you.'"

Chapter 96

1. "'Take hope, O righteous, for soon the sinners will fall, and you will reign over them.'"
2. "'In their times of distress, your children will rise like eagles, soaring above.'"
3. "'You will find refuge in the crevices of the earth and shelter in the rocks, as the wicked mourn.'"
4. "'Do not fear, for healing and light will be yours, and a comforting voice from heaven will reach you.'"
5. "'Woe to sinners who are misled by wealth into thinking themselves just, for their own hearts will accuse them.'"
6. "'Woe to those who oppress the weak and indulge in excess, for they will waste away.'"
7. "'Woe to those who abandon the source of life, for they will be consumed.'"
8. "'Woe to the powerful who oppress the righteous, for the day of their destruction is near.'"

Chapter 97

1. "'Know, O righteous, that the sinners will be put to shame and perish in their day of wrongdoing.'"
2. "'Be aware, O sinners, that the Most High has not forgotten your judgment, and the angels rejoice at your downfall.'"
3. "'What will you do, O sinners, and where will you hide on the day of judgment when you hear the prayers of the righteous?'"
4. "'You will be treated as those condemned, for you have walked with sinners.'"
5. "'In that time, the prayers of the righteous will reach the Lord, and the days of your judgment will begin.'"
6. "'All your misdeeds will be presented before the Great Holy One, and you will stand in shame. He will cast away all your works built on evil.'"
7. "'Woe to you sinners who reside by land and sea, for your memory is filled with wrongdoing.'"
8. "'Woe to those who accumulate silver and gold through unjust means, saying, "We are rich and have all we need."'"

9. "'Though you think you are secure, your wealth will slip away like water. For it was gained by unrighteousness, and a great curse awaits you.'"

Chapter 98

1. "I swear to you, both the wise and the foolish, that you will witness many things on earth."
2. "Men will dress themselves in splendor like women, adorning themselves with colored garments, as if they were royalty, in grandeur, power, silver, and gold; their lives will spill out like water."
3. "In their vanity, they will lose wisdom and perish, along with their riches, in shame, destruction, and poverty. Their spirits will be thrown into the furnace of fire."
4. "I declare to you, sinners, as mountains cannot be slaves, nor can hills become a woman's servant, likewise, sin was not sent upon the earth; it is humanity that created it. Those who live in sin will be greatly cursed."
5. "A woman was not destined to be barren, but by her own actions, she may pass without children."
6. "I swear by the Great Holy One that every evil deed you do is revealed in the heavens; no act of oppression is hidden."
7. "Do not think in your heart that you are unknown or unseen, for every sin is recorded daily before the Most High."
8. "Understand that all your oppressions are noted, and you are prepared for the day of ruin."
9. "Woe to you, foolish ones, for your own folly will destroy you. You transgress against the wise, and fortune will not be yours."
10. "Know that you are set for a day of destruction. Do not hope for life, sinners, for you will die and pass with no ransom."
11. "Woe to you, hardened in heart, who indulge in wickedness and violence. You partake of the good things the Lord Most High provides, but peace will not be yours."
12. "Woe to you who delight in the suffering of the righteous, for you will receive no grave."
13. "Woe to you who dismiss the words of the righteous, for life will not be offered to you."
14. "Woe to those who spread false and godless words, misleading others to act against their neighbors."
15. "For this, you will find no peace; you will perish without warning."

Chapter 99

1. "Woe to those who engage in godlessness and take pride in their lies, for they will perish without happiness."
2. "Woe to those who distort words of righteousness, break eternal laws, and turn themselves to evil; they will be trodden down upon the earth."

3. "In those days, O righteous, lift your prayers as a reminder before the angels, so that they may bring the sins of the wicked to the Most High."
4. "The nations will be stirred up, and all the families of the earth will rise on the day of destruction."
5. "The poor will abandon their infants, leaving even the nursing ones to perish without mercy."
6. "I swear to you, O sinners, that an unending day of bloodshed is destined because of your sins."
7. "Those who worship carved idols and serve demons and spirits will find no help in them."
8. "They will turn godless, blinded by fear and foolishness, and will perish swiftly for their false worship."
9. "Blessed are those who follow wisdom and righteousness, for they will not fall among the godless; they will be saved."
10. "Woe to those who spread evil to their neighbors; they will descend into Sheol."
11. "Woe to those who bring bitterness upon the earth through deception; they will be consumed."
12. "Woe to those who build homes through others' hard labor and with sin-stained materials; peace will elude them."
13. "Woe to those who forsake their fathers' heritage and pursue idols; they will find no rest."
14. "Woe to those who practice oppression and harm their neighbors; the day of judgment is near."
15. "The Lord will humble your pride, bring grief to your hearts, and bring all your glory to ruin. The righteous will remember your sins."

Chapter 100

1. "In that day, fathers and sons will fall together, and brothers will strike down one another, staining rivers with their blood."
2. "Sinners will not restrain themselves, killing from dawn until nightfall."
3. "Horses will wade in the blood of sinners, and chariots will be soaked in it."
4. "In that day, the angels will descend to gather those who caused sin, and the Most High will judge them among the sinners."
5. "The righteous will be protected by holy angels as treasured ones, and though they rest a long sleep, they will not fear."
6. "The wise will be at peace, and understanding will increase, for the wealth of sinners will not save them in their fall."
7. "Woe to you, sinners, in the day of anguish! You afflict the righteous and burn them; you will be repaid for your deeds."
8. "Woe to you, hardened in heart, who plan wickedness; terror will come upon you, and there will be no one to help."

9. "Woe to you, sinners, for your lawless deeds will ignite flames that will burn more intensely than fire."
10. "The sun, moon, and stars will testify against you, for you condemned the righteous unjustly. Clouds, mist, and rain will all stand witness to your sins, withholding themselves from you. "You will offer bribes to bring the rain, but your gifts will be worthless. When frost, snow, and storms come upon you, you will not endure."

Chapter 101

1. "Look to the heavens, O children of the heavens, and observe the works of the Most High; fear Him and avoid evil in His sight."
2. "If He seals the heavens and holds back the rain and dew due to your sins, what then will you do?"
3. "If His wrath falls upon you for your deeds, you cannot plead with Him, for you spoke arrogantly against His justice
4. Thus, peace will evade you."
5. "Look at those who navigate the sea, how their ships are tossed by waves, filling their hearts with dread."
6. "They fear the sea and its dangers, yet you, sinners, do not fear the Most High who made the sea and land."
7. "Do not the ships and their crews fear the sea? But you, sinners, show no reverence for the Creator who set the boundaries of the sea."
8. "The heavens and the earth were crafted by His hand, and He gave wisdom and understanding to all things that move upon the earth."
9. "Yet, despite His mighty works, you sinners do not fear Him."

Chapter 102

1. "In the days when He brings a grievous fire upon you, where will you escape? Where will you find safety?"
2. "When He speaks His judgment upon you, will you not tremble with fear?"
3. "The stars of heaven will quake, and the earth will tremble
4. While you sinners shall be cursed forever, without peace."
5. "But you, righteous ones, fear not. Be hopeful, even in death, if you have lived in righteousness."
6. "Do not grieve if your soul descends into Sheol, for your goodness will not go unrewarded."
7. "When you die, the wicked may mock, saying, 'The righteous die like us, gaining nothing from their deeds.'"
8. "But I tell you, sinners, while you live in pleasure and sin without fear, your end will be unlike the righteous."

9. "Though the righteous suffer in death, their spirits do not perish,
10. While you sinners will endure torment in Sheol eternally."

Chapter 103

1. "Now, I swear to you, O righteous ones, by the glory of the Mighty One who reigns above all, I reveal to you a great mystery."
2. "I have read the heavenly tablets and the holy books written on high." "In them, I found truth concerning those who have died in righteousness."
3. "They are promised joy, glory, and reward for their works on earth, their reward surpassing that of the living, with blessings manifold."
4. "The spirits of the righteous, though they have passed, will live and rejoice before the Great One, and their memory shall not fade but endure forever."
5. "Do not fear the insults of the wicked, for your place is secure before the Holy One."
6. "Woe to you, sinners, who die in sin, departing with the wealth of your iniquity. Though others say, 'Blessed are the sinners who prospered,'"
7. "Though they die in honor and ease, their souls will descend to Sheol, where torment and judgment await."
8. "Into darkness and chains, they will be cast, into flames where grievous punishment endures across generations." "Woe to you, sinners, for you will have no peace."
9. "Do not say of the righteous who live, 'We have labored in vain, enduring hardship and sorrow, as sin surrounded us.'"
10. "'We were destroyed, left without help, tortured, and lost hope.'"
11. "'We tried to lead but became the tail, burdened by the wicked's yoke.'" "'We bowed before them, but they showed no mercy, offering no refuge.'"
12. "'They aided those who robbed and scattered us, forgetting their guilt against the righteous.'"

Chapter 104

1. "I swear to you, righteous ones, by the holy angels in heaven: Your names are inscribed for good before the Great One."
2. "Your deeds are recorded, and your trials are remembered in the presence of the Mighty One on high."
3. "Be hopeful, for although you have endured shame and suffering, you will shine like the lights of the heavens." "You will be visible, and the gates of heaven will open wide to receive you."
4. "Cry out for justice, and it will be granted to you, for your hardships will be avenged, and those who wronged you will face the Most High's judgment."
5. "Do not let go of your hope, O righteous ones."

6. "Great joy awaits you as the angels of heaven rejoice. Why would you need to hide on the day of judgment? You will not be counted among sinners."
7. "The eternal judgment is not for you, but for those who have strayed far from righteousness, through every generation." "Do not fear the prosperity of the sinful, and do not join them in their wickedness."
8. "Remain distant from their violence and unrighteousness, for you are companions to the heavenly hosts."
9. "Even if sinners say, 'Our sins will not be found out, nor will they be recorded,' know that their wrongdoings are written down every day."
10. "The Great One who sees all keeps a record of light and darkness, day and night, as witnesses to all deeds."
11. "Do not be godless in your hearts. Speak truthfully and do not accuse the Great Holy One of wrongdoing."
12. "Avoid putting trust in idols, for lies and godlessness lead to sin." "I know this mystery: sinners will twist the words of righteousness and spread lies, writing books filled with deceit."
13. "But when they finally record my words truthfully, without change or omission, a new mystery will be revealed."
14. "Books will be given to the righteous and wise, bringing them joy, uprightness, and wisdom."
15. "The righteous will believe in these words, rejoice over them, and find the path of righteousness." "Then those who have learned from these books will be rewarded, for they have walked in the way of truth."

Chapter 105

1. "In those days, the Lord will command the righteous to bear witness to their wisdom. They will be shown the reward for guiding the earth."
2. "I, along with My Son, will be with them forever, walking in the paths of righteousness." "You, children of integrity, will find joy and live in eternal peace. Amen."

Chapter 106

1. "After some days, Methuselah, my son, took a wife for his son Lamech, who bore him a son."
2. "The child's skin was as white as snow, with a rosy glow, and his hair was as white as wool."
3. "His eyes were bright, and when he opened them, the entire house was illuminated as if by the sun."
4. "Immediately, the child spoke to the Lord of righteousness."

5. "Lamech, terrified, ran to his father Methuselah and said, 'I have fathered a strange child, unlike any human."
6. "'His appearance is divine, and I fear he may not be my own, but born of the angels.'"
7. "'Please, father, go to Enoch, who dwells with the angels, and seek the truth about this child.'"
8. "Hearing this, Methuselah came to me at the ends of the earth. He called out, and I heard his voice."
9. "I went to him and asked, 'Why have you come to me, my son?'"
10. "Methuselah replied, 'I am deeply troubled by a vision and the birth of a strange child to my son Lamech."
11. "'This child's appearance is like no man's, with skin as white as snow, eyes bright as the sun, and hair like wool.'"
12. "I, Enoch, answered, 'The Lord is about to do something new on the earth."
13. "'The angels have sinned by mingling with women and producing giant offspring.
14. A great judgment will come upon the earth because of this sin.'"
15. "'The earth will be cleansed by a flood, but this child will be spared.
16. Tell Lamech to name him Noah, for he will be a survivor.'"
17. "'Noah will be the remnant left on earth after the flood, and through him, the earth will be repopulated.'"

Chapter 107

1. "I saw written on the heavenly tablets that generation after generation would continue to transgress until a time of righteousness would arise." "In that day, all wickedness will be destroyed, and sin will be eradicated from the earth, bringing only goodness upon it."
2. "Go now, my son, and let your son Lamech know that this child truly is his, and this is no lie."
3. "When Methuselah heard these words from his father Enoch, who revealed these secrets to him, he returned to Lamech." "He named the child Noah, saying, 'This one will bring comfort to the earth after the devastation.'"

Chapter 108

1. "Here is another message that Enoch wrote for his son Methuselah and those who would come after him, keeping the law in the last days."
2. "'You who have acted righteously, await the time when an end will come for those who commit wickedness; for the downfall of mighty transgressors is certain.'"
3. "'Wait for sin to pass away, for the names of the wicked will be blotted out from the book of life and from the holy records, and their lineage will be destroyed forever.'"

4. "'Their spirits will be cut off, and they will cry out in anguish in a desolate wilderness, suffering in flames with no rest.'"
5. "I saw a cloud too deep to see beyond, with a blazing fire burning brightly, and mountains of light sweeping to and fro."
6. "I asked one of the holy angels beside me, 'What is this bright, fiery place? It is not heaven but appears as a blazing fire.'"
7. "He replied, 'This is where the spirits of sinners and blasphemers are cast. Here suffer those who twisted the words spoken by the prophets.'"
8. "Their deeds are recorded in the heavens, for the angels to see and understand the fate of the wicked."
9. "Among them are also the spirits of the humble and righteous who have suffered much, yet their reward is great." "These ones were shamed by the wicked, yet they did not desire earthly riches. They endured hardship, viewing life as fleeting."
10. "The Lord tested them greatly, finding their spirits pure, that they might bring honor to His name. Their blessings are written in the records."
11. "Because they valued heaven over earthly life, even when trampled by others, they continued to bless My name."
12. "I will summon the righteous spirits from the generation of light. Those born in darkness who were denied honor for their faith will be transformed."
13. "They will be brought into the light, and those who loved My holy name will sit upon thrones of honor, shining in eternal brightness." "In God's righteous judgment, He will reward the faithful. The righteous will see the fate of those born in darkness, as they are cast into eternal night."
14. "The sinners will cry out in despair when they see the righteous shining, while they themselves are cast into a place where suffering is everlasting."

The Book of Jasher

Also known as Sefer haYashar

The *Sefer haYashar*, first published in 1552, is a Hebrew midrash, also referred to as *Toledot Adam* and *Dibre ha-Yamim be-'Aruk*. Its Hebrew name, *Sefer haYashar*, translates to "Book of the Upright" or "Book of the Correct Record." However, in English tradition, it is widely known as the *Book of Jasher*, named after the reference to a "Book of Jasher" in the biblical books of *Joshua* and *2 Samuel*.

Though the English translations, such as Moses Samuel's 1840 version, often present it as the original *Book of Jasher*, rabbinical Judaism does not regard it as such, and the original Hebrew text makes no claim of being the ancient "Book of Jasher." Still, the midrash is valued for its high-quality narrative and chronological alignment with the *Masoretic Text* in Genesis. Some scholars even speculate that it could date back to before the 6th century AD.

CHAPTER 1

1. And God said, "Let Us make man in Our image, after Our likeness," and thus, God created man in His own image.
2. God formed man from the ground, breathing life into his nostrils, and man became a living soul with the gift of speech.
3. Then the LORD declared, "It is not good for man to be alone; I will make a helper suitable for him."
4. The LORD caused a deep sleep to fall upon Adam, and while he slept, He took one of his ribs and fashioned it into a woman, whom He presented to Adam.
5. Upon awakening, Adam saw the woman and proclaimed, "This is bone of my bones, and it shall be called Woman, for it has been taken out of Man." Adam named her Eve, as she was the mother of all living.
6. God blessed them and named them Adam and Eve on the day of their creation, saying, "Be fruitful and multiply; fill the earth."
7. The LORD God placed Adam and his wife in the Garden of Eden to tend and care for it, commanding them, "You may eat from every tree of the garden, but from the Tree of Knowledge of Good and Evil, you shall not eat, for on the day you eat of it, you will surely die."
8. Having blessed and instructed them, God left, and Adam and his wife lived in the garden, obeying His command.
9. Among the creatures was the serpent, who approached to tempt them into disobeying God's command.
10. The serpent persuaded the woman to eat from the Tree of Knowledge, and she listened, taking the fruit and eating, then gave some to her husband, who also ate.

11. Adam and his wife transgressed God's command, and God, knowing this, was angered and cursed them.
12. The LORD drove them out of the Garden of Eden that day to work the ground from which they were taken, settling them east of the garden. Adam knew his wife, and she bore two sons and three daughters.
13. She named the firstborn Cain, saying, "I have acquired a man from the LORD," and the other Abel, saying, "In vanity we came into the earth, and in vanity we will leave it."
14. As the boys grew, Adam gave them land. Cain became a tiller of the ground, while Abel tended sheep.
15. After a few years, they each brought an offering to the LORD. Cain offered the fruits of the ground, and Abel offered the firstborn of his flock with their fat. The LORD accepted Abel's offering with fire from heaven.
16. But the LORD did not accept Cain's offering, for he brought inferior fruit. This caused Cain to grow jealous of Abel, and he sought a reason to kill him.
17. One day, while in the field, Cain, angered by Abel's flock grazing on his land, approached his brother.
18. Cain said to Abel, "Why do you come to feed your flock on my land?"
19. Abel replied, "Why do you eat the flesh of my flock and wear their wool?
20. Return to me the wool and flesh you have taken, and I will leave your land."
21. Cain retorted, "If I slay you, who will hold me accountable?"
22. Abel answered, "God, who made us, will judge between us.
23. He knows your heart and will judge the wicked."
24. Hearing this, Cain's anger burned, and he struck Abel with an iron part of his plow, killing him.
25. Abel's blood spilled upon the earth.
26. Filled with regret, Cain wept
27. And buried Abel's body in the ground.
28. God then appeared to Cain, asking, "Where is your brother Abel?"
29. Cain replied, "I do not know. Am I my brother's keeper?"
30. The LORD said, "What have you done?
31. Your brother's blood cries out to Me from the ground."
32. The LORD cursed Cain, saying, "The ground will no longer yield its strength to you. You will wander the earth until your death."
33. Cain departed from the LORD's presence, moving east of Eden, where he and his family settled.
34. Cain knew his wife, and she bore a son named Enoch.
35. Cain built a city named after his son, Enoch.
36. Enoch fathered Irad, who fathered Mehujael, who fathered Methusael.

CHAPTER 2

1. In the one hundred and thirtieth year of Adam's life on earth, he again knew his wife Eve. She conceived and bore a son in Adam's likeness and image, naming him Seth, saying, "God has granted me another offspring in place of Abel, whom Cain killed."
2. Seth lived one hundred and five years and fathered a son. He named his son Enosh, for during this time, the sons of men began to multiply, afflicting their souls by turning against God.
3. In the days of Enosh, humanity continued to rebel, further inciting the LORD's anger.
4. The people served other gods, forgetting the LORD who had created them. They crafted idols of brass, iron, wood, and stone, bowing down in worship.
5. Each man created his own god, abandoning the LORD throughout Enosh's days. The LORD's anger was kindled by the abominations they committed.
6. The LORD caused the waters of the River Gihon to overwhelm them, destroying a third of the earth. Yet, the people did not turn from their evil ways, continuing in defiance.
7. In those days, there was neither sowing nor reaping; the famine was great, leaving the sons of men without food.
8. The seeds they planted grew only into thorns and thistles, a curse upon the earth from Adam's sin before the LORD.
9. As humanity continued in rebellion, the earth itself grew corrupt.
10. Enosh lived ninety years and fathered Cainan.
11. Cainan, growing in wisdom, ruled over humanity, guiding them in knowledge and leading them to understanding, even having mastery over spirits and demons.
12. Through his wisdom, Cainan foresaw that God would one day destroy humanity for their sins, bringing a flood upon them.
13. In those days, Cainan inscribed future events on stone tablets, storing them in his treasures.
14. Cainan ruled over the earth, turning some people back to the service of God.
15. At seventy years old, Cainan fathered three sons and two daughters.
16. Cainan's children were Mahalaleel, Enan, Mered, Adah, and Zillah.
17. Lamech, son of Methusael, married two of Cainan's daughters. Adah bore him a son, Jabal.
18. She bore another son, naming him Jubal. Zillah, her sister, remained barren at this time.
19. During this period, the sons of men began to transgress the commands given to Adam to be fruitful and multiply.
20. Some men gave their wives a potion to render them barren, wishing to preserve their wives' beauty.
21. Among those who drank the potion was Zillah.
22. Wives who bore children became undesirable to their husbands, while the barren women were preferred.

23. In her old age, Zillah's womb was opened by the LORD, and she bore a son named Tubal-Cain, saying, "The Almighty has granted him to me after I had withered."
24. She bore again, naming her daughter Naamah, saying, "After withering away, I have found pleasure and joy."
25. Lamech, now advanced in years and nearly blind, went into the field one day with his son Tubal-Cain.
26. While in the field, Cain, son of Adam, approached them. Lamech, unable to see well, relied on Tubal-Cain to guide him.
27. Tubal-Cain advised his father to draw his bow, and Lamech, shooting, struck Cain, mistaking him for an animal, and Cain fell dead.
28. The LORD repaid Cain's wickedness for killing Abel, fulfilling His word.
29. Lamech and Tubal-Cain went to see the creature they had killed and discovered it was their ancestor Cain.
30. Grief-stricken, Lamech clapped his hands in despair, accidentally striking Tubal-Cain, who then died.
31. Hearing of these events, Lamech's wives sought to kill him.
32. From that day, Lamech's wives harbored resentment toward him for the deaths of Cain and Tubal-Cain, separating themselves from him.
33. Lamech pleaded with his wives, explaining that his actions had been unintentional due to his old age and failing sight.
34. His wives eventually listened to him, heeding the counsel of their father Adam, but bore him no more children, sensing God's wrath growing.
35. Knowing of humanity's evil deeds, they understood that the LORD's judgment through a flood was near.
36. Mahalaleel, son of Cainan, lived sixty-five years and fathered Jared.
37. Jared, in turn, lived sixty-two years and fathered Enoch.

CHAPTER 3

1. Enoch was sixty-five years old when he fathered Methuselah. After Methuselah's birth, Enoch walked closely with God, serving the LORD and turning away from the wickedness of humanity.
2. Enoch's soul became deeply immersed in God's teachings, knowledge, and understanding. He withdrew from society, hiding himself from others for many days.
3. After many years, as Enoch was praying in his house, a messenger from the LORD called to him from Heaven, and Enoch answered, "Here I am."
4. The messenger instructed him, "Go out from your place of hiding and show yourself to the people, that you may teach them the path they must follow and the work they should do to walk in God's ways."

5. Obeying the word of the LORD, Enoch left his house and went to the people, teaching them the ways of the LORD. He gathered the sons of men and shared with them God's instruction.
6. He proclaimed throughout the land, "Whoever desires to learn the ways of the LORD and pursue good works, let him come to Enoch."
7. All who sought guidance came to Enoch, who reigned over them according to the LORD's word. They bowed before him and listened to his teachings.
8. Filled with God's Spirit, Enoch instructed them in divine wisdom, and they served the LORD during Enoch's lifetime, coming often to hear his words.
9. Kings, princes, and judges from every region came to Enoch for his wisdom, bowing before him and asking him to be their leader. Enoch agreed to reign over them.
10. A total of one hundred and thirty kings and princes assembled, placing themselves under Enoch's rule and authority.
11. Enoch taught them wisdom, knowledge, and God's ways, establishing peace among them. Harmony prevailed on earth during Enoch's lifetime.
12. Enoch reigned over humanity for two hundred and forty-three years, ruling with justice and righteousness and guiding them in the LORD's ways.
13. Enoch's children were Methuselah, Elisha, and Elimelech; he also had two daughters, Melca and Nahmah. Methuselah, at the age of eighty-seven, fathered Lamech.
14. In Lamech's fifty-sixth year, Adam passed away at nine hundred and thirty years old. His sons, along with Enoch and Methuselah, buried him with great honor in the cave where God had directed them.
15. Humanity mourned Adam deeply, establishing a tradition of honoring his memory to this day.
16. Adam's death was due to eating from the Tree of Knowledge, fulfilling the LORD's words about the consequences of his actions.
17. In the year of Adam's death, during Enoch's two hundred and forty-third year as king, Enoch decided to withdraw from public life to devote himself fully to serving the LORD.
18. Although he secluded himself, he did not entirely hide from the people, choosing to spend three days in isolation and then appearing before them on the fourth day.
19. During his days of seclusion, Enoch prayed and praised the LORD. When he reappeared, he answered their questions and taught them about the LORD.
20. Enoch continued this practice for many years. Later, he increased his seclusion, appearing only once a week, then once a month, and eventually only once a year. The people longed to see him, but were in awe of his divine presence, which struck fear in their hearts.
21. Desiring to see him once more, the kings and leaders gathered the people, hoping to speak with him during one of his appearances.
22. When Enoch finally appeared, they assembled before him, and he shared with them the teachings of the LORD. They bowed to him, proclaiming, "May the king live!"

23. While Enoch was teaching, a messenger from the LORD called to him from Heaven, inviting him to ascend to reign with the sons of God as he had with the sons of men on earth.
24. Hearing this, Enoch gathered the people and shared his divine teachings, saying, "I am to ascend to Heaven, though I do not know when."
25. Enoch then imparted wisdom, guiding them on how to live in alignment with God's will.
26. He gave them statutes, judgments, and instructions for peace and continued to live among them, teaching these principles.
27. While Enoch was speaking, the people saw the likeness of a great horse descending from Heaven, moving in the air.
28. They told Enoch what they saw, and he said, "This horse has come for me; my time to leave is near, and you will not see me again."
29. The horse descended and stood before Enoch, visible to all the people.
30. Enoch then proclaimed, "Let anyone who desires to know the ways of the LORD come to me this day before I am taken from you."
31. Many gathered that day, including kings, princes, and counselors, who received Enoch's final teachings on wisdom and devotion to God.
32. Afterward, Enoch mounted the horse, and a great assembly of about eight hundred thousand men followed him for a day's journey.
33. On the second day, Enoch urged them, "Return to your tents, lest you die." Some heeded his warning, while others continued with him.
34. Each day Enoch warned them to turn back, yet many persisted until, on the sixth day, only a few remained, pledging to stay with him no matter the cost.
35. Seeing their resolve, Enoch stopped discouraging them, and they continued on together.
36. When the kings returned, they conducted a census to know how many had followed Enoch to the end.
37. On the seventh day, Enoch ascended into Heaven in a whirlwind, with chariots and horses of fire.
38. On the eighth day, the kings sent men to the place of Enoch's ascent. They found the ground covered with snow and large stones. Some suggested digging through the snow to see if Enoch's followers lay beneath, but they found nothing, for Enoch had been taken up into Heaven.

CHAPTER 4

1. Enoch lived on earth for a total of three hundred and sixty-five years.
2. After Enoch ascended to Heaven, the kings of the earth came together and appointed his son, Methuselah, as their ruler, anointing him to reign in his father's place.
3. Methuselah lived uprightly in the sight of God, following the teachings of his father, Enoch. He devoted his life to instructing people in wisdom, knowledge, and the fear of the LORD, remaining steadfast in the righteous path.

4. However, in the later years of Methuselah's life, humanity turned away from God. The people corrupted the earth, plundering one another, rebelling against God, and refusing to heed Methuselah's voice.
5. The LORD grew exceedingly angry with them, and He caused destruction upon their seed, so there was no sowing or reaping.
6. When they planted crops, only thorns and thistles grew, providing no sustenance.
7. Despite these hardships, the people did not abandon their evil ways, continuing to provoke the LORD, who began to regret creating mankind.
8. God considered eradicating them and took steps toward this end.
9. During this time, Lamech, Methuselah's son, was one hundred and sixty years old when Seth, the son of Adam, passed away.
10. Seth lived nine hundred and twelve years before he died.
11. At one hundred and eighty years old, Lamech married Ashmua, the daughter of his uncle Enoch's son, Elisha, and she conceived.
12. During these days, the people continued to sow the ground, yet only a little food grew, and they persisted in their rebellion against God.
13. Lamech's wife gave birth to a son around the new year.
14. Methuselah named the child Noah, saying, "In his days, the earth will be free from corruption." Lamech named him Menachem, saying, "This one will bring us comfort in our labors and struggles on the cursed earth."
15. The child grew and was weaned, walking in the ways of his grandfather Methuselah and remaining righteous before God.
16. Meanwhile, humanity continued to stray from the LORD, filling the earth with children and teaching one another wicked practices.
17. Every man made a god for himself, and they plundered one another, filling the earth with violence and corruption.
18. Their judges and rulers took wives by force from others, taking daughters of men as they pleased. They even engaged in unnatural practices, mixing species of animals to provoke the LORD. God saw the earth's corruption, as all flesh—both men and animals—had turned from His ways.
19. God declared, "I will blot out man whom I created from the face of the earth, along with the birds of the air, cattle, and wild animals, for I regret creating them."
20. In those days, all who followed the ways of the LORD passed away before the coming judgment, as it was ordained by the LORD that they should not witness the evil He had foretold for humanity.
21. However, Noah found favor with the LORD, who chose him and his descendants to continue the human race on earth.

CHAPTER 5

1. In Noah's eighty-fourth year, Enoch, the son of Seth, died at the age of nine hundred and five years.
2. In Noah's one hundred and seventy-ninth year, Cainan, the son of Enosh, passed away, having lived nine hundred and ten years.
3. In the two hundred and thirty-fourth year of Noah's life, Mahalaleel, son of Cainan, died at the age of eight hundred and ninety-five years.
4. Jared, the son of Mahalaleel, died in Noah's three hundred and thirty-sixth year, having lived nine hundred and sixty-two years.
5. All those who faithfully followed the LORD passed away before witnessing the evil that God would bring upon the earth.
6. Many years later, in Noah's four hundred and eightieth year, all the remaining righteous had passed except Methuselah. God then spoke to Noah and Methuselah,
7. "Tell the people, 'Thus says the LORD, turn from your wicked ways and forsake your evil deeds, and the LORD will withhold the disaster He has planned.'"
8. The LORD proclaimed, "I grant a period of one hundred and twenty years. If they repent and abandon their evil, I will turn away from My judgment."
9. Noah and Methuselah spread the message, repeatedly warning the people to turn back to God.
10. But the people refused to listen, hardening their hearts against the words of Noah and Methuselah.
11. For one hundred and twenty years, the LORD extended His patience, hoping they would return to Him.
12. Noah refrained from taking a wife, thinking, "God may destroy the earth soon, so why should I have children?"
13. Noah, a just man, remained blameless in his generation, and the LORD chose him to continue humanity on earth.
14. God then commanded Noah, "Take a wife and have children, for I have seen you as righteous."
15. Obediently, Noah took a wife, choosing Naamah, the daughter of Enoch, who was five hundred and eighty years old.
16. Noah was four hundred and ninety-eight years old when he married Naamah.
17. Naamah bore a son, whom Noah named Japheth, saying, "God has enlarged me on the earth." She bore another son, Shem, whom Noah named as a remnant to preserve life.
18. Noah was five hundred and two years old when Shem was born, and both sons grew up in the ways of the LORD, following the teachings of Methuselah and their father, Noah.
19. In those days, Lamech, Noah's father, passed away, not fully following in his ancestors' ways, at one hundred and ninety-five years of Noah's life.
20. Lamech lived a total of seven hundred and seventy years before his death.
21. Those who knew the LORD all passed away before witnessing the calamity God had planned for their kin, as He wished to spare them from the suffering to come.

22. At that time, the LORD instructed Noah and Methuselah, "Once more, declare My message to the people, that they may turn from their evil, and I will withhold judgment."
23. Noah and Methuselah delivered God's words
24. But the people paid no heed to their warnings.
25. The LORD then said to Noah, "The end of all flesh has come before Me because of their evil; I will destroy the earth."
26. God instructed Noah, "Build an ark of gopher wood in a specific place, following these dimensions
27. Three hundred cubits in length, fifty cubits in width, and thirty cubits in height.
28. Construct a door on the side and cover the ark with pitch inside and out.
29. I will bring a flood upon the earth, destroying all life under Heaven. But you and your family will be saved.
30. Gather two of every kind of living creature, male and female, to preserve life on earth.
31. Collect food for yourselves and the animals to sustain you during the flood.
32. Choose three women from among the daughters of men to be wives for your sons."
33. Noah followed God's commands
34. Beginning the ark's construction in his five hundred and ninety-fifth year, completing it in five years.
35. He also took three daughters of Eliakim, son of Methuselah, as wives for his sons.
36. Around this time, Methuselah, son of Enoch, died at the age of nine hundred and sixty years.

CHAPTER 6

1. After Methuselah's death, the LORD spoke to Noah, saying, "Go into the Ark with your household, for I will gather all the animals of the earth to you—beasts of the field and birds of the air—and they will come to surround the Ark."
2. "Sit by the doors of the Ark, and as the animals arrive, those that crouch before you, you will bring into the Ark. Those that stand will remain outside."
3. The next day, just as the LORD had said, animals, beasts, and birds arrived in great numbers, encircling the Ark.
4. Noah sat by the door of the Ark, and of all the creatures that crouched before him, he brought them inside, leaving the others on the earth.
5. A lioness came with her two cubs, a male and a female, and all three crouched before Noah.
6. Suddenly, the cubs turned against the lioness, striking her so that she fled, returning to stand with the other lions.
7. Noah observed this with amazement, and he took the two cubs into the Ark.
8. Thus, Noah brought into the Ark all living creatures on earth; none were left behind except those the LORD had instructed him not to bring.

9. Two by two, they came to Noah, while he brought seven pairs of the clean animals and clean birds, as God commanded him.
10. The animals and birds continued to surround the Ark, and the rains did not begin for another seven days.
11. On the seventh day, the LORD shook the whole earth; darkness covered the sun, the foundations of the earth trembled, lightning flashed, thunder roared, and all the fountains of the earth broke open—events beyond anything the people had seen. God did this to stir fear in the hearts of men and end evil on earth.
12. Despite these signs, humanity did not turn from their wickedness, and they only intensified the LORD's anger, ignoring the warnings.
13. After seven days, in the six hundredth year of Noah's life, the floodwaters came upon the earth.
14. All the fountains of the deep burst open, and the windows of Heaven poured forth rain upon the earth for forty days and forty nights.
15. Noah, his family, and all the creatures in the Ark took shelter from the floodwaters, and the LORD sealed the Ark.
16. Those left on earth were overwhelmed by the rain, as it poured relentlessly, driving animals and people toward the Ark.
17. About seven hundred thousand men and women gathered near the Ark, calling out to Noah
18. "Open the door for us, that we may come inside and live!"
19. Noah responded loudly from within the Ark, "Have you not rejected the LORD, denying His existence? This disaster has come upon you because of your rebellion, cutting you off from the face of the earth.
20. Did I not warn you of this day one hundred and twenty years ago, and yet you refused to heed the voice of the LORD?"
21. They answered, "We are now ready to return to the LORD; open the door, that we may live."
22. Noah replied, "Now that you face calamity, you wish to return to the LORD. Why did you not repent during the hundred and twenty years the LORD gave you as a grace period?
23. Now, in your desperation, you turn to me, but the LORD will not listen to you today, and your plea will not be answered."
24. The crowd, desperate to escape the rain, attempted to break into the Ark.
25. But the LORD commanded the surrounding animals to defend the Ark, and they drove the people away. Scattered, each went his way, yet the rain continued.
26. For forty days and forty nights, the waters prevailed over the earth, and all flesh perished—men, animals, beasts, creeping things, and birds of the air—leaving only Noah and those with him in the Ark.
27. The floodwaters rose greatly, lifting the Ark high above the earth.

28. The Ark floated on the surface of the waters, tossed about as though its occupants were like stew in a cauldron.
29. Inside the Ark, fear and anxiety gripped the creatures
30. And they cried out in distress—the lions roared, the oxen bellowed, the wolves howled, and every animal lamented in its own way. Their cries reached far and wide, and Noah and his sons wept and prayed, terrified that they had come to the gates of death.
31. In his fear, Noah prayed fervently to the LORD, "O LORD, help us, for we are unable to endure this trial. The waters surround us, torrents terrify us, and the snares of death threaten us. Answer us, O LORD; shine Your face upon us and be merciful. Save and deliver us!"
32. The LORD heard Noah's prayer and remembered him.
33. A wind swept across the earth, calming the waters, and the Ark came to rest.
34. The fountains of the deep and the windows of Heaven were closed, and the rain ceased.
35. The waters began to recede, and the Ark settled on the mountains of Ararat.
36. Noah opened a window of the Ark and prayed again, saying, "O LORD, Creator of heaven and earth, release us from this confinement, for I am weary with longing."
37. The LORD heard Noah's plea and replied, "When the year is complete, you will be free to go out."
38. When the full year had passed, the waters dried from the earth, and Noah removed the Ark's covering.
39. On the twenty-seventh day of the second month, the earth was dry, but Noah and his family waited until the LORD commanded them to leave the Ark.
40. At the appointed time, the LORD instructed them to go out, and they exited the Ark.
41. Each creature returned to its natural habitat, and Noah and his sons settled in the land God directed them to inhabit, serving the LORD faithfully.
42. The LORD blessed Noah and his sons as they left the Ark, saying, "Be fruitful and fill the earth. Grow strong and multiply abundantly across the land."

CHAPTER 7

1. These are the sons of Noah: Japheth, Ham, and Shem. Each had children after the flood, as they had taken wives beforehand.
2. The sons of Japheth were Gomer, Magog, Madai, Javan, Tubal, Meshech, and Tiras—a total of seven sons.
3. Gomer's sons were Askinaz, Rephas, and Tegarmah.
4. Magog's sons were Elichanaf and Lubal.
5. The sons of Madai were Achon, Zeelo, Chazoni, and Lot.
6. Javan's sons were Elisha, Tarshish, Chittim, and Dudonim.
7. Tubal's sons were Ariphi, Kesed, and Taari.
8. Meshech's sons were Dedon, Zaron, and Shebashni.

9. Tiras's sons were Benib, Gera, Lupirion, and Gilak. These were Japheth's descendants, numbering about four hundred and sixty men.
10. The sons of Ham were Cush, Mitzraim, Phut, and Canaan.
11. Cush's sons were Seba, Havilah, Sabta, Raama, and Satecha; Raama's sons were Sheba and Dedan.
12. Mitzraim's sons were Lud, Anom, Pathros, Chasloth, and Chaphtor.
13. Phut's sons were Gebul, Hadan, Benah, and Adan.
14. Canaan's sons were Zidon, Heth, Amori, Gergashi, Hivi, Arkee, Seni, Arodi, Zimodi, and Chamothi. These descendants of Ham numbered about seven hundred and thirty men.
15. Shem's sons were Elam, Asshur, Arphaxad, Lud, and Aram.
16. Elam's sons were Shushan, Machul, and Harmon.
17. Asshur's sons were Mirus and Mokil. Arphaxad's sons were Salah, Anar, and Ashcol.
18. Lud's sons were Pethor and Bizayon, while Aram's sons were Uz, Chul, Gather, and Mash. These descendants of Shem numbered about three hundred men.
19. The lineage of Shem continued: Shem begot Arphaxad, who begot Salah, and Salah begot Eber.
20. Eber had two sons: Peleg, named so because in his time, humanity was divided, and Yoktan, as in his days, the lives of men were shortened.
21. Yoktan's sons were Almodad, Shelaf, Chazarmoves, Yerach, Hadurom, Ozel, Diklah, Obal, Abimael, Sheba, Ophir, Havilah, and Jobab.
22. Peleg's line continued with his son Yen, who fathered Serug, who fathered Nahor, who fathered Terah. Terah, at thirty-eight, fathered Haran and Nahor.
23. Cush, son of Ham, took a wife in his old age and had a son named Nimrod, for in those days, people once again began to rebel against God.
24. Nimrod grew to be greatly loved by his father, as he was born in Cush's old age. Cush also possessed the garments of skin that God had made for Adam and Eve upon their expulsion from Eden.
25. After Adam and Eve's death, these garments passed to Enoch, who gave them to Methuselah before his ascension.
26. At Methuselah's death, Noah took the garments and brought them onto the Ark, keeping them until he left.
27. Upon leaving the Ark, Ham secretly stole the garments from Noah and hid them from his brothers.
28. When Ham's firstborn, Cush, was born, he secretly gave him the garments, and Cush kept them for many years.
29. When Cush begot Nimrod, he passed these garments to him, and when Nimrod was twenty, he wore them, gaining great strength from them.
30. With God's favor, Nimrod became a mighty hunter on earth, offering animals on altars to the LORD.

31. Nimrod grew strong, rising among his brothers, and fought their battles, delivering them from their enemies.
32. The LORD granted him victory, and Nimrod prospered, becoming a renowned leader and ruler.
33. People began to use Nimrod's name as a blessing, saying, "May God strengthen us as He did Nimrod, the mighty hunter and defender of his people."
34. When Nimrod turned forty, a war broke out between his brothers and the descendants of Japheth.
35. Nimrod gathered the sons of Cush, about four hundred and sixty men, along with eighty hired men from his friends.
36. He encouraged them, saying, "Do not fear; our enemies will fall into our hands, and you may do with them as you please."
37. Nimrod and his men, totaling about five hundred, fought and defeated their enemies, placing officials over the conquered people.
38. He took captives, who became servants to Nimrod and his brothers, and he returned home victorious.
39. Following his victory, Nimrod's brothers and supporters crowned him king.
40. He established a royal administration with princes, judges, and rulers, appointing Terah, son of Nahor, as the head of his army.
41. Nimrod honored Terah, elevating him above all his princes.
42. Once secure in his reign, Nimrod decided to build a city for his palace, with his counselors' support.
43. They found a vast valley to the east and constructed a great city, which Nimrod named Shinar, as the LORD had shaken his enemies.
44. Nimrod settled in Shinar, ruling securely, and conquered surrounding enemies, expanding his kingdom.
45. His fame spread among nations, and people from every language and land gathered to Shinar, bringing offerings and acknowledging him as king.
46. Nimrod ruled over all the descendants of Noah, and they all looked to him for leadership.
47. At this time, all people spoke one language. But Nimrod did not follow the ways of the LORD; he became more wicked than any man before him.
48. He made idols of wood and stone, leading his people in rebellion against the LORD. His son Mardon was even more wicked than he.
49. People would say, "From the wicked comes wickedness," a saying that began with Mardon and spread across the earth.
50. Terah, son of Nahor, greatly respected by Nimrod and his princes, was highly favored.
51. Terah married Amthelo, daughter of Cornebo, and she bore him a son when he was seventy years old. Terah named his son Abram, as the king had honored and elevated Terah above all his princes.

CHAPTER 8

1. On the night Abram was born, Terah's servants, as well as Nimrod's wise men and conjurers, gathered at Terah's house to celebrate. They feasted, drank, and rejoiced together.
2. As the wise men and conjurers left the house, they looked up at the night sky and observed a remarkable sight—a single large star rising from the east, which moved across the heavens, consuming four other stars from each of the four directions.
3. The king's wise men and conjurers were astonished at the sight and pondered its meaning.
4. They spoke among themselves, saying, "This can only signify the child born to Terah tonight. He will grow, prosper, and his descendants will fill the earth, conquering mighty kings and possessing their lands."
5. The wise men and conjurers returned home that night, but in the morning
6. They assembled to discuss the sight they had witnessed.
7. They said, "If we do not tell the king of this omen, he may later question why we concealed it, and we will suffer punishment."
8. Agreeing on this course, they went to the king, bowing before him and proclaiming, "May the king live!"
9. They told him, "We learned that a son was born last night to Terah, the prince of your host. We visited his house, celebrated with him, and rejoiced in his honor."
10. They continued, "After leaving Terah's home, we looked to the heavens and saw a great star coming from the east, which moved swiftly and consumed four other stars."
11. "We were astonished and, understanding the sight through our wisdom, realized it foretells the destiny of the child born to Terah. This child will grow, multiply, and rise to power, conquering all the kings of the earth and inheriting their lands forever."
12. The wise men concluded, "Now, our lord and king, we have revealed this matter to you.
13. If it pleases you, give Terah a reward for this child, that we may kill him before he grows and his influence endangers us all."
14. Hearing their words, the king approved of their plan, and he summoned Terah, who appeared before him.
15. The king said, "I have been told that you have had a son, and a great sign was seen in the heavens on the night of his birth."
16. "Therefore, give me the child, that we may end his life before his evil rises against us. In return, I will fill your house with silver and gold."
17. Terah responded respectfully, "My lord and king, I have heard your command, and I am your servant, ready to fulfill your wishes."
18. "However," Terah continued, "let me share an incident from last night and seek your advice on it. Then, I will answer your request."
19. The king encouraged him, "Speak."

20. Terah said, "Last night, Ayon, son of Mored, came to me, saying, 'Give me the magnificent horse that the king gifted you, and in exchange, I will give you silver, gold, and food for its value.'"
21. "I replied to him, 'Wait until I consult the king regarding your offer, and whatever the king decides, I will do.'"
22. "Now, my lord and king, I seek your counsel on this matter."
23. The king, angered by what he saw as foolishness, replied, "Are you so ignorant as to exchange such a fine horse for silver, gold, or food? Are you so lacking in wealth that you would trade it away?"
24. "What is silver, gold, or food compared to such a rare horse that I gave you? There is no other like it on earth."
25. Terah replied, "The king speaks wisely, my lord. And yet, what is this that you ask of me?"
26. "You ask me to give up my son in exchange for silver and gold. What purpose would the wealth serve after my son's death? Who would inherit it? Upon my death, it would return to the king."
27. Hearing this, the king was troubled by Terah's words and felt greatly displeased.
28. Realizing the king's anger, Terah said, "All that I have is at the king's command. Do with me as you wish, and take my son, for he and his two older brothers are in your power."
29. The king responded, "No, I desire only your youngest son, for I will purchase him from you at a price."
30. Terah respectfully replied, "Please, my lord and king, allow me three days to consider this matter and consult with my family. Then I will answer your request."
31. The king agreed, granting him three days. Terah returned to his home, shared the king's words with his family, and they were filled with fear.
32. On the third day, the king sent for Terah, saying, "Send me your son in exchange for the agreed price. If you refuse, I will destroy all you have, leaving not even a dog alive."
33. Terah, knowing the urgency of the king's command, took a child born that day to one of his servants and presented him to the king, receiving payment for the child.
34. The LORD was with Terah, ensuring that Nimrod would not bring harm upon Abram. The king took the child, believing it to be Abram, and struck his head against the ground to kill him. This act was hidden from the king, as it was God's will that Abram's life be spared.
35. Meanwhile, Terah secretly took Abram, along with his mother and nurse, and hid them in a cave, bringing them provisions each month.
36. The LORD was with Abram in the cave, and he grew up there. Abram remained hidden in the cave for ten years, and the king, along with his princes and wise men, believed that he had killed Abram.

CHAPTER 9

1. During these days, Haran, the eldest son of Terah and brother of Abram, took a wife.
2. At thirty-nine years old, Haran's wife bore him a son named Lot.
3. She conceived again and bore a daughter named Milca, and once more, bearing another daughter, whom she named Sarai.
4. Haran was forty-two when Sarai was born, which was in the tenth year of Abram's life. Around this time, Abram, along with his mother and nurse, emerged from the cave where they had been hiding, as the king and his subjects had forgotten about Abram.
5. After coming out, Abram went to live with Noah and Shem, Noah's son, to learn the ways and instructions of the LORD. No one knew of his whereabouts, and Abram remained with Noah and Shem for a long period.
6. Abram spent thirty-nine years in Noah's household, learning and walking in the ways of the LORD, from the age of three until his death, following the guidance of Noah and Shem. Meanwhile, the people of the earth were increasingly rebelling against the LORD, turning to other gods and forsaking their Creator.
7. The inhabitants of the earth, each in their own way, created gods of wood and stone, which could neither hear, see, nor save. These became the idols that the people served.
8. Even the king, his servants, Terah, and his entire household were among the first to worship these false gods.
9. Terah had twelve large idols made from wood and stone, each representing one month of the year. Every month, Terah offered meat and drink offerings to his gods, following this ritual throughout his days.
10. That generation was utterly wicked before the LORD, each man creating his own god while abandoning the One who created them.
11. During this time, no one knew the LORD, for everyone served their own idols, except Noah and his household, who held true to the LORD's ways. Abram, growing up in Noah's house, also grew in wisdom and understanding of the LORD.
12. The LORD granted Abram a discerning heart, helping him realize the futility of his generation's practices and the powerlessness of their idols.
13. One day, Abram saw the sun shining and said to himself, "Surely this sun, which shines upon the earth, must be God, and I will worship it."
14. Abram devoted himself to the sun that day, praying to it. However, when evening came and the sun set, he realized, "This cannot be God."
15. Continuing to seek the truth, Abram pondered, "Who is the One who created the heavens and the earth? Where is He?"
16. As night fell, Abram looked around and saw the sun had disappeared, leaving only darkness.
17. Observing the stars and the moon, Abram thought, "Perhaps this is the God who created the earth and mankind, and the stars are His servants." Abram prayed to the moon throughout the night.

18. But when morning came and the sun rose again, Abram reconsidered, saying, "These cannot be the creators of the earth and humankind. They are only servants of the true God." Abram continued to seek understanding of the LORD in Noah's house and served Him all his days, though his generation had forgotten God and worshipped idols of wood and stone.
19. Meanwhile, King Nimrod reigned securely over a united earth, as all people shared one language and common purpose.
20. Nimrod's princes, including Phut, Mitzraim, Cush, and Canaan, gathered to discuss a plan to build a great city and a tower reaching the heavens.
21. They reasoned, "By doing this, we will make ourselves famous, establish our rule over the world, end the conflicts of our enemies, and prevent ourselves from being scattered."
22. They presented their plan to the king, who approved, and the families gathered, numbering about six hundred thousand men, and set out to find a suitable location.
23. After searching, they found a vast valley to the east in the land of Shinar, which they considered ideal, and they settled there.
24. They began making bricks and burning fires to build the city and the tower, which they intended to complete.
25. Their project was a direct rebellion against the LORD God of Heaven, as they sought to challenge Him and ascend to Heaven itself.
26. The people divided into three factions: one declared, "We will ascend and wage war against Him"; another said, "We will place our own gods in Heaven and serve them"; and the third said, "We will go up and strike Him with bows and spears." God observed their intentions and the city and tower they were building.
27. The city was large and the tower exceedingly tall and strong, so much so that it took an entire year for builders to carry materials up to the higher levels.
28. Each day, workers ascended and descended. If a brick fell and broke, the people mourned, but if a man fell and died, they paid him no attention.
29. The LORD saw their intentions and, as they shot arrows toward Heaven, He caused the arrows to return stained with blood, deceiving them into believing they had struck those in Heaven.
30. This deception from the LORD led them into further error, ultimately resulting in their downfall.
31. Over many days and years, they continued to build the tower and the city, until God acted to disrupt their work.
32. God spoke to seventy of His messengers, saying, "Let us descend and confuse their language, so they will no longer understand one another."
33. The messengers descended, and from that day forward, each person forgot his neighbor's language, causing great confusion. When one asked for mortar or stones, his neighbor, unable to understand, would hand him something else, leading to frustration and even violence.

34. This chaos continued for many days, with countless people being killed by their own companions.
35. The LORD dealt with each of the three factions according to their intentions: those who sought to ascend and serve their own gods were transformed into apes and elephants; those who aimed to strike Heaven with arrows were slain by their companions; and those who intended to fight God were scattered across the earth.
36. Realizing the calamity that had befallen them, the survivors abandoned the tower, scattering across the world.
37. The city and tower were left incomplete, and the place was named Babel, for it was there that the LORD confused the language of the entire earth, creating disunity among them.
38. As for the tower, the earth opened up and swallowed a third of it, fire from Heaven consumed another third, and the final third still stands today, with a circumference of a three-day journey.
39. Many people perished in the tower—a vast number beyond counting.

CHAPTER 10

1. In the forty-eighth year of Abram's life, Peleg, the son of Eber, passed away, having lived a total of two hundred and thirty-nine years.
2. After the LORD scattered humanity for their transgression at the tower, people spread out across the earth in various groups and directions.
3. Each family established its own language, land, and city, settling across the four corners of the earth.
4. The sons of men constructed numerous cities wherever they settled, following the places where the LORD had scattered them.
5. Some of these cities were built in areas where they were later uprooted, and they named these cities after themselves, their children, or significant events in their lives.
6. The descendants of Japheth, son of Noah, established cities where they were scattered, naming each after their own families, dividing themselves into various groups and languages.
7. The sons of Japheth and their descendants were: Gomer, Magog, Madai, Javan, Tubal, Meshech, and Tiras. These were Japheth's descendants according to their generations.
8. The descendants of Gomer settled by the River Franza in the land of Franza; these people were known as the Francum.
9. The children of Rephas, known as the Bartonim, settled in Bartonia near the River Ledah, which flows into the great sea Gihon, also known as Oceanus.
10. Togarmah's descendants divided into ten families: Buzar, Parzunac, Balgar, Elicanum, Ragbib, Tarki, Bid, Zebuc, Ongal, and Tilmaz.
11. These families settled in the north, building cities named after themselves.
12. The families of Angoli, Balgar, and Parzunac settled by the River Dubnee, naming their cities after themselves.

13. The descendants of Javan, known as the Javanim, settled in Makdonia, while Madai's descendants, the Orelum, resided in Curson, and Tubal's people settled in Tuskanah near the River Pashiah.
14. Meshech's descendants, called the Shibashni, and Tiras's descendants, including Rushash, Cushni, and Ongolis, built cities near the Sea of Jabus by the River Cura, which flows into the River Tragan.
15. Elishah's descendants, known as the Almanim, built cities between the mountains of Job and Shibathmo. Among these were the people of Lumbardi, who eventually conquered Italia and settled there.
16. Chittim's descendants, the Romim, lived in the Valley of Canopia by the River Tibreu.
17. Dudonim's descendants settled along the coast of the Sea of Gihon in the land of Bordna.
18. These are the families and cities of Japheth's descendants, established after their scattering from the tower, named after themselves and significant events.
19. The sons of Ham were Cush, Mitzraim, Phut, and Canaan
20. And they built cities according to their generations, naming them after their ancestors.
21. Mitzraim's descendants were the Ludim, Anamim, Lehabim, Naphtuchim, Pathrusim, Casluchim, and Caphturim.
22. These seven families lived by the River Sihor, also known as the brook of Egypt, naming their cities after themselves.
23. The children of Pathros and Casloch intermarried, giving rise to five families: the Pelishtim, Azathim, Gerarim, Githim, and Ekronim. They too built cities named after their forefathers.
24. The descendants of Canaan also built cities, totaling eleven primary cities, along with numerous others.
25. Four men from Ham's lineage—Sodom, Gomorrah, Admah, and Zeboyim—settled in a plain
26. And each built a city, naming them after themselves.
27. They, along with their descendants, prospered in these cities, multiplying and living in peace.
28. Seir, son of Hur and grandson of Hivi, a descendant of Canaan, settled in a valley near Mount Paran. He built a city named Seir, where he lived with his seven sons and household.
29. These are the descendants of Ham, dispersed by language and city after the scattering from the tower.
30. Some descendants of Shem, son of Noah and ancestor of all the children of Eber, also settled and built cities, naming them after themselves.
31. Shem's sons were Elam, Asshur, Arphaxad, Lud, and Aram, and they too constructed cities named after themselves.
32. Asshur and his family, a large group, journeyed to a distant land and found a vast valley where they built four cities.

33. They named these cities Ninevah, Resen, Calach, and Rehoboth, and Asshur's descendants continue to dwell there.
34. The descendants of Aram built a city named Uz, after their eldest brother, which remains the land of Uz to this day.
35. Two years after the tower's fall, a man from Asshur's line named Bela left Ninevah with his household, seeking a place to settle.
36. Bela traveled until he reached the cities of the plain near Sodom and built a small city named Bela, known today as Zoar.
37. These are the families of Shem's descendants, scattered across the earth with their languages and cities after the tower.
38. Every kingdom, city, and family from Noah's descendants established multiple cities.
39. They also set up governance within their cities to maintain order, a practice carried on by all the families of Noah's descendants throughout the earth.

CHAPTER 11

1. Nimrod, son of Cush, remained in Shinar, reigning over the land and establishing cities there.
2. The names of the four cities he built reflected events surrounding the Tower of Babel.
3. He named the first city *Babel*, saying, "Here the LORD confounded the language of the whole earth."
4. The second city he called *Erech*, marking the place where God dispersed them.
5. The third city was named *Eched*, because a great battle occurred there, and the fourth was named *Calnah*, as his princes and mighty men were consumed there, provoking the LORD with rebellion.
6. After building these cities, Nimrod settled his people, princes, and remaining warriors there. He established his rule securely in Babel and was called *Amraphel* by his subjects, as his men had fallen due to his actions at the tower.
7. However, Nimrod did not repent and continued his wicked ways, leading the people astray, and his son Mardon was even more corrupt, adding to his father's transgressions.
8. This gave rise to the saying, "From the wicked comes wickedness."
9. Around this time, a conflict arose among the families of Ham's descendants over the cities they had built.
10. Chedorlaomer, king of Elam, waged war against them, subduing them, and extended his control to the five cities of the plain
11. Which served him for twelve years, paying him tribute.
12. During this period, Nahor, son of Serug, died in the forty-ninth year of Abram's life.
13. In Abram's fiftieth year, he returned from Noah's household to his father Terah's home.
14. Abram, who knew the LORD and followed His ways, had the LORD's presence with him.

15. However, Terah, still serving as captain of Nimrod's army, remained devoted to idol worship.
16. When Abram entered his father's house and saw twelve idols, he became enraged at the sight of them.
17. Swearing by the LORD, he vowed to destroy the idols within three days.
18. With his anger stirred, Abram left the chamber and went to his father's courtyard, where he found Terah sitting with his servants.
19. Abram sat down before his father and asked, "Father, where is the God who created the heavens, the earth, and all people, including you and me?"
20. Terah answered, "They are all here in the house."
21. Abram requested to see them, so Terah led him to the inner chamber filled with idols of wood and stone—twelve large ones and countless smaller images.
22. "These are the creators of all you see," Terah said, bowing to them before leaving the room.
23. After Terah departed, Abram went to his mother
24. And requested a young goat to prepare savory meat as an offering for the idols.
25. His mother prepared the meat, which Abram brought before the idols
26. But as he waited, none of them moved or ate.
27. Abram mocked them, saying, "Perhaps the meal displeased them; tomorrow, I'll bring more to see if they will eat."
28. The next day, he asked his mother to prepare a feast of three fine young goats, which she did, unaware of Abram's intentions.
29. Abram placed the food before the idols, watching all day
30. But still, none moved or responded. That evening, filled with the Spirit of God
31. Abram cried out, "Woe to this generation who worship these lifeless idols!"
32. Enraged, he took a hatchet and destroyed all the idols, leaving only the largest with the hatchet in its hand.
33. When Terah returned and saw the broken idols, his anger flared, and he confronted Abram.
34. Abram claimed that the large idol had destroyed the others after a dispute over the offering, placing the blame on it.
35. Furious, Terah accused Abram of lying, stating, "These idols are wood and stone. They cannot move or strike anything."
36. Abram responded, "Then why do you worship them? Can they save you or respond to your prayers? Why forsake the LORD who created all things?"
37. He warned Terah of the consequences of idolatry, urging him to abandon these false gods.
38. Terah, outraged, reported Abram's actions to King Nimrod, requesting justice.
39. The king summoned Abram, who reiterated his story about the large idol destroying the others, questioning the wisdom of serving powerless idols.

40. Nimrod, angered by Abram's words, rebuked him, but Abram warned the king of the LORD's judgment, reminding him of the flood's destruction upon those who sinned.
41. Declaring that he served the God who held power over life and death, Abram cautioned Nimrod and his people against continuing in their idolatrous ways.
42. Finishing his words, Abram looked to the heavens and said, "The LORD sees all wickedness and will judge justly."
43. Nimrod, seething with rage, dismissed Abram's warning, perceiving it as an affront to his authority and his gods.
44. Nimrod turned to his advisors and ordered that Abram be imprisoned, intending to determine a severe punishment for his defiance.
45. While Abram was held in captivity, Nimrod consulted with his council, many of whom urged that Abram be put to death to set an example.
46. Yet, some among them hesitated, aware of Abram's wisdom and fearing that shedding innocent blood might provoke the wrath of Abram's God.
47. Ultimately, Nimrod ordered that Abram be cast into a furnace, believing that if Abram's God were truly powerful, He would save him from the flames.
48. The furnace was prepared, and Abram was brought forth, yet he remained steadfast, showing no fear as he approached the fire.
49. Abram prayed quietly to the LORD, placing his life in God's hands and trusting Him fully.
50. When Abram was cast into the furnace, the flames roared and consumed everything around him, but to the astonishment of all who watched, Abram stood unharmed in the midst of the fire.
51. The people marveled, some exclaiming that Abram's God must indeed be the true God, for He had delivered Abram from the flames.
52. Nimrod, shaken by this display, was filled with both fear and wonder but remained defiant, refusing to acknowledge the LORD.
53. After three days, Nimrod ordered Abram to be brought out of the furnace, having hoped he would perish, but when Abram emerged unscathed, the king was left speechless.
54. Abram stood before Nimrod, unburned and unharmed, and with a calm resolve, he declared, "The LORD, my God, whom I serve, delivered me from your fire. He alone is sovereign over life and death."
55. Some of Nimrod's advisors, witnessing this miracle, began to question their own loyalty to Nimrod's gods and privately marveled at the power of Abram's God.
56. Nimrod, however, was overcome by pride and dismissed Abram, fearing the influence he might hold over the people if he continued to live openly.
57. He ordered Terah to take Abram away, commanding that Abram not return to his court.
58. Terah, concerned for his son's safety, took Abram and removed him from Nimrod's sight, guiding him to a safe place.

59. Abram continued to grow in wisdom, walking in the ways of the LORD, and began to influence those around him, teaching them of the LORD's power and goodness.
60. Though Nimrod's kingdom remained steeped in idolatry, a quiet movement began among some of the people, as Abram's faith and resilience inspired them to seek the true God.
61. In this way, the LORD protected Abram and allowed him to grow in strength and influence, preparing him for the greater calling that lay ahead.

CHAPTER 12:

1. When the king heard Abram's words, he commanded that Abram be imprisoned, where he remained for ten days.
2. At the end of these days, the king summoned all the rulers, princes, governors, and sages from the surrounding regions to gather. With Abram still in confinement, they assembled before the king.
3. The king addressed the gathering, saying, "You have heard what Abram, son of Terah, has done. He was brought before me, and despite his actions and words, he did not waver. Now he is confined, and I seek your judgment on his case."
4. The advisors responded, "The law dictates that anyone who defies the king should be hanged. Since Abram also scorned our gods, he must be burned. If it pleases the king, let a fire be prepared in the furnace for three days and nights, and then Abram can be cast into it."
5. Agreeing, the king ordered his servants to prepare the fire in Kasdim's furnace. They built it up for three days and nights, then brought Abram from his confinement.
6. Word of Abram's impending fate spread, and a crowd of about nine hundred thousand men, women, and children gathered to witness the event.
7. Among the crowd, the king's sages recognized Abram and reminded the king that he was the child marked by the star's appearance at birth, a sign they had interpreted years ago. The king, angered by this revelation, summoned Terah, Abram's father.
8. The king demanded an explanation, and Terah, seeing the king's anger, admitted that he had presented another child to the king out of love for his son, Abram.
9. Furious, the king sentenced Haran, Terah's eldest, who Terah had named as an accomplice, to share Abram's fate.
10. Both Abram and Haran were stripped of all but their lower garments, bound, and thrown into the furnace. But while Haran was consumed by the fire, Abram remained unharmed, walking freely within the flames.
11. The LORD had compassion on Abram, burning away only the cords binding him while protecting him from harm.
12. For three days and nights, Abram walked unscathed in the fire, to the amazement of the king's servants, who reported back what they saw.
13. The king himself went to witness this, astonished to see Abram alive amidst the flames. He ordered Abram's release, but the flames prevented anyone from approaching him.

14. Finally, the king called out directly, and Abram emerged from the furnace unharmed, his lower garments intact, while only the cords had burned.
15. The king asked how he survived, and Abram replied, "The God of Heaven and Earth, in whom I trust, delivered me from the fire."
16. Haran's remains were searched for, but he was found burned to ashes. Upon seeing Abram's miraculous survival, the king and his subjects marveled, bowing before Abram.
17. Abram stopped them, urging them to bow instead to the God who created them, who alone delivered him from the fire.
18. The king, deeply moved, gifted Abram with treasures and two servants, Oni and Eliezer. Abram left peacefully, joined by about three hundred men who chose to follow him.
19. Returning to his father's house, Abram continued to serve the LORD faithfully, encouraging others to follow His ways.
20. Around this time, Abram and his brother Nahor married the daughters of their late brother, Haran. Abram's wife, Sarai, however, remained barren.
21. Two years later, King Nimrod, troubled by a dream, saw a man resembling Abram rising from a furnace and overpowering him and his armies. In his dream, the man threw an egg, which transformed into a river, drowning the king's troops. Only Nimrod and three other kings escaped.
22. Disturbed, Nimrod sought the counsel of his wise men, who interpreted the dream as a warning that Abram's descendants would threaten his reign.
23. The wise men advised Nimrod to kill Abram, and the king secretly sent servants to capture him. However, Eliezer, Abram's loyal servant, overheard and warned Abram.
24. Abram fled to the safety of Noah's house, hiding there until the king's anger faded.
25. After a month, Terah visited his son, and Abram urged him to leave for Canaan, far from Nimrod's reach. He cautioned Terah that Nimrod's favor was a means of control and that only the LORD was worthy of true allegiance.
26. Noah and Shem supported Abram's plea, and Terah agreed, recognizing the LORD's guidance in sparing Abram from Nimrod's wrath.
27. After listening to Abram's plea, Terah was deeply moved by his son's wisdom and resolve. He agreed that leaving was the best course of action.
28. Together, they gathered their family and set out toward the land of Canaan, as Abram had advised.
29. As they journeyed, Abram continued to strengthen his family's faith in the LORD, encouraging them to turn away from idols and trust in the Creator of heaven and earth.
30. Along the way, they encountered various tribes and people, and Abram spoke to them about the LORD, encouraging others to turn from false gods and find strength in the one true God. Many were drawn to his words and joined them in faith.
31. By the time they reached Canaan, Abram had already begun spreading knowledge of the LORD among those who listened to him.

32. Upon arriving in Canaan, Abram and his family settled in the land. Abram devoted his life to serving the LORD and helping others understand His ways.
33. Abram's steadfastness, even in the face of great trials, inspired others, and he became known for his faith and wisdom.
34. Throughout his life, Abram continued to grow in faith and trust in the LORD, always seeking guidance and strength. His influence spread far and wide, touching the hearts of many.
35. The LORD blessed Abram, and his family multiplied in the land, laying the foundation for a people devoted to serving God.
36. Thus, Abram's journey, marked by trials and unwavering faith, would go on to shape generations to come, fulfilling the promises the LORD had for him and his descendants.
37. Abram and Terah journeyed onward, drawing ever closer to the land of Canaan, as Abram had proposed. As they traveled, Abram continued to speak to those they met along the way about the LORD, the Creator of heaven and earth, urging them to turn away from their idols and to worship the true God. Many people were touched by his words and joined them on their journey.
38. When they finally reached Canaan, Abram felt deep gratitude for the LORD's guidance and protection along the way. He established an altar and worshiped, offering prayers of thanks for their safe arrival and for the guidance the LORD had provided.
39. Settling in the land, Abram continued to teach his family and those who joined him about the ways of the LORD, drawing people toward faith in the one true God. His words and deeds inspired all who heard him, and his wisdom and kindness became known throughout the region.
40. Abram's influence spread beyond his family, reaching the hearts of many who had not known of the LORD. His steadfast dedication to God earned him respect, and he became a guiding light to those who sought truth and understanding.
41. In the years that followed, Abram's family grew and prospered in the land of Canaan. Each member of his household embraced the faith, and they became known as a people devoted to God.
42. Terah, grateful for the wisdom of his son, looked upon the changes in their lives with a heart full of pride and peace. He knew that this path was the one that God had blessed and that Abram's vision and courage had preserved their family.
43. Abram's life was filled with faith and service, and his name became renowned for his dedication to God. His example inspired generations, laying the groundwork for a people who would carry forward the knowledge and love of the LORD.
44. Throughout the land, people spoke of Abram's faithfulness, and he was revered as a wise and righteous man, chosen by God. The blessings upon him and his family multiplied, and the LORD's favor was evident in all that they undertook.

45. Abram's teachings continued to spread, and his influence extended beyond his immediate family. He became known as a teacher and leader of faith, guiding others toward a life dedicated to the LORD.
46. From the day they left the influence of Nimrod and the idolatry of their homeland, Abram's family grew stronger in their faith. The LORD's presence was with them, blessing their steps and guiding them through every trial they faced.
47. And Abram's descendants would remember these days of their journey and his faith, passing down the stories of his courage and devotion to God, keeping alive the memory of his unwavering dedication to the LORD.
48. Thus, the legacy of Abram's faith was secured, and he became a symbol of righteousness and steadfastness for all who would come after him. His name would be remembered for generations as a man who stood firm in the face of adversity, trusting in God's promises.
49. Abram's life was a testament to the power of faith, and the people of Canaan came to respect and honor him, seeing the favor of the LORD upon him in all things.
50. His family flourished in the land, and they became a beacon of light to the surrounding peoples, who witnessed the strength of their faith and the blessings that followed them.
51. The LORD's promise to Abram began to unfold, and his family grew in number, wealth, and influence. They lived in peace and prosperity, honoring the God who had brought them out of Ur and into the promised land.
52. Abram continued to worship and serve the LORD, always seeking His guidance and thanking Him for every blessing. His life became a model of devotion, inspiring those around him to draw nearer to God.
53. Abram's household was filled with joy, faith, and gratitude, for they recognized that they were chosen and blessed by God, who had led them on this journey.
54. As Abram's family grew, he took great care to teach them the ways of the LORD, ensuring that each generation understood the faith and honored the covenant with God.
55. Abram became known for his wisdom, not only among his family but also among the people of Canaan, who came to respect his guidance and moral integrity.
56. His life of righteousness and service to God became an example for others, drawing people from all around to hear his teachings and seek his counsel.
57. Abram's teachings were passed down through generations, becoming a cornerstone of faith for all who followed in his footsteps.
58. And in the land of Canaan, Abram was known as a man of God, whose faith and devotion brought blessings upon his family and all who joined them.
59. Abram's influence extended far and wide, touching the hearts of countless people and leading them to a greater understanding of the LORD.
60. His life of faith would leave a legacy that endured, as his descendants continued in the ways he had taught them, remaining faithful to the covenant with God.
61. Throughout his life, Abram demonstrated the power of unwavering trust in God, setting a standard for righteousness that would inspire all who came after him.

62. The LORD blessed Abram's family, as they multiplied and prospered in the land, becoming a people who honored God in all they did.
63. And so, Abram's journey from Ur to Canaan marked the beginning of a new CHAPTER, one that would shape the future of his family and the generations to come.
64. Terah marveled at the wisdom of his son and the strength of his faith, grateful that they had left behind the land of idols and found a place of peace in Canaan.
65. Abram's unwavering faith continued to shine brightly, a light to all who sought to know the LORD and follow His ways.
66. In the land of Canaan, Abram's family established themselves as a people set apart, dedicated to serving the LORD and living according to His commands.
67. The LORD's hand was upon them, guiding their steps and blessing their lives, as they flourished in the land they had been promised.
68. Abram's journey was one of courage, faith, and devotion, and his life served as a testimony to the power of God's love and guidance.
69. And thus, Abram's legacy of faith was secure, passed down through generations as a testament to his trust in the LORD, who had led him out of Ur and into the land of promise.
70. And Terah listened to the voice of his son Abram, and heeded his words, for he recognized that they were from the LORD. Together, they departed from the influence of Nimrod, seeking the land of Canaan, that they might live in peace and serve the LORD. Thus, by God's will, Abram's life and journey marked the beginning of a lasting legacy of faith, a testament to those who would come after him.

CHAPTER 13

1. Terah, along with his son Abram, his grandson Lot (the son of Haran), and his daughter-in-law Sarai, who was Abram's wife, took all their household and set out from Ur-Kasdim with the intention of going to the land of Canaan. When they arrived at Haran, they decided to settle there, as it was an excellent place for pasturing their flocks and suitable for the company they brought with them.
2. The people of Haran saw that Abram was a good and upright man who walked faithfully with God. Observing that the Lord was with Abram, some people from Haran joined him, and he taught them the ways of the Lord. They chose to remain with him, becoming a part of his household.
3. Abram lived in Haran for three years. At the end of this period, the Lord appeared to him and said, "I am the Lord who brought you out of Ur-Kasdim and protected you from all your enemies.
4. "Now, if you heed My voice, keep My commandments, statutes, and laws, I will make your enemies fall before you. I will multiply your descendants as numerous as the stars in the sky and bless all the works of your hands, so you will lack nothing.

5. "Now arise, take your wife and all that belongs to you, and go to the land of Canaan. I will be your God there, and I will bless you." Following the Lord's direction, Abram took his wife and all his possessions and set out for Canaan. Abram was over fifty years old at the time.
6. Abram arrived in Canaan and settled in the midst of the land, pitching his tent among the Canaanites who inhabited the land.
7. There, the Lord appeared to Abram and said, "This is the land I am giving to you and your descendants forever. I will make your descendants as numerous as the stars in the sky, and all the land you see will be your inheritance."
8. Abram built an altar at the place where God had spoken to him and called upon the name of the Lord.
9. Around this time, three years into Abram's stay in Canaan, Noah passed away. Abram was fifty-eight years old when Noah died, and Noah had lived nine hundred and fifty years.
10. Abram, along with his wife and those who accompanied him, continued to live in Canaan, where more people joined his household and followed his teachings about the Lord. However, Abram's brother Nahor, along with Terah, Lot, and their households, remained in Haran.
11. In the fifth year of Abram's stay in Canaan, the people of Sodom, Gomorrah, and other cities of the plain rebelled against Chedorlaomer, king of Elam. For twelve years, they had served him and paid an annual tribute, but in the thirteenth year, they rose up against him.
12. In Abram's tenth year in Canaan, a conflict arose between Nimrod, king of Shinar, and Chedorlaomer, king of Elam. Nimrod went to battle to defeat Chedorlaomer and subjugate him once more.
13. At the time, Chedorlaomer was one of Nimrod's powerful allies. However, after the dispersion from the tower, he had taken control of Elam and turned against Nimrod's rule.
14. When Nimrod saw that the cities of the plain had rebelled, he mobilized his forces, gathering about seven hundred thousand men, and marched against Chedorlaomer. Chedorlaomer, with five thousand men, met Nimrod in the Valley of Babel, located between Elam and Shinar.
15. The two armies clashed, and Chedorlaomer's forces defeated Nimrod's, resulting in the loss of around six hundred thousand of Nimrod's men, including his son Mardon.
16. Nimrod retreated in disgrace to his land and remained under Chedorlaomer's control for a long time. Chedorlaomer returned to his kingdom, securing alliances with nearby kings, including Arioch of Ellasar and Tidal of Goyim, establishing dominance over them.
17. In Abram's fifteenth year in Canaan, at the age of seventy, the Lord appeared to him and declared, "I am the Lord who brought you out of Ur-Kasdim to give you this land as your inheritance.

18. "Walk before Me and be blameless, and I will give this land to you and your descendants from the River of Egypt to the great River Euphrates.
19. You will come to your ancestors in peace, and your descendants in the fourth generation will return here to inherit the land forever."
20. Abram, moved by God's promise, built an altar and called upon the name of the Lord, offering sacrifices there.
21. Afterward, Abram returned to Haran to visit his father, mother, and their household. Abram, along with his wife and those with him, resided in Haran for five years.
22. During this time, about seventy-two people from Haran joined Abram, drawn to his teachings about the Lord.
23. One day, the Lord appeared to Abram in Haran, reminding him, "Twenty years ago, I commanded you to leave your land, birthplace, and father's house for the land I had prepared for you and your descendants.
24. "Now arise, take your wife, household, and all who are with you, and return to Canaan. There, I will make you a great nation, bless you, and through you, all families of the earth will be blessed."
25. Abram, heeding the Lord's command, gathered his household and followers, along with Lot, his nephew, and set out for Canaan.
26. Abram returned to Canaan as the Lord instructed. He settled in the plain of Mamre, accompanied by Lot and all their possessions.
27. Once again, the Lord appeared to Abram and reaffirmed His promise, saying, "To your descendants, I will give this land."
28. Abram built another altar to the Lord in the plains of Mamre, dedicating it to the God who had guided and blessed him, a legacy that endures to this day.

CHAPTER 14

1. In those days, a wise man lived in the land of Shinar. Skilled in all forms of wisdom and possessing a pleasing appearance, he was nonetheless poor and struggled to sustain himself. His name was Rikayon.
2. In hopes of finding favor and securing support, Rikayon decided to travel to Egypt to present his wisdom to Oswiris, the son of Anom and king of Egypt. Rikayon believed that perhaps the king might look favorably upon him and grant him the means to live.
3. Upon arriving in Egypt, Rikayon inquired about the king. He learned that it was the custom of the Egyptian king to leave his palace only once a year to address public matters.
4. On that day, he would hear petitions and pass judgment, then return to the palace for the rest of the year.
5. Saddened by this custom, Rikayon realized he would not be able to see the king soon, and he became disheartened and troubled.

6. That night, Rikayon found shelter in an abandoned bakehouse in Egypt. There, he spent the night, his heart heavy with sorrow, hunger gnawing at him, and unable to sleep.
7. As he lay awake, he contemplated his situation and pondered how he might sustain himself in Egypt while he awaited the king's appearance.
8. At dawn, Rikayon went out and observed people selling vegetables and seeds, essential provisions for the city's inhabitants.
9. Inspired by this, Rikayon decided to try selling vegetables himself to earn a livelihood. However, he was unfamiliar with the ways of the Egyptians and felt as though he was wandering blindly among them.
10. Nevertheless, Rikayon managed to acquire vegetables to sell. But as he tried to earn an income, crowds gathered around him, mocking him. They took his goods, leaving him with nothing.
11. Disheartened, Rikayon returned to the same abandoned bakehouse where he had spent the previous night, and there he rested again.
12. That night, Rikayon devised a new plan to sustain himself.
13. The next morning, he took a bold step. He hired thirty men from among the local rabble, men armed with weapons, and led them to a prominent tomb in Egypt.
14. He instructed them, "By the king's command, stand firm and let no one be buried here unless two hundred pieces of silver are paid." Rikayon's men followed this order, enforcing the fee throughout Egypt that year.
15. Within eight months, Rikayon and his men had amassed considerable wealth in silver and gold. Rikayon then purchased horses and other goods and employed more men, outfitting them with horses as well.
16. When the year came around and the day approached when the king made his annual public appearance, the Egyptians gathered to voice their grievances about Rikayon's activities.
17. On the designated day, as the king went out, the people of Egypt approached him, crying out,
18. "May the king live forever! What is this injustice imposed upon us? Why must we pay such high fees just to bury our dead? This is unprecedented! Since ancient times, no such demand has ever been made."
19. "We know that kings levy taxes on the living, but now even the dead are not spared from these charges.
20. The entire city suffers because of this."
21. Hearing their complaint, the king grew furious, for he had been unaware of Rikayon's actions.
22. "Who has dared to commit this evil without my command?" he demanded.
23. The people informed him of all that Rikayon and his men had done. Enraged, the king summoned Rikayon and his followers.

24. To gain the king's favor, Rikayon prepared gifts, including a thousand children dressed in fine clothes, a grand horse, and a wealth of silver, gold, and precious stones. He presented these offerings to the king and bowed before him.
25. The people of Egypt were awestruck by Rikayon's wealth and generosity. Even the king was impressed by the offerings.
26. As Rikayon was brought before him, the king questioned him about his actions. Rikayon responded with wisdom, presenting himself eloquently.
27. The king and his officials were captivated by Rikayon's wisdom, and he found favor in their eyes. The Egyptians grew fond of Rikayon, admiring his insight and skillful speech.
28. The king then declared, "Your name will no longer be Rikayon. From this day forward, you shall be called Pharaoh, for you have brought tribute even from the dead."
29. The king and his subjects grew to love Rikayon, and they conferred with each other, deciding to make him a governor under the king's rule.
30. The people of Egypt made this decision official, establishing it as a new law. Rikayon, now known as Pharaoh, governed Egypt, administering daily justice to the city, while Oswiris, the king, would judge the people only on his annual appearance day.
31. Over time, Rikayon Pharaoh subtly consolidated his authority over Egypt, even collecting taxes from the people.
32. The Egyptians held him in high esteem, and they decreed that every king who reigned after him should also bear the title "Pharaoh."
33. Thus, from that time forward, all rulers of Egypt have been called Pharaoh, a title that continues to this day.

CHAPTER 15

1. That year, a severe famine struck the land of Canaan, making it difficult for people to survive. Due to the harsh conditions, Abram and everyone with him traveled to Egypt to escape the famine. They rested for a while by the brook of Mitzraim to recover from their journey.
2. As Abram and Sarai walked near the brook, Abram noticed Sarai's beauty and became concerned.
3. Abram said to Sarai, "Since God has given you such beauty, I fear that the Egyptians, lacking reverence for God, might kill me to take you."
4. He continued, "To protect ourselves, please tell them you are my sister so that they will treat me well and spare my life."
5. Abram gave this instruction to everyone traveling with him, including Lot, emphasizing that they should say Sarai was his sister if questioned by the Egyptians.
6. Despite these precautions, Abram was still anxious for Sarai's safety due to Egypt's reputation, so he placed her inside a chest, hiding her among their belongings.

7. After leaving the brook, Abram and his group entered Egypt. Upon arrival, they encountered city guards who required a tithe for the king before allowing entry. Abram and his companions complied.
8. The Egyptians noticed the chest Abram brought with him and grew curious about its contents. The king's officers approached him, demanding to see what was inside to collect the appropriate tithe.
9. Abram offered to pay whatever amount was required if they refrained from opening it, suspecting they might uncover Sarai inside.
10. However, the officers insisted, forcing the chest open, and were struck by Sarai's beauty. Word of her beauty spread quickly, and Pharaoh's officials reported to him, describing Sarai with admiration.
11. Fascinated, Pharaoh ordered her brought before him. Sarai's appearance pleased him immensely, and he rewarded those who brought her.
12. Meanwhile, Abram was distressed and prayed for Sarai's safety. Sarai, too, prayed, recalling God's promise to bless them in Canaan. She implored God for mercy and deliverance from Pharaoh's hands.
13. God heard Sarai's plea and sent a messenger to protect her. As Pharaoh approached Sarai, the messenger appeared, reassuring her not to fear.
14. Pharaoh questioned Sarai about her relationship with Abram. She replied, "He is my brother."
15. Satisfied, Pharaoh resolved to honor Abram, sending him silver, gold, livestock, and servants. That night, the king summoned Abram to the court, elevating him in status.
16. When Pharaoh attempted to approach Sarai again, the messenger struck him, terrifying the king and preventing him from touching her. This continued throughout the night, leaving Pharaoh in great fear.
17. That same night, the messenger afflicted Pharaoh's household as well, filling the palace with cries of anguish.
18. Realizing Sarai was the cause of this misfortune, Pharaoh spoke kindly to her and sought the truth. Sarai revealed, "He is indeed my husband. I claimed he was my brother out of fear that you might harm him."
19. Upon learning the truth, Pharaoh kept his distance from Sarai. The plagues lifted, and he marveled at the events.
20. The following morning, Pharaoh confronted Abram, questioning why he had concealed Sarai's true identity and caused such calamity. He returned Sarai to Abram and urged them to leave Egypt.
21. To ensure Abram's safety, Pharaoh provided him with more servants, livestock, and gifts. He also sent a young woman from his household, Hagar, as Sarai's maidservant.
22. Pharaoh told Hagar, "It is better to serve in the house of this man than to remain here, especially after the misfortune brought upon us."

23. Abram gathered his belongings and departed from Egypt, escorted by some of Pharaoh's men.
24. He returned to the land of Canaan, to the altar he had previously set up, where he first pitched his tent.
25. Lot, Abram's nephew, who had traveled with him, possessed a great wealth of livestock and tents, as God's favor was upon them through Abram.
26. As their flocks grew, conflicts arose between Lot's and Abram's herdsmen, as the land could not sustain both groups.
27. Abram's herdsmen kept to their land, but Lot's herdsmen allowed their animals to graze in neighboring fields, angering the local people who complained to Abram.
28. Abram confronted Lot, saying, "Why are your herdsmen grazing on others' land? Remember, I am a stranger here. Please don't tarnish my reputation."
29. Despite Abram's repeated requests, Lot's herdsmen continued, leading to further disputes with the locals.
30. Abram then approached Lot, suggesting, "Let there be no strife between us. We are family. Please choose another place to settle so we can live in peace."
31. After considering Abram's words, Lot looked out over the well-watered plains of the Jordan, ideal for his livestock, and chose to settle there, moving his tents near Sodom.
32. Abram remained in the plain of Mamre in Hebron, pitching his tent there and dwelling in the land for many years.
33. Abram settled in the land of Canaan, content to live in peace. Meanwhile, Lot moved his tents toward the fertile plains near Sodom, a land known for its wealth but also for the wickedness of its people.
34. The inhabitants of Sodom and Gomorrah were steeped in corruption, their deeds displeasing to the Lord. Yet, Lot, enticed by the prosperity of the region, continued to dwell there, despite the troubling nature of the city's people.
35. Time passed, and Abram remained steadfast in his faith, often building altars and calling on the name of the Lord. He grew in wisdom, revered by those around him for his integrity and devotion.
36. As he lived in the plains of Mamre, Abram continued to prosper. God's blessings were evident in his life, and those who joined him witnessed his faith and were drawn to his ways.
37. Lot, however, faced ongoing challenges in Sodom. The city's residents, known for their unrighteousness, began to test his resolve and values, leaving him increasingly isolated.
38. Abram, hearing of Lot's circumstances, prayed for his nephew, seeking protection and guidance for him amidst the turmoil of Sodom.
39. Lot's decision to settle near Sodom continued to have consequences, as he faced the daily trials of living among a corrupt people. Yet, his heart remained torn between the comforts of the land and the troubles of the city.

40. Meanwhile, Abram's name spread across the region as a man of honor and faith, respected by the neighboring tribes and sought after for counsel and blessings.
41. Abram's days were marked by peace and purpose, his life a testament to the covenant he held with God, who continued to bless him and all who followed in his ways.
42. Seeing the continued quarrels between their herdsmen, Abram approached Lot once again, urging him for peace. "We are family," he said gently, "Let there be no strife between us or between our herdsmen, for we are kin."
43. Abram proposed a solution. "Look around," he said, pointing to the land before them. "Let us separate so we may each have peace. If you choose the left, I will go to the right. If you choose the right, I will go to the left."
44. Lot lifted his eyes and saw the lush, fertile plain of the Jordan, well-watered and bountiful, like the garden of the Lord. He saw it would be a good place to settle with his family and herds.
45. Choosing for himself, Lot moved his tents toward the plain of Jordan, settling near the cities of Sodom and Gomorrah, where the people were known for their wickedness.
46. Abram, watching Lot depart, turned his steps toward the land of Canaan, content with the land that remained. He trusted fully in the Lord's provision, knowing his path was guided by God's promises.
47. Abram made his home in the plain of Mamre, near Hebron, and he built an altar there, dedicating the place to the Lord. Abram dwelt in Mamre for many years, his life rich in faith, peace, and purpose, and the Lord continued to bless him in all things.

CHAPTER 16

1. During this period, Chedorlaomer, king of Elam, reached out to nearby rulers, including Nimrod, king of Shinar, who was under his influence, along with Tidal, king of Goyim, and Arioch, king of Ellasar. He urged them, "Join me so we may attack the towns of Sodom and its people, for they have defied my rule these past thirteen years."
2. In response, these four kings gathered their armies, totaling around eight hundred thousand men. As they advanced, they struck down anyone they encountered along the way.
3. The five kings of Sodom and Gomorrah—Shinab, king of Admah; Shemeber, king of Zeboyim; Bera, king of Sodom; Bersha, king of Gomorrah; and Bela, king of Zoar—gathered their forces and went out to face the invaders in the Valley of Siddim.
4. These nine kings clashed in battle within the Valley of Siddim, but the forces of Sodom and Gomorrah were defeated by the coalition led by Elam.
5. The Valley of Siddim, filled with lime pits, became a trap for the fleeing kings of Sodom and Gomorrah. Many fell into the pits, while others fled to the mountains for refuge. The victorious kings pursued them to Sodom's gates, capturing everything within the city.
6. They looted all the cities of Sodom and Gomorrah, seizing goods, and even taking Lot, Abram's nephew, along with his possessions. When Abram's servant, Unic, who had

been in the battle, witnessed this, he quickly informed Abram of the fate that had befallen Lot and the cities.

7. Upon hearing this, Abram took immediate action. With three hundred and eighteen men, he pursued the invading kings through the night and struck them down, leaving no one remaining except the four kings, who fled in separate directions.
8. Abram retrieved all the possessions of Sodom, as well as Lot, his family, and all his belongings, ensuring that nothing was lost.
9. As Abram and his men returned from their victory, they passed through the Valley of Siddim, where the kings had clashed.
10. Emerging from the lime pits, Bera, the king of Sodom, and his remaining men went out to meet Abram and his company.
11. Adonizedek, the king of Jerusalem (who was also Shem), joined them in the Valley of Melech, bringing bread and wine to meet with Abram and his men.
12. Adonizedek blessed Abram, who, in turn, gave a tenth of his recovered spoils to Adonizedek, recognizing him as a priest before God.
13. The kings of Sodom and Gomorrah, accompanied by their servants, approached Abram, pleading with him to return their people, even offering him all the reclaimed property.
14. Abram responded, "As surely as the Lord lives, who made heaven and earth, who has delivered me from hardship and saved me from my foes, I will not take anything that belongs to you, so you cannot claim tomorrow that Abram grew wealthy from your property.
15. "The Lord, in whom I trust, promised me that I would lack nothing, for He will bless all that I do. Therefore, take what belongs to you and go, for as the Lord lives,
16. I will not take even a thread or a strap, aside from provisions for those who joined me in battle—Anar, Ashcol, and Mamre—and also for those who stayed back to guard our supplies; they shall have their share of the spoils."
17. The kings of Sodom followed Abram's terms, urging him to take anything he wished, yet he remained steadfast in his refusal.
18. Abram then sent away the kings of Sodom and their men, issuing instructions regarding Lot. They departed for their lands.
19. Lot, too, was sent off with his belongings, returning to Sodom, while Abram and his people returned to their home in the plains of Mamre in Hebron.
20. At this time, the Lord appeared to Abram in Hebron, assuring him
21. "Do not fear, for I am your great reward. I will bless you abundantly, making your descendants as countless as the stars in the sky.
22. "I will grant to your descendants all the lands that you see, giving them as an everlasting inheritance. Be strong and walk before Me, and be perfect."
23. In the seventy-eighth year of Abram's life, Reu, the son of Peleg, passed away at the age of two hundred and thirty-nine.

24. Sarai, Abram's wife, remained childless. Desiring children, she presented her handmaid, Hagar, a gift from Pharaoh, to Abram as a wife.
25. Hagar, having learned Sarai's ways, faithfully followed her teachings.
26. Sarai said to Abram, "Here is my maid Hagar; go to her that she may bear a child on my behalf, that I may have children through her."
27. After ten years in Canaan, at the age of eighty-five, Abram took Hagar as Sarai had suggested, and Hagar conceived.
28. When Hagar realized she was pregnant, she rejoiced, feeling favored over her mistress Sarai, who had not conceived.
29. This realization caused Hagar to look down on Sarai, believing herself more blessed in God's eyes.
30. Seeing this, Sarai grew envious, feeling Hagar's attitude stemmed from her conceiving. She spoke to Abram, saying, "My wrong be upon you! When you prayed for children, why did you not pray on my behalf as well?"
31. Sarai continued, "When I speak, Hagar disregards me because she has conceived, and you say nothing. Let the Lord judge between us."
32. Abram replied, "Behold, your handmaid is in your power; do as you see fit." Sarai then dealt harshly with Hagar, leading her to flee into the wilderness.
33. There, a messenger of the Lord found Hagar by a well and assured her, "Do not fear; I will greatly multiply your descendants, and you will bear a son named Ishmael."
34. The Lord instructed her, "Return to your mistress Sarai and submit to her."
35. Hagar named the well Beer-lahai-roi, located between Kadesh and the wilderness of Bered.
36. Hagar returned to Abram's household, and, in due time, bore a son named Ishmael. Abram was eighty-six years old at Ishmael's birth.

CHAPTER 17

1. During the ninety-first year of Abram's life, the people of Chittim waged war against the people of Tubal. This conflict arose after the Lord had dispersed humanity across the earth. The children of Chittim settled in the plains of Canopia, where they built cities and resided near the River Tibreu.
2. Meanwhile, the descendants of Tubal lived in Tuscanah, whose borders extended to the River Tibreu as well.
3. They established a city there, naming it Sabinah after Sabinah, the son of Tubal, and have continued to dwell there to this day.
4. At that time, the people of Chittim engaged in battle with the people of Tubal, inflicting significant casualties, with around three hundred and seventy of Tubal's people falling in the fight.
5. The people of Tubal then made a vow to the people of Chittim, stating, "We will not intermarry with you, nor will we give our daughters to any of your sons."

6. The daughters of Tubal were known for their beauty, unmatched throughout the land, and many men—kings, princes, and others—sought wives from among them.
7. Those who admired beauty greatly were drawn to the daughters of Tubal and took them as wives, leading to the custom of men, both noble and common, marrying women from Tubal.
8. After three years, twenty men from Chittim attempted to take wives from Tubal but found that none were available, as the people of Tubal remained faithful to their vow.
9. During the harvest season, while the people of Tubal were gathering their crops, young men from Chittim gathered, went to Sabinah, and each took a young woman back to their city.
10. When the people of Tubal learned of this, they prepared for war, but they found it difficult to retaliate due to the high mountain terrain, and thus, they returned to their land.
11. The following year, the people of Tubal hired around ten thousand warriors from nearby cities and prepared for another confrontation with Chittim.
12. This time, the forces of Tubal succeeded in overwhelming the people of Chittim, causing great distress among them.
13. In desperation, the people of Chittim lifted the children they had borne from Tubal's daughters onto the city walls, calling out, "Would you wage war against your own kin?"
14. Hearing this, the people of Tubal ceased their attack and returned to their cities.
15. Following this, the people of Chittim established two cities along the coast, naming them Purtu and Ariza.
16. Abram, son of Terah, was ninety-nine years old at this time.
17. The Lord appeared to him, saying, "I am making a covenant with you, promising to multiply your descendants exceedingly.
18. "As a sign of this covenant, every male child among you shall be circumcised, starting at eight days old. This will be a sign of our everlasting covenant."
19. The Lord continued, "No longer will you be called Abram, but Abraham; and your wife shall no longer be called Sarai, but Sarah.
20. "I will bless you both, and your descendants will become a great nation, and even kings will come from among them."

CHAPTER 18

1. Abraham obeyed God's command, circumcising every male in his household, both those born in his home and those he had acquired.
2. He left no one uncircumcised, and both he and his son Ishmael were circumcised as God had instructed, with Ishmael being thirteen years old at the time.
3. On the third day after the procedure
4. Abraham sat at the entrance of his tent to enjoy the warmth of the sun, enduring the pain of healing.

5. The Lord appeared to him in the plains of Mamre and sent three heavenly messengers to visit him as he rested at the tent's entrance.
6. Looking up, Abraham saw three men approaching from afar, and he quickly rose to meet them, bowing in welcome.
7. "If I have found favor with you," he said, "please stay and refresh yourselves with a meal."
8. He urged them to rest, offering water for their feet, and they sat under the tree at his tent's entrance.
9. Abraham hurried to prepare a meal, choosing a tender calf and giving it to his servant Eliezer to prepare
10. Then instructed Sarah to make cakes from fine flour.
11. He brought them butter, milk, and portions of beef and lamb, serving these before the calf was fully ready, and they ate.
12. After they finished, one of the men told Abraham, "I will return to you in due season, and your wife Sarah will have a son."
13. Then the visitors departed, each going to fulfill his mission.
14. At this time, Sodom, Gomorrah, and the neighboring cities were exceedingly sinful
15. Engaging in acts that provoked the Lord's wrath with their corrupt behavior.
16. These cities had a large valley, lush with springs and vegetation, and the people would gather there four times a year with their families to celebrate.
17. During these festivals, men would openly take their neighbor's wives and daughters without objection.
18. From morning until night, they engaged in revelries before returning to their homes
19. Repeating this behavior each season.
20. When merchants entered Sodom to sell their goods, the townsfolk would gather
21. Seize the merchandise by force, and distribute it among themselves, leaving the trader empty-handed.
22. If the merchant protested, they would taunt him, each claiming only a small portion, leaving the trader to depart in despair.
23. On one occasion, a man from Elam traveling with a multicolored mantle bound to his donkey entered Sodom at dusk.
24. As he sought lodging for the night, no one offered him shelter, for the people of Sodom were known for their cruelty.
25. A man named Hedad, known for his wickedness, saw the traveler and approached him, asking,
26. "Where are you from, and where are you going?"
27. The traveler replied, "I am journeying from Hebron to Elam and hoped to rest here, but no one has offered me a place."
28. Hedad responded, "I will give you all you need; come to my home for the night."

29. Hedad then took the man's mantle and cord from his donkey, providing the animal with fodder while the traveler ate and drank.
30. The following morning, as the traveler prepared to depart,
31. Hedad urged him to stay, offering him food once more, and the man agreed.
32. They spent another day together, and when evening came, Hedad again convinced him to stay the night.
33. The next day, as the man prepared to leave, Hedad insisted he remain, saying, "Stay a while longer and enjoy another meal."
34. The traveler agreed, but on the third day, he rose early, determined to continue his journey.
35. As he saddled his donkey, Hedad's wife remarked, "This man has stayed with us, eating and drinking, but has given us nothing in return."
36. Hedad dismissed her concern, but as the traveler readied his donkey, he asked for his cord and mantle.
37. Hedad replied, "The cord you dreamt of represents a long life, and the mantle's colors signify a vineyard filled with fruit trees."
38. The traveler protested, saying he was awake when he gave Hedad the items for safekeeping
39. But Hedad insisted, demanding payment for the "dream interpretation."
40. Frustrated, the traveler appealed to the judge, Serak, who ruled in favor of Hedad, supporting his claim as a skilled interpreter of dreams.
41. The man, outraged, shouted, "This is not so! I gave him my cord and mantle in plain sight, not as part of any dream!"
42. They quarreled, but the judge's verdict stood, and the man was forced to leave in bitterness.
43. As he departed, the people of Sodom mocked him, and he left the city lamenting his mistreatment.

CHAPTER 19

1. In the cities of Sodom and its neighbors, there were four judges presiding over four cities. Their names were Serak in Sodom, Sharkad in Gomorrah, Zabnac in Admah, and Menon in Zeboyim.
2. Abraham's servant, Eliezer, gave them other names: he called Serak "Shakra," Sharkad "Shakrura," Zabnac "Kezobim," and Menon "Matzlodin."
3. Under the direction of these judges, beds were set up in the streets. When strangers arrived, they were forced to lie on these beds.
4. If the traveler was shorter than the bed, several men would stretch him out; if he was longer, they would compress his body until he reached the limits of pain.
5. Despite the cries of these strangers, the people of Sodom would reply only, "This is the custom for any who enter our land."

6. Upon hearing of these terrible practices, people began to avoid coming to Sodom.
7. When a poor man entered the city, they would give him silver and gold, yet announce throughout the city that no one should offer him food.
8. If the stranger died of hunger, the citizens would then retrieve the silver and gold they had given him, taking even his clothes.
9. They would fight over these belongings, the victor claiming them all.
10. Afterward, they would bury him in a shallow grave under the bushes outside the city—a practice they maintained consistently.
11. One day, Sarah sent Eliezer to visit Lot in Sodom to check on his welfare.
12. Upon entering Sodom, Eliezer witnessed a local man robbing a stranger of his clothing and leaving him with nothing.
13. The victim, seeing Eliezer, pleaded for help against the injustice he'd suffered.
14. Eliezer rebuked the man of Sodom, asking why he would treat a poor stranger in such a way.
15. The man retorted, "Is he your brother, or have you been made a judge over us?"
16. Eliezer persisted, attempting to recover the stolen clothes, but the man struck him on the forehead with a stone, drawing blood.
17. Seeing the blood, the Sodomite demanded payment, saying, "Give me my fee for cleansing you of this bad blood."
18. Eliezer was outraged, replying, "You wound me and expect me to pay?" Refusing to comply, he was dragged before Shakra, the judge of Sodom.
19. The man repeated his complaint to the judge, demanding his payment.
20. The judge agreed, declaring that Eliezer should pay, as this was their custom.
21. In response, Eliezer took a stone and struck the judge, causing him to bleed, and said, "If this is your law, then pay this man from your own blood."
22. Leaving the man and judge behind, Eliezer departed.
23. Later, when the kings of Elam waged war against Sodom and its allies, Lot and his property were taken.
24. Abraham rescued Lot and his goods, restoring them.
25. During this time, Lot's wife bore a daughter whom they named Paltith, meaning "deliverance," as she was born after Lot's rescue from the Elamite kings.
26. As Paltith grew, a man of Sodom took her as his wife.
27. In Sodom, when a poor man entered seeking sustenance, the people would again enforce their cruel custom, withholding all food until he perished.
28. Paltith noticed a starving man in the street and, moved with compassion, began to feed him secretly.
29. Each day, as she fetched water, she hid bread in her pitcher, giving it to the man.
30. The man's strength returned, and the people of Sodom marveled, wondering how he survived so long without food.
31. Suspecting someone was helping him, they placed three men in hiding to observe him.

32. When Paltith came with her pitcher, they saw her take bread from it and give it to the man.
33. The men seized both Paltith and the poor man, bringing her before the city's judges.
34. The people condemned her for breaking the law by aiding the stranger and decided on her punishment.
35. They kindled a fire in the city square, cast her into it, and she perished in the flames.
36. A similar event occurred in the city of Admah. A traveler stopped to rest outside the house of a young woman as evening fell.
37. The man requested water, and she gave him bread and water.
38. When the townspeople discovered this, they brought her before their judges.
39. The judge declared, "For violating our law, her punishment shall be death."
40. The young woman was coated with honey from head to toe and placed near a beehive.
41. Bees stung her until she was swollen, and her cries ascended to the heavens, though no one showed her mercy.
42. Seeing the cruelty of Sodom and its sister cities, the LORD's wrath was stirred.
43. Despite their abundance and prosperity, the people refused to aid the poor and practiced extreme wickedness.
44. In response, the LORD sent two messengers, who had previously visited Abraham, to bring destruction upon Sodom and its cities.
45. The messengers arrived in Sodom in the evening, where Lot sat at the gate. Seeing them, he bowed low and insisted they stay at his home.
46. They accepted his hospitality, ate, and spent the night there.
47. Before dawn, they warned Lot, saying, "Take your family and leave this city, for the LORD is about to destroy it."
48. The messengers took hold of Lot, his wife, and his daughters, leading them outside the city.
49. They urged Lot to escape quickly, and he fled with his family.
50. Then, the LORD rained fire and brimstone on Sodom, Gomorrah, and the neighboring cities, destroying everything, including the vegetation.
51. Lot's wife, Ado, looked back, longing for her daughters who stayed behind, and she became a pillar of salt, which remains to this day.
52. Oxen that pass by lick the salt each morning, and by evening, the pillar reappears anew.
53. Lot and his two daughters took refuge in a cave near Adullam, where they lived for a time.
54. Early in the morning, Abraham looked out and saw the smoke of the destroyed cities rising like that of a furnace.
55. While in the cave, Lot's daughters, believing they were the last survivors, gave their father wine to drink.
56. Each lay with him to preserve their family line, and both conceived sons.

57. The elder daughter named her son Moab, saying, "He was conceived by my father." Moab became the ancestor of the Moabites.
58. The younger daughter named her son Ben-Ammi, ancestor of the Ammonites.
59. Eventually, Lot left the cave, dwelling on the other side of the Jordan with his daughters and their sons.
60. These sons took wives from the land of Canaan, raising families and multiplying greatly.

CHAPTER 20

1. Around this time, Abraham left the plain of Mamre and traveled to the land of the Philistines, settling in Gerar. This occurred in the twenty-fifth year of his stay in Canaan, during Abraham's one-hundredth year of life.
2. As they entered the Philistine territory, Abraham instructed his wife, Sarah, "Tell everyone you are my sister, so we may avoid any harm from the people here."
3. While Abraham was living in the land of the Philistines, the servants of Abimelech, king of the Philistines, noticed Sarah's remarkable beauty
4. And inquired about her relationship to Abraham. Abraham confirmed, "She is my sister."
5. The servants brought this news to Abimelech, saying, "A man from Canaan has arrived, and he has a sister of exceptional beauty."
6. Hearing his servants' praise, Abimelech sent for Sarah, and she was brought before him.
7. Sarah was brought to Abimelech's palace, and upon seeing her, the king was captivated by her beauty.
8. Approaching her, Abimelech asked, "What relation do you have to the man with whom you traveled here?" Sarah replied, "He is my brother, and we came from Canaan to find a place to settle."
9. Abimelech offered generously, "My land is open to you. Allow your brother to choose any place he desires, and we will honor him on account of you."
10. Abimelech then summoned Abraham and expressed, "I have instructed that you be treated with great respect, considering your relationship with Sarah."
11. Abraham departed from the king, accompanied by gifts from Abimelech.
12. Later that night, as the king sat on his throne, he fell into a deep sleep and remained there until morning.
13. During this sleep, he dreamed that a messenger of the LORD appeared with a sword drawn, standing over him with intent to strike.
14. Terrified, Abimelech asked in his dream, "What offense have I committed that you come to harm me with your sword?"
15. The messenger replied, "You are about to die because of the woman you took into your house, for she is a married woman—the wife of Abraham, who arrived with her.
16. Now, return her to her husband, or you and all you own will surely perish."
17. That night, the Philistine land was filled with a dreadful cry, as the people saw a figure with a drawn sword, striking down those nearby.

18. The messenger of the LORD swept over the entire land, bringing turmoil and confusion upon the Philistines, and every womb was closed in response to the LORD's wrath over Sarah's captivity.
19. When morning came, Abimelech awoke, shaken and confused. He summoned his servants and recounted the dream, filling the people with fear.
20. One of the king's servants, who had witnessed similar events in Egypt, stepped forward, advising,
21. "Return this woman to her husband, for she is indeed his wife. A similar situation arose with Pharaoh in Egypt when he took this woman, believing she was Abraham's sister, and the LORD struck Egypt with severe plagues until Pharaoh restored her to her husband.
22. "Reflect on the turmoil and suffering we experienced last night throughout the land, which surely occurred because of the woman you took."
23. Fearing a fate like Egypt's, Abimelech quickly summoned Sarah and Abraham. He confronted them, saying, "What have you done by claiming you are siblings, causing me to unknowingly take a married woman?"
24. Abraham responded, "I feared that harm would come to me because of her."
25. Abimelech, wishing to make amends, offered Abraham flocks, herds, servants, and a thousand pieces of silver as restitution, returning Sarah to him.
26. He said, "Here is the land; settle anywhere you choose."
27. Abraham and Sarah departed from Abimelech with respect and honor, settling in the land of Gerar.
28. Meanwhile, the people of the Philistine land, including Abimelech's household, continued to suffer from the affliction brought by the messenger throughout the night due to Sarah's presence.
29. Abimelech sent for Abraham again, pleading, "Pray to the LORD on behalf of my people that we may be spared from this plague."
30. Abraham prayed to the LORD for Abimelech and his people, and in response, the LORD healed Abimelech and his household, restoring health to the entire land.

CHAPTER 21

1. During Abraham's stay of one year and four months in the Philistine city of Gerar, the LORD visited Sarah, fulfilling His promise to her, and she conceived, giving birth to a son for Abraham.
2. Abraham named his son, born to him by Sarah, Isaac.
3. As God had commanded, Abraham circumcised Isaac when he was eight days old. At the time of Isaac's birth, Abraham was one hundred years old, and Sarah was ninety.
4. As Isaac grew and was eventually weaned, Abraham hosted a grand feast to celebrate this occasion.

5. Many people attended, including Shem, Eber, Abimelech (the Philistine king), his servants, and Phicol, his army commander. They all gathered to eat, drink, and celebrate Isaac's weaning.
6. Abraham's father, Terah, and his brother Nahor also traveled from Haran with their households, having heard of the birth of Isaac and wanting to join in the celebration.
7. They ate and drank at the feast and remained with Abraham in the land of the Philistines for some time, sharing in his joy.
8. During that period, Terah and Nahor rejoiced with Abraham, staying many days in Gerar.
9. Around that time, Serug, son of Reu, passed away, the same year Isaac was born.
10. Serug lived a total of 239 years before his death.
11. Meanwhile, Ishmael, Abraham's son through Hagar, had grown to the age of fourteen by the time of Isaac's birth.
12. God's presence was with Ishmael as he grew; he learned to use the bow and became a skilled archer.
13. When Isaac turned five, he was playing near the entrance of the tent with Ishmael.
14. Ishmael, however, sat opposite Isaac with his bow drawn, intending to harm him.
15. Sarah, noticing Ishmael's actions, was deeply distressed and immediately called for Abraham, urging him, "Send away this bondwoman and her son, for her son will not share the inheritance with my son, Isaac, especially after his actions today."
16. Abraham heeded Sarah's words and rose early the next morning, providing Hagar with twelve loaves of bread and a bottle of water before sending her and Ishmael away. They settled in the wilderness of Paran, where Ishmael grew and became a skilled archer, living among the people of the wilderness.
17. Later, Hagar and Ishmael traveled to Egypt, where Hagar found a wife for Ishmael named Meribah.
18. Meribah bore Ishmael four sons and two daughters, and they eventually returned to the wilderness, where they established a nomadic life.
19. In time, they set up tents and frequently moved, resting during specific months and years as needed.
20. God blessed Ishmael with livestock, tents, and prosperity for Abraham's sake, leading Ishmael to accumulate wealth in the wilderness.
21. Living a life of travel and rest, Ishmael did not see his father for an extended period.
22. Eventually, Abraham expressed to Sarah his desire to visit Ishmael, whom he hadn't seen for a long time.
23. Abraham mounted one of his camels and journeyed into the wilderness to seek out Ishmael, having heard that his son lived in a tent with his family.
24. Upon reaching Ishmael's tent around midday, Abraham inquired about Ishmael's whereabouts and found Ishmael's wife inside the tent with their children, though Ishmael and his mother were absent.
25. Abraham asked Ishmael's wife where he had gone, and she responded

26. "He is in the fields hunting." Abraham remained seated on his camel, as he had promised Sarah he would not dismount.
27. He then requested, "My daughter, may I have some water, as I am weary from my journey."
28. Ishmael's wife, however, responded, "We have neither water nor bread," and she continued sitting, paying little attention to Abraham, not inquiring about his identity.
29. Abraham observed her neglecting her children and cursing both them and Ishmael, which greatly displeased him.
30. Abraham called the woman to step outside, and she stood before him as he continued to sit on his camel.
31. He said to her, "When your husband Ishmael returns, tell him that an elderly man from the land of the Philistines came seeking him, with the following appearance," and Abraham described himself.
32. Abraham added, "The man told me to tell you: When your husband comes home, remove the tent's nail and replace it with a new one."
33. Having finished his message, Abraham departed on his camel.
34. Later, when Ishmael returned from hunting, his wife relayed the message, saying, "An elderly man from the Philistine land came to see you.
35. He described himself, and because you were absent, he instructed me to tell you that you should replace the tent's nail with another."
36. Realizing that the man was his father, Ishmael understood his wife's lack of respect toward Abraham.
37. Ishmael grasped the message behind his father's words, and he listened, dismissing the woman, who then left.
38. Ishmael later traveled to Canaan and remarried, bringing his new wife to their tent.
39. Three years passed, and Abraham expressed a renewed desire to visit Ishmael.
40. He mounted his camel and again traveled into the wilderness, reaching Ishmael's tent around noon.
41. He inquired about Ishmael, and his wife, seeing him, greeted Abraham warmly, saying, "My lord, Ishmael is not here. He is in the fields, hunting and tending the camels."
42. She then invited Abraham to rest, offering, "Please, come into the tent and eat, as you must be tired from your journey."
43. Abraham declined, saying, "I must continue, but may I have some water to drink, as I am thirsty?" The woman quickly fetched water and bread, bringing them to Abraham. He ate and drank, feeling refreshed, and he blessed Ishmael in his heart.
44. Before leaving, Abraham instructed her, "When Ishmael returns, tell him that an elderly man from Philistine land came seeking him. Since he wasn't here, I was given water and bread, and my heart was comforted."
45. Abraham added, "Tell your husband, 'The nail of the tent is good; do not remove it.'"

46. After delivering his message, Abraham returned to the Philistines. When Ishmael returned, his wife joyfully recounted the visit, saying, "An elderly man came looking for you. Since you weren't here, I provided him with water and bread, and his heart was comforted."
47. She repeated his message about the tent nail, and Ishmael, recognizing it was his father, was pleased that his wife had shown kindness and respect to him.
48. As a result, the LORD blessed Ishmael and his family.

CHAPTER 22

1. Ishmael gathered his wife, children, livestock, and belongings and set off to visit his father, Abraham, in the land of the Philistines.
2. When he arrived, Abraham recounted to Ishmael the events surrounding his first marriage and the actions of his former wife.
3. Ishmael and his family stayed with Abraham for a while, and they all dwelt together in the Philistine land for an extended period.
4. As time passed, twenty-six years went by, and then Abraham, along with his servants and all his possessions, left the land of the Philistines and journeyed to a place near Hebron. There, they settled, and Abraham's servants dug wells.
5. However, the servants of Abimelech, king of the Philistines, learned of these wells and came to confront Abraham's servants, seizing a major well that had been dug.
6. When Abimelech heard of the situation, he, along with Phicol, the commander of his army, and twenty of his men, went to speak with Abraham about it. Abraham rebuked Abimelech for his servants' actions.
7. Abimelech replied, "As surely as the LORD, who made the earth, lives, I had not heard of what my servants did to yours until today."
8. Abraham then took seven ewe lambs and gave them to Abimelech, saying, "Please accept these as a witness that I dug this well."
9. Abimelech accepted the seven lambs, along with an abundance of cattle and herds from Abraham, and he swore an oath concerning the well.
10. Hence, they named the well "Beersheba," as it marked their sworn agreement.
11. The two men then established a covenant at Beersheba. Abimelech, Phicol, and all their men then returned to Philistine territory, while Abraham remained in Beersheba for a considerable time.
12. Abraham planted a large grove in Beersheba, creating four gates that faced each direction.
13. He also established a vineyard so that any traveler approaching could enter, find sustenance, and depart satisfied.
14. Abraham's home was always open to those passing by, and people came daily to eat and drink there.

15. If anyone was hungry and came to Abraham's house, he would provide food and drink until they were satisfied.
16. Likewise, anyone lacking clothing would receive garments, and Abraham would give them silver and gold, teaching them about the LORD, the Creator of all. This was Abraham's practice throughout his life.
17. Abraham, his children, and all his household lived in Beersheba, setting up tents that extended as far as Hebron.
18. Abraham's brother Nahor and their father Terah, along with their families, remained in Haran and did not accompany Abraham to Canaan.
19. Nahor's wife, Milcah, the daughter of Haran (and sister to Abraham's wife, Sarah), bore Nahor several children.
20. These were the names of Nahor's sons: Uz, Buz, Kemuel, Kesed, Chazo, Pildash, Tidlaf, and Bethuel—eight sons in total, born to Milcah.
21. Nahor also had a concubine, Reumah, who bore him four sons: Zebach, Gachash, Tachash, and Maacha.
22. In total, Nahor had twelve sons besides his daughters, who also had children in Haran.
23. The descendants of Uz, Nahor's firstborn, were Abi, Cheref, Gadin, Melus, and their sister Deborah.
24. The sons of Buz were Berachel, Naamath, Sheva, and Madonu.
25. Kemuel's sons were Aram and Rechob.
26. Kesed's sons included Anamlech, Meshai, Benon, and Yifi. Chazo's sons were Pildash, Mechi, and Opher.
27. Pildash's sons were Arud, Chamum, Mered, and Moloch.
28. Tidlaf's sons included Mushan, Cushan, and Mutzi.
29. Bethuel's children were Sechar, Laban, and their sister, Rebekah.
30. These families, the descendants of Nahor, were born and settled in Haran.
31. Aram, Kemuel's son, and his brother Rechob eventually left Haran and found a place to settle by the Euphrates River.
32. There they built a city, naming it after Pethor, Aram's son, which is known as Aram Naherayim to this day.
33. Meanwhile, the descendants of Kesed also relocated, finding a valley near Shinar, where they built a city they named Kesed after their ancestor.
34. This area became known as Kasdim, where they prospered and multiplied greatly.
35. Terah, Abraham's father, remarried in his old age, and his new wife, Pelilah, bore him a son named Zoba.
36. Terah lived for twenty-five years after Zoba's birth.
37. Terah passed away in the thirty-fifth year after Isaac's birth, having lived a total of 205 years, and he was buried in Haran.
38. Zoba, Terah's son, had a son named Aram, along with Achlis and Merik.

39. Aram, Zoba's son, married three wives and had twelve sons and three daughters, and the LORD blessed him with great wealth and prosperity.
40. Eventually, Aram, his brother, and their families left Haran due to their growing wealth, which made it difficult for them to remain there together.
41. They traveled eastward, eventually building a city they named after Aram, their eldest brother, which is called Aram Zoba to this day.
42. Meanwhile, Isaac, Abraham's son, was growing up, and Abraham taught him about the LORD and His ways.
43. The LORD was with Isaac as he grew.
44. When Isaac was thirty-seven years old, he conversed with his brother Ishmael in the tent.
45. Ishmael boasted, saying, "I was thirteen when the LORD commanded my father to circumcise us, and I obeyed the LORD's command without hesitation."
46. Isaac replied, "Why do you boast about such a small act of obedience, a small part of your flesh, in fulfilling the LORD's command?
47. As surely as the LORD lives, if He commanded my father to offer me as a sacrifice, I would gladly accept it."
48. The LORD heard Isaac's words and was pleased with his devotion, deciding to test Abraham in this matter.
49. One day, the heavenly beings came to present themselves before the LORD, and Satan also came among them.
50. The LORD asked Satan, "From where have you come?" And Satan answered, "From wandering through the earth."
51. The LORD then asked, "What have you observed concerning humanity?" Satan replied, "I have seen that people remember You when they need something, but after receiving it, they quickly forget You."
52. He then continued, "Have You considered Abraham, who once had no children yet faithfully served You and built altars everywhere he went? Now, with a son, he has forgotten You. He made a grand feast for the people of the land when his son was weaned, yet offered no sacrifices to You."
53. Satan continued accusing, saying, "Since Isaac's birth, Abraham has not built an altar or offered sacrifices to You."
54. The LORD responded, "Have you considered Abraham, who is upright and reverent? If I were to ask him to offer Isaac as a sacrifice, he would not refuse."
55. Satan challenged, "Then test him, and You will see if he remains steadfast."

CHAPTER 23

1. The LORD called out to Abraham, saying, "Abraham," and Abraham replied, "Here I am."
2. The LORD instructed, "Take your son, your only son whom you love, Isaac, and go to the land of Moriah. There, on a mountain that I will show you, offer him as a burnt

offering. You will recognize the place by a cloud and the glory of the LORD resting upon it."

3. Abraham pondered how he might separate Isaac from Sarah without revealing his intentions.
4. Entering the tent, he sat beside Sarah and said, "Isaac has grown, and he has not spent enough time studying the ways of the LORD. Tomorrow, I will bring him to Shem and Eber, who will teach him to understand and serve the LORD, that he may know the blessings of a life devoted to prayer."
5. Sarah agreed, saying, "Do as you have said, but please, my lord, do not keep him too far from me, nor for too long, for my soul is bound to his."
6. Abraham asked Sarah to pray that the LORD might bless their journey.
7. Sarah held Isaac close that night, kissing and instructing him until dawn.
8. She said, "My son, how will I bear this separation from you?" She kissed him again and gave Abraham many instructions for Isaac's care.
9. Sarah pleaded with Abraham, "Take care of our son. Give him bread if he is hungry, water if he thirsts. Do not let him walk in the sun or go alone on the road. Please, my lord, protect him."
10. She wept the whole night, overcome with worry for Isaac, and in the morning, she dressed him in a fine garment Abimelech had given her.
11. She wrapped a precious stone in his turban and gave him provisions for the road. Isaac then left with Abraham, accompanied by some servants who traveled partway with them.
12. Sarah walked with them, weeping as she bid her son farewell, saying, "Who knows if I will ever see you again, my child?"
13. The whole household wept with them, and at last, Sarah returned to the tent, still grieving.
14. Abraham, accompanied by Isaac, set off to fulfill the LORD's command.
15. Alongside them were two young men—Abraham's servant Eliezer and Ishmael, son of Hagar.
16. Along the way, Ishmael whispered to Eliezer, "When my father returns, surely he will grant me the inheritance, for I am his firstborn."
17. Eliezer replied, "No, he will not. Abraham cast you and your mother away, vowing that you would not inherit. As for me, I have been faithful, serving him day and night; surely, he will give all he has to me."
18. As they traveled, Satan appeared to Abraham, disguised as an old man. "Are you truly going to sacrifice your only son, whom you love? This cannot be the LORD's will. He gave you this son in your old age, only to take him away?"
19. Recognizing the tempter, Abraham rebuked Satan, refusing to listen to him. Satan left but soon appeared before Isaac as a young man, saying, "Your old father intends to sacrifice you. Do not go along with his plan."

20. Isaac told his father of the stranger's words, and Abraham explained, "That was Satan trying to deter us from obeying the LORD's command. Pay him no mind."
21. Satan, frustrated, transformed into a large brook of water blocking their path.
22. They entered the brook, which grew deeper as they waded through. As the waters rose to their necks, Abraham recognized the place and realized it was Satan's doing.
23. He rebuked Satan again, commanding him to leave. At Abraham's words, the waters receded, and the brook dried up, allowing them to continue their journey.
24. On the third day, Abraham lifted his eyes and saw the mountain in the distance, marked by a pillar of fire and a cloud of glory.
25. Abraham asked Isaac, "Do you see what I see?" and Isaac answered, "Yes, I see the glory of the LORD on the mountain."
26. Abraham turned to Eliezer and Ishmael, asking if they saw anything unusual. They responded, "We see only a mountain like any other." Knowing they were not chosen to proceed, Abraham instructed them, "Stay here with the donkey while Isaac and I go up to worship."
27. Abraham placed wood for the offering on Isaac's back, while he carried the fire and knife, and they continued alone.
28. As they walked, Isaac asked, "I see the fire and the wood, but where is the lamb for the offering?"
29. Abraham replied, "The LORD has chosen you, my son, as the offering."
30. Isaac, with a joyful heart, said, "I am willing to fulfill the LORD's will." Abraham asked if Isaac held any doubts or reservations, but Isaac assured him, "There is nothing in my heart but obedience."
31. Abraham, deeply moved, rejoiced at Isaac's faith.
32. They arrived at the place, and together they built the altar, Abraham shedding tears as they worked.
33. He placed the wood on the altar, then bound Isaac and laid him on top. Isaac urged his father, "Bind me securely so I do not flinch and dishonor the sacrifice."
34. Abraham, sorrowful yet resolute, took the knife to slay his son.
35. At that moment, angels of mercy interceded, pleading with the LORD to spare Isaac, who was bound like a lamb for the slaughter.
36. The LORD called out to Abraham from heaven, "Do not lay your hand on the boy. Now I know that you fear God, for you did not withhold your son, your only son, from Me."
37. Abraham looked up and saw a ram caught in a thicket. This was the ram the LORD had prepared from the beginning to take Isaac's place.
38. Abraham freed Isaac and offered the ram in his place, saying, "May this be as though it were my son's blood."
39. After completing the offering, Abraham and Isaac returned to the young men waiting for them, and they all returned to Beersheba.

40. Meanwhile, Satan went to Sarah, disguised as a humble old man, and told her that Abraham had sacrificed Isaac.
41. Overcome with grief, Sarah mourned bitterly, casting herself to the ground and crying, "O my son, my son Isaac! I should have died instead of you."
42. She continued to weep, remembering how she had longed and prayed for Isaac, her joy now turned to mourning.
43. Afterward, she resolved to seek out Abraham and Isaac. With her servants, she traveled to Hebron, inquiring about her son's fate, but no one had news of them.
44. Satan appeared once more, this time revealing that Isaac was alive. Sarah, overwhelmed by joy, passed away.
45. When Abraham and Isaac returned, they searched for Sarah and learned that she had gone to Hebron. Traveling there, they found her lifeless body.
46. Abraham and Isaac wept over Sarah, mourning deeply. Isaac, in grief, cried out, "O my mother, how have you left me?"
47. Together, Abraham, Isaac, and their servants mourned the loss of Sarah with a great lamentation.
48. Abraham was filled with sorrow, for he could not bear the loss of his beloved wife, Sarah. Together with Isaac, they mourned deeply, and their grief was shared by all those in their household.
49. Isaac fell upon his mother's face, and he wept bitterly, saying, "Oh, my mother, my dear mother! How have you left me, and where have you gone?"
50. Abraham, too, mourned beside her, saying, "My beloved Sarah, who stood by me through all trials and wanderings, how has the LORD taken you from me?"
51. And all their servants and the men and women of Abraham's household wept with them, for Sarah had been beloved by all, and her absence left a void in their hearts.
52. After many days of mourning, Abraham and Isaac prepared to honor her memory by laying her to rest.
53. Abraham sought a burial place for Sarah and approached the sons of Heth, seeking to purchase a suitable tomb for his beloved wife.
54. He spoke to them, saying, "I am a foreigner and a visitor among you. Grant me property for a burial place among you, that I may bury my dead out of my sight."
55. The sons of Heth responded, "Hear us, my lord; you are a mighty prince among us. Bury your dead in the choicest of our burial places. None of us will withhold from you his burial place."
56. However, Abraham insisted on purchasing the land with honor and fairness, saying, "Let me pay for it, that it may rightfully belong to me and my descendants."
57. Ephron the Hittite, who owned the field and cave of Machpelah, was present, and he offered it freely to Abraham in the presence of the people, yet Abraham still insisted on paying a fair price for it.

58. So Ephron finally named a price, and Abraham weighed out four hundred shekels of silver, as agreed upon, in the presence of the sons of Heth.
59. And thus, the field and the cave of Machpelah, which is before Mamre, became Abraham's possession as a burial site.
60. After the purchase was complete, Abraham buried Sarah, his beloved wife, in the cave of Machpelah.
61. This became the resting place of Sarah, where she was honored and remembered by her family and all who knew her goodness.
62. Isaac remained by his mother's side in spirit, cherishing her teachings, love, and kindness.
63. The people of the land also remembered Sarah's compassion and faithfulness, for she had blessed many and was deeply revered.
64. Abraham often visited her tomb, reflecting on their journey together and finding solace in the legacy of love and faith that Sarah had left behind.
65. Thus, Sarah's life became a beacon of hope and faith for her family and generations to come.
66. And Abraham continued to teach Isaac the ways of the LORD, preserving the memory and faith that he and Sarah had built together.
67. They were comforted by the LORD's promises, knowing that their legacy would continue through Isaac and the generations that would follow.
68. Abraham and Isaac, surrounded by their household and many friends, continued to mourn deeply for Sarah, honoring her memory and the love she had shown throughout her life.
69. The entire community shared in their sorrow, as Sarah's kindness and faith had touched many, and she was remembered as a woman of great compassion and strength.
70. Abraham instructed his servants to prepare a beautiful memorial service, inviting all those who had known and loved Sarah to join them in honoring her life.
71. Together, they recalled her acts of generosity, her devotion to God, and the wisdom she had shared with so many, bringing comfort to all who mourned her.
72. Isaac, who had been closest to his mother, found solace in remembering her teachings and the love she had instilled in him.
73. He would often visit her resting place, bringing flowers and spending time in prayer, feeling her presence near him as he honored her memory.
74. Abraham, though deeply grieved, continued to place his trust in the LORD, knowing that Sarah's spirit was with God and that he would one day be reunited with her.
75. He found strength in his faith, carrying on the legacy they had built together, and fulfilling the promises God had made to him and his descendants.
76. The sons of Heth and many others who had respected Abraham and Sarah came to pay their respects, reflecting on the legacy of faith and integrity that Sarah had left behind.
77. Abraham's household continued to grow in faith, following the example of love and devotion that Sarah had set for them all.

78. As time passed, Abraham shared stories of Sarah with Isaac, ensuring that her memory lived on through the generations.
79. Isaac treasured these stories, cherishing his mother's wisdom, which became a source of strength for him as he grew into a man of faith.
80. Abraham often prayed at her graveside, thanking God for the years he had shared with Sarah and seeking guidance for the future.
81. He felt her spirit with him, guiding him as he prepared Isaac to carry forward the promises that God had made to their family.
82. Even as Abraham and Isaac moved forward, Sarah's memory remained a source of inspiration, shaping their lives and the lives of all who would follow.
83. The LORD, seeing Abraham's unwavering faith, continued to bless him and his descendants, fulfilling His promise to make them a great nation.
84. Sarah's legacy of faith, love, and kindness became a foundation for future generations, reminding them of the power of steadfast devotion to God.
85. As Isaac grew, he embraced his mother's values, carrying her spirit with him in all he did, and teaching his own children to honor the LORD.
86. Abraham and Isaac found peace, knowing that Sarah's life and faith would forever be remembered.
87. Through their continued faith and obedience, God's promises remained alive, fulfilling the legacy that Abraham and Sarah had envisioned for their family.
88. The LORD continued to walk with Abraham and Isaac, guiding them on the path that had been set for them, in honor of Sarah's memory and devotion.
89. As generations passed, Sarah's influence and legacy endured, shaping the destiny of her family and blessing all those who followed in her footsteps.
90. And thus, Sarah was remembered as a mother of nations, her life and faith inspiring countless generations to trust in the LORD and live with love and compassion.

CHAPTER 24

1. Sarah lived for 127 years before she passed away. Abraham mourned her deeply and sought a place to bury her. He approached the Hittites, the inhabitants of the land, saying,
2. "I am a stranger and sojourner among you. Grant me a burial site among you, so that I may lay my wife to rest."
3. The Hittites responded kindly, "You are welcome to use any of our tombs; no one will deny you this."
4. Abraham then asked, "If you are willing, please speak to Ephron, son of Zochar, on my behalf, to request the cave of Machpelah at the edge of his field.
5. I am willing to buy it at full value as a permanent burial place."
6. Ephron, who was nearby, was called forward and, standing before Abraham, he said, "I am at your service; I will do as you ask."

7. Although Ephron offered the land freely, Abraham insisted on purchasing it, saying, "I wish to own it fully so that it may remain ours forever."
8. Ephron and his kinsmen agreed, and Abraham weighed out 400 shekels of silver in their presence. This transaction was documented, and four witnesses were called to testify.
9. The witnesses to this transaction were Amigal, son of Abishna the Hittite; Adichorom, son of Ashunach the Hivite; Abdon, son of Achiram the Gomerite; and Bakdil, son of Abudish the Zidonite.
10. Abraham wrote the deed of purchase, which stated:
11. "The cave and the field Abraham purchased from Ephron the Hittite, and from his descendants and kin, as a burial site forever." This was sealed with Abraham's signet and witnessed by the four men.
12. The cave, the field, and all its boundaries became Abraham's property in the presence of the Hittites near Mamre in Hebron.
13. Afterward, Abraham buried Sarah in the cave, establishing it as a family burial place.
14. Abraham held an elaborate burial for Sarah, fit for royalty, dressing her in beautiful garments.
15. Notable figures like Shem, Eber, Abimelech, Anar, Ashcol, and Mamre joined the procession, along with many others.
16. Abraham mourned deeply for Sarah, observing seven days of mourning rituals.
17. After the mourning period, the people of the land comforted Abraham and Isaac.
18. Once the days of mourning concluded, Abraham sent Isaac to stay with Shem and Eber to study the ways of the LORD, where he remained for three years.
19. Abraham then returned with his servants to Beersheba, where they lived for a time.
20. During that year, Abimelech, king of the Philistines, passed away at the age of 193.
21. Abraham went to the Philistines to console Abimelech's household before returning home.
22. Abimelech's son, Benmalich, was crowned king in his place, continuing the family tradition by adopting his father's name.
23. Around this time, Lot, Abraham's nephew, also passed away at the age of 140.
24. Lot's descendants, born of his daughters, were Moab and Benami.
25. Moab's sons were Ed, Mayon, Tarsus, and Kanvil, who became the patriarchs of the Moabites.
26. Lot's family settled and thrived in various regions, building cities named after themselves.
27. Abraham's brother, Nahor, also died in these years, reaching the age of 172. He was buried in Haran.
28. Upon learning of Nahor's death, Abraham mourned for his brother.
29. He then called his servant, Eliezer, and gave him instructions about his household, saying,

30. "I am aging and may soon die. Do not take a wife for my son from the Canaanites among whom we dwell."
31. Instead, Abraham asked Eliezer to journey to his homeland to find a wife for Isaac from his own kin.
32. Eliezer questioned if he should bring Isaac back to Abraham's birthplace if the woman was unwilling to come,
33. but Abraham replied, "No, the LORD will send His messenger before you to ensure success."
34. Eliezer took an oath to fulfill his master's wishes, then gathered ten camels and a company of men to travel to Haran, the city of Abraham and Nahor.
35. In the meantime, Abraham sent for Isaac to return to Beersheba from the house of Shem and Eber.
36. Arriving at a well, Eliezer prayed, "God of my master Abraham, grant me success today by guiding me to the right woman."
37. God answered his prayer, and he encountered Rebekah, daughter of Bethuel, the son of Milcah and Nahor, who welcomed Eliezer to her home.
38. Eliezer explained his mission to her family, who rejoiced, seeing God's hand in the arrangement.
39. Rebekah, a beautiful and virtuous young woman, was offered as Isaac's bride.
40. That evening, the household celebrated with a feast, and Eliezer's men joined in the joy.
41. The next morning, Eliezer requested leave to return to his master.
42. Rebekah's family blessed her and sent her, along with her nurse, Deborah, and gifts of silver, gold, and servants, on her journey.
43. Eliezer and his company took Rebekah and returned to Abraham's household in Canaan.
44. Isaac took Rebekah as his wife, bringing her into his mother Sarah's tent, signifying the continuity of the family legacy.
45. Isaac was 40 years old when he married Rebekah, daughter of Bethuel, Abraham's nephew, beginning a new chapter in the family's journey in faith.

CHAPTER 25

1. In Abraham's later years, he took another wife named Keturah, a woman from the land of Canaan. She bore him six sons: Zimran, Jokshan, Medan, Midian, Ishbak, and Shuach. Zimran's sons were Abihen, Molich, and Narim.
2. Jokshan's sons were Sheba and Dedan, while Medan's sons were Amida, Joab, Gochi, Elisha, and Nothach. Midian's sons were Ephah, Epher, Chanoch, Abida, and Eldaah.
3. Ishbak's sons were Makiro, Beyodua, and Tator. Shuach's sons were Bildad, Mamdad, Munan, and Meban. These were the families born to Keturah, the Canaanite woman, who bore children for Abraham, known as the Hebrew.
4. Abraham sent Keturah's sons away, giving them gifts before they left Isaac to find their own dwelling places.

5. These sons went eastward, building six cities where they and their descendants live to this day.
6. However, the children of Sheba and Dedan, descendants of Jokshan, did not settle in these cities. They chose instead to live in camps across distant lands and wildernesses, where they remain even now.
7. Midian's descendants went east of the land of Cush, found a valley there, and established a city that became known as the land of Midian.
8. Midian and his five sons settled in the city they had built, along with their households.
9. The sons of Midian, each of whom established his own family, were Ephah, Epher, Chanoch, Abida, and Eldaah.
10. Ephah's sons were Methach, Meshar, Avi, and Tzanua. Epher's sons were Ephron, Zur, Alirun, and Medin.
11. Chanoch's sons were Reuel, Rekem, Azi, Alyoshub, and Alad. Abida's sons were Chur, Melud, Kerury, and Molchi.
12. Eldaah's sons were Miker, Reba, Malchiyah, and Gabol. These were the families of the Midianites, who later spread throughout the land of Midian.
13. Ishmael, Abraham's son through Hagar, also had descendants. His first wife, Ribah (also called Meribah), bore him children in Egypt: Nebayoth, Kedar, Adbeel, Mibsam, and their sister Bosmath.
14. However, Ishmael eventually sent Ribah away due to discord between them. She returned to her father's house in Egypt.
15. Ishmael then married a Canaanite woman named Malchuth, who bore him several sons: Nishma, Dumah, Masa, Chadad, Tema, Yetur, Naphish, and Kedma.
16. These twelve sons of Ishmael became the heads of distinct nations, each forming their own tribes and families. Ishmael gathered his family and possessions and moved to a place near the wilderness of Paran.
17. Ishmael's territory extended from Havilah to Shur, near Egypt, in the direction of Assyria.
18. His sons had numerous descendants and continued to prosper and grow.
19. Nebayoth's sons were Mend, Send, and Mayon. Kedar's sons were Alyon, Kezem, Chamad, and Eli.
20. Adbeel's sons were Chamad and Jabin, while Mibsam's sons were Obadiah, Ebedmelech, and Yeush.
21. Mishma's sons were Shamua, Zecaryon, and Obed. Dumah's sons were Kezed, Eli, Machmad, and Amed.
22. Masa's sons were Melon, Mula, and Ebidadon. Chadad's sons were Azur, Minzar, and Ebedmelech.
23. Tema's sons were Seir, Sadon, and Yakol, while Yetur's sons were Merith, Yaish, Alyo, and Pachoth.

24. Naphish's sons were Ebed-Tamed, Abiyasaph, and Mir. Kedma's sons were Calip, Tachti, and Omir. These were the descendants of Malchuth, Ishmael's wife, grouped by family.
25. Ishmael's descendants settled in the lands where they established cities, and these cities remain inhabited by their descendants.
26. Meanwhile, Rebekah, Isaac's wife and daughter of Bethuel, struggled with barrenness, having no children.
27. Isaac continued to dwell with Abraham in Canaan, and the LORD was with him. Around this time, Arphaxad, the son of Shem, Noah's son, passed away.
28. Arphaxad lived a total of 438 years, and he died in the 48th year of Isaac's life.

CHAPTER 26

1. In the fifty-ninth year of Isaac's life, his wife Rebekah remained barren.
2. She said to Isaac, "I have heard that your mother, Sarah, was once barren until your father Abraham prayed for her, and she conceived.
3. So, please, rise and pray to God; perhaps He will hear and remember us in His mercy."
4. Isaac replied, "My father Abraham already prayed for God to multiply his descendants; perhaps this barrenness is coming from you."
5. Rebekah pleaded, "Still, please pray so that the LORD may grant us children." Isaac listened, and together, they journeyed to the land of Moriah to seek the LORD's favor.
6. Upon reaching Moriah, Isaac prayed for Rebekah, asking the LORD to bless her with children.
7. "O LORD, God of heaven and earth," Isaac prayed, "You who promised to multiply my father's descendants as the stars in the sky and the sand on the shore, may Your word to him be fulfilled.
8. We look to You alone to give us the gift of children, as You promised." The LORD heard Isaac's prayer, and Rebekah conceived.
9. Several months later, Rebekah felt intense movement within her, causing her great discomfort.
10. She asked the women of the land if they had experienced anything similar, but they had not.
11. Troubled, she went to seek guidance from Shem and Eber and to inquire of the LORD through them.
12. They sought God on her behalf, and the message came: "Two nations are within your womb; one will be stronger than the other, and the elder shall serve the younger."
13. When the time came, Rebekah gave birth to twins, just as the LORD had said.

14. The first child was red and covered with hair, so they named him Esau, signifying that he was fully formed.
15. His brother followed, grasping Esau's heel, so he was named Jacob.
16. Isaac was sixty years old when his sons were born.
17. As the boys grew, Esau became a skilled hunter and a man of the field, while Jacob was wise, dwelling peacefully in tents and learning the ways of the LORD as taught by his parents.
18. Isaac and his household lived alongside Abraham in the land of Canaan, as God had commanded.
19. Ishmael, Abraham's other son, returned to the land of Havilah with his family, where they settled.
20. Abraham's other sons from his concubines also settled in the east, after he sent them away with gifts, leaving Isaac as his primary heir.
21. Abraham gave all his treasures to Isaac, instructing him to honor the LORD.
22. He said, "Know that the LORD alone is God in heaven and on earth, and there is no other.
23. He delivered me from my father's house, gave me blessings, and protected me.
24. He promised to give this land to my descendants if they follow His ways and obey His commands."
25. Abraham continued, "Therefore, my son, follow the LORD's commands, as I have taught you.
26. Remember His kindness in delivering us from enemies and guiding us here.
27. Serve Him faithfully so that it may go well with you and your children forever."
28. Isaac pledged to keep these commands and never to depart from the path his father had shown him.
29. Abraham blessed Isaac and his family, instructing Jacob in God's ways.
30. In the fifteenth year of Jacob and Esau's lives, Abraham passed away at the age of 175. He was gathered to his people, having lived a full and blessed life.
31. Isaac and Ishmael buried him with honor, and all the inhabitants of Canaan, including kings and princes, attended his funeral.
32. Abraham's kindness was remembered, and many came to pay their respects, including those from Haran and the family of his concubines.
33. The people mourned Abraham for a full year, grieving the loss of a man who had been good to all and had walked faithfully with God.
34. Even the children of the land wept for Abraham, as he had shown love and fairness to all.
35. He had feared God from his youth, and there arose no one else who matched his devotion to the LORD.
36. The LORD had delivered him from enemies, and Abraham had taught many to know and serve the LORD.
37. Abraham's home was always open to strangers, and he provided generously for travelers.

38. Through Abraham's life, God blessed the whole earth.
39. After Abraham's death, God blessed Isaac, as he followed his father's example, keeping all the LORD's commands.

CHAPTER 27

1. Following Abraham's death, Esau often went hunting in the fields.
2. Meanwhile, Nimrod, king of Babel, who was also known as Amraphel, would frequently go out with his mighty men to hunt and stroll in the fields.
3. Nimrod had developed a jealousy toward Esau and observed him closely.
4. One day, Esau went out hunting and encountered Nimrod walking in the wilderness with only two of his men.
5. Nimrod's other men had scattered in various directions to hunt. Seizing the opportunity, Esau concealed himself, lying in wait for Nimrod.
6. Unaware of Esau's presence, Nimrod and his companions wandered through the field, as they often did, to observe their hunting parties.
7. When Nimrod and his two men approached, Esau sprang from his hiding place, drew his sword, and quickly killed Nimrod by striking off his head.
8. Esau then engaged in a fierce battle with the two men, ultimately killing them both.
9. Nimrod's other warriors, who had been hunting nearby, heard the commotion and recognized the voices of their fallen comrades. They rushed toward the sound and discovered their king and his men dead in the wilderness.
10. Seeing Nimrod's men approaching, Esau fled, taking with him the valuable garments that had been passed down to Nimrod from his father, garments that had given Nimrod dominance over the land.
11. Esau brought these garments back to his father's house, exhausted and fearing for his life. When he saw his brother Jacob, he sat down, saying, "I am at the point of death; what use is the birthright to me?"
12. Recognizing an opportunity, Jacob wisely persuaded Esau to sell his birthright, which Esau agreed to. The sale was in line with the LORD's plan.
13. Esau also transferred his portion in the burial site at the Cave of Machpelah, which Abraham had purchased, to Jacob.
14. Jacob recorded the transaction on a scroll, witnessed and sealed, and kept the document for safekeeping.
15. After Nimrod's death, his followers buried him in his city. He had lived for 215 years, ruling his people for 185 of them.
16. Nimrod died by Esau's hand, fulfilling a prophecy of his downfall by Abraham's descendants.
17. Upon Nimrod's death, his kingdom fractured into multiple regions, with the territories he once controlled returning to their original rulers. Nimrod's household faced years of subjugation to these other kings.

CHAPTER 28

1. After Abraham's death, a severe famine struck the land of Canaan.
2. As the famine worsened, Isaac decided to go to Egypt, as his father Abraham had done.
3. However, that night, the LORD appeared to Isaac, instructing him, "Do not go to Egypt. Instead, go to Gerar, to Abimelech, king of the Philistines, and remain there until the famine subsides."
4. Obediently, Isaac traveled to Gerar and stayed for a year.
5. During his time in Gerar, the people noticed Rebekah's beauty and asked Isaac about her.
6. Fearing for his life, he told them, "She is my sister."
7. Although some of Abimelech's men spoke of her beauty, the king ignored their remarks.
8. After three months, Abimelech saw Isaac displaying affection toward Rebekah and realized she was his wife, not his sister.
9. Confronting Isaac, Abimelech said, "Why did you deceive us by claiming she was your sister? Someone could have taken her, bringing guilt upon us."
10. Isaac explained, "I feared for my life, believing they would kill me because of her."
11. Abimelech then commanded his men to bring Isaac and Rebekah to him. He ordered that they be dressed in royal garments and paraded through the city with a proclamation
12. "Anyone who harms this man or his wife shall be put to death."
13. Isaac returned to Abimelech's house, enjoying favor in the king's eyes.
14. The LORD blessed Isaac, who prospered in Gerar, recalling the covenant between Abimelech and Abraham.
15. Abimelech offered Isaac land and resources, saying, "Settle where you wish until the famine ends." Isaac accepted, sowing and reaping a hundredfold that year.
16. When the famine lifted, the LORD instructed Isaac to return to Canaan.
17. Isaac obeyed, taking his household back to Hebron.
18. In the same year, Shelah, son of Arphaxad, passed away at 433 years.
19. Isaac sent Jacob, his younger son, to the house of Shem and Eber to learn the LORD's ways.
20. Jacob remained with them for thirty-two years, while Esau, choosing not to go, stayed behind in Canaan.
21. Esau became a skilled hunter and grew adept at deception, manipulating others to his advantage.
22. He spent time in Seir, later known as Edom, and hunted there for a year and four months.
23. During his time in Seir, Esau married Jehudith, daughter of Beeri the Hittite, from the descendants of Heth.
24. Esau was forty years old when he married her and brought her back to Hebron.
25. In the 110th year of Isaac's life, which was the fiftieth year of Jacob's, Shem, son of Noah, passed away at 600 years old.
26. After Shem's death, Jacob returned to his father in Hebron.

27. In the fifty-sixth year of Jacob's life, news reached Rebekah about her brother Laban in Haran.
28. Laban's wife had been childless, but the LORD remembered her, and she bore twin daughters, Leah and Rachel.
29. When Rebekah heard of her brother's good fortune, she rejoiced, grateful that the LORD had blessed him with children.

CHAPTER 29

1. As Isaac grew old, his eyesight weakened with age.
2. One day, he called for his son Esau, saying, "Take your quiver and bow, go out to the field, hunt some game, and prepare a savory meal for me.
3. Afterward, I will bless you before I pass."
4. Esau took his weapons and set out to hunt, following his father's request to bring back food so that he could receive Isaac's blessing.
5. Rebekah overheard Isaac's instructions to Esau and quickly called Jacob to her.
6. She explained what she had heard and devised a plan.
7. She instructed Jacob, "Go to the flock and bring me two young goats.
8. I'll prepare a savory dish for your father, and you'll present it to him before Esau returns, so he will bless you instead."
9. Jacob obeyed his mother's command, preparing the food and bringing it to Isaac before Esau returned from hunting.
10. Isaac, unaware, asked, "Who are you, my son?"
11. Jacob replied, "I am Esau, your firstborn. I have done as you asked; please eat, and bless me as you promised."
12. Isaac ate, drank, and blessed Jacob.
13. Afterward, Jacob left.
14. As soon as he departed, Esau returned from the hunt with his own prepared meal for Isaac.
15. Esau approached Isaac, saying, "Here, Father, eat of my game so that you may bless me."
16. Isaac asked, "Then who was it who brought me food earlier? I have already blessed him."
17. Realizing what had happened, Esau grew furious with Jacob, saying, "Is he not rightly named Jacob, for he has deceived me twice—first taking my birthright, and now my blessing!"
18. Isaac explained, "Your brother came with guile and received the blessing."
19. Esau wept bitterly, and his anger toward Jacob grew intense.

20. Fearing Esau's wrath, Jacob fled to the house of Eber, son of Shem, where he hid for fourteen years, continuing to learn the ways of the LORD.
21. Esau, realizing Jacob had fled, grew even more resentful. He blamed his father and mother and moved to Seir with his first wife.
22. There, he took a second wife, Bosmath, daughter of Elon the Hittite, whom he renamed Adah.
23. Esau returned to Canaan six months later with his two wives, who provoked Isaac and Rebekah by practicing idolatry, serving their gods of wood and stone.
24. Their behavior distressed Isaac and Rebekah.
25. Frustrated, Rebekah lamented, "I cannot bear these Hittite women. If Jacob marries one of them, my life will be bitter."
26. Around this time, Esau's wife Adah bore him a son named Eliphaz.
27. Meanwhile, Ishmael, Abraham's son, passed away at the age of 137, and Isaac mourned his passing for many days.
28. After fourteen years, Jacob left Eber's house to visit his parents in Hebron.
29. By then, Esau had forgotten his anger toward Jacob.
30. However, seeing Jacob rekindled his rage, and he planned to kill him.
31. Learning of Esau's intentions, Rebekah advised Jacob to flee to her brother Laban in Haran until Esau's anger subsided.
32. Isaac called Jacob, cautioning him, "Do not marry a Canaanite woman. The LORD has promised this land to our descendants if they remain faithful. Go to Haran, find a wife from Laban's family, and keep the LORD's commandments."
33. Isaac continued, "May God guide you and bless you as He did Abraham, and may He make you fruitful and return you safely to this land with joy."
34. Isaac blessed Jacob, bestowed gifts of silver and gold, and sent him to Padan-Aram.
35. Esau, hearing of Jacob's departure, instructed his son Eliphaz, "Take your sword, pursue Jacob, ambush him in the mountains, and kill him."
36. Eliphaz, a skilled hunter at thirteen, gathered ten of his mother's relatives and pursued Jacob to the border near Shechem.
37. Jacob saw Eliphaz approaching with armed men and inquired, "Why do you approach with swords?"
38. Eliphaz answered, "My father ordered me to kill you." Realizing the danger, Jacob pleaded, "Take everything I own, but spare my life, and let this mercy be credited to you."
39. The LORD softened Eliphaz's heart, and he agreed to Jacob's plea, taking his possessions but sparing his life.
40. Eliphaz and his men returned to Esau, delivering Jacob's belongings.
41. Furious that they hadn't killed Jacob, Esau demanded an explanation. They explained, "Jacob begged us, and we were moved with compassion."
42. Esau stored the silver and gold taken from Jacob in his house.

43. Upon realizing Isaac and Rebekah disapproved of Canaanite wives, Esau married Machlath, daughter of his uncle Ishmael, in addition to his other wives.

CHAPTER 30

1. Jacob continued his journey toward Haran and reached Mount Moriah, where he stayed the night near the city of Luz.
2. During that night, the LORD appeared to Jacob, saying, "I am the LORD, the God of Abraham and Isaac. The land where you rest will be yours and your descendants'.
3. "I am with you, and I will protect you wherever you go. I will make your descendants as numerous as the stars, and your enemies will not prevail against you.
4. I will bring you back to this land with joy, children, and great riches."
5. Jacob awoke, deeply moved by the vision, and named the place Bethel. Filled with joy, he continued his journey with a light heart until he arrived in the eastern lands and came to a well near Haran.
6. There, Jacob met shepherds who were from Haran and asked them about Laban, the son of Nahor. They informed him that they knew Laban and pointed out his daughter Rachel, who was approaching with her father's sheep.
7. Jacob saw Rachel, ran to her, kissed her, and wept with joy. He told her that he was Rebekah's son, her father's sister's child. Rachel ran to tell her father, while Jacob, saddened by his lack of wealth, continued to weep.
8. When Laban heard about Jacob's arrival, he welcomed him warmly, embraced him, and brought him into his home, providing food and a place to stay.
9. Jacob recounted his story to Laban, sharing his troubles with Esau and Eliphaz.
10. Jacob stayed with Laban for a month, working around the household.
11. Laban eventually said to Jacob, "You should not work for me without wages. Tell me, what shall your payment be?"
12. Laban had no sons, only two daughters, Leah and Rachel. Leah had gentle eyes, but Rachel was beautiful and Jacob loved her.
13. Jacob offered, "I will serve you for seven years in exchange for your younger daughter Rachel." Laban agreed, and Jacob began his service.
14. During the second year of Jacob's stay in Haran, Eber, the son of Shem, passed away at 464 years old.
15. Jacob mourned deeply for him.
16. In Jacob's third year there, Esau's wife, Bosmath, the daughter of Ishmael, gave birth to a son, Reuel.
17. By the fourth year, the LORD blessed Laban on account of Jacob's presence, granting him wealth, honor, and several sons: Beor, Alib, and Chorash.
18. The LORD's blessing extended over all of Laban's household, and both his house and fields flourished due to Jacob's diligent work.

19. In the fifth year, Esau's wife Jehudith passed away in Canaan, leaving him two daughters, Marzith and Puith.
20. With Jehudith's death, Esau went to Seir to continue hunting as he often did, staying there for a long time.
21. In the sixth year, Esau took a new wife, Aholibamah, the daughter of Zebeon the Hivite, and brought her back to Canaan.
22. She bore him three sons: Yeush, Yaalan, and Korah.
23. Esau's wealth grew significantly, creating conflict between his herdsmen and the inhabitants of Canaan.
24. Eventually, the land could no longer sustain both Esau's and the local inhabitants' livestock.
25. Facing continued strife, Esau moved his household, family, and possessions to Seir, where he settled with his people.
26. However, he still visited his parents in Canaan periodically.
27. Esau intermarried with the Horites, forming alliances by giving his daughters in marriage to Seir's sons.
28. He married his elder daughter, Marzith, to Anah, the son of Zebeon, and his younger daughter, Puith, to Azar, son of Bilhan the Horite.
29. Esau's family prospered in the mountains of Seir, becoming a fruitful and numerous people, expanding in their new homeland.

CHAPTER 31

1. In the seventh year, Jacob's service to Laban was complete, and he asked Laban, "Give me my wife, for I have fulfilled my service."
2. Laban gathered the people of the place, and they held a feast.
3. That evening, Laban went into the house, and Jacob followed with the guests from the feast.
4. Laban then extinguished all the lights in the house.
5. Jacob asked Laban, "Why have you done this?" Laban replied, "This is our custom in this land."
6. Laban then brought his daughter Leah to Jacob, and Jacob was unaware it was Leah.
7. Laban also gave Leah his maid, Zilpah, as her handmaid.
8. Everyone at the feast knew of Laban's plan, but they did not inform Jacob.
9. Throughout the night, the guests sang and danced before Leah, chanting, "Heleah, Heleah."
10. Jacob heard them but did not understand their words, assuming it was a local custom.
11. When daylight came, Jacob turned to his wife and realized it was Leah.
12. He said, "Now I understand what the guests meant by 'Heleah' last night."

13. Jacob called out to Laban, "What have you done? I served you for Rachel.
14. Why did you deceive me and give me Leah?"
15. Laban responded, "In our land, it is not customary to give the younger daughter before the elder.
16. If you desire Rachel, serve me another seven years, and she will be yours as well."
17. Jacob agreed, and after completing another seven years of service, he married Rachel, whom he loved more than Leah.
18. Laban also gave Rachel his maid, Bilhah, as her handmaid.
19. When the LORD saw Leah was unloved, He opened her womb, and she bore Jacob four sons
20. Reuben, Simeon, Levi, and Judah. Afterward, she stopped bearing children.
21. During this time, Rachel remained childless, which caused her great distress.
22. Envious of Leah, she gave Jacob her maid Bilhah as a wife, and Bilhah bore two sons: Dan and Naphtali.
23. Leah, seeing she had stopped bearing, also gave her maid Zilpah to Jacob, who bore him two sons: Gad and Asher.
24. Leah conceived again, giving Jacob two more sons, Issachar and Zebulun, and a daughter, Dinah.
25. Rachel, still barren, prayed fervently to the LORD, saying, "O LORD, remember me and grant me children, lest my husband cast me off."
26. The LORD heard her prayer, opened her womb, and she bore a son, whom she named Joseph
27. Saying, "The LORD has taken away my shame; may He add another son to me." Jacob was ninety-one years old when Joseph was born.
28. During this time, Rebekah sent her nurse, Deborah, and two of Isaac's servants to Jacob in Haran.
29. They brought word from Rebekah, saying, "Your mother desires that you return to Canaan to your father's house."
30. Jacob listened to his mother's message, and after completing the fourteen years of service, he asked Laban,
31. "Release me, that I may return to my homeland."
32. Laban replied, "If I have found favor in your eyes, please stay. Set your wages, and I will give them to you."
33. Jacob agreed, saying, "Allow me to pass through the flock today, and I will take every speckled, spotted, and brown lamb and goat as my payment."
34. Laban agreed, and Jacob took these animals and placed them under the care of his sons, while he continued tending Laban's flock.
35. Isaac's servants returned to Canaan without Jacob
36. But Deborah stayed with Jacob, Rachel, Leah, and their children in Haran.

37. Jacob served Laban another six years, taking the speckled and spotted animals from the flock, as agreed
38. And the LORD blessed him with abundant wealth, livestock, servants, camels, and donkeys.
39. Jacob's livestock flourished, and his wealth attracted people who desired his flocks, offering him servants, donkeys, or camels in exchange.
40. Through these trades, Jacob amassed great wealth, causing envy among Laban's children.
41. Laban's sons began saying, "Jacob has taken everything that belonged to our father and gained all his wealth from him."
42. Jacob noticed Laban's attitude toward him had changed.
43. Then the LORD spoke to Jacob, "Return to your homeland, and I will be with you."
44. Jacob gathered his family and possessions, mounted them on camels, and set off toward Canaan.
45. Laban was shearing his sheep when Jacob left.
46. Meanwhile, Rachel took her father's household idols, hiding them among her belongings.
47. Laban's household idols were believed to speak to those who worshipped them, revealing hidden truths.
48. Rachel took these idols to prevent Laban from discovering Jacob's whereabouts.
49. When Laban returned and found Jacob gone, he searched for the idols to find out where Jacob had gone but could not locate them.
50. Laban gathered his family and servants and pursued Jacob, overtaking him at Mount Gilead.
51. Laban confronted Jacob, asking, "Why have you deceived me, taking my daughters like captives?
52. Why didn't you let me send them off with joy? You've stolen my gods and left."
53. Jacob replied, "I feared you might take your daughters from me by force. Whoever has your gods shall not live."
54. Laban searched all Jacob's tents but found no idols.
55. Laban then proposed a covenant with Jacob, saying
56. "Let us make a pact. If you afflict my daughters or take other wives, let God witness between us."
57. They gathered stones to mark the covenant, calling the place Gilead, meaning "witness heap."
58. Jacob and Laban offered sacrifices on the mountain, eating together by the heap, and spent the night there.
59. Early in the morning, Laban kissed his daughters and grandchildren, then departed.
60. Laban sent his son Beor, along with Abichorof, the son of Uz, and ten men to Seir to inform Esau of Jacob's return.
61. They traveled quickly, meeting Esau and saying, "Your uncle Laban has sent us.
62. Do you know what your brother Jacob has done?"

63. They told Esau, "Jacob came to Laban with nothing, and Laban honored him, giving him his daughters as wives.
64. The LORD blessed Jacob, and he grew wealthy.
65. Now, Jacob has fled, taking his wives, children, and all his property without allowing Laban to bid farewell."
66. They continued, "Jacob stole Laban's gods and departed while Laban was shearing his sheep."
67. Hearing this, Esau's anger burned, and he gathered sixty of his own men and three hundred forty of Seir's men, forming a group of four hundred to confront Jacob.
68. Esau divided his forces, placing his son Eliphaz over one group and assigning the others to Seir's sons.
69. Meanwhile, Laban's messengers returned to Rebekah, reporting Esau's approach with an armed force.
70. Rebekah quickly sent seventy-two of Isaac's men to meet Jacob, fearing Esau might attack him on the road.
71. These men met Jacob at the Brook of Jabbok, and Jacob, seeing them, said,
72. "This must be God's camp," and he named the place Mahanaim.
73. Jacob welcomed his father's men, asking of his parents' well-being, and they assured him all was well.
74. They then conveyed Rebekah's message
75. "Esau has come with a force. Show him honor and present him with gifts.
76. Answer him honestly, and perhaps his anger will subside."
77. When Jacob heard his mother's words, he wept and followed her instructions.

CHAPTER 32

1. At that time, Jacob sent messengers to his brother Esau in the land of Seir with words of humility.
2. He told them, "Say to my lord Esau: 'This is what your servant Jacob says: Do not think that our father's blessing has made me prosperous.
3. I spent twenty years with Laban, and he deceived me, changing my wages ten times.
4. I worked hard in his house, but God saw my struggle and granted me favor and mercy.
5. Through God's kindness, I gained oxen, donkeys, cattle, servants, and maids.
6. Now I am returning to my homeland, to my father and mother in Canaan, and I send this message to you to find favor in your sight."
7. Jacob's messengers went to Esau and found him near the land of Edom, approaching with four hundred men.
8. They relayed all of Jacob's words to Esau.
9. Esau replied with pride and anger, saying, "I have heard what Jacob did to Laban, gaining wealth through him.

10. When he saw his riches were great, he left without telling Laban, taking Laban's daughters.
11. Jacob also took advantage of me twice, and I will not remain silent."
12. Esau continued, "I am coming with my men to meet him, and I will act as my heart desires."
13. The messengers returned to Jacob, saying, "We met your brother, Esau, and he comes to meet you with four hundred men."
14. Jacob was greatly afraid and distressed; he prayed to God,
15. "O LORD, God of my fathers Abraham and Isaac, You said,
16. 'I am the LORD, the God of Abraham and Isaac. I will give this land to your descendants, as numerous as the stars, to bless all families on earth.'
17. You have given me riches, children, and livestock, all that I could ask for.
18. You also told me to return to my birthplace, promising to bless me.
19. But now I fear Esau will destroy me and my family. Deliver me, I pray, for the sake of Abraham and Isaac."
20. Jacob added, "In Your mercy, I have gained all I have. Save me with Your kindness, I implore You."
21. Jacob then divided his people and flocks into two groups, entrusting one group to Damesek, son of Eliezer, and the other to Elianus, another son of Eliezer.
22. He instructed them to keep their distance so if one group was attacked, the other might escape.
23. That night, Jacob stayed with his servants and continued preparing for Esau's approach.
24. God heard Jacob's prayer and sent three angels, who went before Esau.
25. These angels appeared as a great army, causing fear in Esau and his men, who scattered in terror.
26. Esau questioned them, "Is Jacob your lord? After twenty years, I come to see him, and this is my reception?"
27. The angels replied, "If Jacob were not your brother, we would not spare you. For his sake, we do you no harm."
28. Each group of angels approached Esau and his men, increasing their fear.
29. Esau's anger turned to peace, and he hid his resentment toward Jacob.
30. Jacob arranged a gift for Esau from his livestock, choosing two hundred forty animals.
31. He divided them into ten groups, each led by a servant, with space between each group.
32. Jacob instructed the servants to say, "We are Jacob's servants, bringing a gift to Esau."
33. Each group would add, "Jacob follows behind us with joy, hoping for peace with his brother."
34. That night, Jacob led his family across the Brook of Jabuk, remaining behind alone.
35. A Man appeared and wrestled with Jacob until dawn, dislocating Jacob's thigh.
36. As dawn broke, the Man blessed Jacob and departed, and Jacob crossed the brook, limping.

37. As the sun rose, Jacob continued his journey, seeing Esau approaching with four hundred men.
38. Jacob divided his children among his wives and servants, hiding Dinah in a chest for protection.
39. He went ahead to meet Esau, bowing seven times as he approached.
40. God granted Jacob favor, and Esau's anger melted into kindness.
41. Esau ran to meet Jacob, embraced him, and they wept together.
42. God moved the hearts of Esau's men, and they embraced Jacob with kindness.
43. Even Eliphaz, Esau's son, and his brothers embraced Jacob, feeling awe and reverence.
44. Esau noticed Jacob's children and asked, "Who are these with you, my brother?"
45. Jacob replied, "These are the children God graciously gave me."
46. Esau then asked about the livestock he encountered, and Jacob said, "They are a gift, to find favor with you."
47. Though Esau initially refused, Jacob insisted, and Esau accepted.
48. Esau offered to accompany Jacob to Seir, but Jacob expressed concern for his family and flocks, saying they could not travel quickly.
49. Esau offered his men to assist, but Jacob politely declined, assuring Esau he would follow slowly.
50. Satisfied, Esau returned to Seir with his men, while Jacob continued on to Canaan.
51. Jacob settled in a place near the border, remaining there for a while.
52. Later, Jacob rose with his family and continued traveling, preparing his people and livestock.
53. As he journeyed, Jacob looked up and saw Esau at a distance, approaching with many men.
54. Jacob hastily arranged his children with their mothers and hid Dinah in a chest for protection.
55. Jacob then went forward to meet Esau, bowing to the ground seven times as he approached.
56. God caused Esau to feel kindness toward Jacob, remembering his love for his brother.
57. When Esau saw Jacob, he ran to him, embracing him warmly, and they wept together.
58. God stirred the hearts of Esau's men with fear and kindness toward Jacob.
59. Esau's sons, including Eliphaz, came forward to embrace Jacob, moved by the sight.
60. Esau looked at the women and children with Jacob and asked, "Who are these with you, my brother?"
61. Jacob answered, "These are my children, gifts from God to your servant."
62. As they spoke, Esau looked over the camp and said, "Where did you get all the animals I saw last night?"
63. Jacob replied, "They are a gift to find favor in my lord's sight."
64. Jacob urged Esau to accept the gifts, saying, "Since I see you still live in peace, I am blessed to offer these gifts."

65. Though Esau hesitated, Jacob insisted, and finally, Esau took the gifts.
66. Esau then divided the livestock, giving half to his men and keeping the other half for his family.
67. The silver, gold, and jewels Jacob had given, Esau handed to his eldest son, Eliphaz.
68. Esau then said to Jacob, "Let us travel together slowly so we can stay close."
69. Jacob replied, "The children and flocks are delicate; we must travel at their pace."
70. Esau offered some of his men to assist Jacob, but Jacob declined, saying, "I will come to Seir in due time."
71. Jacob thanked Esau and assured him he would visit in peace, suggesting Esau go on ahead.
72. Esau agreed and returned to Seir with his men, while Jacob continued his journey with his family.
73. Jacob reached the borders of Canaan, where he stayed for a time, settling with his people and resting from the journey.

CHAPTER 33

1. Some time after Jacob left the borderlands, he arrived in Shalem, a city in the land of Shechem, within Canaan, and set up camp near the city.
2. He purchased a piece of land there from the sons of Hamor, the locals, for five shekels.
3. Jacob built a house and pitched his tents, also constructing shelters for his livestock. He named the place Succoth.
4. Jacob and his family settled in Succoth, remaining there for a year and six months.
5. At that time, some women from the city of Shechem gathered for a festival with dancing and celebration. Rachel, Leah, and their families went to see the festivities.
6. Dinah, Jacob's daughter, went along, joining the other women and observing the festivities while the people of the city looked on.
7. Shechem, son of Hamor, the prince of the region, was also there and noticed Dinah.
8. Shechem was captivated by Dinah and asked his friends, "Who is this girl among the women? I do not know her."
9. They told him, "This is Dinah, daughter of Jacob, son of Isaac, who has been living here. She came with her family to watch the celebrations."
10. Shechem became deeply infatuated with Dinah.
11. He seized her and took her to his house, where he violated her, but his heart was filled with love for her, and he kept her with him.
12. When Jacob heard what had happened to Dinah, he sent twelve servants to retrieve her from Shechem's house.
13. The servants arrived, but Shechem and his men drove them away, refusing to let them see Dinah.
14. The servants returned to Jacob and said, "Shechem drove us away and held Dinah before our eyes."

15. Jacob knew Dinah had been defiled, but he kept silent until his sons returned from the field.
16. Before his sons came home, Jacob sent two maidens from among his servants to stay with Dinah in Shechem's house.
17. Meanwhile, Shechem sent friends to his father, Hamor, requesting that he arrange for Dinah to be his wife.
18. Hamor went to Shechem and said, "Is there no woman among our people that you would take a foreigner, a Hebrew?"
19. But Shechem insisted, "I must have her, for I am deeply fond of her." So Hamor, loving his son, agreed.
20. Hamor then went to Jacob to discuss the matter, but on his way, Jacob's sons returned from the field, having heard what Shechem had done.
21. Jacob's sons were furious, grieving over the disgrace done to their sister, and gathered around their father, speaking in anger.
22. They said, "The law of God condemns such acts; Shechem has violated our sister, and no one in the city has spoken against it."
23. They continued, "By God's law, Shechem and his father deserve judgment."
24. While they were speaking, Hamor arrived to discuss Shechem's proposal with Jacob and his sons.
25. Hamor said, "My son Shechem desires your daughter. Please, give her to him as his wife and intermarry with us. We will give you our daughters in marriage, and you can give us yours."
26. He added, "Our land is broad and open. Live, trade, and prosper here as you wish."
27. Hamor finished speaking, and Shechem arrived, joining his father.
28. Shechem spoke, "Let me find favor in your eyes, and give me your daughter. Name the dowry, and I will meet your price for her hand."
29. Simeon and Levi responded deceitfully, saying, "We agree to your terms. Our sister is in your care, but let us first consult our father Isaac."
30. They added, "Our father Isaac follows the ways of Abraham, and whatever he directs, we will tell you."
31. Their words were a strategy, intended to buy time as they sought a way to deal with Shechem and his city.
32. Shechem and Hamor accepted the words of Simeon and Levi, returning home with a sense of approval.
33. After they left, Jacob's sons said to their father, "These men deserve judgment for their wickedness, for they have acted against God's commands to Noah and his descendants."
34. They continued, "Shechem defiled our sister; such a thing must not be tolerated among us. Let us plan what to do to them and to their city."
35. Simeon suggested, "Here is my counsel: tell them to be circumcised as we are. If they refuse, we can take Dinah and go.

36. But if they agree, when they are in pain from the circumcision, we can attack and kill all the men."
37. The others agreed to Simeon's plan, resolving to carry it out.
38. The next morning, Shechem and Hamor returned to Jacob and his sons to hear their answer.
39. The sons of Jacob answered deceitfully, "We spoke with our father Isaac, and he approved. But he reminded us of God's command to Abraham that anyone wishing to join our family must be circumcised."
40. They added, "Therefore, if every male in your city is circumcised as we are, then we will give you our daughter."
41. They continued, "If you refuse to be circumcised, we will take our sister and leave."
42. Shechem and Hamor found these words favorable, eager for Shechem's desire to be fulfilled.
43. They hastened back to the city, assembling all the men at the gate to relay the words of Jacob's sons.
44. They told the men, "We spoke to Jacob's sons, and they will intermarry with us and live among us if we agree to be circumcised."
45. They added, "Their land is vast, and we will share in their wealth. Only let us follow their custom and circumcise every male as they are."
46. The men of the city, respecting Hamor and Shechem as leaders, agreed to their proposal and were willing to undergo circumcision.
47. The following morning, all the men gathered in the city center, and Jacob's sons circumcised every male in the city over the next two days.
48. Shechem, his father Hamor, and Shechem's five brothers were circumcised along with the other men, and afterward, each returned to his home.
49. This action was in accordance with the LORD's plan against Shechem's city, for Simeon's suggestion came from God.
50. Thus, God intended to deliver Shechem's city into the hands of Jacob's sons.
51. As the men lay in pain from the circumcision, Simeon and Levi prepared to carry out their plan.
52. In the weakness of Shechem and his people, Jacob's sons would find justice for their sister's defilement, according to their resolve and the LORD's will.

CHAPTER 34

1. The total number of circumcised males was six hundred forty-five men and two hundred forty-six boys.
2. However, Chiddekem, son of Pered, along with his six brothers, refused to follow Shechem and Hamor's request, declining circumcision as they found Jacob's sons' proposal offensive.

3. On the evening of the second day, eight young boys were found uncircumcised, as their mothers had hidden them from Shechem, Hamor, and the townsmen.
4. Shechem and Hamor tried to bring them for circumcision, but Chiddekem and his brothers, armed with swords, attempted to kill them.
5. They sought to kill Shechem, Hamor, and even Dinah over this matter.
6. They said to Shechem, "Are there not women among your own people? Why would you choose a Hebrew woman, unfamiliar to our customs, going against your father's teachings?"
7. They continued, "Do you think such a choice will go unnoticed by your fellow Canaanites when they question your actions tomorrow?"
8. "If your actions are seen as unjust by them, how will you justify yourselves? They may retaliate."
9. "And if all the people of the land and your Canaanite kin hear of this, what refuge will you have when they condemn your choice?"
10. "We cannot bear the shame of this offense against our customs; neither can we support this act, for our ancestors never commanded such a thing."
11. "Tomorrow, we will gather our fellow Canaanites and confront you, Shechem, and those who support this offense, leaving none of you."
12. When Hamor, Shechem, and the city's residents heard Chiddekem and his brothers' words, fear took hold of them, and they regretted their actions.
13. Shechem and his father answered, "Your words are true. We did not do this out of love for the Hebrews."
14. "We acted only because they refused our request for Dinah unless we complied with their terms."
15. "We only agreed to circumcision to gain Dinah, and once we succeed, we will turn against them as you wish."
16. "We ask that you be patient until our wounds heal and we regain our strength, and then we will join you in confronting them."
17. Dinah overheard the exchange between Chiddekem, his brothers, Hamor, Shechem, and the city's people.
18. She quickly sent one of her maidservants—whom Jacob had sent to care for her in Shechem's house—with a message for her father and brothers.
19. She told them, "Chiddekem and his brothers have declared their intentions, and here is how Hamor, Shechem, and their people responded."
20. Upon hearing this, Jacob was filled with anger and indignation.
21. Simeon and Levi swore, "As surely as the LORD lives, by tomorrow, no one in that city will remain."
22. Twenty young men had hidden themselves from the circumcision. They fought Simeon and Levi, who killed eighteen of them, though two escaped into nearby pits. Simeon and Levi searched for them but could not find them.

23. They continued through the city, killing every male they encountered by the sword, leaving none alive.
24. The city was thrown into chaos as cries rose to the heavens from the people. Women and children wailed in fear.
25. Simeon and Levi left no males alive, killing every one in Shechem.
26. They also killed Hamor and Shechem by the sword, rescued Dinah from Shechem's house, and departed.
27. Returning to the city, the sons of Jacob took all the spoils from the city and the surrounding fields.
28. While collecting the spoils, three hundred men resisted, throwing dust and stones at them. Simeon turned back and slew them with his sword, rejoining Levi in the city.
29. They seized sheep, oxen, cattle, and took the remaining women and children captive, opening a gate and leading them out to their father Jacob.
30. When Jacob saw what they had done and all the spoils they took, he became furious, saying, "What have you done to me? I had peace with the Canaanites, and none had troubled me."
31. "Now you have brought trouble upon me with the inhabitants of the land, the Canaanites and Perizzites. We are few, and they will join together against us, wiping out me and my household."
32. Simeon, Levi, and the others replied, "We live here, and shall Shechem do this to our sister? Why should we remain silent after what he did?"
33. They added, "Shall our sister be treated as a common woman in the streets?"
34. The number of women Simeon and Levi spared from Shechem was eighty-five, all untouched by men.
35. Among them was a beautiful young woman named Bunah, whom Simeon took as his wife.
36. They captured forty-seven men, leaving no others alive.
37. The men and women Simeon and Levi took captive served Jacob's family and descendants until they left Egypt.
38. When Simeon and Levi departed the city, two hidden young men who had survived emerged and found the city empty except for grieving women.
39. These young men cried out, "This is the destruction that Jacob's sons brought upon Shechem, a Canaanite city, without fear of retribution from the land."
40. The men traveled to the nearby city of Tapnach and told its residents all that Jacob's sons had done in Shechem.
41. King Jashub of Tapnach sent men to verify this report, as he doubted that two men could destroy such a large city alone.
42. His messengers returned, confirming, "We found the city destroyed, without a single man, only mourning women, and the livestock taken."

43. Jashub was astonished, asking, "How could two men destroy a city, with no one resisting?"
44. He declared, "This has not been seen since the days of Nimrod, nor in all time since."
45. Jashub rallied his people, saying, "Gather courage! We will go and fight these Hebrews to avenge Shechem's destruction."
46. He consulted with his advisors, who warned, "If two men could do this to a city, we alone will not prevail against them."
47. "If you go alone, they will rise up and destroy us. Send word to nearby kings, and together we can face them."
48. Jashub followed their advice, sending messages to the kings of the Amorites surrounding Shechem and Tapnach.
49. He urged them, "Join me in fighting Jacob and his sons, for they have destroyed Shechem, and you are aware of this."
50. When the Amorite kings heard of the devastation in Shechem, they were shocked at the power of Jacob's sons.
51. Seven Amorite kings gathered their armies, assembling about ten thousand men with drawn swords, preparing to fight Jacob's family.
52. Jacob learned of the Amorite kings' assembly and was deeply troubled.
53. He turned to Simeon and Levi, saying, "Why did you bring this trouble upon me? I lived in peace, but now all of Canaan is set against us."
54. Judah replied, "Our brothers struck Shechem because Shechem violated our sister, breaking the command of God given to Noah and his descendants."
55. "The people of Shechem allowed him to take our sister by force, so the LORD delivered Shechem into our hands."
56. Judah assured Jacob, "Trust in the LORD, who delivered Shechem to us. He will also deliver these kings into our hands."
57. Judah sent a servant to spy on the Amorite kings' camps.
58. The servant went as far as Mount Sihon, seeing their massive encampment, and reported back, "The kings' armies are as numerous as sand on the seashore."
59. Judah encouraged his brothers, "Stand strong and ready. The LORD is with us; do not fear these uncircumcised men."
60. Each of Jacob's sons prepared for battle, arming themselves with swords and bows.
61. They were joined by Isaac's servants from Hebron, all equipped with weapons of war, making a force of one hundred twelve men.
62. Jacob joined his sons, and they sent word to Isaac, who was in Hebron, asking him to pray for them.
63. They requested, "Pray to the LORD for protection from these Canaanites, who are set against us."
64. Isaac prayed, "O LORD, You promised Abraham, saying You would multiply his descendants like the stars. Fulfill Your word now, for my sons have committed no sin."

65. "O LORD, protect my sons from these kings. Deliver their enemies into their hands."
66. Jacob and his sons placed their trust in God, setting out in faith while Jacob prayed, "O God, You are mighty; You cause wars to start and cease. Show mercy upon us."
67. "Turn the hearts of these kings and instill fear of my sons in their camps."
68. "Deliver my sons and those who trust in You, bringing the nations under our hand."
69. Jacob and his sons continued their journey, placing their full trust in the LORD. As they went, Jacob prayed, "O LORD, God Almighty, who has reigned from the beginning and will reign forever, You alone can calm or stir the nations."
70. "In Your hands are power and might to humble or exalt. May my plea come before You, that You might turn the hearts of these kings with fear and awe of my sons, and deliver them by Your great mercy."

CHAPTER 35

1. All the Amorite kings gathered in a field, discussing with their counselors what action to take against Jacob's sons, still fearful after learning that only two of them had destroyed the city of Shechem.
2. The LORD heard Isaac and Jacob's prayers, filling the advisors of these kings with intense fear, causing them to say,
3. "Are you truly wise, or are you inviting your own ruin by challenging the Hebrews?
4. Remember, two of them entered Shechem without fear and wiped out the entire city. How can you hope to defeat them all?"
5. "Their God is strongly devoted to them, performing mighty deeds for them unseen before among any nation's gods."
6. "Remember how He saved their forefather Abraham from King Nimrod and all his followers who wanted to kill him."
7. "Their God even delivered Abraham from the flames when Nimrod cast him into a fire."
8. "Who else has such power? It was Abraham who defeated the five kings of Elam when they attacked his nephew who was living in Sodom."
9. "He pursued them with only a few servants, yet they conquered and restored everything taken from his nephew."
10. "The God of the Hebrews favors them, and they hold Him in great love because He has saved them from their foes."
11. "Out of devotion to their God, Abraham was willing to sacrifice his only son until God intervened."
12. "God witnessed this act and swore to deliver Abraham's descendants from any trouble because he had shown such loyalty."
13. "Have you not heard what their God did to Pharaoh in Egypt and Abimelech of Gerar after they tried to take Abraham's wife, whom he called his sister?"
14. "Even Esau, Jacob's own brother, came with four hundred men to kill him, but their God saved him."

15. "Esau intended to attack Jacob's entire family, but God intervened and protected them."
16. "It was also their God who empowered them to destroy Shechem as you have heard."
17. "Could two men alone devastate such a large city if their God hadn't helped them?"
18. "If you go to battle, you won't only be fighting them but their powerful God who chose them. This fight could bring disaster upon you."
19. "Therefore, avoid this danger and spare yourselves from a ruinous battle. Though they are few, their God is with them."
20. When the Amorite kings heard this advice, they were deeply shaken and decided against fighting the sons of Jacob.
21. Listening to their advisors' warnings, the kings felt relieved and satisfied, choosing to avoid battle.
22. Terrified of Jacob's sons, the kings withdrew, unwilling to engage them in war, as they feared what might happen.
23. These kings then left, each returning to his city, leaving the sons of Jacob unchallenged.
24. This outcome was the LORD's doing, for He had heard the prayers of His servants, Isaac and Jacob, who trusted in Him. And so the kings returned to their cities without engaging in battle with Jacob's sons.
25. Jacob's sons stayed near Mount Sihon that day until evening, observing that the kings made no move to fight. Seeing this, they returned home.

CHAPTER 36

1. At that time, the LORD appeared to Jacob and commanded, "Go to Bethel and settle there, building an altar to the LORD who appeared to you and saved you and your sons from trouble."
2. Jacob obeyed, gathering his sons and everyone with him to journey to Bethel as the LORD had instructed.
3. Jacob was ninety-nine years old when he went to Bethel. He and his household, including all his followers, remained in Bethel, also known as Luz, where he built an altar to the LORD. They stayed in Bethel for six months.
4. During this period, Deborah, the nurse of Rebekah, passed away. Jacob buried her beneath an oak tree in Bethel.
5. Around this time, Rebekah, Jacob's mother, also died in Hebron, also called Kirjath-Arba, and was buried in the cave of Machpelah, which Abraham had bought from the Hittites.
6. Rebekah lived to the age of one hundred thirty-three. When Jacob learned of her death, he mourned her deeply along with his mother's nurse, Deborah, beneath the oak tree, naming the place Allon-bachuth, meaning "Oak of Weeping."
7. Laban, the Syrian, also died around this time. God struck him because he had broken the covenant he had made with Jacob.

8. Jacob was one hundred years old when the LORD appeared to him, blessed him, and renamed him Israel. Rachel, Jacob's wife, conceived during this time.
9. Jacob and his entire household set out from Bethel to return to his father's home in Hebron.
10. On the way, as they neared Ephrath, Rachel went into labor and suffered greatly. She passed away during childbirth.
11. Jacob buried her on the road to Ephrath, which is now called Bethlehem, marking her grave with a pillar that still stands. Rachel was forty-five when she died.
12. Jacob named their newborn son Benjamin, meaning "Son of the Right Hand," as he was born in the land on the right side.
13. After Rachel's death, Jacob pitched his tent in the quarters of her maidservant, Bilhah.
14. Reuben, Leah's son, became jealous on his mother's behalf and, filled with anger, went to Bilhah's tent and moved his father's bed.
15. Due to this act, Reuben lost the rights to the birthright and the roles of king and priest. The birthright was given to Joseph, the kingship to Judah, and the priesthood to Levi.
16. These are the descendants of Jacob born to him in Padan-Aram. Jacob had twelve sons.
17. Leah's sons were Reuben, Jacob's firstborn, and Simeon, Levi, Judah, Issachar, Zebulun, along with their sister Dinah. Rachel's sons were Joseph and Benjamin.
18. Zilpah, Leah's servant, bore Gad and Asher, and Bilhah, Rachel's servant, bore Dan and Naphtali. These are Jacob's children, born in Padan-Aram.
19. Jacob, his sons, and all his household traveled to Mamre, also known as Kirjath-Arba, in Hebron, where Abraham and Isaac had lived. Jacob and his family settled there with his father.
20. Meanwhile, Esau, along with his sons and household, settled in Seir, where they accumulated possessions. Esau's descendants flourished and multiplied in Seir.
21. These are Esau's descendants, born to him in Canaan. Esau had five sons.
22. Esau's wife Adah bore his firstborn, Eliphaz, and another son, Reuel. Aholibamah bore Jeush, Yaalam, and Korah.
23. These children were born to Esau in Canaan. Eliphaz's sons were Teman, Omar, Zepho, Gatam, Kenaz, and Amalek. Reuel's sons were Nahath, Zerah, Shammah, and Mizzah.
24. Jeush's children were Timnah, Alvah, and Jetheth. Yaalam's sons were Alah, Phinor, and Kenaz.
25. Korah's children were Teman, Mibzar, Magdiel, and Eram. These were the clans of Esau's sons in the land of Seir.
26. The sons of Seir the Horite, who lived in Seir, were Lotan, Shobal, Zibeon, Anah, Dishon, Ezer, and Dishan, seven sons in total.
27. Lotan's children were Hori, Heman, and their sister Timna. (This is the same Timna who came to Jacob's sons, seeking refuge, but was rejected. She later became Eliphaz's concubine, bearing him Amalek.)

28. Shobal's children were Alvan, Manahath, Ebal, Shepho, and Onam. Zibeon's children were Ajah and Anah.
29. This Anah is known for discovering the Yemim in the wilderness while tending his father Zibeon's donkeys.
30. Anah would often lead his father's donkeys into the wilderness, guiding them along the seashore opposite the people's territory.
31. One day, a severe storm rose from the sea, startling the donkeys, causing them to freeze in place.
32. Suddenly, about one hundred twenty strange and terrifying creatures emerged from the wilderness on the other side of the sea, approaching the donkeys.
33. These creatures were human-like below the waist, with the upper bodies resembling bears and keephas. Each had a tail that stretched from its shoulders to the ground, like that of a ducheepha. The creatures mounted the donkeys, riding them away, and they have not been seen since.
34. One of these creatures struck Anah with its tail before fleeing, leaving him terrified. He escaped to the city.
35. Anah shared this tale with his family, and several men went to search for the donkeys but found none. From that day, Anah and his brothers avoided that place, fearing for their lives.
36. Anah's children were Dishon and his sister Aholibamah. Dishon's children were Hemdan, Eshban, Ithran, and Cheran. Ezer's children were Bilhan, Zaavan, and Akan. Dishon's children were Uz and Aran.
37. These were the families of Seir's descendants, living in Seir and organized by their clans.
38. Esau and his family dwelled in Seir alongside the Horite families, growing and prospering in the land. Meanwhile, Jacob and his household lived with Isaac in Canaan, fulfilling the LORD's promise to Abraham.

CHAPTER 37

1. In the one hundred fifth year of Jacob's life, marking the ninth year since he had settled with his family in Canaan after leaving Padan-Aram,
2. Jacob and his family journeyed from Hebron to Shechem, along with all their possessions. They found fertile pastures for their cattle, as Shechem had been rebuilt and was home to about three hundred residents.
3. Jacob and his family settled in the section of land Jacob had purchased from Hamor, father of Shechem, before Simeon and Levi had attacked the city.
4. When the Canaanite and Amorite kings nearby heard that Jacob's sons had returned to Shechem, they grew concerned.
5. They questioned, "Will these Hebrews come again to inhabit the city they previously destroyed? Will they now expel or kill the current residents?"

6. In response, the Canaanite kings gathered, preparing to wage war against Jacob and his family.
7. Jashub, king of Tapnach, sent messages to other kings nearby: Elan of Gaash, Ihuri of Shiloh, Parathon of Chazar, Susi of Sarton, Laban of Bethchoran, and Shabir of Othnaymah.
8. He urged them, "Come and aid me in defeating Jacob, his sons, and all their people. They have returned to Shechem to take possession and may harm its residents once more."
9. These kings assembled with their armies—a multitude as vast as the sand on the shore—and gathered opposite Tapnach.
10. Jashub led his army to join them, camping outside Tapnach, and arranged the assembled kings into seven divisions, forming seven camps against Jacob's sons.
11. They sent a message to Jacob and his family: "Come out to the plains and meet us. We seek justice for the men of Shechem you killed, as you have returned to reclaim the city and may harm its people again."
12. Jacob's sons were infuriated by this message. Ten of them quickly readied their weapons, joined by one hundred and two of their servants prepared for battle.
13. Together, Jacob and his sons, along with their servants, approached the assembled kings, gathering at the hill overlooking Shechem.
14. Jacob raised his hands in prayer to the LORD, saying, "O Almighty God, our Creator and Father, we are the work of Your hands. In Your mercy, deliver my sons from these enemies who have come to attack us, for You alone have the power to save the few from the many."
15. "Grant my sons courage and strength to overcome their foes. May their enemies fall before them, and protect them from death at the hands of the Canaanites."
16. "But if it is Your will to take their lives, may You do so mercifully by Your own hand, rather than let them perish by the hands of these Amorite kings."
17. When Jacob finished praying, the earth trembled, and the sun grew dim. The kings were struck with fear and confusion.
18. The LORD heard Jacob's plea and instilled terror in the hearts of the kings and their armies,
19. causing them to hear sounds like chariots, mighty horses, and a vast army accompanying Jacob's sons.
20. The kings were seized with fear, and as Jacob's sons advanced with one hundred twelve men and a resounding battle cry,
21. the sight of them approaching only heightened the kings' panic, and they considered retreating rather than face them.
22. However, they hesitated, saying, "It would bring shame upon us to flee a second time from the Hebrews."
23. Jacob's sons advanced toward the kings and their armies, seeing their enemies' vast numbers spread like the sand of the sea.

24. They called out to the LORD, saying, "Help us, LORD! We place our trust in You; do not let us fall to these uncircumcised men who come against us today."
25. Each son of Jacob took up his shield and javelin, preparing for battle.
26. Judah, the son of Jacob, led the charge, accompanied by ten of his servants, moving toward the kings.
27. Jashub, king of Tapnach, also advanced with his army to confront Judah. When Judah saw Jashub and his forces, he was filled with anger and readied himself for the fight, even at the risk of his own life.
28. Jashub, a formidable warrior clad in iron and brass armor, rode forward on a powerful horse, shooting arrows in all directions.
29. He was highly skilled with the bow, able to shoot accurately both ahead and behind, a tactic he used in every battle.
30. As Jashub approached Judah, he unleashed a volley of arrows. But the LORD intervened, causing Jashub's arrows to miss and strike his own men instead.
31. Undeterred, Jashub continued his attack, trying to close the distance, which was about thirty cubits. Judah, fueled by wrath, charged toward Jashub.
32. Judah lifted a large stone, weighing about sixty shekels, and hurled it at Jashub's shield, striking it so hard that Jashub was knocked from his horse to the ground.
33. The impact sent Jashub's shield flying about fifteen cubits, landing near the second camp.
34. Observing Judah's strength and his attack on Jashub, the allied kings were terrified of Judah.
35. They gathered around Jashub's camp as he lay stunned, while Judah drew his sword and struck down forty-two of Jashub's men, causing the entire camp to flee in panic.
36. Seeing his men abandon him, Jashub quickly rose, trembling, and stood to face Judah once more.
37. He engaged Judah in a one-on-one fight, their shields clashing, while his men fled in fear.
38. Jashub tried to strike Judah's head with his spear, but Judah raised his shield just in time, blocking the blow. The force split Judah's shield.
39. Seeing his shield broken, Judah drew his sword and swiftly struck Jashub's ankles, severing his feet and causing him to fall to the ground, dropping his spear.
40. Judah then seized Jashub's spear and used it to decapitate him, placing his head beside his feet.
41. When Jacob's sons saw Judah's victory over Jashub, they charged into the ranks of the remaining kings and fought fiercely.
42. The sons of Jacob struck down fifteen thousand of their enemies, cutting through them as one harvests ripe gourds, while the rest fled for their lives.
43. Judah stood over Jashub's body, removing his armor.
44. Nine of Jashub's captains approached to fight Judah, but he quickly grabbed a stone and struck one on the head, shattering his skull and knocking him from his horse.

45. Seeing Judah's strength, the remaining eight captains fled. Judah pursued them with his ten men, overtaking and killing them.
46. Jacob's sons continued to battle the armies of the kings, killing many of them, while the kings, though unwilling to retreat, found no way to rally their fleeing men.
47. After defeating the armies, Jacob's sons gathered around Judah, who was still fighting the last of Jashub's captains and stripping their armor.
48. Levi spotted Elon, king of Gaash, advancing toward him with fourteen captains, but at first, he did not realize they were approaching him.
49. As Elon and his captains neared, Levi turned and saw the danger.
50. With twelve of his servants, Levi charged at Elon and his captains, striking them down with the sword.

CHAPTER 38

1. King Ihuri of Shiloh joined the fight to support Elon, but as he neared Jacob, Jacob drew his bow and struck Ihuri with an arrow, ending his life.
2. With Ihuri's death, the remaining four kings and their captains fled, admitting, "We lack the strength to defeat these Hebrews after they have slain three of our mightiest kings and their warriors."
3. Seeing the kings retreat, the sons of Jacob pursued them. Jacob left his post at Shechem's mound to join his sons, and together they advanced on the fleeing kings and their armies.
4. The kings and their soldiers, fearing for their lives, fled until they reached the city of Chazar.
5. Jacob's sons pursued them to the gate of Chazar, where they engaged the kings' forces in a fierce battle, killing about four thousand men. Meanwhile, Jacob focused on using his bow, aiming at the kings and striking them down one by one.
6. Near the gate of Chazar, Jacob killed King Parathon, and afterward, he targeted and killed Kings Susi of Sarton, Laban of Bethchorin, and Shabir of Machnaymah, each falling to Jacob's arrows.
7. With the kings slain, the sons of Jacob continued to strike the armies remaining outside Chazar's gate, killing an additional four hundred men.
8. During this battle, three of Jacob's servants fell. Judah was deeply grieved over their deaths, and his anger against the Amorites intensified.
9. The rest of the Amorites, terrified, rushed into Chazar's gates, breaking them open to gain entry and seek refuge within the city's walls.
10. Chazar, a large and well-fortified city, concealed the armies within its vast area. Jacob's sons arrived at the city, determined to pursue their enemies.
11. Four experienced warriors emerged from Chazar's entrance, brandishing swords and spears, blocking the sons of Jacob from entering.
12. Naphtali rushed forward, striking down two of the guards with a single swing, severing their heads.

13. The remaining two guards attempted to flee, but Naphtali chased them down and killed them as well.
14. Entering the city, the sons of Jacob encountered another wall within. Unable to locate the entrance, Judah climbed to the top, followed by Simeon and Levi, and the three descended into the city.
15. Simeon and Levi attacked all those who had sought safety within the city, including the residents and their families, leaving no man alive. The city's cries rose up to the heavens.
16. Dan and Naphtali scaled the wall, alarmed by the noise, and looked down, hearing the townspeople pleading, "Take all that we own and leave us in peace."
17. Once Judah, Simeon, and Levi stopped the attack, they climbed the wall to call their brothers, informing them of a way into the city, so the rest of Jacob's sons entered to gather spoils.
18. They seized all of Chazar's goods, livestock, and valuable property, taking everything of worth before departing the city that day.
19. The following day, the sons of Jacob went to Sarton, having heard that the remaining men there were rallying to avenge their slain king. Sarton was a fortified city with a tall and strong wall.
20. The wall surrounding Sarton was fifty cubits high and forty cubits wide, making it impossible to enter directly.
21. The only way into Sarton was through a rear gate, requiring a circuitous route around the city.
22. Angered by the obstacle, Jacob's sons looked for a way in but found none, while Sarton's inhabitants watched from within, terrified by the sons of Jacob's approach, having heard of their victory at Chazar.
23. The people of Sarton, fearing an attack, gathered within the city but dared not engage the sons of Jacob outside, knowing their formidable strength.
24. In their fear, Sarton's people removed the city bridge, preventing entry and retreating into the city's depths.
25. Jacob's sons searched for an entrance but were thwarted, and when Sarton's people saw them trying to enter, they taunted and cursed them from atop the wall.
26. Enraged by the insults, Jacob's sons mustered their strength, leaping across the wide wall to the city's entrance.
27. Using their might, they traversed the forty-cubit-wide rampart,
28. only to find the city's gates barred by heavy iron doors.
29. Attempting to break through, they were met by a hail of stones and arrows from above, as around four hundred defenders stood on the walls.
30. Judah led the charge, scaling the east side of the city, followed by Gad and Asher on the west, with Simeon and Levi approaching from the north and Dan and Reuben from the south.

31. The men atop the walls, seeing the sons of Jacob advance, abandoned their positions, retreating into the city's center to hide.
32. Issachar and Naphtali stayed behind and managed to break open the city gates, setting a fire that weakened the iron, allowing Jacob's sons and their men to enter and engage Sarton's inhabitants in battle.
33. In the ensuing fight, about two hundred men fled, hiding within a tower in the city. Judah pursued them, toppling the tower, which collapsed on the men, killing them.
34. Climbing atop the fallen tower, Jacob's sons saw another tall structure nearby, reaching into the sky. They descended quickly and headed for the tower,
35. where they found around three hundred people—men, women, and children—taking refuge.
36. They launched a fierce assault, causing the remaining men to flee once more.
37. As Simeon and Levi pursued them, twelve valiant warriors emerged to confront them.
38. These twelve men fiercely resisted, even shattering Simeon and Levi's shields. One attacker nearly struck Levi's head, but Levi blocked the blow with his hand, narrowly escaping injury.
39. Levi retaliated, grabbing the man's sword and beheading him in a swift counterattack.
40. The remaining eleven warriors, seeing their fallen comrade, continued their resistance, proving to be formidable opponents.
41. Recognizing the struggle, Simeon let out a powerful shout, momentarily startling their foes.
42. Judah, hearing Simeon's call, and Naphtali rushed over with new shields for Simeon and Levi, whose own were now broken.
43. Together, Simeon, Levi, and Judah fought the remaining eleven warriors until sunset, though they couldn't overpower them.
44. News of the struggle reached Jacob, who grieved deeply, praying to the LORD and then setting out with Naphtali to join the fight.
45. Jacob, bow in hand, approached the battle and swiftly struck down three of the mighty men, causing the remaining eight to panic.
46. Surrounded and overwhelmed, the eight men tried to retreat but found themselves trapped, and they were ultimately defeated by Jacob's sons.
47. As they fled, they encountered Dan and Asher, who engaged them, killing two before Judah and his brothers arrived to finish off the last of the men.
48. With the battle over, Jacob's sons scoured the city, finding twenty young men hiding in a cave, whom Gad and Asher swiftly defeated, while Dan and Naphtali dealt with those who had escaped the second tower.
49. Every man of Sarton was slain, sparing only the women and children, who remained untouched.
50. The inhabitants of Sarton were powerful warriors, renowned for their strength, with one man able to face a thousand and two able to hold their ground against ten thousand.

51. Despite this, Jacob's sons destroyed every man in the city with their swords, sparing only the women.
52. They claimed the city's riches, livestock, and possessions, taking all they desired and treating Sarton as they had Chazar, before departing.

CHAPTER 39

1. As the sons of Jacob departed from Sarton, they had traveled only a short distance when they encountered the inhabitants of Tapnach advancing to confront them, for these people sought revenge for the death of their king and soldiers.
2. Every remaining warrior in Tapnach came out to challenge Jacob's sons, hoping to reclaim the spoils taken from Chazar and Sarton.
3. The Tapnach fighters engaged Jacob's sons but soon fell back, fleeing toward the city of Arbelan, with Jacob's sons in pursuit, striking them down along the way.
4. Returning to Tapnach, Jacob's sons intended to gather its remaining treasures. But upon arrival, they learned that the people of Arbelan had advanced to defend Tapnach's wealth. So, Jacob's sons left ten men in Tapnach to continue the plunder, while the rest went out to meet Arbelan's forces.
5. The people of Arbelan, including their wives, came out in strength, prepared to battle, for their women were seasoned warriors; a force of roughly four hundred men and women confronted Jacob's sons.
6. With a thunderous shout, Jacob's sons charged the inhabitants of Arbelan, their voices echoing like lions' roars and the rumbling of ocean waves.
7. Terrified by the sound, the Arbelan forces grew panicked, overwhelmed with fear, and quickly retreated back into their city with Jacob's sons close behind, chasing them to the city gates.
8. Jacob's sons entered Arbelan and fought within the city walls, where women also joined the fray, hurling stones and slings against them in fierce combat that lasted all day.
9. Despite their strength, Jacob's sons struggled to gain the upper hand and faced near defeat. At last, they cried out to the Lord, receiving renewed strength that allowed them to overcome their foes by evening, slaughtering Arbelan's inhabitants—men, women, and children alike.
10. Those who had previously escaped from Sarton also fell under the swords of Jacob's sons in Arbelan.
11. Following the massacre, the surviving women of the city climbed onto the rooftops, casting down stones like heavy rain on Jacob's sons below.
12. Jacob's sons stormed through the city, seizing the women and killing them as well, capturing livestock, valuables, and all forms of plunder before departing.
13. They treated Machnaymah in the same ruthless manner, as they had done with Tapnach, Chazar, and Shiloh, leaving ruin in their wake as they moved on.

14. Five days later, news reached them that Gaash's people had gathered an army, determined to avenge their slain king and his fourteen captains, all of whom Jacob's sons had killed in a previous encounter.
15. Girded with weapons, Jacob's sons prepared for battle and advanced toward Gaash—a well-fortified Amorite city protected by three formidable walls and housing a powerful army.
16. Upon reaching Gaash, they found its gates securely barred and a force of around five hundred men stationed atop the outer wall. At the same time, a vast number of soldiers lay in ambush outside the city to encircle Jacob's sons.
17. As Jacob's sons neared the gates, the hidden forces emerged, surrounding them and blocking both their advance and retreat.
18. The men of Gaash attacked from the front and rear, with others raining down arrows and stones from the wall above.
19. Seeing the assault grow fiercer, Judah let out a resounding cry so intense that it caused men on the wall to fall in terror, spreading panic throughout Gaash's forces.
20. As Jacob's sons attempted to breach the city gates, the defenders intensified their assault from above, forcing them to pull back.
21. Jacob's sons regrouped and turned on the ambushers outside, striking them down as easily as one might break fragile gourds. Overwhelmed with fear from Judah's powerful shout, the men of Gaash stood little chance.
22. Jacob's sons killed all outside the city walls before renewing their attack on Gaash itself. Yet, those remaining within fortified the walls, preventing any further advance by Jacob's sons.
23. When they attempted to fight from beneath the walls, a shower of arrows and stones from Gaash's defenders forced them back repeatedly.
24. Emboldened by their defense, the inhabitants of Gaash taunted Jacob's sons from the walls, mocking their inability to conquer a truly fortified city.
25. "What holds you back from victory now?" they jeered. "Do you think to overcome mighty Gaash as easily as those weaker towns? You'll all perish here, and we will avenge our fallen allies."
26. The defenders of Gaash continued hurling insults, calling upon their gods and pelting Jacob's sons with arrows and stones.
27. Infuriated by their mockery and moved to jealousy for the Lord's honor, Judah shouted a prayer, "Lord, send help to us and to our brothers!"
28. He then sprinted with all his might, leaping to the wall with sword drawn. Yet as he ascended, his sword slipped from his grip.
29. Reaching the top, Judah let out a fierce shout, terrifying the men on the wall, causing some to fall to their deaths within the city.

30. Others, mustering courage, advanced on Judah, seeing he was unarmed, and aimed to throw him over the wall. Twenty reinforcements joined them, but Judah called to his brothers below for aid.
31. Jacob and his sons drew their bows from beneath the wall, shooting three men who had encircled Judah. Meanwhile, Judah called on the Lord for strength, his voice carrying far and wide.
32. The sound of Judah's shout unnerved his opponents, causing them to drop their swords and flee.
33. Judah seized the fallen swords and, wielding them skillfully, struck down twenty men atop the wall.
34. Eighty more men and women ascended the wall to attack Judah, but the Lord instilled a fear of Judah in their hearts, keeping them at bay.
35. Below, Jacob and his sons continued to shoot, killing ten more of the defenders, whose bodies tumbled to the ground.
36. Observing their losses, more men on the wall launched an assault on Judah but dared not approach, their fear of him growing ever stronger.
37. One warrior named Arud tried to strike Judah's head with his sword, but Judah blocked it with his shield, splitting the blade.
38. Terrified, Arud attempted to flee but stumbled, falling from the wall where Jacob's sons killed him.
39. The blow had injured Judah, causing severe pain, and he cried out, alerting Dan below. Hearing his brother, Dan's anger ignited, and he ascended the wall with fierce strength.
40. As Dan joined Judah, the men on the wall retreated to a second wall, throwing stones and arrows at the brothers from above.
41. Dan and Judah barely dodged the projectiles, suffering injuries as they tried to evade the attacks.
42. From below, Jacob and his sons couldn't shoot at the defenders atop the second wall, who remained hidden from view.
43. At last, Dan and Judah leapt to the second wall, facing the defenders head-on. Terrified, the men of Gaash abandoned their posts, descending between the walls.
44. Jacob's sons heard the noise of their enemies' retreat and grew anxious for their brothers, whom they could not see on the second wall.
45. With fierce resolve, Naphtali climbed the first wall to investigate the shouting, while Issachar and Zebulun forced open the city gates, allowing them to enter.
46. Naphtali leapt from the first wall to the second, joining Dan and Judah. Seeing him, the defenders panicked, fleeing into the city below.
47. Now united, Jacob, his sons, and their men pursued the fleeing inhabitants, engaging them from all directions.
48. Simeon and Levi, unaware the gate was open, climbed the wall and descended to aid their brothers.

49. Surrounded by Jacob's sons, Gaash's inhabitants were struck down on all sides. Around twenty thousand men and women fell, unable to withstand the assault.
50. Blood flowed through the city like a river, reaching beyond Gaash's borders toward the Bethchorin desert.
51. Observing the bloodshed, seventy men from Bethchorin approached, tracing the river of blood to Gaash's wall and hearing the inhabitants' cries rise to the heavens.
52. Jacob's sons continued the battle, killing nearly twenty thousand people by nightfall. The onlookers from Bethchorin realized the Hebrews were responsible and hurried back to gather their warriors.
53. As Jacob's sons completed their attack, they circled Gaash to strip the dead, venturing deeper into the city where they encountered three formidable men, unarmed yet defiant.
54. These powerful men attempted to flee, but one seized Zebulun, a young and small figure, throwing him to the ground.
55. Jacob struck this man below the waist, cleaving him in two, and the body fell onto Zebulun.
56. The second man turned on Jacob, but Simeon and Levi struck him, knocking him down. Judah delivered a final blow, splitting his head.
57. The third mighty warrior, witnessing the defeat of his companions, tried to escape from Jacob's sons, but they pursued him through the city streets. In desperation, he found a sword from a fallen soldier and turned to face them, prepared to fight.
58. He charged at Judah, aiming a blow at his head. Judah, unarmed, narrowly avoided the strike, but Naphtali quickly intervened, holding up a shield to protect Judah. The enemy's sword hit Naphtali's shield, allowing Judah to escape harm.
59. Simeon and Levi rushed in, each wielding a sword, and struck the powerful man simultaneously. Their blades cut deep, dividing him in two.
60. With the fall of the three mighty men, Jacob's sons fought on, cutting down all who remained in the city of Gaash. The day drew to a close as they went through the city, leaving no man standing.
61. Moving through the streets of Gaash, Jacob's sons claimed the spoils. They spared no one except for the city's women and children.
62. Blood ran through the city like a river, eventually spilling outside Gaash's walls. The sight and sound of such destruction reached as far as the desert lands of Bethchorin.
63. At Bethchorin, a group of seventy men saw the river of blood flowing from Gaash and heard the cries of its people. They followed the trail, arriving at the city wall where they witnessed the aftermath of the conflict.
64. These men from Bethchorin realized the destruction was wrought by the sons of Jacob, known across the land for their strength and ferocity. They swiftly returned to Bethchorin, rallying their warriors and preparing for battle.

65. Meanwhile, Jacob's sons, after securing all the wealth and valuables within Gaash, completed their conquest as they had in other cities before. When the city lay in silence, they gathered their plunder and prepared to depart, leaving Gaash in ruin.

CHAPTER 40

1. Jacob's sons gathered all the loot they had taken from Gaash and left the city under cover of night.
2. They traveled toward the fortress of Bethchorin, where the inhabitants prepared to confront them. That night, Jacob's sons engaged in battle with the people of Bethchorin within the fortress walls.
3. The people of Bethchorin were known for their strength; a single warrior from among them could face a thousand men without retreating. Throughout the night, the sounds of battle echoed far and wide, causing the earth to tremble.
4. Fighting in the dark was unfamiliar to Jacob's sons, and the might of the men of Bethchorin left them disoriented. They prayed to the Lord, saying, "Help us, O Lord! Do not let us fall to these uncircumcised men."
5. The Lord heard their cries and caused confusion among the people of Bethchorin, leading them to turn against each other in the darkness, each one attacking his neighbor.
6. Recognizing that the Lord had sown discord among their enemies, Jacob's sons moved away from the confused crowd, descending to the lower areas of the fortress where they could rest safely.
7. Throughout the night, the people of Bethchorin continued to fight one another, their shouts ringing out and shaking the ground with their intensity. Their voices could be heard from great distances.
8. The clamor was so loud that it reached the surrounding regions, and the Canaanites, Hittites, Amorites, Hivites, and other Canaanite kings across the Jordan heard the noise and were filled with fear.
9. They speculated, "This must be the Hebrews battling those seven cities. Who can possibly withstand them?"
10. The inhabitants of Canaan, along with those beyond the Jordan, were seized with fear, saying, "If these Hebrews could do such things to other cities, what hope do we have against their power?"
11. The cries of Bethchorin's people grew louder as the night wore on, with many casualties among them.
12. At dawn, Jacob's sons rose and ascended the fortress, finishing off the remaining inhabitants of Bethchorin.
13. On the sixth day, the people of Canaan saw from a distance the bodies of Bethchorin's people lying like sheep across the fortress.

14. Jacob's sons took the spoils from Gaash and made their way to Bethchorin, where they encountered yet more people, as numerous as the sand by the sea, and fought them until evening.
15. They treated Bethchorin as they had the other cities, striking it down and seizing its riches.
16. Afterward, they gathered all the valuables from Bethchorin and surrounding cities and began their journey back to Shechem.
17. Jacob's sons camped outside Shechem, keeping their loot and resting after the battles.
18. They left the spoils outside the city, not bringing them within, saying, "We must be cautious in case we face another attack."
19. Jacob, his sons, and their servants stayed in the field they had purchased from Hamor for five shekels, guarding their considerable bounty.
20. The treasure they had accumulated from their campaigns was vast, stretching across the field like sand on a shore.
21. Observing from a distance, the neighboring people feared Jacob's sons, for none had ever seen such deeds before.
22. The seven Canaanite kings decided to make peace with Jacob's sons, fearing for their lives.
23. On the seventh day, Japhia, king of Hebron, sent a message to other kings—of Ai, Gibeon, Shalem, Adullam, Lachish, Chazar, and others under his rule—urging them,
24. "Join me in meeting with Jacob's sons to make peace with them, or they may bring destruction to our lands just as they did to Shechem and nearby cities."
25. He advised that each king bring only three chief officers and each officer three attendants, and that they meet in Hebron to discuss a treaty with Jacob's sons.
26. The kings complied, gathering as instructed under Japhia's guidance, intending to seek peace with Jacob's family. Meanwhile, Jacob's sons continued to stay near Shechem, wary of possible deception.
27. They camped in the fields outside Shechem for ten days without encountering opposition.
28. When it was clear no one planned to fight them, they finally returned to the city of Shechem.
29. After forty days, the Amorite kings gathered in Hebron, led by Japhia.
30. In all, twenty-one kings assembled with sixty-nine captains and 189 men, camping at the foot of Mount Hebron.
31. The king of Hebron, accompanied by his three captains and nine attendants, led the kings in a plan to approach Jacob's sons peacefully.
32. "We will go first and speak on your behalf to Jacob's sons," he advised, and the other kings agreed.
33. Jacob's sons, upon learning of the assembly in Hebron, sent four servants as scouts, telling them, "Count the numbers of these kings and their men to determine if they are few or many, then return."

34. The servants went unnoticed and returned to report, "They are not numerous; there are only 288 of them altogether."
35. Seeing that their numbers were small, Jacob's sons chose 62 men and ten of Jacob's sons, equipping them for battle, as they still suspected an attack.
36. They met the Hebron delegation at Shechem's gate, with Jacob himself among them.
37. From a distance, they saw Japhia, king of Hebron, approaching with his men. Jacob's sons took their stand at the gate, waiting.
38. Japhia and his captains bowed low before Jacob and his sons, then seated themselves respectfully.
39. Jacob's sons asked, "Why have you come to us? What do you want from us today?"
40. The king of Hebron replied, "We have come in peace. All the Canaanite kings wish to make a treaty with you."
41. Yet, Jacob's sons were cautious, doubting the sincerity of Hebron's king.
42. Seeing their mistrust, the king of Hebron assured them, "We bring no army or weapons, only ourselves to offer peace."
43. Jacob's sons then proposed, "Send for each of these kings to come before us individually. If they come unarmed, we will know their intentions are peaceful."
44. Japhia sent word, and each king approached Jacob's sons, bowing to the ground, then seated themselves before them.
45. They said, "We have heard of your strength and your victories, and we fear your power. None can withstand you, and so we seek peace."
46. The kings expressed their desire for a lasting covenant, swearing not to harm Jacob's sons if they, in turn, would refrain from attacking their lands.
47. Understanding their genuine desire for peace, Jacob's sons accepted, establishing a treaty.
48. They swore not to interfere with the Canaanite kings, who likewise pledged loyalty and tribute from that day forward.
49. The kings brought gifts for Jacob and his sons, bowing low and paying respect.
50. They then requested the return of captives and loot from the Amorite cities. Jacob's sons agreed, restoring the people and goods they had taken.
51. The kings, grateful, bestowed further gifts, and with blessings, Jacob's sons sent them peacefully back to their cities.
52. From that day forward, peace reigned between Jacob's family and the Canaanite kings, a peace that endured until the Israelites came to settle in Canaan.

CHAPTER 41

1. As the year came full circle, Jacob's sons journeyed from Shechem to Hebron, where they settled with their father Isaac. They kept their flocks in Shechem's fertile pastures, as it was a rich grazing land at the time, and Jacob and his entire household lived peacefully in the Valley of Hebron.

2. It was in this period, the one hundred and sixth year of Jacob's life and ten years after his return from Padan-Aram, that Leah, Jacob's wife, passed away at the age of fifty-one.
3. Jacob and his sons buried Leah in the cave at Machpelah in Hebron, which Abraham had bought from the Hittites as a family burial place.
4. Afterward, Jacob's sons remained with him in the Valley of Hebron, and their strength and reputation became well known throughout the land.
5. Joseph and his younger brother Benjamin, sons of Rachel, were still young during those days and didn't join their brothers in any of their battles across the Amorite cities.
6. Watching his brothers' strength and valor, Joseph admired them but held himself in higher regard, seeing himself as superior. Jacob loved Joseph more than his other sons because Joseph had been born to him in his old age, and he expressed this love by gifting him a richly colored coat.
7. Seeing the special affection his father showed him, Joseph continued to exalt himself above his brothers and often reported on their activities to their father, sometimes bringing bad reports.
8. Witnessing Joseph's behavior and the favoritism he received from their father, his brothers grew to resent him deeply, and they could not speak to him peacefully.
9. At seventeen, Joseph continued to think highly of himself, often dreaming of greatness.
10. One day, he had a dream and shared it with his brothers, saying, "I dreamed we were in the field binding sheaves, and my sheaf rose and stood upright, while your sheaves gathered around and bowed down to mine."
11. His brothers responded with frustration, "Do you really believe this dream? Do you expect to reign over us?"
12. Joseph then shared his dream with their father, and Jacob embraced him, pleased by the words he heard, and blessed Joseph.
13. Observing their father's affection for Joseph, his brothers grew increasingly jealous and their resentment intensified.
14. Later, Joseph had another dream and told it to his father and brothers, saying, "I dreamed again, and this time the sun, the moon, and eleven stars were bowing down to me."
15. Recognizing the jealousy this was causing, Jacob gently rebuked Joseph in front of his brothers, asking, "What meaning do you see in this dream? Do you think that I, along with your mother and brothers, will come and bow before you?"
16. His brothers' jealousy only deepened because of his dreams and his words, yet Jacob quietly kept Joseph's dreams in his heart, pondering them.
17. One day, Jacob's sons went to pasture their father's flocks in Shechem, where they continued to work as shepherds. They remained in the field past the usual time, and the herds had not been gathered as expected.
18. Growing concerned, Jacob wondered, "Could the people of Shechem have confronted them in battle, causing their delay?"

19. Jacob then called Joseph and instructed him, "Your brothers are tending the flock in Shechem, but they have not returned. Go and check on their well-being and that of the flock, then bring me word."
20. Following his father's instruction, Joseph set out from the Valley of Hebron toward Shechem to find his brothers.
21. Arriving in Shechem, he searched the fields for any sign of them but could not locate them. Wandering in the area, he lost his way.
22. While he was wandering, a messenger of the Lord appeared and asked him, "What are you seeking?" Joseph replied, "I am searching for my brothers; have you seen where they may be pasturing?"
23. The messenger answered, "I overheard them saying they were going to Dothan to feed the flock."
24. Heeding the messenger's words, Joseph made his way to Dothan, where he found his brothers tending their sheep.
25. When his brothers saw Joseph approaching from a distance, they conspired to harm him.
26. Simeon suggested to his brothers, "Look, here comes the dreamer. Let us kill him and throw his body into one of these pits. Then we'll say a wild animal has devoured him when our father asks about him."
27. Reuben, however, intervened, saying, "Let's not shed his blood. Instead, we can put him in this pit and leave him there to die, but we shouldn't lay a hand on him." He suggested this plan with the hope of rescuing Joseph later and returning him to their father.
28. When Joseph arrived, his brothers seized him, threw him to the ground, and stripped him of his multicolored coat.
29. They then cast him into an empty pit, though it was full of snakes and scorpions. Fearing these creatures, Joseph cried out, but the Lord hid the snakes and scorpions within the pit's walls, sparing him from harm.
30. From the bottom of the pit, Joseph pleaded with his brothers, asking, "What have I done to you? Why would you do this to me? Do you not fear God concerning me? Am I not of your own flesh, a son of our father Jacob? How will you explain this to him?"
31. He continued calling out, saying, "Judah, Simeon, Levi, my brothers! Lift me from this darkness where you have cast me! Show me compassion. If I have wronged you, forgive me for our father's sake."
32. His brothers, unmoved by his cries, moved away from the pit so they could no longer hear his pleas, ignoring his continued calls and cries from below.
33. Joseph, filled with sorrow, exclaimed, "If only our father knew what my brothers have done to me today, and the words they have spoken!"
34. But his brothers, hardened by jealousy, would not listen to him. Instead, they distanced themselves from the pit to escape his cries and lamenting.

CHAPTER 42

1. As they sat at a distance, about a bow's shot away from the pit, the brothers began eating and discussing what they should do with Joseph—whether to kill him or to bring him back to their father.
2. While they were deep in discussion, they noticed a caravan of Ishmaelites approaching from Gilead, heading down to Egypt.
3. Judah spoke to his brothers, saying, "What benefit would there be for us to kill our brother? Perhaps God will demand an account from us. Instead, let's try another plan.
4. Look, here is a caravan of Ishmaelites heading to Egypt. Why not sell him to them, sparing us from having his blood on our hands?
5. They will take him far from here, lost among strangers, without us having to be responsible for his death." His brothers agreed with Judah's idea, deciding to follow his suggestion.
6. As they were still discussing this, a group of Midianite traders happened by. These traders, thirsty from their journey, saw the pit where Joseph was confined, expecting it to hold water.
7. When they reached the pit, they heard Joseph's cries and looked inside, spotting a young man of striking appearance.
8. They called down to him, "Who are you? How did you come to be in this pit?" Then, working together, they pulled Joseph from the pit, taking him along as they resumed their journey. As they walked, they crossed paths with Joseph's brothers.
9. The brothers called out, "What are you doing, taking away our servant? We put him in that pit because he disobeyed us, and now you are stealing him away!"
10. The Midianites replied, "This man is your servant? He looks nobler and finer than any of you. Why do you deceive us with such a story?
11. We found him alone in the wilderness, and he is ours now. We will not heed your words."
12. The brothers then approached them, threatening, "Give him back to us, or prepare to fight!" and drew their swords, preparing to defend their claim.
13. Seeing this, Simeon leaped forward, drew his sword, and shouted with such power that the earth trembled, echoing his voice far and wide.
14. Terrified by Simeon's fierce display, the Midianites fell to the ground, overcome by fear.
15. Simeon warned them, "I am Simeon, son of Jacob the Hebrew, who with my brother leveled Shechem and the cities of the Amorites.
16. I tell you, if all of Midian and even the kings of Canaan stood against me, they would fall.
17. Return the youth, or I will feed your bodies to the birds and beasts."
18. The Midianites, struck with fear, tried to reason with the brothers, saying, "If this young man is truly your servant, and he rebelled against you, why not sell him to us instead? We will pay whatever you demand." The Lord had guided these words to prevent Joseph's death.

19. The Midianites, admiring Joseph's appearance, were eager to buy him, and the brothers, seeing their persistence, agreed to sell Joseph for twenty pieces of silver.
20. At that moment, Reuben was not with them.
21. The Midianites took Joseph and continued toward Gilead, but as they journeyed, they began to second-guess their decision to buy him.
22. One said, "What have we done? This youth, so fine-looking—could he be stolen from his own land? What if he brings misfortune on us?"
23. Another added, "Indeed, these were strong men who sold him. They may have seized him from his homeland. We should not keep him."
24. While they discussed their concerns, the original caravan of Ishmaelites approached, and the Midianites decided to sell Joseph to them to avoid any ill fate.
25. They met with the Ishmaelites, trading Joseph for the twenty pieces of silver they had paid to his brothers.
26. The Midianites continued their journey to Gilead, while the Ishmaelites took Joseph, setting him on a camel and leading him to Egypt.
27. Realizing he was bound for Egypt, far from his home in Canaan, Joseph mourned his fate, weeping bitterly.
28. As he wept on the camel, one of the Ishmaelites forced him down to walk instead, yet Joseph continued crying, calling out, "Father! My father!"
29. Seeing his persistence, one of the Ishmaelites struck him on the cheek, trying to silence his cries.
30. Exhausted and grieved, Joseph struggled to keep pace, his spirit heavy with sorrow.
31. The Lord saw Joseph's suffering and sent darkness and confusion upon his captors; their hands withered, and they were filled with dread.
32. They wondered aloud, "What has God done to us? Could this be because of him?"
33. They did not realize it was because of their mistreatment of Joseph.
34. Continuing, they passed the region of Ephrath, where Rachel, Joseph's mother, was buried.
35. Spotting her grave, Joseph hurried over, falling upon it as he wept, "Mother, awaken! See how I am enslaved, separated from home and family, with no one to comfort me!
36. Rise and see how my brothers have treated me! Stand and make your plea for me before the Lord!"
37. Joseph continued, "If I have done any wrong, may my bones find rest here with you. Rise, mother, and seek justice for me!"
38. He cried until he was exhausted, lying motionless on the grave, overcome by grief.
39. As he lay silent, he heard a voice from the ground saying, "My son, my son, Joseph! I have heard your cries and seen your sorrow. It pains me deeply to witness your suffering.
40. Trust in the Lord, my child. Wait on Him, for He is with you. He will rescue you from this trial.
41. Rise, my beloved. Go to Egypt without fear, for the Lord's presence goes with you."

42. Hearing this voice, Joseph was astounded and continued weeping, filled with wonder. But his captors, growing impatient, pulled him away from the grave, berating and striking him.
43. Joseph pleaded with them, "Please, take me back to my father's home, and he will reward you greatly."
44. They scoffed, replying, "Are you not a slave? If you had a father, you would not have been sold." With that, they struck him again, their anger unrelenting.
45. The Lord, seeing Joseph's suffering, again brought a storm upon his captors—thunder and lightning filled the sky, and the ground quaked.
46. The camels stopped in their tracks, refusing to move, even as the men struck them.
47. Trembling with fear, the Ishmaelites wondered aloud, "What sin have we committed to deserve this?"
48. One said, "Perhaps it is because of this youth we have mistreated. Let us ask his forgiveness and see if this calamity is lifted."
49. So, they approached Joseph with remorse, pleading for his forgiveness and asking him to pray to his God to lift the darkness surrounding them.
50. Joseph prayed, and the Lord relented, restoring peace to the skies and calming the earth. The men recognized their troubles had come upon them because of Joseph.
51. They debated among themselves, saying, "We cannot continue on this path with him. Should we return him to his family?"
52. But one argued, "The journey back is too far. Let us reach Egypt and sell him there, where he might fetch a good price."
53. Agreeing on this plan, they continued their journey toward Egypt, intending to sell Joseph upon their arrival.

CHAPTER 43

1. After selling Joseph to the Midianites, Jacob's sons felt deep remorse and sought to find him and bring him back, but he was nowhere to be found.
2. Reuben, hoping to retrieve Joseph from the pit, returned to where he had last seen him. Standing by the pit, he called out, "Joseph! Joseph!" Yet, there was no response.
3. Reuben thought, "Perhaps Joseph has perished from fear, or a serpent may have harmed him." He climbed down into the pit, searching, but found nothing.
4. Tearing his clothes in sorrow, Reuben lamented, "The child is gone! How will I face my father if he has truly died?" He returned to his brothers, who were grieving and discussing how they would explain this to Jacob.
5. Reuben told them, "I checked the pit, but Joseph is not there. What will we tell our father? He will ask me about his son first."
6. The brothers confessed, "We did this, and our hearts are heavy with guilt. Now we are planning what to say to ease our father's grief."

7. Reuben rebuked them, "What have you done? This may bring our father down to his grave in sorrow."
8. They all sat together, then took an oath, agreeing not to reveal the truth to Jacob. "If anyone tells our father or his household, or spreads this word to anyone in the land, we will all stand against him."
9. With this pact, the brothers feared each other and kept the matter concealed.
10. They deliberated further, searching for a plan to explain Joseph's absence.
11. Issachar offered a suggestion, "Take Joseph's coat, tear it, kill a young goat, and dip the coat in its blood.
12. Then we can send it to our father. When he sees it, he will believe a wild animal has attacked him, and this will end his questions."
13. The brothers agreed with Issachar's idea.
14. They tore Joseph's coat, soaked it in goat's blood, and rubbed it in dust to make it appear damaged. They handed the coat to Naphtali, instructing him on what to say.
15. "Tell our father, 'We found this coat on the road, stained with blood and dirt. Examine it to see if it belongs to your son.'"
16. Naphtali brought the coat to Jacob and delivered the message.
17. Upon seeing the coat, Jacob recognized it immediately. Falling to the ground in grief, he cried out, "This is my son's coat!"
18. Jacob then sent a servant to call his sons, who arrived later that evening, their garments torn and dust on their heads, meeting their father in mourning.
19. Jacob confronted them, "What tragedy have you brought upon me this day?"
20. They replied, "We found this coat on the road as we returned from the fields. We recognized it and sent it to you to confirm if it was Joseph's."
21. Hearing their words, Jacob cried aloud, "It is my son's coat! Surely a wild beast has torn him apart! I sent him today to check on you, and now he is lost!"
22. The brothers responded, "He did not reach us, and we have not seen him since we left you."
23. Jacob, stricken with grief, tore his garments, wore sackcloth, and mourned bitterly, crying out,
24. "Oh, my son Joseph! I sent you today to see to your brothers' welfare, and now you are gone.
25. Through my own actions, this calamity has come upon you!"
26. Overwhelmed, he lamented, "Joseph, you were so precious to me in life; how bitter is your loss in death!
27. If only I had taken your place, my son!"
28. Unable to be consoled, he called out, "My son, where are you? Can you not come back and witness my sorrow?"
29. He implored Joseph's spirit, "Count my tears as they fall, let them reach heaven, that the Lord may turn His wrath from me."

30. Reflecting on his son's innocence, Jacob continued, "My son was gentle and committed no wrong. How could fate be so cruel? God has taken you back, and I am left desolate."
31. Over many days, Jacob wept with these words, collapsed in grief.
32. His sons, seeing his anguish, were filled with remorse and joined in weeping.
33. Judah lifted Jacob's head into his lap, wiping his father's tears, and sobbed deeply as Jacob lay still as stone.
34. The sons of Jacob, overwhelmed by their father's sorrow, wept aloud, yet Jacob remained motionless on the ground.
35. Servants and their children gathered, attempting to console him, but Jacob could not be comforted.
36. News reached Isaac, who also mourned deeply for Joseph, traveling to Hebron with his household to comfort Jacob, yet Jacob refused to be consoled.
37. After some time, Jacob rose, tears streaming down, and addressed his sons, "Go and search the fields for my son's body, that I may give him a proper burial.
38. Also, hunt the creature that may have attacked him and bring it to me, for I will avenge my son's loss."
39. His sons did as he commanded, each arming themselves with bows and swords, setting out to search.
40. Meanwhile, Jacob paced the house, his hands clasped in grief, repeatedly calling, "My son Joseph!"
41. In the wilderness, a wolf approached them. The brothers captured it, bringing it back to Jacob, saying, "This is what we found; your son's body was not among the remains."
42. Jacob took hold of the beast and, with a voice filled with anguish, cried, "Why have you devoured my son Joseph? Did you not fear God, or my sorrow over my son?"
43. Speaking to the creature, he continued, "My son had committed no harm; yet, you took him from me without mercy."
44. Moved by Jacob's pain, the Lord opened the wolf's mouth, allowing it to speak,
45. The beast replied, "As God lives, and as your soul lives, I did not harm your son. I, too, have come searching for my lost young one, who has not returned."
46. The wolf continued, "Your sons found me and brought me here, but I have not seen your son, nor harmed any man."
47. Jacob, astounded by the creature's words, released it. The wolf left, and Jacob resumed his mourning.
48. For many days, Jacob continued to weep bitterly for Joseph, unable to move past his sorrow.

CHAPTER 44

1. The sons of Ishmael, who had bought Joseph from the Midianites, traveled with Joseph toward Egypt, and they arrived on the borders of Egypt.

2. When they neared Egypt, they encountered four men from the sons of Medan, the son of Abraham, who had come out from Egypt on their journey.
3. The Ishmaelites asked them, "Do you desire to purchase this servant from us?" And the men replied, "Deliver him over to us," and they bought Joseph for twenty shekels.
4. The Ishmaelites continued on their journey to Egypt, and the Medanites also returned to Egypt that day.
5. The Medanites said to one another, "We have heard that Potiphar, an officer of Pharaoh, is seeking a trustworthy servant to oversee his household."
6. They went to Potiphar and offered to sell Joseph, if he would pay their price.
7. Potiphar asked to see the servant, and when they brought Joseph before him, he was pleased by Joseph's appearance and abilities.
8. Potiphar asked, "What price do you request for this youth?" And they responded, "We desire four hundred pieces of silver."
9. Potiphar agreed, provided they could show proof of his sale and tell his background, to ensure he was not a stolen man.
10. The Medanites brought the Ishmaelites who had sold Joseph, and they confirmed that he was indeed a servant sold to them.
11. Potiphar paid the price to the Medanites, who took the silver and departed, and the Ishmaelites also returned home.
12. Potiphar took Joseph into his house, where Joseph found favor, and Potiphar trusted him with the management of all he possessed.
13. God blessed Potiphar's house for Joseph's sake, and Potiphar placed all he had in Joseph's care.
14. Joseph, now eighteen, was a young man of beautiful form and appearance, and none in Egypt was like him.
15. Zelicah, Potiphar's wife, noticed Joseph's beauty and began to desire him.
16. She spoke to him each day, seeking his attention, but Joseph kept his eyes from her and avoided her advances.
17. She praised his appearance, but Joseph replied, "God who created me created all mankind."
18. She admired his eyes, but he said, "These eyes will not be as beautiful in the grave."
19. She asked him to play the harp and sing, but he said, "I will sing only in praise to my God."
20. She complimented his hair, suggesting he use a golden comb, but he replied, "Cease these words and attend to your tasks."
21. Zelicah insisted, "There is no one else here, only you and me," but Joseph turned his gaze downward.
22. Zelicah's desire for him grew daily, and she threatened to have him punished if he did not yield.
23. Joseph replied, "God who made me can deliver me from your threats and judgment."

24. Despite her persistence, Joseph resisted, and Zelicah's unfulfilled longing made her fall ill.
25. The women of Egypt came to visit her and asked why she was sick, saying she lacked nothing.
26. Zelicah answered, "Today I will reveal the cause of my sickness," and she arranged for food to be served to all the women.
27. She commanded her servants to dress Joseph in fine clothing and bring him before her guests.
28. When Joseph entered, the women were so entranced by his beauty that they accidentally cut their hands with the knives they held.
29. Zelicah asked them why they had done so, and they replied, "This slave has overcome us with his beauty."
30. Zelicah admitted, "If seeing him once affects you so, imagine how I feel seeing him every day in my home."
31. The women advised her to act on her desires, but Zelicah explained that she had already tried and failed.
32. Her love for Joseph deepened, making her weaker, and yet no one in her household knew the reason for her sickness.
33. Zelicah's servants and friends continued to question her, but she gave no answer.
34. Finally, she confided in her closest friends, who encouraged her to pursue Joseph again.
35. She grew sicker, weakened by unrequited love, but her household remained oblivious to her feelings.
36. Each day, she visited Joseph in confinement, urging him to listen to her.
37. She promised to secure his release if he would yield to her wishes, but he refused, staying faithful to God and Potiphar.
38. As Egypt celebrated an annual festival, Potiphar and his entire household left for the occasion, except for Zelicah.
39. Claiming illness, she stayed behind, adorning herself and preparing perfumes in her chamber, awaiting Joseph.
40. When he returned from his work, Zelicah called out to him, but Joseph turned away.
41. She insisted, "Come and fulfill your duties; I will make way for you."
42. Joseph entered the house, passing her on his way to his assigned duties.
43. Dressed in her finest garments, Zelicah approached him, her scent filling the air.
44. She grabbed his garment, saying, "If you refuse, you will die this day," and drew a hidden sword.
45. Frightened, Joseph tried to escape, and his garment tore in her hand as he fled.
46. Realizing she held his garment, Zelicah feared exposure and quickly changed her clothes.
47. She called her servants and accused Joseph of attempting to assault her.
48. When Potiphar returned, Zelicah repeated her accusation, displaying the torn garment as proof.

49. Enraged, Potiphar ordered that Joseph be beaten.
50. As he was struck, Joseph called out to God, proclaiming his innocence.
51. At that moment, a young child in the house miraculously spoke, revealing Zelicah's deception.
52. Potiphar, hearing the child's words, was deeply ashamed and ordered the beating to stop.
53. Potiphar brought Joseph before the priests, who served as the king's judges, for a formal judgment.
54. Joseph defended his innocence, reminding Potiphar of his loyalty and service.
55. Potiphar questioned him, asking why he would betray such trust.
56. Joseph reaffirmed his integrity, noting he had served honorably in Potiphar's house for a year.
57. The priests asked for the torn garment, examining it to determine the truth.
58. Seeing the tear on the front, they deduced that Zelicah had pressed herself upon Joseph.
59. The priests declared that Joseph was innocent but suggested imprisonment to protect Potiphar's honor.
60. Potiphar placed Joseph in prison, where he remained for twelve years.
61. Yet, Zelicah did not abandon her pursuits, continuing to visit him daily in confinement.
62. Each time, Joseph refused her advances, holding firm to his faith and loyalty.
63. Eventually, she ceased her attempts, and Joseph remained steadfast in his prison cell.
64. Meanwhile, Jacob and his family, believing Joseph to be dead, continued to mourn him in Canaan.
65. Jacob's sorrow for Joseph grew deeper each day, refusing any comfort from his family.
66. Reuben and Judah also grieved, regretting their role in Joseph's fate.
67. Even the servants in Jacob's household mourned alongside him, sharing in his sorrow.
68. Isaac, Jacob's father, also wept upon hearing of Joseph's loss.
69. Isaac traveled from Hebron to offer comfort, but Jacob's grief remained unyielding.
70. Each day, Jacob wept aloud, crying for his son Joseph.
71. In his sorrow, he would call out to God, praying for understanding and strength.
72. Jacob's mourning became so intense that his friends and family worried for his health.
73. Despite his pain, Jacob refused to move from his home, remaining in mourning.
74. He would often sit alone, lamenting the absence of his beloved son.
75. His sons tried to console him, but he turned away, lost in his grief.
76. For days and nights, Jacob cried out, lamenting the loss of Joseph.
77. He would walk through his home, calling out his son's name in desperation.
78. The entire household shared in his sorrow, unable to ease his pain.
79. Isaac returned to Hebron, still grieving for his grandson.
80. The people of Canaan heard of Jacob's loss and marveled at his devotion.
81. Despite the passage of time, Jacob's heart remained broken, and he could not find peace.

CHAPTER 45

1. In that time, in the same year that Joseph was sold and taken down to Egypt, Reuben, the son of Jacob, traveled to Timnah and took Eliuram, daughter of Avi the Canaanite, as his wife.
2. Eliuram, wife of Reuben, conceived and bore him four sons: Hanoch, Palu, Chetzron, and Carmi. Simeon, his brother, also took their sister Dinah as his wife, and she bore him five sons: Memuel, Yamin, Ohad, Jachin, and Zochar.
3. Simeon then took Bunah, the Canaanite woman he had captured in Shechem, as a second wife. Bunah had served Dinah, and to Simeon, she bore a son named Saul.
4. Around this time, Judah went to Adulam, where he met Hirah, a man of Adulam. Judah saw and took Aliyath, daughter of Shua the Canaanite, and with her, he had three sons: Er, Onan, and Shiloh.
5. Levi and Issachar journeyed east and took as wives the daughters of Jobab, son of Yoktan, son of Eber. Jobab had two daughters: Adinah, whom Levi took, and Aridah, whom Issachar married.
6. Levi and Issachar returned to Canaan to their father's home, where Adinah bore Levi three sons: Gershon, Kehas, and Merari.
7. Aridah bore Issachar four sons: Tola, Puvah, Job, and Shomron. Dan went to Moab, where he married Aphlaleth, daughter of Chamudan the Moabite, and brought her back to Canaan.
8. Aphlaleth was initially barren, but God remembered her, and she later bore Dan a son named Chushim.
9. Gad and Naphtali went to Haran and took wives from the daughters of Amuram, son of Uz, son of Nahor.
10. Amuram's daughters were Merimah, whom Naphtali married, and Uzith, who became Gad's wife. They returned with them to their father's home in Canaan.
11. Merimah bore Naphtali four sons: Yachzeel, Guni, Jazer, and Shalem. Uzith bore Gad seven sons: Zephion, Chagi, Shuni, Ezbon, Eri, Arodi, and Arali.
12. Asher took as a wife Adon, daughter of Aphlal, son of Hadad, son of Ishmael, and brought her to Canaan.
13. Adon, Asher's wife, died childless, and after her death, Asher went beyond the river and married Hadurah, daughter of Abimael, son of Eber, son of Shem.
14. Hadurah, a wise and beautiful woman, had been previously married to Malkiel, son of Elam, son of Shem.
15. With Malkiel, Hadurah had a daughter named Serach. After Malkiel died, Hadurah returned to her father's home.
16. Following his first wife's death, Asher married Hadurah and brought her and her three-year-old daughter Serach to Jacob's household in Canaan.
17. Serach was beautiful and raised in the ways of Jacob's family, lacking nothing, and God granted her wisdom and understanding.
18. Hadurah bore Asher four sons: Yimnah, Yishvah, Yishvi, and Beriah.

19. Zebulun traveled to Midian and married Merishah, daughter of Molad, son of Abida, son of Midian, and brought her to Canaan.
20. Merushah bore Zebulun three sons: Sered, Elon, and Yachleel.
21. Jacob sent to Aram, son of Zoba, son of Terah, for a wife for his youngest son Benjamin, and they brought Mechalia, daughter of Aram, to Jacob's home in Canaan. Benjamin, then ten years old, married her.
22. Mechalia bore Benjamin five sons: Bela, Becher, Ashbel, Gera, and Naaman. Later, Benjamin took another wife, Aribath, daughter of Shomron, son of Abraham, at age eighteen. With Aribath, he had five more sons: Achi, Vosh, Mupim, Chupim, and Ord.
23. Judah, during this time, went to the house of Shem and took Tamar, daughter of Elam, son of Shem, as a wife for his eldest son Er.
24. Er married Tamar, but when he came to her, he committed an evil act by wasting his seed, displeasing God, who struck him down.
25. After Er's death, Judah instructed his second son Onan to fulfill the duty of a brother-in-law and marry Tamar to raise up offspring for Er.
26. Onan also acted wickedly with Tamar, displeasing God, and was struck down.
27. Judah, wary of giving Tamar to his youngest son Shiloh, told her to remain in her father's house until Shiloh grew up, fearing he might die like his brothers.
28. Tamar returned to her father's home and lived there for some time.
29. The following year, Judah's wife Aliyath died, and after mourning her, Judah and his friend Hirah went to Timnah to shear their sheep.
30. Tamar learned Judah was going to Timnah, saw that Shiloh had grown, and noticed that Judah had not called her back.
31. Tamar removed her widow's garments, veiled herself entirely, and went to sit in the public road leading to Timnah.
32. When Judah passed by, he saw her and, not recognizing her, went to her. Tamar conceived from this union, and when the time came, she gave birth to twin sons, whom Judah named Perez and Zerah.

CHAPTER 46

1. In those days, Joseph remained imprisoned in Egypt.
2. During that time, Pharaoh's chief butler and chief baker, both serving the king of Egypt, were also in confinement.
3. The butler brought wine to Pharaoh, and the baker brought bread for the king to eat, as well as for the servants who dined at the royal table.

4. While they were eating and drinking, many flies were found in the butler's wine, and stones of niter were found in the baker's bread.
5. The captain of the guard appointed Joseph as an attendant over Pharaoh's officers, and they were held in confinement for a full year.
6. At the end of that year, both the butler and the baker each had a dream on the same night in their place of confinement, which left them troubled.
7. When Joseph attended to them the next morning, he noticed their sad and dejected expressions.
8. Joseph asked them, "Why are your faces downcast today?" and they replied, "We each dreamed a dream, but no one is here to interpret it." Joseph said, "Please, share your dreams with me, and God will grant you peace."
9. The butler spoke first, saying, "In my dream, I saw a vine with three branches. The vine quickly blossomed, grew tall, and produced ripe clusters of grapes.
10. I took the grapes, pressed them into Pharaoh's cup, and handed it to him." Joseph responded, "The three branches represent three days.
11. In three days, Pharaoh will restore you to your position, and you will again serve him wine. When this happens, please remember me and speak to Pharaoh on my behalf to get me out of this prison, for I was unjustly taken from Canaan.
12. What they said about me and my master's wife is false, and I am imprisoned without cause." The butler replied, "If I am indeed restored as you have said, I will fulfill your request and mention you to Pharaoh."
13. The baker, seeing that Joseph had interpreted the butler's dream favorably, also shared his own dream with Joseph.
14. "In my dream," said the baker, "there were three white baskets on my head. In the top basket were all sorts of baked goods for Pharaoh, but birds were eating from it."
15. Joseph replied, "The three baskets signify three days. In three days, Pharaoh will order your execution, and the birds will consume your flesh."
16. At this time, Pharaoh's queen was expecting a child, and she bore a son on the third day. The birth of the king's firstborn was announced throughout Egypt.
17. On the third day after the birth, Pharaoh held a great feast for his officers and servants, as well as the citizens of Zoar and Egypt.
18. People from all over Egypt and Pharaoh's servants celebrated for eight days in honor of the birth, with music, dancing, and feasting at the royal palace.
19. However, the butler forgot Joseph and did not mention him to Pharaoh, as Joseph had requested, because this lapse was ordained by the LORD to test Joseph's patience and faith.
20. Thus, Joseph remained in prison for two additional years, bringing his total time in confinement to twelve years.

CHAPTER 47

1. At this time, Isaac, the son of Abraham, was still living in Canaan. He was very old, reaching the age of one hundred and eighty years, while his son Esau was residing in the land of Edom.
2. When Esau heard that his father was nearing the end of his life, he, along with his sons and household, traveled to Canaan to see Isaac.
3. Jacob and his sons also left their home in Hebron to visit Isaac, and they found Esau and his family gathered with their father.
4. Jacob brought his sons before Isaac, who was still in mourning over the loss of Joseph.
5. Isaac asked Jacob to bring his grandsons to him, so Jacob presented his eleven sons to his father, who embraced and blessed each one.
6. Isaac prayed over them, saying, "May the God of your forefathers bless you abundantly and make your descendants as numerous as the stars."
7. Isaac then turned to Esau's sons, blessing them by saying, "May God instill fear and respect for you among all who encounter you and all your enemies."
8. He then called Jacob and his sons to sit before him, saying, "The LORD, God of the whole earth, has promised to grant this land to your descendants if they obey His statutes and ways."
9. He continued, "Teach your children and their children to revere the LORD and follow His ways, for if they do, He will keep His covenant with Abraham and bless you all your days."
10. After giving his blessings and advice, Isaac's spirit departed, and he passed away, joining his ancestors in rest.
11. Jacob and Esau mourned deeply for their father, who had lived one hundred and eighty years. They prepared his body and took him to the cave of Machpelah, where Abraham had purchased a burial place from the Hittites.
12. Kings from across Canaan came to honor Isaac at his death, joining Jacob and Esau in mourning.
13. The sons of Jacob and Esau, along with the Canaanite kings, walked barefoot and mourned as they made their way to Kirjath-Arba.
14. At Kirjath-Arba, they buried Isaac in the cave of Machpelah, with great honor fitting a king's funeral.
15. After Isaac's death, his possessions were divided between Jacob and Esau. Esau proposed that they split the inheritance equally, allowing him first choice.
16. Jacob agreed, so he divided Isaac's property, livestock, and other possessions into two portions and set them before Esau to choose from.
17. Jacob reminded Esau of God's promise to Abraham and Isaac, saying, "To our descendants, He has granted this land as an inheritance forever."
18. Jacob continued, "Therefore, take what you desire—either the land or the possessions. If you choose the land, I will take the riches; if you take the riches, I will inherit the land."

19. At that time, Nebayoth, the son of Ishmael, was in Canaan with his family, and Esau consulted with him on the matter.
20. Esau asked for Nebayoth's advice, explaining Jacob's offer.
21. Nebayoth replied, "All the Canaanite people dwell securely in their land, and Jacob claims it will belong to him and his descendants forever."
22. He advised, "Take your father's wealth and let Jacob have the land, as he wishes."
23. Esau returned to Jacob, agreeing to the arrangement and taking all the possessions Isaac had left behind, including livestock, slaves, and riches.
24. Jacob retained the land of Canaan, from the river of Egypt to the Euphrates, as an inheritance for himself and his descendants forever.
25. Jacob also took ownership of the cave of Machpelah, which Abraham had purchased for a burial site for himself and his family.
26. To formalize this transaction, Jacob recorded it in a scroll, signed it, and witnessed it with four reliable witnesses.
27. The document stated: "The land of Canaan, from the river of Egypt to the Euphrates, and the cities of the seven nations—the Hittites, Hivites, Jebusites, Amorites, Perizzites, Girgashites, and Canaanites—are the perpetual inheritance of Jacob and his descendants."
28. Jacob stored this scroll of purchase, along with its legal documents, in an earthen vessel to preserve them for future generations.
29. Esau took his inheritance, including all the livestock, wealth, and property that Isaac had left, and moved back to Seir, the land he had claimed for himself.
30. Esau and his family settled among the people of Seir, never again returning to live in Canaan.
31. From that time onward, the entire land of Canaan belonged to Jacob and his descendants, becoming their eternal possession, while Esau and his descendants held the mountain of Seir as their own.

CHAPTER 48

1. In those days, following the death of Isaac, the LORD brought a great famine upon the earth.
2. Pharaoh, king of Egypt, was lying on his throne in the land of Egypt, and he dreamed while he slept.
3. In his dream, he saw himself standing beside the river in Egypt.
4. As he stood, he saw seven fat and healthy cows rising from the river.
5. Afterward, seven other cows came up behind them, but these were thin and sickly.
6. The thin cows devoured the fat cows, yet they looked just as sickly as before.
7. Pharaoh awoke, disturbed by what he saw, but then he lay down and fell asleep again.
8. He dreamed a second time, seeing seven ears of grain growing on one stalk, full and rich.
9. Afterward, seven thin and blasted ears appeared and devoured the seven full ears.
10. Pharaoh awoke, troubled by these dreams and unable to understand their meaning.

11. In the morning, he remembered his dreams, and his spirit was deeply disturbed.
12. Pharaoh called for all the magicians and wise men of Egypt to come before him.
13. Pharaoh shared his dreams with them, but none could interpret them to his satisfaction.
14. The wise men spoke to Pharaoh, saying, "The seven healthy cows signify seven daughters who will be born to you."
15. They continued, "But the seven thin cows mean these daughters will all die in your lifetime."
16. The magicians said, "The seven full ears of grain represent seven cities that you will build in Egypt."
17. They added, "The seven thin ears show that these cities will be destroyed in the future."
18. Pharaoh was displeased with their answers, sensing they were not correct.
19. He said to them, "You have spoken falsely. I require the true interpretation of my dreams."
20. Pharaoh commanded that anyone who could not interpret his dream would face death.
21. Another proclamation was sent throughout Egypt, promising wealth and favor to anyone who could interpret the dream.
22. All the wise men and magicians in Egypt's cities gathered before Pharaoh.
23. Yet, their interpretations were varied, and none pleased Pharaoh.
24. Some said the cows represented future kings who would rise and fall.
25. Others claimed the cows represented strong cities of Egypt that would later be destroyed.
26. Still, others suggested wars or other interpretations that failed to satisfy Pharaoh.
27. Pharaoh knew that none had given the correct interpretation, as the LORD was preventing them from understanding.
28. Enraged by their false interpretations, Pharaoh ordered all magicians to leave his presence.
29. He considered executing the wise men of Egypt in his anger.
30. But his chief butler, recalling Joseph, approached Pharaoh and spoke of his time in prison.
31. The butler explained how Joseph had interpreted both his and the baker's dreams accurately.
32. Pharaoh decided to summon Joseph and ordered his servants to bring him without frightening him.
33. Joseph was brought from prison, and he stood before Pharaoh, who was eager for answers.
34. Pharaoh told Joseph of his dreams and requested their true interpretation.
35. Joseph replied, "Pharaoh's dreams are one; God has shown Pharaoh what He is about to do."
36. Joseph explained that the seven fat cows and seven full ears represented seven years of plenty.

37. He also revealed that the seven thin cows and blasted ears signified seven years of severe famine.
38. Joseph advised Pharaoh to appoint a wise overseer to manage Egypt's food during the years of plenty.
39. This overseer would store surplus grain to provide for the years of famine.
40. Pharaoh was deeply impressed with Joseph's wisdom and decided to elevate him to a position of authority.
41. He declared that Joseph would be second in command, with authority over all of Egypt.
42. Pharaoh gave Joseph a new name, Zaphenath-Paneah, and arranged his marriage to Asenath, daughter of Potiphera, priest of On.
43. Joseph was thirty years old when he entered into Pharaoh's service and began preparing Egypt for the famine.
44. Joseph traveled throughout Egypt, gathering and storing grain in preparation for the years to come.
45. Under Joseph's guidance, Egypt was able to store an abundant supply of food.
46. The seven years of plenty passed, and the years of famine began as Joseph had foretold.
47. The famine spread over the entire earth, affecting all lands.
48. Only Egypt had stored food and was prepared for the famine due to Joseph's foresight.
49. People from many lands came to Egypt to buy grain from Joseph.
50. Pharaoh witnessed the fulfillment of Joseph's interpretations and was grateful for his wisdom.
51. Pharaoh's respect for Joseph grew, and he entrusted him with even more authority.
52. The people of Egypt admired Joseph's leadership and wisdom, knowing that he had saved them.
53. Joseph's reputation spread throughout Egypt and beyond.
54. Even in the midst of famine, Egypt prospered due to Joseph's careful planning.
55. Joseph's family in Canaan also felt the effects of the famine and began to seek aid.
56. Jacob sent his sons to Egypt to buy grain, not knowing they would encounter Joseph.
57. Joseph recognized his brothers when they arrived, but they did not recognize him.
58. Joseph tested his brothers to learn about their character and their treatment of Benjamin.
59. He accused them of being spies, which they denied.
60. Joseph held Simeon as a guarantee and sent the others back to bring Benjamin.
61. Jacob was distressed by the news but eventually sent Benjamin with his brothers.
62. When they returned, Joseph hosted them, yet he still did not reveal his identity.
63. After further testing, Joseph finally revealed himself to his brothers.
64. His brothers were astonished and fearful, but Joseph reassured them.
65. Joseph forgave his brothers, recognizing that God had used their actions for good.
66. He invited his entire family to come to Egypt, where they would be provided for during the famine.

CHAPTER 49

1. After these events, Pharaoh gathered all his officers, servants, nobles, and the high-ranking officials of Egypt.
2. Pharaoh addressed them, saying, "You have all witnessed the wisdom of this Hebrew man and seen that every word he has spoken has proven true."
3. He continued, "This man has correctly interpreted my dreams, and they are about to be fulfilled. Consider what we must do to save the land from famine."
4. Pharaoh urged them, "Look among yourselves for a man of great wisdom who can carry out the Hebrew's advice to preserve the land."
5. The officials replied, "The Hebrew's counsel is indeed wise; let the king do what seems best to him."
6. Pharaoh considered this and said, "Since God has revealed all this to the Hebrew man, there is no one wiser than he in the entire land."
7. He asked his officials, "What do you say about appointing him over the land of Egypt to implement his own advice?"
8. The officers agreed, "This is good in our sight. The Hebrew man has shown wisdom beyond any of us."
9. However, they added, "It is written in the laws of Egypt that only one who knows all the languages of the earth may rule over us or serve as second in command."
10. They suggested, "Let us bring the Hebrew man and test him in every language, to see if he meets this requirement."
11. Pharaoh replied, "Very well. Tomorrow, we shall summon him and proceed as you suggest."
12. That night, the LORD sent an angel to visit Joseph in the prison where he was confined.
13. The angel appeared to Joseph as he lay sleeping, and Joseph awoke to find the angel standing before him.
14. The angel of the LORD taught Joseph all the languages of mankind in a single night.
15. He also gave Joseph the name "Jehoseph" and then departed from him.
16. When morning came, Pharaoh's officials and servants gathered before him, and he ordered Joseph to be brought from the prison.
17. Joseph was brought before Pharaoh, and as he ascended the steps toward Pharaoh, he spoke fluently in all the languages of Egypt.
18. Pharaoh and his officials were greatly impressed with Joseph's abilities.
19. Recognizing the wisdom of Joseph's counsel, Pharaoh appointed him as second in command over all of Egypt.
20. Pharaoh said to Joseph, "Since God has revealed all this to you, there is none as discerning and wise as you are in the land."
21. Pharaoh continued, "You shall be called Zaphnath-Paaneah, and all the matters of my government will be under your authority."
22. He decreed, "At your word, the people of Egypt will come and go. Only I, in the throne, will be greater than you."

23. Pharaoh removed his royal ring and placed it on Joseph's hand, symbolizing Joseph's new authority.
24. He dressed Joseph in fine garments and placed a golden chain around his neck.
25. Pharaoh commanded that Joseph be escorted through the streets of Egypt in his second chariot.
26. Musicians with timbrels, harps, and other instruments played in celebration as they followed Joseph.
27. Pharaoh had heralds announce, "This is the man whom the king has chosen as his second in command!"
28. The people of Egypt were commanded to bow before Joseph as he passed by.
29. The people proclaimed, "Long live the king and his chosen second!" as they bowed in reverence.
30. Joseph looked up to Heaven and praised the LORD, saying, "Blessed is the one who lifts the lowly from the dust."
31. Joseph continued throughout Egypt, with officials showing him all the storehouses and resources of the land.
32. When he returned to Pharaoh, the king gave him estates and appointed him to oversee the collection of grain.
33. Pharaoh awarded Joseph with treasures of silver, gold, and precious stones.
34. Pharaoh declared that anyone who disregarded Joseph's authority would be punished severely.
35. The king arranged a marriage between Joseph and Asenath, daughter of Potiphera, priest of On.
36. Asenath was a young woman of great beauty and virtue, and Joseph took her as his wife.
37. Pharaoh proclaimed, "I am Pharaoh, and only in the throne shall I be greater than Joseph."
38. Joseph was thirty years old when he was placed in authority over Egypt, and he began organizing the land's resources.
39. Joseph appointed officers to assist him and established a system to store surplus grain.
40. Over the next seven years, Egypt experienced great abundance, as Joseph had foretold.
41. Joseph traveled throughout Egypt, ensuring that every region stored enough food for the coming famine.
42. During these years of plenty, Joseph collected and stored immense quantities of grain.
43. The stored grain was like the sands of the sea, beyond measure.
44. The years of plenty ended, and soon the years of famine began, affecting all lands.

CHAPTER 50

1. In that time, the people of Tarshish came up against the sons of Ishmael and waged war with them, successfully overtaking the Ishmaelites for many years.

2. Because the sons of Ishmael were few in number during those days, they could not withstand the strength of Tarshish and were greatly oppressed.
3. So, the elders of the Ishmaelites sent a message to the king of Egypt, saying, "We plead with you, send us officers and an army to assist us in fighting against the people of Tarshish, as we have been enduring much hardship."
4. In response, Pharaoh sent Joseph along with the strong men and soldiers from the royal guard to support the Ishmaelites.
5. Joseph and the Egyptian forces journeyed to Havilah, joining with the Ishmaelites to stand against the Tarshishites. Joseph fought and defeated the Tarshishites, taking control of their territory, which the Ishmaelites occupy to this day.
6. After subduing Tarshish, the people of Tarshish fled and settled near their relatives, the descendants of Javan. Joseph and his forces returned safely to Egypt with all soldiers accounted for.
7. As the year turned, marking the second year of Joseph's authority in Egypt, the LORD granted an abundant harvest across the land, fulfilling Joseph's prediction of seven years of plenty.
8. During this time, Joseph appointed officers to gather food each year and store it, creating vast reserves of grain.
9. Following Joseph's instructions, the food was gathered with ears of corn and soil, helping prevent spoilage.
10. Year by year, Joseph continued this work, amassing a stockpile of grain as vast as the sand on the seashore, with supplies too numerous to count.
11. Likewise, the Egyptians also stored provisions during these years of plenty, although they did not preserve their grain as carefully as Joseph.
12. Thanks to Joseph's preparations, Egypt had ample supplies stored in anticipation of the coming years of famine.
13. Each household in Egypt filled their storage places with corn, preparing for the difficult years ahead.
14. Joseph ensured that all the food he had gathered was secured in various cities and placed under guard.
15. During this time, Joseph's wife, Asenath, the daughter of Potiphera, gave birth to two sons, Manasseh and Ephraim, when Joseph was thirty-four years old.
16. As the boys grew, they followed Joseph's teachings and lived according to his wisdom, never straying from the path he set.
17. The LORD blessed them with insight, skill, and understanding in all things, especially in government affairs. The Egyptians held them in high regard, raising them alongside the children of the royal court.
18. When the seven years of abundance concluded, the predicted years of famine began, spreading across Egypt as Joseph had foretold.

19. With the famine's onset, the people of Egypt opened their stores of grain, but soon found themselves in great need as the scarcity increased.
20. To their dismay, they discovered that much of their stored grain had spoiled, becoming infested and unfit for consumption. The famine grew severe throughout the land, and the people of Egypt cried out to Pharaoh for relief.
21. They pleaded with Pharaoh, saying, "Give us food, lest we and our children perish from hunger before your eyes."
22. Pharaoh responded, "Why do you come to me with these pleas? Did not Joseph advise all to prepare during the years of abundance? Why did you not heed his instructions?"
23. The Egyptians answered, "Our lord, we followed Joseph's counsel and gathered the harvests from our fields during the prosperous years, storing it as he commanded.
24. Yet, when the famine began and we opened our stores, we found our grain filled with vermin, making it unfit to eat."
25. Hearing this, Pharaoh was troubled and fearful of the famine's severity. He directed them, "Go to Joseph and do as he commands; do not disobey his instructions."
26. The Egyptians heeded Pharaoh's command and went to Joseph, pleading with him, "Provide us with food, or we will surely die. We gathered during the years of plenty as you ordered, yet all has turned to ruin."
27. Joseph, understanding their plight, ordered the opening of his own stores, and he began to sell grain to the people of Egypt.
28. The famine worsened across the land, yet Egypt had provisions available, unlike the other nations.
29. People from all regions—Canaan, Philistia, the land beyond the Jordan, and other distant places—heard of the available grain and traveled to Egypt to buy food.
30. Joseph oversaw the distribution of grain, appointing officers to manage the sales and ensure that provisions were sold daily to all who came.
31. Anticipating that his brothers would also come to buy food due to the widespread famine, Joseph issued a decree throughout Egypt.
32. The decree stated that anyone wishing to buy grain in Egypt should not send servants, but rather their sons.
33. Furthermore, it was proclaimed that those who came to buy food were not to resell it but were to buy only what was needed for their households.
34. Joseph warned that anyone who brought more than one beast to carry grain or who attempted to sell it would be punished by death.
35. He posted guards at Egypt's gates, instructing them to record the names of all who entered to buy grain, along with the names of their fathers and grandfathers, and to report these names to him each evening.
36. Throughout the land, Joseph's officers implemented these commands to ensure that only those in genuine need would purchase grain.

37. By establishing these rules, Joseph hoped to identify his brothers when they arrived, and the regulations were proclaimed each day as directed.
38. Word of these decrees reached distant lands, and people from all over the world came to Egypt to buy grain, abiding by Joseph's rules.
39. Each day, the names of those who entered Egypt were recorded and delivered to Joseph by evening.

CHAPTER 51

1. At this time, Jacob learned that there was grain available in Egypt, and he called on his sons to go there and buy food, as the famine was affecting them as well.
2. Jacob said to his sons, "I hear that there is grain in Egypt, and people from all over are traveling there to buy it.
3. Why do you stand here without action? Go down to Egypt and purchase some food so that we may survive."
4. Listening to their father, Jacob's sons prepared to go down to Egypt to buy grain, joining those who were also going for the same purpose.
5. Jacob instructed them, saying, "When you enter the city, do not go in together through one gate, but each of you go through a different gate, considering the people of that land."
6. Thus, Jacob's ten sons set out for Egypt, obeying their father's guidance.
7. However, Jacob did not send Benjamin, fearing harm might come to him as it had to Joseph.
8. While on the journey, the brothers began to feel remorseful about their treatment of Joseph, discussing among themselves their plan to search for him in Egypt.
9. They resolved to search for Joseph wherever they could, and if they found him, they would either buy his freedom or rescue him by force if necessary.
10. Strengthened in their resolve, the brothers entered Egypt, but they went through separate gates to avoid drawing attention.
11. At each gate, they gave their names to the gatekeepers, who recorded their entries and later reported to Joseph that evening.
12. That night, Joseph reviewed the list of names brought by the gatekeepers and recognized the names of his brothers who had entered through the various gates.
13. The next day, Joseph commanded his officers to close all but one storehouse, allowing grain to be sold only from that specific location.
14. Joseph instructed the official in charge of this open storehouse, "Ask for the names of each man who comes, and if any bear the names of my brothers, detain them and bring them to me."

15. Meanwhile, Joseph's brothers gathered in the city to search for him before buying grain for their family.
16. They went to different places, including areas known for entertainment and gathering, hoping to find some trace of Joseph, as he had been young and attractive when they last saw him.
17. For three days, the brothers searched throughout the city, looking in places where they thought Joseph might be, but they could not find him.
18. The officer managing the open storehouse also looked for the names Joseph had specified, but the brothers had not yet come to buy grain.
19. On the fourth day, some of Joseph's servants found the brothers in a public area.
20. Recognizing them, they detained them and brought them before Joseph.
21. As the brothers stood before him, they bowed low, not recognizing him, as he was now dressed in royal attire and seated on a throne.
22. Joseph observed his brothers, noting their unfamiliarity with his identity, and said to them, "Where do you come from?"
23. They replied, "We have come from the land of Canaan to buy food, as the famine has afflicted our land, and we heard there is food here in Egypt."
24. Joseph responded, "If you are here to buy food, why did you each enter through different gates? Surely, this can only mean that you are spies."
25. The brothers answered, "No, my lord, we are not spies.
26. We are honest men, brothers from the same family, all sons of one father in Canaan. Our father advised us to enter the city separately to avoid suspicion."
27. Still accusing them, Joseph said, "No, I am certain you have come to spy on the vulnerabilities of the land."
28. They insisted, "We are truthful men, twelve in number, though only ten of us have come here.
29. One brother is with our father, and the other is missing."
30. Joseph replied, "Your words only confirm my suspicions. You are spies seeking to uncover the weaknesses of Egypt."
31. The brothers protested, "We are simply looking for food.
32. The younger brother you speak of is with our father, and the one who is missing is our lost brother, for whom we have searched."
33. Joseph said, "If you are truthful, leave one brother here, and the rest of you return with grain for your family.
34. Then, bring your youngest brother back as proof of your honesty."
35. Joseph then summoned his guards, ordering them to place the brothers in custody. They were kept in confinement for three days.
36. On the third day, Joseph released them and spoke to them again, saying,
37. "If you are truthful men, one brother will remain here in prison, while the others return with food for your family."

38. He added, "Bring your youngest brother to me to verify your claim. If you do this, I will know that you are honest men and not spies."
39. Joseph departed from them briefly, overwhelmed with emotion, and wept privately before returning to them.
40. He then selected Simeon to be detained, binding him before the others.
41. Though Simeon resisted at first, he was eventually restrained by Joseph's guards.
42. Joseph ordered his officials to fill each brother's sack with grain, secretly returning each man's payment to his sack, and giving them supplies for their journey home.
43. He warned them, "Remember my instructions. Bring your youngest brother back to me to prove your honesty.
44. Then, I will release your detained brother and allow you to conduct trade here freely."
45. The brothers agreed, saying, "We will do as you command," and they bowed before him in submission.
46. Loading the grain onto their donkeys, they set out for home. When they reached a resting place, one of them opened his sack to feed his donkey and discovered his money at the top of the sack.
47. Fearful, he called out to his brothers, "My payment has been returned; it is here in my sack." The brothers, startled, looked in their sacks and found their money as well, and they were filled with dread.
48. They said to one another, "What has God done to us? How could this happen?"
49. Arriving home, they recounted the entire event to their father Jacob, including how they had been accused of spying and how Simeon had been detained.
50. They explained, "The man who governs Egypt demanded we bring our youngest brother back to prove our honesty and secure Simeon's release."
51. Jacob replied with sorrow, "You have taken away my children. Joseph is gone, Simeon is now gone, and you would take Benjamin from me as well. Everything seems against me."
52. Reuben tried to reassure him, saying, "You may hold my own sons accountable if I fail to bring Benjamin back safely. I will personally ensure his return."
53. But Jacob refused, saying, "My son will not go with you. His brother is already lost, and if harm should come to him, it would bring me down to my grave in sorrow."
54. Though the brothers pleaded, Jacob remained resolute, refusing to let Benjamin accompany them to Egypt.

CHAPTER 52

1. The brothers returned to their house, and each man opened his sack to find his bundle of money still there. Both they and their father were filled with fear upon seeing it.
2. Jacob asked them, "What have you done to me? I sent Joseph to seek your welfare, and you claimed he was devoured by a wild beast."

3. He continued, "Then you went with Simeon to buy food, and now you say the king of Egypt has imprisoned him. Now you want to take Benjamin, causing his death too, bringing my gray hairs to the grave in sorrow."

4. Jacob then declared, "Benjamin will not go down with you, for his brother is dead, and he alone remains. Harm might befall him on the journey, just as it did his brother."

5. Reuben responded, "Take the lives of my two sons if I fail to bring your son back to you." Yet Jacob insisted, "Stay here and do not go down to Egypt, for Benjamin shall not die as his brother did."

6. Judah then suggested, "Wait until the corn is all consumed. Only then, when he faces hunger himself, will he say, 'Take your brother down to Egypt to save us all.'"

7. In those days, the famine intensified, affecting all the people of the earth, who came to Egypt to buy food. Meanwhile, the sons of Jacob stayed in Canaan for a year and two months until their provisions ran out.

8. When their food was depleted, hunger grew severe in Jacob's household. The children of Jacob's sons surrounded him, pleading for bread to avoid starvation.

9. Hearing their cries, Jacob wept deeply, his heart moved with compassion. He called his sons to sit before him.

10. Jacob said, "Do you not see your children weeping for food? They beg for bread, yet we have none to give. Go, buy us a little more to sustain us."

11. Judah replied, "If you send our brother with us, we will go and buy food. But if you do not, we will not go, for the king of Egypt clearly commanded us not to return without him."

12. Judah added, "This king is powerful, and if we approach him without Benjamin, he may put us all to death. Surely, you have heard of his strength and wisdom, unequaled by any on earth."

13. "Father, you have not seen the grandeur of his palace, his throne, nor the splendor in which he sits, wearing a golden crown, clothed in majesty beyond any king we have encountered."

14. He continued, "You have not witnessed the wisdom that God has placed in him, nor heard his gracious voice when he inquired after you, asking if our father was still alive and well."

15. "This king governs Egypt with wisdom, without even consulting Pharaoh, and commands great respect from the people."

16. "When we departed, we even threatened to respond against Egypt as we had done to the Amorite cities. But now, if we return without our brother, we cannot stand before him."

17. "Father, please send the young one with us, and we will buy food for you, for otherwise, we will all perish of hunger."

18. Jacob asked them, "Why did you tell the king you had another brother? What trouble have you brought upon me?"

19. Judah pleaded, "Entrust him to my care, and we will go to buy food. If we do not bring him back, I will bear the blame forever."
20. "Have you not seen the little ones crying out in hunger? Let your compassion move you to send him with us, so we may not all perish."
21. "How can the LORD's covenant with our forefathers be fulfilled if you fear that the king of Egypt will take away Benjamin?"
22. Jacob finally said, "I entrust in the LORD God to protect you and grant you favor before the king of Egypt."
23. "Rise, take the man a gift from what remains in the land, and may God's mercy allow you to bring back your brothers, Benjamin and Simeon."
24. Jacob's sons took Benjamin, along with a large gift of the land's best and double the silver needed, and prepared to leave.
25. Jacob strictly instructed them to watch over Benjamin, not to separate from him along the way or in Egypt.
26. Jacob lifted his hands and prayed, "O LORD God of heaven and earth, remember Your covenant with Abraham, and my father Isaac, and show kindness to my sons."
27. The wives and children of Jacob's sons also looked to Heaven, weeping and praying for their fathers' safety and deliverance from Egypt.
28. Jacob wrote a letter to the king of Egypt, giving it to Judah and his sons to deliver.
29. The letter read, "From Jacob, son of Isaac, son of Abraham, servant of God, to the mighty and wise king of Egypt, greetings."
30. "The famine has struck hard in Canaan, and I sent my sons to you to buy us a little food for our survival."
31. "My sons surrounded me, and I, an old man with failing sight and sorrowful heart, thought to seek my lost son Joseph in Egypt."
32. "Thus, I commanded them not to enter the city through one gate but to search the land for my son."
33. "I heard of your wisdom in interpreting Pharaoh's dream. How then could you consider my sons as spies?"
34. "My lord, I have sent my youngest son with them, as you requested. I plead that you show him mercy and return him safely with his brothers."
35. "Do you not know what God did to Pharaoh and Abimelech when they took my mother Sarah?"
36. "And what my father Abraham did to the kings of Elam, and what my sons Simeon and Levi did to the Amorite cities?"
37. "Likewise, my sons now mourn Joseph and console themselves with their brother Benjamin. How will they respond if anyone dares to harm him?"
38. "King of Egypt, know that the power of God rests with us, and He hears our prayers without fail."

39. "When my sons told me of your treatment toward them, I held back my prayer, not seeking the LORD's judgment against you, hoping for mercy."
40. "Now my son Benjamin comes with them. May God bless you and keep you in His sight."
41. "I have shared my heart with you. May God's protection be upon you as you receive my sons in peace."
42. With this, Jacob handed the letter to Judah for delivery to the king of Egypt.

CHAPTER 53

1. Jacob's sons took Benjamin, along with their gifts, and went down to Egypt. They stood before Joseph.
2. When Joseph saw his brother Benjamin with them, he greeted them, and they came to Joseph's house.
3. Joseph instructed his steward to prepare food for his brothers, and they all sat down to eat.
4. At midday, Joseph called his brothers to him, along with Benjamin, and they informed the steward about the money returned in their sacks.
5. The steward reassured them, saying, "Peace be with you, do not fear," and he brought Simeon to join them.
6. Simeon greeted his brothers, saying, "The lord of Egypt has shown me kindness; he did not keep me bound but treated me well."
7. Judah held Benjamin's hand, and they all bowed before Joseph.
8. They presented their gifts to Joseph, and Joseph asked, "Is it well with you? Is it well with your children? Is it well with your father?"
9. They answered, "It is well," and handed Joseph the letter from Jacob.
10. Joseph read the letter, recognized his father's handwriting, and went into a private room to weep.
11. He composed himself, returned, and looked at Benjamin, saying, "Is this your younger brother of whom you spoke?"
12. Benjamin came forward, and Joseph placed his hand on his head, blessing him, "May God be gracious to you, my son."
13. Seeing his brother, Joseph's heart was moved again, and he withdrew to weep, washing his face before returning.
14. Joseph then ordered food to be served, and he had a special silver cup brought to him, adorned with precious stones.
15. He struck the cup as a signal, and his brothers were seated in order of their birth, which surprised them greatly.
16. Joseph said, "This youngest brother, like me, has no other full brother. He shall sit with me."

17. Benjamin took a seat next to Joseph, and the brothers watched in astonishment at Joseph's actions.
18. They ate and drank with Joseph, and he gave Benjamin additional gifts, each from his own household.
19. Joseph poured them wine, but they declined, saying, "We have not drunk wine or eaten delicacies since losing Joseph."
20. Joseph insisted, urging them to drink, and they finally drank and enjoyed a meal with him.
21. After the meal, Joseph turned to Benjamin, asking, "Have you any children?"
22. Benjamin replied, "Yes, your servant has ten sons, whom I have named in memory of my lost brother."
23. Joseph then showed Benjamin a special chart, saying, "Look here and tell me if you find anything concerning your brother."
24. Benjamin examined it, noting the stars, and realized that the man before him was Joseph, which astonished him.
25. Joseph, noticing Benjamin's amazement, asked, "What do you see that has surprised you so?"
26. Benjamin replied, "By this chart, I see that you, my brother Joseph, are here with me."
27. Joseph responded, "I am indeed your brother. Do not reveal this to the others yet."
28. He instructed Benjamin, "When you return home, I will arrange for you all to be brought back, and I will test their loyalty."
29. Joseph said, "If they fight for you, I will reveal myself to them; if not, you shall remain with me."
30. Joseph commanded his steward to fill their sacks with food and return their money, along with his silver cup placed in Benjamin's sack.
31. The next morning, they set out for Canaan with Benjamin.
32. They had not gone far when Joseph's steward pursued them, accusing them of stealing the silver cup.

CHAPTER 54

1. When Judah saw how Joseph was dealing with them, he approached him, broke open the door, and came with his brothers before Joseph.
2. Judah said to Joseph, "Please, my lord, may I speak a word in your hearing? Do not let it be grievous to you."
3. Joseph replied, "Speak," and Judah began to speak while his brothers stood before Joseph.
4. Judah said, "When we first came to you to buy food, you accused us of being spies, and even though we brought Benjamin, you still mock us today."
5. "Now let the king hear my words and send our brother with us, lest you perish along with all the people of Egypt."

6. "Do you not know what Simeon and Levi did to Shechem and seven Amorite cities for our sister Dinah? They would do the same for Benjamin."
7. "I am stronger than both of them, and if you refuse, I will come upon you and your land today."
8. "Have you not heard what our God did to Pharaoh because of our mother Sarah? He struck him with plagues for taking her from our father."
9. "So our God will remember His covenant with Abraham and bring calamity upon you if you continue to oppress us today."
10. "Now listen to my words, send our brother back with us, lest you and your land perish."
11. Joseph responded, "Why do you boast about your strength? If I commanded my men to fight, you and your brothers would sink in the mire."
12. Judah said, "As the LORD lives, if I draw my sword, I will not put it away until all of Egypt is slain, starting with you and ending with Pharaoh."
13. Joseph replied, "Strength does not belong to you alone; I am stronger than you. If you draw your sword, I'll put it to your neck and all your brothers' necks."
14. Judah answered, "If I open my mouth, I would swallow you and your kingdom off the face of the earth."
15. Joseph said, "If you open your mouth, I have the power to close it with a stone so you cannot utter a word; see these stones before us?"
16. "I could force one into your mouth and break your jaws."
17. Judah said, "God is witness that we have not come here to fight with you; just return our brother and we'll leave."
18. Joseph replied, "As Pharaoh lives, even if all the kings of Canaan came with you, you would not take him from my hand."
19. Judah said, "Does it matter to you or the king that you accuse us over a cup you claim our brother stole?"
20. "Surely the king of Egypt sends out silver and gold as gifts throughout the land; would he miss a mere cup?"
21. "God forbid that Benjamin or any of Abraham's seed would steal from you or anyone else."
22. "Stop this accusation, lest all the world hears that Egypt's king wrestled with men over a cup and enslaved a brother."
23. Joseph replied, "Take the cup and leave. Your brother will remain a slave, as a thief should be."
24. Judah said, "How can you be so dishonorable as to keep our brother and give us your cup?"
25. "Even if you offered a thousand times the cup's value, we would not leave without him."
26. Joseph said, "Why, then, did you sell your brother Joseph for twenty pieces of silver and leave him?"

27. Judah said, "The LORD is witness; we don't seek to fight you. Give us our brother, and we will depart without conflict."
28. Joseph replied, "Even if all the kings of the land gathered, they would not take him from my hand."
29. Judah said, "What shall we say to our father when he sees our brother is not with us? He will grieve."
30. Joseph replied, "Tell him, 'The rope has gone after the bucket.'"
31. Judah said, "Surely you are a king, yet you judge falsely. Woe to the king who speaks as you do."
32. Joseph replied, "There is no falsehood in what I've said; you sold Joseph to the Midianites for twenty pieces of silver and denied it to your father."
33. Judah said, "The fire of Shem burns in my heart; I will burn your land with fire."
34. Joseph replied, "Didn't Tamar, your sister-in-law, extinguish the fire of Shechem by taking your sons?"
35. Judah said, "If I pluck a single hair from my flesh, I'll fill all of Egypt with blood."
36. Joseph replied, "Such is your way, as you did to Joseph, dipping his coat in blood and bringing it to your father."
37. Hearing this, Judah's anger burned, and he took a stone weighing four hundred shekels and cast it to the heavens, catching it with his left hand.
38. He placed the stone under his feet and sat on it with all his strength until it turned to dust.
39. Seeing Judah's strength, Joseph was afraid and ordered his son Manasseh to do likewise with another stone.
40. Judah said to his brothers, "This man is not an Egyptian, but of our father's family."
41. Joseph said, "Strength is not yours alone. We are powerful too. Why do you boast over us?"
42. Judah said, "Send our brother, or face the ruin of your country."
43. Joseph replied, "Tell your father an evil beast devoured him, as you said about your brother Joseph."
44. Judah spoke to Naphtali, "Go, count all the streets of Egypt and tell me."
45. Simeon said, "I will go to the mountain, take a stone, and level it at everyone in Egypt."
46. Joseph, overhearing his brothers, was afraid they might destroy Egypt, so he ordered Manasseh to gather Egypt's people and soldiers.
47. Manasseh gathered troops, and they came with horses, infantry, and musicians, as Joseph commanded.
48. Naphtali, swift as a stag, counted the twelve streets of Egypt and reported back to Judah.
49. Judah said, "Each of us shall destroy a street."
50. Judah prepared to destroy three streets by himself, but then Egyptian troops surrounded them with a great shout.
51. There were five hundred cavalry, ten thousand infantry, and four hundred unarmed fighters.

52. The Egyptians surrounded Joseph's brothers, causing the ground to quake.
53. Seeing the troops, Jacob's sons were afraid for their lives, as Joseph had intended to calm them.
54. Judah reassured his brothers, "Why fear? God's grace is with us."
55. Judah drew his sword, screamed loudly, struck the ground, and continued to shout.
56. The LORD caused terror to fall upon Egypt's mighty men, and they fled, trampling each other, many dying in their escape.
57. Judah and his brothers pursued them to Pharaoh's house, then Judah roared at Joseph like a lion.
58. The roar was heard afar, and Egypt quaked, walls fell, and even Pharaoh fell from his throne.
59. Pharaoh sent for Joseph, saying, "You brought Hebrews here to destroy Egypt. Send them away or Egypt will perish."
60. Pharaoh added, "If you won't let them go, give up your wealth and join them, for they will destroy us all."
61. Joseph heard Pharaoh's words and grew afraid, as Judah and his brothers were enraged.
62. Manasseh approached Judah, placing a hand on his shoulder, and Judah's anger calmed.
63. Judah told his brothers, "This man's actions are not those of an Egyptian; he belongs to our father's house."
64. Seeing Judah's anger was stilled, Joseph spoke kindly, saying, "Your strength is evident. May God bless you."
65. "But tell me, why are you the only one to plead for Benjamin?"
66. Judah replied, "I am responsible for the boy; I promised our father I would return him."
67. "So, I beg you, allow Benjamin to leave, and I will remain as your servant."
68. "Send me to fight any enemy, and I will bring victory."
69. Joseph replied, "Indeed, I've heard of Abraham's strength, inherited by his descendants."
70. "On one condition, I will release Benjamin: if you bring me his lost brother, Joseph."
71. Judah's anger flared again; his eyes burned with fury.
72. Simeon spoke, "We don't know where Joseph is; why do you demand this?"
73. Joseph said, "If I call for Joseph now, would you give him in exchange for Benjamin?"
74. Joseph called out, "Joseph, come forth before your brothers."
75. His brothers looked around, bewildered.
76. Joseph said, "Why look around? I am Joseph, whom you sold to Egypt."
77. "Do not grieve, for God sent me here to preserve life during this famine."
78. His brothers were terrified at his words, and Judah was especially afraid.
79. Benjamin ran to Joseph, embraced him, and they wept together.
80. Seeing this, the other brothers embraced Joseph, and they all wept greatly.
81. News of Joseph's reunion with his brothers spread, and Pharaoh rejoiced.
82. Pharaoh sent servants to congratulate Joseph on his family's arrival.

83. Pharaoh said to Joseph, "Tell your family to come to Egypt; I will give them the best land."
84. Joseph commanded his steward to bring royal garments and gifts for his brothers.
85. He gave each a change of fine garments and three hundred pieces of silver.
86. Pharaoh saw Joseph's brothers were valiant men and was greatly pleased.
87. They set out to return to Canaan, rejoicing, with Benjamin among them.
88. Joseph gave them eleven chariots from Pharaoh and his own chariot to fetch their father.
89. Joseph sent gifts for his brothers' children and his father's household.
90. He gave his sister Dinah and the wives of his brothers many precious gifts.
91. Joseph's brothers departed, with ten servants each to accompany them.
92. Joseph went with them to the Egyptian border, reminding them not to quarrel on the way.
93. As they neared their home, they considered how to tell their father the news.
94. They met Serach, daughter of Asher, who was skilled in playing the harp.
95. They asked her to play and gently tell Jacob the news of Joseph.
96. She played and sang, "Uncle Joseph lives! He rules in Egypt."
97. Jacob listened to her song, and joy entered his heart.
98. He blessed her, saying, "May death never prevail over you, for you've revived my spirit."
99. Serach continued her song, and Jacob rejoiced.
100. While she sang, Jacob's sons arrived in royal garments, with treasures.
101. Jacob rose to meet them, and they told him, "Joseph is alive! He rules in Egypt."
102. Jacob's heart leapt with joy, and he believed them after seeing the gifts.
103. He said, "It is enough. My son Joseph lives; I will go to see him before I die."
104. His sons told him all that had happened in Egypt.
105. Jacob declared, "I will go to Egypt to see my son and his children."
106. Jacob put on the royal garments Joseph had sent, having washed and shaved.
107. His household rejoiced that Joseph lived and ruled in Egypt.
108. The news spread, and the people of Canaan came to rejoice with Jacob.
109. Jacob hosted a feast for three days, and all the kings of Canaan celebrated with him.
110. They ate, drank, and rejoiced in Jacob's house, celebrating Joseph's life and rule.

CHAPTER 55:

1. After these events, Jacob said, "I will go to see my son in Egypt and then return to the land of Canaan, as God promised to Abraham, for I cannot leave the land of my birth."
2. The word of the LORD came to Jacob, saying, "Go down to Egypt with all your household, and do not fear, for there I will make you a great nation."
3. And Jacob thought, "I will go to see if the fear of his God is still within Joseph, despite his life in Egypt."
4. The LORD assured Jacob, saying, "Fear not for Joseph; he remains true in his heart to serve Me, as you will see."

5. Rejoicing, Jacob called his sons and household to prepare for their journey to Egypt, as the LORD had instructed.
6. And Jacob, with his family, rose from Beersheba in Canaan, setting out joyfully toward Egypt.
7. As they neared Egypt, Jacob sent Judah ahead to Joseph, so he might prepare a place for them.
8. Judah ran ahead to Joseph, who then arranged for their family to settle in the land of Goshen.
9. Judah returned to guide Jacob along the way.
10. Joseph harnessed his chariot, gathered his servants, officers, and a mighty host of Egypt to meet his father.
11. A proclamation went out in Egypt that all should accompany Joseph to meet Jacob, and any who did not join would face death.
12. The next day, Joseph and a vast procession, richly dressed and bearing instruments of gold and silver, went out to greet Jacob.
13. Women of Egypt gathered on rooftops and city walls to witness the arrival, and Joseph wore Pharaoh's crown, which he had been given for the occasion.
14. When Joseph came within fifty cubits of his father, he stepped down from the chariot and walked towards him.
15. Seeing this, all Egyptian officers and nobles also descended and walked with Joseph toward Jacob.
16. Jacob observed the approaching camp of Egypt and was astonished at the sight.
17. Jacob asked Judah, "Who is this man in royal attire, with a red robe and crown, coming on foot towards us?"
18. Judah replied, "It is your son, Joseph, the king." And Jacob rejoiced at the honor of his son.
19. Joseph came before his father, bowing low, as did the entire camp of Egypt.
20. Then Jacob hurried to his son, embraced him, and they wept together.
21. Joseph kissed his father, and they wept, as did all who were with them.
22. Jacob said to Joseph, "Now I can die in peace, having seen that you are alive and in glory."
23. The sons of Jacob, their wives, children, and all of Jacob's household embraced Joseph and wept.
24. Then Joseph and his people returned to Egypt, taking Jacob and his family to settle in Goshen.
25. Joseph told his father and brothers, "I will inform Pharaoh that you and all your household have arrived."
26. Joseph then selected Reuben, Issachar, Zebulun, and Benjamin, presenting them to Pharaoh.

27. He explained to Pharaoh, "My brothers and father's household have come to Egypt from Canaan to sojourn, as the famine was severe there."
28. Pharaoh said to Joseph, "Settle your family in the best land, sparing no goodness, so they may eat of Egypt's abundance."
29. Joseph replied, "I have stationed them in Goshen to keep their flocks separate, as they are shepherds."
30. Pharaoh agreed, "Do as you see fit," and Jacob's sons bowed before Pharaoh, departing in peace.
31. Afterward, Joseph brought his father Jacob to meet Pharaoh.
32. Jacob came before Pharaoh, bowed, and blessed him, and then departed.
33. Jacob and all his sons took up residence in Goshen, and Joseph provided for his family throughout the famine.
34. Joseph secured for them the choicest land, and they prospered greatly, lacking nothing.
35. Each year, Joseph provided new garments for them and took care of their needs.
36. Jacob and his sons lived securely, and Joseph's two sons, Ephraim and Manasseh, remained close to their grandfather, learning God's ways and His laws.

CHAPTER 56:

1. Jacob lived in Egypt for seventeen years, and his total years were one hundred and forty-seven.
2. As Jacob's illness worsened, he called for his son Joseph, who came quickly to his side.
3. Jacob said to Joseph, "Behold, I am about to die, but God will surely bring you back to the land promised to Abraham."
4. He then commanded, "Swear to bury me in the cave of Machpelah in Hebron, beside my ancestors."
5. Joseph and his brothers vowed to fulfill Jacob's wish.
6. Jacob gathered all his sons to his side, blessing each according to God's promise.
7. He then blessed them again on the following day, speaking words over each son's future.
8. To Judah, he said, "You are mighty among your brothers; your descendants will rule over them."
9. "Teach your sons the ways of the bow and all skills of war for the protection of their brothers."
10. He instructed, "When I pass, carry me in the manner I've commanded, with each tribe taking its place."
11. Judah, Issachar, and Zebulun would carry the bier from the east.
12. Reuben, Simeon, and Gad would carry from the south.
13. Ephraim, Manasseh, and Benjamin would carry from the west.
14. Dan, Asher, and Naphtali would carry from the north.
15. Levi would refrain, for he and his descendants would carry the Ark of God's Covenant.
16. Joseph, as ruler, would not carry the bier; Ephraim and Manasseh would represent him.

17. Jacob said, "Do all I command and receive the Lord's blessing and remembrance forever."
18. Jacob reminded them, "Honor each other, and instruct your descendants to serve God faithfully."
19. He then spoke to Joseph, "Forgive your brothers for their wrongs, for God intended it for good."
20. He advised, "Do not leave your brothers in Egypt nor hold resentment, but protect them."
21. Jacob's sons promised to do all he commanded, trusting in God's blessing.
22. Jacob blessed them, "May God guide and save you, now and in future trials."
23. "Teach your children to know God, so He will deliver them in affliction."
24. Jacob finished speaking, drew his feet into bed, and passed peacefully.
25. Joseph fell upon his father, weeping and kissing him, calling out in sorrow.
26. All Jacob's household wept and mourned deeply.
27. Jacob's sons tore their clothes, wore sackcloth, and cast dust upon themselves in grief.
28. News reached Osnath, Joseph's wife, who joined with the Egyptian women to mourn Jacob.
29. Egyptians who knew Jacob also gathered, mourning with his family for many days.
30. Women from Canaan joined in mourning upon hearing of Jacob's passing.
31. After seventy days of weeping, Joseph requested permission from Pharaoh to bury his father.
32. Pharaoh granted his request, saying, "Go and fulfill your oath to bury your father."
33. Joseph departed with his brothers and all Pharaoh's officials, traveling to Canaan.
34. Pharaoh's proclamation commanded that all Egypt should join in mourning.
35. The sons of Jacob carried his bier as he had instructed, each tribe in its place.
36. The bier, adorned with gold and precious stones, was covered in woven garments.
37. Joseph placed a golden crown on his father's head and a scepter in his hand, honoring him.
38. Egyptian warriors led the procession, armed and prepared.
39. Mourning women and mourners followed at a respectful distance.
40. Joseph, barefoot and grieving, walked near the bier, accompanied by his household.
41. Jacob's servants scattered myrrh and aloes on the path as they moved toward Canaan.
42. They mourned deeply at the threshing floor of Atad, beyond the Jordan.
43. Thirty-one Canaanite kings joined to mourn Jacob, placing their crowns on his bier.
44. These kings joined in the sons' mourning, for Jacob's valor was renowned.
45. Esau learned of Jacob's death and came with his people to mourn.
46. Esau wept with Egypt and Canaan over Jacob's passing.
47. Joseph and his brothers moved Jacob's body to Hebron, preparing for burial.
48. As they arrived at the cave, Esau and his sons blocked their way, claiming the burial site.
49. Joseph confronted Esau, asserting Jacob's rightful purchase of the land.

50. Esau denied the sale, hoping to deceive Joseph, knowing he wasn't present for the transaction.
51. Joseph insisted, "The transaction is recorded; it awaits in Egypt."
52. Esau challenged, "Bring the record and prove your claim."
53. Joseph called Naphtali, instructing him to retrieve the record from Egypt.
54. Naphtali, swift as a stag, departed to fetch the evidence.
55. Meanwhile, Esau and his sons resisted, blocking access to the cave.
56. A battle ensued between Jacob's sons and Esau's men, with forty of Esau's men falling.
57. Chushim, son of Dan, though mute and deaf, sensed the conflict and asked why they delayed burying Jacob.
58. Learning of Esau's obstruction, he charged forward, slaying Esau and scattering his people.
59. With Esau defeated, Jacob's sons buried him in the cave as planned.
60. Jacob was buried in Hebron with his ancestors, dressed in regal garments.
61. No king had received such honor as Joseph bestowed on his father.
62. Joseph's brothers observed a seven-day mourning period for Jacob.
63. Egypt, Canaan, and all who revered Jacob mourned his passing.
64. Joseph provided his father with a burial of kingly reverence, fulfilling his oath.
65. The Egyptian people respected Jacob's memory, honoring him for his righteousness.
66. With Jacob laid to rest, his sons and family returned to Egypt, carrying his legacy forward.
67. Joseph remained in Egypt, ruling wisely and securing peace for Jacob's descendants.

CHAPTER 57

1. After these events, the sons of Esau waged war against the sons of Jacob at Hebron, where Esau lay dead and unburied.
2. The battle was fierce, and the sons of Esau were defeated by Jacob's sons, who killed eighty men without suffering any losses.
3. Joseph's forces captured Zepho, son of Eliphaz, along with fifty men, binding them in iron chains and taking them to Egypt.
4. Seeing Zepho and his men taken captive, the remaining sons of Esau feared for their lives and fled with Esau's body to Mount Seir.
5. Upon reaching Mount Seir, they buried Esau, though they left his head in Hebron, where the battle had occurred.
6. Jacob's sons pursued them to the borders of Seir but refrained from further killing, turning back to Hebron.
7. On the third day, the sons of Seir and the children of the east, numbering like the sands of the sea, assembled and marched to Egypt to free their captured brothers.
8. Joseph, his brothers, and Egypt's strong men met them in battle at Rameses, striking the sons of Esau and the eastern armies with a tremendous blow.

9. Six hundred thousand were killed, including the mighty men of Seir and many of Esau's kin, while the survivors, including Eliphaz, fled.
10. Joseph and his brothers pursued them to Succoth, killing thirty more men, with the rest escaping to their cities.
11. Joseph, his brothers, and the Egyptian forces returned victorious and in high spirits, having subdued their enemies.
12. Zepho and his men remained as slaves in Egypt, enduring increasing hardships.
13. Upon returning to Seir, the sons of Seir realized they had suffered greatly because of Esau's battle with Jacob's sons.
14. The sons of Seir addressed Esau's descendants, saying, "This battle was because of you, and now we are left without mighty warriors."
15. "Depart from our land," they said, "return to the land of your forefathers, for why should your children inherit our lands?"
16. Esau's descendants refused to leave, prompting the sons of Seir to prepare for war against them.
17. The children of Esau secretly requested aid from Angeas, king of Africa, also known as Dinhabah.
18. "Send warriors to join us," they urged, "and together, we will defeat the sons of Seir."
19. Angeas, friendly toward Esau's lineage, sent five hundred foot soldiers and eight hundred cavalry.
20. Meanwhile, the sons of Seir sent word to the eastern tribes and the Midianites, saying,
21. "See what Esau's descendants have done, nearly destroying us in their battle against Jacob's sons. Join us to drive them from our land."
22. Hearing this, eight hundred eastern men armed with swords joined the sons of Seir, and they fought Esau's descendants in Paran.
23. The sons of Seir prevailed, killing about two hundred of Angeas's men and many of Esau's people.
24. On the second day, Esau's men launched another attack, but again faced a fierce resistance from the sons of Seir.
25. Some men from Esau's ranks defected, siding with the sons of Seir against their own kin.
26. Another fifty-eight of Angeas's forces perished in the second battle.
27. On the third day, Esau's men learned that some of their own had joined Seir's forces, which saddened and troubled them.
28. They asked, "What should we do about our kin who have betrayed us to fight alongside Seir?"
29. Esau's descendants again appealed to Angeas, requesting more soldiers.
30. Angeas sent an additional six hundred men to support Esau's descendants in their battle.
31. Ten days later, Esau's descendants clashed with the sons of Seir once more in Paran, this time gaining the upper hand.
32. They killed two thousand of Seir's warriors, leaving only young children in Seir's cities.

33. Witnessing the intense battle, the eastern tribes and Midianites abandoned Seir, fleeing the scene.
34. Esau's men pursued the eastern tribes, killing two hundred and fifty before they escaped, while losing thirty of their own.
35. After the battle, Esau's men returned to Seir, where they killed the remaining men, women, and children, sparing only fifty young boys and girls.
36. These captives became servants and wives for Esau's descendants, who then settled in Seir, taking full possession of the land.
37. They divided the land among Esau's five sons, claiming it as their inheritance.
38. In time, Esau's descendants resolved to appoint a king over them to lead and defend them in battle.
39. They swore never to choose a king from among themselves, due to past betrayals, instead selecting a stranger.
40. This oath reflected the deep resentment among Esau's descendants, each distrusting his own kin.
41. They found a man named Bela, son of Beor, from the people of Angeas. Wise, brave, and handsome, he was renowned for his counsel and skill.
42. Esau's descendants crowned Bela as their king, declaring, "Long live the king!"
43. They brought him gifts of gold, silver, and jewels, bestowing wealth upon him.
44. After celebrating his coronation, Angeas's people returned to Dinhabah.
45. Bela ruled over Esau's descendants for thirty years, with Esau's lineage securely dwelling in Seir.

CHAPTER 58

1. In the thirty-second year of the Israelites' residence in Egypt, which was also the seventy-first year of Joseph's life, Pharaoh, the king of Egypt, died, and his son Magron succeeded him.
2. Before his death, Pharaoh appointed Joseph to be a fatherly advisor to Magron, entrusting him with the young king's guidance.
3. All of Egypt agreed to this, for they held Joseph in high esteem, and although Magron ruled, Joseph managed all affairs.
4. Magron was forty-one when he ascended the throne, reigning for forty years, and the Egyptians referred to him as Pharaoh, following their custom.
5. Pharaoh placed Egypt's laws and government affairs in Joseph's hands, as his father had instructed before him.
6. Thus, Joseph effectively governed Egypt, exercising authority and gaining the people's favor after Pharaoh's passing.
7. However, a few Egyptians resisted, saying, "A foreigner shall not rule over us," though Joseph held supreme authority.

8. Joseph commanded Egypt, fought and subdued neighboring enemies, and brought the Philistine lands under his rule, extending to Canaan.
9. Pharaoh sat on the throne in Egypt, but his reign was subject to Joseph's counsel, as in his father's time.
10. Pharaoh's rule extended only within Egypt's borders, while Joseph held sway over surrounding lands, including regions by the River Perath.
11. The Lord blessed Joseph with continued wisdom, honor, and influence throughout Egypt and beyond.
12. Lands like Philistia, Canaan, and Zidon offered annual tributes to Joseph, acknowledging his authority.
13. All of Jacob's sons lived in security in Egypt under Joseph's rule, growing and prospering in the land.
14. Over time, Esau's descendants multiplied and, emboldened, planned to rescue Zepho, son of Eliphaz, who remained enslaved in Egypt.
15. Esau's descendants made peace with eastern tribes, uniting to march against Egypt.
16. They received support from Angeas, king of Dinhabah, and from the Ishmaelites, who joined their ranks.
17. Gathering in Seir, this vast alliance numbered about eight hundred thousand, prepared to march on Egypt.
18. Joseph and his brothers, accompanied by Egypt's mightiest warriors, met Esau's forces in Rameses.
19. In the ensuing battle, the Lord granted victory to Joseph and his brothers, who defeated Esau's forces.
20. Around two hundred thousand of Esau's allies perished, including their king, Bela, son of Beor, weakening their resolve.
21. Joseph and his brothers pressed their attack, routing Esau's army, who fled in terror.
22. Joseph's forces pursued them a day's journey, killing three hundred more before withdrawing.
23. Upon returning to Egypt, Joseph ordered Zepho and his men further restrained, intensifying their suffering.
24. Esau's survivors returned home in disgrace, having lost all their valiant men.
25. Seeing their king slain, Esau's people elected Jobab, son of Zarach from Botzrah, as their new ruler.
26. Jobab reigned in Edom for ten years, and from that time, Esau's people avoided further conflict with Jacob's descendants.
27. However, deep-seated enmity festered between Esau's and Jacob's lines, enduring for generations.
28. Ten years into Jobab's rule, he passed away, and Esau's people installed Chusham from Teman as king.

29. Chusham reigned over Edom for twenty years, and during this period, Joseph and his family lived peacefully in Egypt.
30. Under Joseph's guidance, the Israelites and Egyptians enjoyed tranquility and prosperity, free from the threat of war.

CHAPTER 59

1. These are the names of the sons of Israel who settled in Egypt, those who came with Jacob; all of Jacob's sons brought their households with them.
2. The sons of Leah were Reuben, Simeon, Levi, Judah, Issachar, Zebulun, and their sister Dinah.
3. The sons of Rachel were Joseph and Benjamin.
4. The sons of Zilpah, Leah's handmaid, were Gad and Asher.
5. The sons of Bilhah, Rachel's handmaid, were Dan and Naphtali.
6. These were the descendants born to Jacob's sons in Canaan before they came to Egypt with their father.
7. Reuben's sons were Chanoch, Pallu, Chetzron, and Carmi.
8. Simeon's sons were Jemuel, Jamin, Ohad, Jachin, Zochar, and Saul, the son of a Canaanite woman.
9. Levi's children were Gershon, Kehas, and Merari, and their sister was Jochebed, born during their journey to Egypt.
10. Judah's sons were Er, Onan, Shelah, Perez, and Zarach.
11. Er and Onan died in Canaan; Perez's sons were Chezron and Chamul.
12. Issachar's sons were Tola, Puvah, Job, and Shomron.
13. Zebulun's sons were Sered, Elon, and Jachleel, and Dan's son was Chushim.
14. Naphtali's sons were Jachzeel, Guni, Jetzer, and Shilam.
15. Gad's sons were Ziphion, Chaggi, Shuni, Ezbon, Eri, Arodi, and Areli.
16. Asher's children were Jimnah, Jishvah, Jishvi, Beriah, and their sister Serach; Beriah's sons were Cheber and Malchiel.
17. Benjamin's sons were Bela, Becher, Ashbel, Gera, Naaman, Achi, Rosh, Mupim, Chupim, and Ord.
18. Joseph's sons born in Egypt were Manasseh and Ephraim.
19. All those descended from Jacob who came with him to Egypt numbered seventy souls, and they settled there together.
20. Joseph lived in Egypt for ninety-three years and ruled over Egypt for eighty years.
21. As Joseph's end drew near, he summoned his brothers and his father's household, and they all gathered before him.
22. Joseph told them, "I am dying, but God will surely visit you and bring you up from this land to the one He promised to your forefathers."
23. "When God visits you to lead you to the land of your fathers, carry my bones with you from here."

24. Joseph made the sons of Israel swear to do this, saying, "God will visit you, and you shall carry my bones up from here."
25. Joseph passed away in the seventy-first year after Israel's arrival in Egypt.
26. He was one hundred and ten years old at his death, and his brothers and servants embalmed him as was custom; all Egypt mourned him for seventy days.
27. Joseph was placed in a coffin with spices and perfumes, and he was buried by the river Sihor. His family mourned him for seven days.
28. After Joseph's death, the Egyptians began to rule over the Israelites, and Pharaoh took control of Egypt's governance, reigning securely over his people.

CHAPTER 60

1. In the seventy-second year after Israel's descent into Egypt, after Joseph's death, Zepho, son of Eliphaz, grandson of Esau, fled from Egypt with his men.
2. He went to Dinhabah in Africa, where Angeas, king of Africa, welcomed him with honor, appointing Zepho as the captain of his host.
3. Zepho gained favor with Angeas and his people, serving as captain of the host for many years.
4. Zepho tried to persuade Angeas to gather his forces to wage war against the Egyptians and the sons of Jacob to avenge his brothers.
5. Angeas, however, refused, knowing the strength of the sons of Jacob and recalling their victory over his army when they fought Esau's descendants.
6. Zepho, though greatly honored, continued to urge Angeas to attack Egypt, but Angeas would not relent.
7. At that time, in the land of Chittim, a man named Uzu from Puzimna was highly revered, and he passed away, leaving only one daughter, Jania.
8. Jania was known throughout the land for her beauty, wisdom, and intelligence, unlike any other.
9. Angeas' people spoke of her, and Angeas sent messengers to Chittim to seek her as a wife, and they agreed.
10. Meanwhile, Turnus, king of Bibentu, also sent messengers to Chittim to ask for Jania's hand in marriage, having heard of her qualities.
11. Turnus' messengers requested Jania as a wife for their king, but the people of Chittim refused.
12. They replied, "Angeas, king of Africa, has already requested her, and we fear to displease him."
13. They added, "We fear Angeas' wrath more than we trust Turnus to protect us."
14. The messengers returned to Turnus and relayed Chittim's response.
15. Chittim then sent word to Angeas, warning him that Turnus planned to attack and pass through Sardunia to fight against his brother, Lucus.

16. Angeas was enraged and gathered his army, traveling through islands to Sardunia, where his brother ruled.
17. Niblos, Lucus' son, greeted Angeas with an army, pledging to fight alongside him and asking his father to make him captain of the host.
18. Angeas met his brother Lucus, who welcomed him, and Lucus appointed Niblos as captain of his forces.
19. Angeas and Lucus led their armies against Turnus in the Valley of Canopia, where a fierce battle ensued.
20. The fighting was severe, and Lucus' forces suffered greatly; Niblos, his son, fell in battle.
21. Angeas commanded a golden coffin made for Niblos, and he resumed the fight against Turnus, eventually defeating him.
22. Turnus was slain, and Angeas' forces struck down his people, avenging Niblos and Lucus' army.
23. With Turnus dead, the survivors fled, pursued by Angeas and Lucus to the road between Alphanu and Romah.
24. Angeas and Lucus killed Turnus' remaining forces along this route.
25. Lucus ordered a brass coffin made for Niblos, and he was buried on one side of the high road, Turnus on the other.
26. A tower was built there, named after Niblos, with the graves of Niblos and Turnus marked by a pavement.
27. After burying his son, Lucus returned to Sardunia, and Angeas went to Bibentu, Turnus' city.
28. The people of Bibentu, fearing Angeas, went out to plead for mercy, begging him not to destroy their city.
29. Angeas spared Bibentu, considering it a city of Chittim, and withheld his wrath.
30. However, Angeas' troops frequently raided Chittim, and Zepho, his captain, often joined these expeditions.
31. Later, Angeas took Jania, daughter of Uzu, as his wife, bringing her back to Africa.

CHAPTER 61

1. During this time, Pharaoh, king of Egypt, commanded his people to construct a grand palace in Egypt for him.
2. He required the sons of Jacob to assist the Egyptians in this building, and a beautiful palace was made as a royal residence, where Pharaoh established his reign securely.
3. In the seventy-second year of Israel's descent to Egypt, Zebulun, son of Jacob, passed away at the age of one hundred and fourteen; he was placed in a coffin and entrusted to his children.
4. Three years later, his brother Simeon died at the age of one hundred and twenty, and he, too, was placed in a coffin and given to his children.

5. Meanwhile, Zepho, son of Eliphaz and captain under Angeas, persistently urged Angeas to wage war on the sons of Jacob in Egypt, but Angeas hesitated, remembering their might.
6. Zepho's entreaties continued daily, pressing Angeas to march against Egypt and the sons of Jacob.
7. Eventually, Angeas yielded, assembling his vast army, as numerous as the sand on the seashore, preparing to invade Egypt.
8. Among Angeas' servants was a youth named Balaam, son of Beor, a skilled practitioner of witchcraft.
9. Angeas requested Balaam to perform divinations to reveal the outcome of the impending battle.
10. Balaam used wax figures of chariots and horsemen, symbolizing the armies of Angeas and Egypt, and placed them in enchanted water.
11. With branches of myrtle, Balaam conducted his ritual, and he saw in the water that the image representing Angeas' forces fell before the Egyptians.
12. Balaam reported this to Angeas, who despaired, losing his resolve to proceed against Egypt, choosing instead to remain in his city.
13. Frustrated, Zepho left Angeas and journeyed to Chittim, where he was received with great honor.
14. The people of Chittim employed Zepho to lead their battles, bringing him considerable wealth and esteem.
15. The king of Africa's troops continued raiding, prompting the people of Chittim to seek refuge on Mount Cuptizia.
16. One day, Zepho sought a missing heifer, tracing its calls to a cave near the mountain, where he encountered a creature part-man, part-animal.
17. Zepho slew the beast with his sword, and the people of Chittim, learning of this, rejoiced greatly.
18. In gratitude, they established an annual day of tribute to Zepho, honoring him with gifts and drink offerings each year.
19. During this time, Jania, Angeas' wife, fell gravely ill, and Angeas and his advisors sought a remedy for her.
20. They surmised that her illness stemmed from the different air and water of Africa, as she was accustomed to water from Purmah in Chittim.
21. Angeas ordered that water from Purmah be brought, discovering it lighter than African waters.
22. He commanded the construction of a bridge to transport this water for Jania's use, which included bringing soil and stones from Chittim to Africa. With these resources, they built palaces, and Jania recovered her health.
23. As Angeas' forces continued plundering Chittim, Zepho fought against them, eventually repelling them and delivering Chittim from their oppression.

24. The people of Chittim were so impressed by Zepho's valor that they crowned him king, granting him dominion over their land.
25. Zepho led them in conquests, subjugating the children of Tubal and nearby islands. Upon their victorious return, they built Zepho a magnificent palace and a grand throne, solidifying his rule over Chittim and Italia. Zepho reigned as king over Chittim and Italia for fifty years, establishing peace and prosperity.

CHAPTER 62

1. 1 And in that year, being the seventy-ninth year of the Israelites going down to Egypt, Reuben the son of Jacob died in the land of Egypt; Reuben was one hundred and twenty-five years old when he died, and they put him into a coffin, and he was given into the hands of his children.
2. And in the eightieth year his brother Dan died; he was one hundred and twenty years old at his death, and he was also put into a coffin and given into the hands of his children.
3. And in that year Chusham king of Edom died, and Hadad the son of Bedad reigned after him for thirty-five years; and in the eighty-first year Issachar the son of Jacob died in Egypt, and Issachar was one hundred and twenty-two years old at his death, and he was put into a coffin in Egypt and given into the hands of his children.
4. And in the eighty-second year his brother Asher died; he was one hundred and twenty-three years old at his death, and he was placed in a coffin in Egypt and given into the hands of his children.
5. And in the eighty-third year Gad died; he was one hundred and twenty-five years old at his death, and he was put into a coffin in Egypt, and given into the hands of his children.
6. And it came to pass in the eighty-fourth year, that is the fiftieth year of the reign of Hadad son of Bedad, king of Edom, that Hadad assembled all the children of Esau, and he got his whole army in readiness, about four hundred thousand men, and he directed his way to the land of Moab, and he went to fight with Moab and to make them tributary to him.
7. And the children of Moab heard this thing, and they were very much afraid, and they sent to the children of Midian to assist them in fighting with Hadad son of Bedad, king of Edom.
8. And Hadad came to the land of Moab, and Moab and the children of Midian went out to meet him, and they placed themselves in battle array against him in the field of Moab.
9. And Hadad fought with Moab, and there fell of the children of Moab and the children of Midian many slain ones, about two hundred thousand men.
10. And the battle was very severe on Moab, and when the children of Moab saw that the battle was severe on them, they weakened their hands, and turned their backs, and left the children of Midian to carry on the battle.

11. And the children of Midian did not know the intentions of Moab, but they strengthened themselves in battle and fought with Hadad and all his host, and all Midian fell before him.
12. And Hadad struck all Midian with a heavy striking, and he slew them with the edge of the sword; he left none remaining of those who came to assist Moab.
13. And when all the children of Midian had perished in battle and the children of Moab had escaped, Hadad made all Moab tributary to him at that time, and they came under his hand, and they gave a yearly tax as it was ordered, and Hadad turned and went back to his land.
14. And at the revolution of the year, when the rest of the people of Midian that were in the land heard that all their brothers had fallen in battle with Hadad for the sake of Moab, because the children of Moab had turned their backs in battle and left Midian to fight, then five of the princes of Midian resolved with the rest of their brothers who remained in their land to fight with Moab to avenge the cause of their brothers.
15. And the children of Midian sent to all their brothers, the children of the east, and all their brothers; all the children of Keturah came to assist Midian to fight with Moab.
16. And the children of Moab heard this thing, and they were greatly afraid that all the children of the east had assembled together against them for battle, and they, the children of Moab, sent a memorial to the land of Edom to Hadad the son of Bedad, saying,
17. "Come to us now, and assist us, and we will strike Midian, for they all assembled together and have come against us with all their brothers, the children of the east, to battle, to avenge the cause of Midian that fell in battle."
18. And Hadad son of Bedad, king of Edom, went out with his whole army and went to the land of Moab to fight with Midian, and Midian and the children of the east fought with Moab in the field of Moab, and the battle was very fierce between them.
19. And Hadad struck all the children of Midian and the children of the east with the edge of the sword, and at that time Hadad delivered Moab from the hand of Midian, and those that remained of Midian and of the children of the east fled before Hadad and his army, and Hadad pursued them to their land, and struck them with a very heavy slaughter, and the slain fell in the road.
20. And Hadad delivered Moab from the hand of Midian, for all the children of Midian had fallen by the edge of the sword, and Hadad turned and went back to his land.
21. And from that day forward the children of Midian hated the children of Moab, because they had fallen in battle for their sake, and there was a great and mighty enmity between them all the days.
22. And all that were found of Midian in the road of the land of Moab perished by the sword of Moab, and all that were found of Moab in the road of the land of Midian perished by the sword of Midian; thus Midian did to Moab and Moab to Midian for many days.
23. And it came to pass at that time that Judah the son of Jacob died in Egypt, in the eighty-sixth year of Jacob's going down to Egypt, and Judah was one hundred and twenty-nine

years old at his death, and they embalmed him and put him into a coffin, and he was given into the hands of his children.

24. And in the eighty-ninth year Naphtali died; he was one hundred and thirty-two years old, and he was put into a coffin, and given into the hands of his children.
25. And it came to pass in the ninety-first year of the Israelites going down to Egypt, that is in the thirtieth year of the reign of Zepho the son of Eliphaz, the son of Esau, over the children of Chittim, the children of Africa came on the children of Chittim to plunder them as usual, but they had not come on them for these thirteen years.
26. And they came to them in that year, and Zepho the son of Eliphaz went out to them with some of his men and struck them desperately, and the troops of Africa fled from before Zepho and the slain fell before him, and Zepho and his men pursued them, going on and striking them until they were near to Africa.
27. And Angeas king of Africa heard the thing which Zepho had done, and it vexed him exceedingly, and Angeas was afraid of Zepho all the days.

CHAPTER 63

1. And in the ninety-third year Levi the son of Jacob died in Egypt, and Levi was one hundred and thirty-seven years old when he died, and they put him into a coffin, and he was given into the hands of his children.
2. And it came to pass after the death of Levi, when all Egypt saw that the sons of Jacob, the brothers of Joseph, were dead, all the Egyptians began to afflict the children of Jacob, and to embitter their lives from that day to the day of their going out from Egypt, and they took from their hands all the vineyards and fields which Joseph had given to them, and all the elegant houses in which the people of Israel lived, and all the fat of Egypt; the Egyptians took everything from the sons of Jacob in those days.
3. And the hand of all Egypt became more grievous in those days against the sons of Israel, and the Egyptians injured the Israelites until the sons of Israel were wearied of their lives on account of the Egyptians.
4. And it came to pass in those days, in the one hundred and second year of Israel's going down to Egypt, that Pharaoh king of Egypt died, and his son Melol reigned in his stead, and all the mighty men of Egypt and all that generation which knew Joseph and his brothers died in those days.
5. And another generation rose up in their stead, which had not known the sons of Jacob, and all the good which they had done to them, and all their might in Egypt.
6. Therefore all Egypt began from that day out to embitter the lives of the sons of Jacob and to afflict them with all manner of hard labor, because they had not known their ancestors who had delivered them in the days of the famine.
7. And this was also from the LORD, for the sons of Israel, to benefit them in their latter days, in order that all the sons of Israel might know the LORD their God,

8. And in order to know the signs and mighty wonders which the LORD would do in Egypt on account of His people Israel, in order that the sons of Israel might fear the LORD God of their ancestors and walk in all His ways—they and their seed after them [for] all the days.
9. Melol was twenty years old when he began to reign, and he reigned ninety-four years, and all Egypt called his name Pharaoh after the name of his father as it was their custom to do to every king who reigned over them in Egypt.
10. At that time all the troops of Angeas king of Africa went out to spread along the land of Chittim as usual for plunder.
11. And Zepho the son of Eliphaz, the son of Esau, heard their report, and he went out to meet them with his army, and he fought them there in the road.
12. And Zepho struck the troops of the king of Africa with the edge of the sword and left none remaining of them, and not even one returned to his master in Africa.
13. And Angeas heard of this which Zepho the son of Eliphaz had done to all his troops, that he had destroyed them, and Angeas assembled all his troops, all the men of the land of Africa, a people numerous like the sand by the seashore.
14. And Angeas sent to his brother Lucus, saying, "Come to me with all your men and help me to strike Zepho and all the children of Chittim who have destroyed my men," and Lucus came with his whole army, a very great force, to assist his brother Angeas to fight with Zepho and the children of Chittim.
15. And Zepho and the children of Chittim heard this thing, and they were greatly afraid, and a great terror fell on their hearts.
16. And Zepho also sent a letter to the land of Edom to Hadad the son of Bedad king of Edom and to all the children of Esau, saying,
17. "I have heard that Angeas king of Africa is coming to us with his brother for battle against us, and we are greatly afraid of him, for his army is very great, particularly as he comes against us with his brother and his army likewise.
18. Now therefore, come up with me also and help me, and we will fight together against Angeas and his brother Lucus, and you will save us out of their hands, but if not, know that we will all die."
19. And the children of Esau sent a letter to the children of Chittim and to Zepho their king, saying, "We cannot fight against Angeas and his people for a covenant of peace has been between us these many years, from the days of Bela the first king, and from the days of Joseph the son of Jacob, king of Egypt, with whom we fought on the other side of the Jordan when he buried his father."
20. And when Zepho heard the words of his brothers, the children of Esau, he refrained from them, and Zepho was greatly afraid of Angeas.
21. And Angeas and his brother Lucus arrayed all their forces, about eight hundred thousand men, against the children of Chittim.

22. And all the children of Chittim said to Zepho, "Pray for us to the God of your ancestors; perhaps He may deliver us from the hand of Angeas and his army, for we have heard that He is a great God and that He delivers all who trust in Him."
23. And Zepho heard their words, and Zepho sought the LORD, and he said,
24. "O LORD God of my ancestors Abraham and Isaac, this day I know that you are a true God, and all the gods of the nations are vain and useless.
25. Now this day remember for me Your covenant with our father Abraham, which our ancestors related to us, and do graciously with me this day for the sake of our fathers Abraham and Isaac, and save me and the children of Chittim from the hand of the king of Africa who comes against us for battle."
26. And the LORD listened to the voice of Zepho, and He had regard for him on account of Abraham and Isaac, and the LORD delivered Zepho and the children of Chittim from the hand of Angeas and his people.
27. And Zepho fought Angeas king of Africa and all his people on that day, and the LORD gave all the people of Angeas into the hands of the children of Chittim.
28. And the battle was severe on Angeas, and Zepho struck all the men of Angeas and his brother Lucus with the edge of the sword, and there fell from them to the evening of that day about four hundred thousand men.
29. And when Angeas saw that all his men perished, he sent a letter to all the inhabitants of Africa to come to him, to assist him in the battle, and he wrote in the letter, saying, "Let all who are found in Africa come to me from ten years old and upward; let them all come to me, and behold, if he does not come, he will die, and the king will take all that he has, with his whole household."
30. And all the rest of the inhabitants of Africa were terrified at the words of Angeas, and there went out of the city about three hundred thousand men and boys, from ten years upward, and they came to Angeas.
31. And at the end of ten days Angeas renewed the battle against Zepho and the children of Chittim, and the battle was very great and strong between them.
32. And from the army of Angeas and Lucus, Zepho sent many of the wounded to his hand, about two thousand men, and Sosiphtar, the captain of the host of Angeas, fell in that battle.
33. And when Sosiphtar had fallen, the African troops turned their backs to flee, and they fled, and Angeas and his brother Lucus were with them.
34. And Zepho and the children of Chittim pursued them, and they struck them still heavily on the road, about two hundred men, and they pursued Azdrubal the son of Angeas who had fled with his father, and they struck twenty of his men in the road, and Azdrubal escaped from the children of Chittim, and they did not slay him.
35. And Angeas and his brother Lucus fled with the rest of their men, and they escaped and came into Africa with terror and consternation, and Angeas feared all the days lest Zepho the son of Eliphaz should go to war with him.

CHAPTER 64

1. And at that time Balaam, the son of Beor, was with Angeas in the battle, and when he saw that Zepho prevailed over Angeas, he fled and came to Chittim.
2. And Zepho and the children of Chittim received him with great honor, for Zepho knew Balaam's wisdom and gave him many gifts, and Balaam remained with him.
3. And when Zepho returned from the war, he commanded that all the children of Chittim who had gone into battle with him be numbered, and behold, none were missing.
4. And Zepho rejoiced over this and renewed his kingdom, making a feast for all his subjects.
5. But Zepho did not remember the LORD, nor did he consider that the LORD had helped him in battle, delivering him and his people from the hand of the king of Africa. Instead, he walked in the ways of the children of Chittim and the wicked children of Esau, serving other gods as his brothers, the children of Esau, had taught him. Hence it is said, "From the wicked goes out wickedness."
6. And Zepho reigned securely over all the children of Chittim, yet he did not know the LORD, who had delivered him and his people from the hand of the king of Africa. And the troops of Africa no longer came to Chittim to plunder as usual, for they feared the might of Zepho, the son of Eliphaz, and the children of Chittim.
7. At that time, after Zepho returned from the war and saw his victory over the armies of Africa, he consulted with the children of Chittim to go to Egypt and battle the sons of Jacob and Pharaoh, king of Egypt.
8. For Zepho heard that Egypt's mightiest men were dead, and that Joseph and his brothers, the sons of Jacob, were no more, leaving only their descendants in Egypt.
9. Zepho resolved to fight against Egypt and the children of Jacob, seeking revenge for what Joseph, his brothers, and their ancestors had done to Esau's children in Canaan when they went to bury Jacob in Hebron.
10. And Zepho sent messengers to Hadad, son of Bedad, king of Edom, and to all his brothers, the children of Esau, saying,
11. "Did you not declare that you would not fight against the king of Africa, as he is a part of your covenant? Behold, I have fought him and struck him down, along with all his people."
12. "Now I have resolved to fight against Egypt and the children of Jacob who are there, and I will take vengeance for what Joseph, his brothers, and their ancestors did to us in Canaan when they went up to bury their father in Hebron."
13. "Therefore, if you are willing, come and assist me in this battle against Egypt, so that together we may avenge our people."
14. And the children of Esau agreed to Zepho's words and gathered together a great army to join him and the children of Chittim in the war.
15. Zepho also sent word to all the children of the east and to the children of Ishmael, who gathered and came to aid Zepho and the children of Chittim in their battle against Egypt.

16. Thus, the kings of Edom, the children of the east, the children of Ishmael, and Zepho, king of Chittim, gathered their armies and encamped in Hebron.
17. The encampment stretched for three days' journey, as vast as the sands of the seashore, innumerable in number.
18. And all these kings and their armies advanced toward Egypt, camping in the Valley of Pathros.
19. When Egypt heard of their approach, they gathered all the people of the land and from every city, amassing an army of about three hundred thousand men.
20. The Egyptians also sent to the sons of Israel in Goshen, requesting that they join them in battle against these kings.
21. The men of Israel, numbering around one hundred and fifty, went out to aid the Egyptians.
22. Together, the Egyptians and the sons of Israel, a combined force of three hundred thousand and one hundred fifty men, marched out to confront these kings, positioning themselves outside Goshen, facing Pathros.
23. However, the Egyptians were wary of Israel, fearing they might betray them to Esau and Ishmael, who were their kin.
24. Therefore, the Egyptians said to the sons of Israel, "Stay here in your positions, and we will go forth to battle. If we are overcome, then you shall come to our aid." The sons of Israel agreed to this.
25. And Zepho, son of Eliphaz, king of Chittim, and Hadad, son of Bedad, king of Edom, with all their camps, and all the children of the east, and children of Ishmael, encamped in the Valley of Pathros near Tachpanches.
26. Balaam, son of Beor, the Syrian, was also there in the camp of Zepho, having come with the people of Chittim, and he was highly regarded by Zepho and his men.
27. Zepho said to Balaam, "Seek by divination for us so that we may know who shall prevail in this battle, whether we or the Egyptians."
28. Balaam rose to perform the divination, but his efforts were confounded, and his work failed in his hands.
29. He attempted again, but with the same result. Balaam despaired and ceased, for the LORD had intervened, that Zepho and his forces would fall to the sons of Israel, who trusted in the LORD, the God of their ancestors.
30. Zepho and Hadad arranged their forces for battle, while the Egyptians, numbering around three hundred thousand, faced them alone, with no Israelite fighting alongside them.
31. The Egyptians fought these kings in battle near Pathros and Tachpanches, but the struggle proved intense against them.
32. The kings' forces were stronger, and they inflicted heavy losses upon the Egyptians that day, slaying around one hundred and eighty Egyptian men, while thirty men fell from the kings' armies.

33. All of Egypt fled before the kings of Esau and Ishmael, who pursued them towards the Israelite camp.
34. And the Egyptians cried out to the sons of Israel, saying, "Hasten to us and assist us, and save us from the hand of Esau, Ishmael, and the children of Chittim!"
35. And the one hundred and fifty men of Israel leaped from their positions and joined the battle, crying out to the LORD for deliverance.
36. And the LORD heard their plea and delivered the kings into the hand of Israel, who struck down around four thousand of the enemy.
37. The LORD cast a great terror upon the camp of the kings, and they fled before the sons of Israel, who pursued them to the borders of Cush.
38. And Israel struck down another two thousand along the way, while not a single Israelite fell.
39. Seeing the bravery and strength of Israel, the Egyptians trembled for their lives.
40. Every Egyptian man, fearing the might of Israel, hid along the roadways, abandoning the battle and leaving Israel to fight alone.
41. And the sons of Israel continued their pursuit, driving the kings' forces back to the borders of Cush, and they returned in victory.
42. The Israelites saw what the Egyptians had done in abandoning them in battle, and they returned, seeking to settle matters.
43. As they made their way back, they encountered some Egyptians along the road and struck them down.
44. And as they slew them, they said, "Why did you leave us, a few among many, to face these kings and risk our lives while you fled?"
45. Some they met along the way, calling out, "Strike him, for he is an Ishmaelite or an Edomite or a child of Chittim," while they stood over him and confirmed he was Egyptian.
46. And the sons of Israel dealt shrewdly with the Egyptians for abandoning them in battle, leaving them to face the enemy.
47. The Israelites struck down about two hundred Egyptians they encountered on the road in this way.
48. When all the Egyptians saw the Israelites' power and what they had done, they feared Israel greatly, for they had seen their strength and that not one man had fallen.
49. And all the sons of Israel returned with joy on their road to Goshen, while the rest of Egypt each returned to his own place.
50. And thus the sons of Israel returned victorious to their camp, while Egypt lay in fear, having witnessed their might and God's hand upon them.

CHAPTER 65

1. And it came to pass after these things that all the counselors of Pharaoh, king of Egypt, and all the elders of Egypt assembled and came before the king, bowing down to the ground and sitting before him.
2. And the counselors and elders of Egypt spoke to the king, saying,
3. "Behold, the people of the sons of Israel are greater and mightier than we are, and you know all the evil which they did to us on the road when we returned from battle.
4. And you have also seen their great power, for this strength is with them from their fathers; though they were but a few men, they stood up against a people as numerous as the sand and struck them with the edge of the sword, and not one of them has fallen.
5. Therefore, if they had been a larger number, they would surely have utterly destroyed them. Now therefore, give us counsel on what to do with them, lest they become too numerous for us in the land.
6. For if the sons of Israel increase in the land, they may become a hindrance to us; and if any war should happen, they might join our enemies with their strength, fight against us, and drive us out of the land."
7. So the king answered the elders of Egypt and said to them, "This is the plan against Israel, from which we will not depart.
8. Behold, Pithom and Rameses are in the land, cities unfortified against battle; let us build and fortify them.
9. Now therefore, go and act with cunning toward them. Proclaim throughout Egypt and Goshen that the king commands all to help build Pithom and Rameses for protection.
10. Announce to all Egypt, Goshen, Pathros, and the surrounding areas: 'The king has ordered us to fortify Pithom and Rameses against future threats. Any willing to build will receive daily wages from the king.'
11. Therefore, go and cunningly gather yourselves, and come to Pithom and Rameses to build.
12. While they build with you, declare daily throughout Egypt at the king's command, inviting all to join in fortifying these cities.
13. When the sons of Israel come to work for daily wages, pay them for a few days.
14. But afterward, gradually pull yourselves away one by one, until they alone remain in the work.
15. Then, rise as their taskmasters and officers, forcing them to build without wages. Should they refuse, make them work with all your strength."
16. And all the elders of Egypt listened to the counsel of the king, and it pleased them and the servants of Pharaoh, and all Egypt followed the king's command.
17. And all the servants went out from the king and caused a proclamation throughout Egypt, in Tachpanches and Goshen, and in all the surrounding cities, saying,
18. "You have seen what the children of Esau and Ishmael did to us, who came against us in battle and sought to destroy us.

19. Now the king commands us to build Pithom and Rameses and fortify them for battle, should they come against us again.
20. Whoever of Egypt or the sons of Israel will come to build with us shall receive daily wages as commanded by the king."
21. And when Egypt and all the sons of Israel heard what the servants of Pharaoh proclaimed, many came, both Egyptians and Israelites, to build Pithom and Rameses with Pharaoh's servants. However, none of the children of Levi joined their brothers in the work.
22. At first, the servants of Pharaoh and his princes worked with deceit among the Israelites as hired laborers, paying them their wages.
23. And the servants of Pharaoh worked alongside Israel for a month, giving them their daily wages.
24. At the end of the month, Pharaoh's servants gradually withdrew from Israel daily.
25. Israel continued in the work, still receiving wages, as some Egyptians remained to oversee the work and receive their own pay.
26. After a year and four months, all the Egyptians withdrew, leaving only the sons of Israel to continue the labor.
27. The Egyptians, now their oppressors, placed officers over the sons of Israel, enforcing the work without pay, receiving from them all they could.
28. The Egyptians treated the sons of Israel with cruelty, oppressing them in their work.
29. All the sons of Israel worked alone, and the Egyptians ceased paying them from that time onward.
30. When some of Israel refused to work without wages, the overseers and Pharaoh's servants struck them, forcing them to labor with their brothers.
31. Thus, the Egyptians continued to afflict the sons of Israel, who labored without pay, building Pithom and Rameses.
32. The sons of Israel were left to work, making bricks and building fortifications across Egypt, engaged in hard labor for many years until the LORD remembered them and brought them out of Egypt.
33. But the children of Levi did not join in the work with their brothers of Israel, from the beginning until the day of their departure from Egypt.
34. For the children of Levi understood the deceit of the Egyptians and refrained from working with their brothers.
35. Therefore, the Egyptians did not force the children of Levi to work, as they had not been with their brothers at the start, leaving them alone.
36. The hands of Egypt grew heavier against the sons of Israel, making them work with great rigor.
37. The Egyptians embittered the lives of the sons of Israel with hard labor in mortar and bricks, and in all manner of work in the field.

38. And the sons of Israel called Melol, the king of Egypt, "Meror, king of Egypt," because in his days the Egyptians had embittered their lives with all kinds of harsh labor.

CHAPTER 66

1. At that time, Hadad son of Bedad, king of Edom, died. Samlah of Mesrekah, from the region of the eastern tribes, took his place as king.
2. In the thirteenth year of Pharaoh's reign over Egypt, marking the one hundred and twenty-fifth year since Israel's descent into Egypt, Samlah had reigned over Edom for eighteen years.
3. During his reign, Samlah gathered his forces to wage war against Zepho, son of Eliphaz, and the people of Chittim, who had attacked Angeas, king of Africa, and destroyed his army.
4. However, he refrained from engaging with them, as the descendants of Esau dissuaded him, declaring Zepho as their kin. Samlah listened to their plea, turned back with his troops, and did not proceed against Zepho.
5. Pharaoh, the king of Egypt, heard of Samlah's intent to battle the children of Chittim, and feared that he might later turn his forces against Egypt.
6. With this in mind, the Egyptians intensified their demands on the Israelites, fearing they might rise against them as they had aided the Edomites in the days of Hadad.
7. So the Egyptians urged the Israelites, "Hurry with your work, fulfill your duties, and strengthen our land, lest the children of Esau come against us on your account."
8. The Israelites, burdened by heavy labor, worked relentlessly, as the Egyptians continued to oppress them in hopes of weakening their numbers.
9. Yet, the more the Egyptians increased the labor, the more the Israelites grew in number, filling the land of Egypt.
10. In the one hundred and twenty-fifth year of Israel's sojourn in Egypt, the Egyptians saw their plans to reduce Israel's numbers had failed. Instead, the Israelites continued to flourish, filling both Egypt and the land of Goshen.
11. All the elders and wise men of Egypt gathered before the king, bowed before him, and took their seats.
12. They said to the king, "May you live forever! We have followed your counsel against Israel, yet they grow in strength and number, filling the land."
13. "Despite the increased burdens, they thrive even more, and the land is full of them."
14. "Therefore, O king, the people of Egypt look to you for wisdom, to devise a plan that will diminish or even rid the land of Israel."
15. The king replied, "Offer counsel on how we might proceed with this matter."
16. One of the king's advisors, Job from Mesopotamia in the land of Uz, addressed the king, saying, "If it pleases the king, may he listen to the counsel of his servant."
17. The king nodded, and Job continued before the gathered princes and elders.

18. "The king's former counsel concerning the labor imposed on Israel was indeed wise; such tasks should never be removed from them."
19. "Yet, if the king desires further to lessen them, let them face increased hardship."
20. "For a long time, we have feared the possibility of Israel's prosperity leading them to take over this land if war should come."
21. "If it pleases the king, let a decree be written into the laws of Egypt that every male child born to Israel be put to death."
22. "In doing this, once all male offspring are eliminated, Israel's threat of uprising will cease. Let the Hebrew midwives be ordered to carry out this decree."
23. The king and his princes were pleased with Job's counsel, and the king ordered it to be so.
24. Pharaoh summoned the Hebrew midwives, named Shiphrah and Puah, to stand before him.
25. He instructed them, "When you assist the Hebrew women during childbirth, if it is a boy, kill him; if it is a girl, let her live."
26. "But if you disobey, I will burn your homes and all that you possess."
27. The midwives, however, feared God and did not obey Pharaoh's command. When a Hebrew woman gave birth, they tended to the newborn and let it live, despite the king's orders.
28. The news of this disobedience reached Pharaoh, and he summoned the midwives, questioning, "Why have you spared the children?"
29. The midwives answered, "The Hebrew women are not like Egyptian women; they give birth quickly, even before we arrive."
30. "For many days, we have seen that Hebrew women deliver on their own, not needing our assistance, as they are strong."
31. Pharaoh accepted their explanation, and God blessed the midwives for their obedience. Israel's numbers continued to increase and flourish exceedingly.

CHAPTER 67

1. There was a man in Egypt from the line of Levi, named Amram, son of Kohath, son of Levi, son of Israel.
2. Amram took a wife named Jochebed, the daughter of Levi and his own father's sister, who was one hundred and twenty-six years old.
3. Jochebed conceived and bore a daughter, whom she named Miriam, for at that time the Egyptians had made the lives of the Israelites bitter.
4. She conceived again and bore a son, whom she named Aaron, as Pharaoh had begun to kill the sons of Israel at the time of his birth.

5. During these days, Zepho son of Eliphaz, grandson of Esau and king of Chittim, died, and Janeas succeeded him.
6. Zepho had reigned over the people of Chittim for fifty years before his death and was buried in Nabna, a city in Chittim.
7. Janeas, a mighty man among the children of Chittim, succeeded him and reigned for fifty years.
8. After Zepho's death, Balaam son of Beor fled from Chittim to Egypt, where he came to Pharaoh, king of Egypt.
9. Pharaoh welcomed him with great honor, having heard of Balaam's wisdom, and bestowed upon him gifts, appointing him as a royal counselor.
10. Balaam lived in Egypt, receiving honor from the king's nobles, who admired his wisdom.
11. In the one hundred and thirtieth year of Israel's time in Egypt, Pharaoh had a dream while seated on his throne.
12. He saw an old man standing before him with scales in his hands, like those used by merchants.
13. The old man placed all the elders and nobles of Egypt into one side of the scales.
14. In the other scale, he placed a young goat, which weighed more than all the others combined.
15. Pharaoh awoke, astonished at the vision and wondering why the young goat had outweighed them all.
16. Early the next morning, he summoned his servants and recounted the dream to them, causing them great fear.
17. The king commanded his wise men, "Interpret this dream so I may understand its meaning."
18. Balaam, son of Beor, responded to Pharaoh, "This dream foretells a great calamity for Egypt in the days to come."
19. "A child will be born among the Israelites who will bring devastation to Egypt and lead the people of Israel out with great power."
20. "Therefore, O king, consider how to prevent Israel from achieving this hope before it arises."
21. Pharaoh replied, "What can we do against Israel? Every attempt we've made has failed."
22. "Advise us now on a plan that may succeed in overcoming them."
23. Balaam suggested, "Summon your two advisors, and we shall see what counsel they offer. Afterward, I will speak further."
24. The king called for Reuel the Midianite and Job the Uzite, who came and sat before him.
25. Pharaoh said, "You have heard my dream and its interpretation. Now, advise me on how to overcome Israel before they bring harm upon Egypt."
26. Reuel the Midianite responded, "O king, may you live forever."
27. "If it pleases you, do not harm the Hebrews, for they are chosen by the LORD from among all nations."

28. "Whoever has raised a hand against them has suffered, for their God has always avenged them."
29. "Remember how Pharaoh, a former king of Egypt, took Sarah, Abraham's wife, because Abraham claimed she was his sister out of fear for his life."
30. "When that Pharaoh took Sarah, God struck him and his household with severe plagues until he returned Sarah to Abraham."
31. "Likewise, God punished Abimelech, king of the Philistines, by sealing every womb in Gerar when he took Sarah, until he returned her to Abraham."
32. "And when Abimelech sought forgiveness, Abraham prayed for him, and God healed the people of Gerar."
33. "Abimelech feared the God of Abraham and gave him gifts along with Sarah when he returned her."
34. "Later, when Abimelech drove Isaac away, God dried up all the wells of Gerar and stopped the growth of the land's trees."
35. "Abimelech and his allies came to Isaac, seeking his prayer for restoration, which he granted."
36. "Likewise, Jacob was preserved from the hand of Esau and his uncle Laban and from the kings of Canaan who rose against him."
37. "When these kings attacked, the LORD delivered Jacob and his sons from their hands."
38. "The former Pharaoh raised Joseph, Jacob's son, above all princes of Egypt, recognizing his wisdom, which saved Egypt from famine."
39. 3"Pharaoh then invited Jacob and his family to dwell in Egypt, sparing Egypt and Goshen from the famine through their presence."
40. "If it pleases the king, allow Israel to remain or send them to Canaan, where their ancestors dwelled."
41. Hearing Reuel's words, Pharaoh grew angry, dismissed him in shame, and Reuel returned to Midian, taking Joseph's staff with him.
42. Pharaoh then turned to Job, asking, "What is your advice regarding the Hebrews?"
43. Job replied, "All who dwell here are under your rule; let the king act as he sees fit."
44. Pharaoh then asked Balaam, "What do you suggest?"
45. Balaam responded, "No plan will succeed against the Hebrews, for their God will deliver them."
46. "If you try to harm them with fire, God saved Abraham from Ur's flames. If by the sword, God spared Isaac, substituting a ram in his place."
47. "Even through labor, you will not overcome them, for Jacob thrived despite Laban's harsh treatment."
48. "If it pleases the king, order that every male child born to the Hebrews from this day be thrown into the river to erase their name from this land."
49. This counsel pleased the king and his advisors, and Pharaoh decreed it throughout Egypt.

50. He issued a proclamation that every male child born to the Hebrews should be cast into the river, but daughters would be spared.
51. Pharaoh commanded his officers, "Go to Goshen, and ensure that every Hebrew son is thrown into the river."
52. Hearing of Pharaoh's command, some Israelites separated from their wives, while others stayed with them.
53. During childbirth, Israelite women went to the fields to deliver in secret, leaving their newborns there.
54. The LORD, honoring His promise to their ancestors, sent His angels to wash and care for the infants, feeding them with milk and honey.
55. God caused the children's hair to grow to cover them and protect them from the cold.
56. He commanded the earth to keep them safe, where they remained until they grew.
57. When it was time, the earth released the children, and they returned to their families.
58. The children of Israel multiplied on the earth like grass, by God's grace.
59. The Egyptians, witnessing this, plowed their fields to search for the infants, hoping to harm them.
60. Pharaoh's officers continued searching Goshen daily, forcibly taking infants from their mothers and throwing them into the river.
61. But every daughter was spared, and thus the Egyptians oppressed the Israelites all their days.

CHAPTER 68

1. During that time, the Spirit of God came upon Miriam, the daughter of Amram and sister of Aaron. She prophesied about their family, saying, "Look, a son will soon be born to my parents, and he will save Israel from the hands of Egypt."
2. Hearing his daughter's words, Amram took his wife Jochebed back into his house. He had previously separated from her when Pharaoh ordered all male children of Israel to be thrown into the river.
3. Three years after sending her away, Amram reunited with Jochebed, and she conceived a child.
4. After seven months, she bore a son, and the whole house was filled with a brilliant light, like the brightness of the sun and moon at their fullest.
5. Seeing that her child was beautiful and strong, Jochebed hid him for three months in an inner room.
6. During those days, the Egyptians plotted to destroy all the Hebrews in the land.
7. Egyptian women came to Goshen, where the children of Israel lived, carrying their own infants, who were too young to speak, on their shoulders.
8. The women of Israel would secretly deliver their sons, hiding them from the Egyptians so that they wouldn't be discovered and taken.

9. As the Egyptian women came to Goshen, carrying their young ones on their shoulders, they would enter the homes of Hebrew women, where their infants would start crying.
10. Hearing these cries, the hidden children of the Hebrew women would respond, leading the Egyptian women to report this to Pharaoh's household.
11. Pharaoh sent his officers to seize and kill these children, and the Egyptians continued this practice daily with the Hebrew women.
12. About three months after Jochebed hid her son, news of the child reached Pharaoh's court.
13. Hastily, Jochebed took her son, made a basket of reeds, coated it with tar and pitch, and placed the child in it. She then laid it among the reeds by the riverbank.
14. Miriam, the child's sister, stood at a distance to watch what would happen to him, awaiting the fulfillment of her prophecy.
15. At that time, God sent an intense heatwave over Egypt, scorching the flesh of the people like the burning sun, causing great distress among the Egyptians.
16. To escape the oppressive heat, the Egyptians flocked to the river to bathe and cool themselves.
17. Pharaoh's daughter, Bathia, also went down to the river with her attendants to escape the burning heat, alongside many other Egyptian women.
18. Bathia noticed the basket floating on the river and sent her maid to retrieve it.
19. When she opened the basket and saw the baby, the child began to cry. Bathia felt compassion and said, "This must be one of the Hebrew children."
20. The Egyptian women along the river desired to nurse the child, but he refused to suckle, for the LORD intended to return him to his mother's care.
21. Miriam, who was standing among the Egyptian women, saw what had happened and said to Bathia, "Shall I fetch a Hebrew woman to nurse the child for you?"
22. Bathia agreed, saying, "Go." So Miriam went and brought the child's mother.
23. Bathia told Jochebed, "Take this child, nurse him for me, and I will pay you two silver coins daily." So Jochebed took her son and nursed him.
24. When the child was weaned, around two years later, Jochebed brought him back to Bathia, and Bathia raised him as her own son, naming him Moses, saying, "I drew him out of the water."
25. Amram, his father, called him Chabar, explaining, "For him, I reunited with my wife after having sent her away."
26. His mother Jochebed named him Jekuthiel, saying, "I have trusted in the Almighty, and God has returned my child to me."
27. Miriam, his sister, named him Jered, for she had gone down to the river to watch over him and see what would happen.
28. His brother Aaron called him Abi Zanuch, saying, "For my father left my mother but returned for his sake."

29. Kohath, Moses's grandfather, named him Abigdor, saying, "Because of him, God repaired the breach in Israel's household so that their sons would not be cast into the river."
30. His nurse called him Abi Socho, saying, "For he was hidden in his dwelling for three months to protect him from the Egyptians."
31. All of Israel called him Shemaiah, son of Nethanel, saying, "In his days, God has heard our cries and delivered us from our oppressors."
32. Moses was raised in Pharaoh's house and became as a son to Bathia, growing up among the royal children.

CHAPTER 69

1. When the king of Edom died after eighteen years of reign, he was buried in a temple he had built as his royal residence.
2. The children of Esau then sent to Pethor on the river and brought back a handsome young man named Saul to make him king in Samlah's place.
3. Saul reigned over Edom for forty years.
4. Seeing that Balaam's counsel to reduce the Israelites' numbers had failed, and that they continued to multiply in Egypt, Pharaoh issued a new proclamation.
5. The decree commanded that no man would be allowed to lessen his daily work,
6. And if anyone failed to meet his quota, his youngest son would be taken in his place.
7. This intensified the Egyptians' oppression of the Israelites
8. With harsh punishment for anyone failing to complete their daily task.
9. However, the tribe of Levi did not participate in the labor from the beginning, as they recognized the cunning of the Egyptians toward Israel.

CHAPTER 70

1. In the third year after Moses was born, Pharaoh held a banquet. Queen Alparanith sat on his right, Bathia on his left, and young Moses lay on Bathia's lap. Also present were Balaam, son of Beor, with his two sons, and all the princes of the kingdom.
2. During the feast, Moses stretched out his hand, took the crown from Pharaoh's head, and placed it on his own.
3. The king and princes, seeing this act, were filled with fear and looked at each other in astonishment.
4. Pharaoh then asked his princes, "What do you think of this matter, and what should be done to the boy for this act?"
5. Balaam, the magician, answered, "O king, remember the dream you had long ago, and the interpretation given to you."
6. "This child is a Hebrew, filled with the Spirit of God. Do not think he acted without knowledge."

7. "Though he is still young, he possesses wisdom and has claimed Egypt's kingdom for himself by this act."
8. "It is the way of the Hebrews to cunningly cause fear among kings and nobles."
9. "Remember, their forefather Abraham misled the armies of Nimrod, king of Babel, and Abimelech, king of Gerar, and took for himself lands and kingdoms."
10. "He entered Egypt, calling his wife Sarah his sister, misleading Egypt and its king."
11. "Isaac, his son, also did the same in Gerar, prevailing over the Philistine king Abimelech."
12. "He too deceived the king, claiming that his wife Rebekah was his sister."
13. "Jacob, in turn, dealt deceitfully with his brother, taking his birthright and blessing."
14. "He went to Padan-Aram, to his uncle Laban, cunningly obtaining Laban's daughters, cattle, and property, before fleeing back to Canaan."
15. "Jacob's sons also sold their brother Joseph, who was enslaved in Egypt and later imprisoned for twelve years."
16. "But when Pharaoh dreamed troubling dreams, Joseph was freed from prison and exalted above all the princes for his wisdom."
17. "In time, God brought famine to the land, and Joseph brought his family to Egypt, supporting them without payment and enslaving the Egyptians."
18. "Now, this child has risen in their stead to do as they did, troubling kings and princes."
19. "If it pleases the king, let us shed his blood, lest he grow up to take Egypt's throne and end Egypt's hope."
20. Balaam then advised, "Let the king summon Egypt's judges and wise men to see if death is indeed due to this boy, and if so, we will slay him."
21. Pharaoh called all the wise men of Egypt, and a messenger of the LORD, appearing as one of the wise men, joined them.
22. Pharaoh said to the wise men, "You have seen what this Hebrew boy has done. Balaam has given his judgment—now you too must decide."
23. The messenger, posing as one of the wise men, replied, "If it pleases the king, let him place before the child an onyx stone and a burning coal."
24. "If the child reaches for the onyx, we will know he acted with understanding and must be put to death."
25. "But if he reaches for the coal, we will know it was done without wisdom, and he will live."
26. This idea pleased the king and his princes, so Pharaoh ordered the onyx stone and coal to be brought before Moses.
27. The items were placed before the boy, and he reached toward the onyx stone. But the messenger of the LORD guided his hand to the coal.
28. Moses picked up the coal, which extinguished in his hand, and he put it to his mouth, burning his lips and tongue.

29. Seeing this, the king and princes knew Moses had not acted with knowledge in taking Pharaoh's crown.
30. They refrained from killing him, so Moses remained in Pharaoh's household and continued to grow, with the LORD's presence upon him.
31. While living in Pharaoh's house, Moses wore royal garments and grew up among the king's children.
32. As he grew older, Bathia, Pharaoh's daughter, treated Moses as her son, and the entire household respected him.
33. The Egyptians even feared Moses, for they saw the LORD's favor upon him.
34. Daily, Moses would visit the land of Goshen, where the Israelites labored, and witnessed their hardships.
35. One day, he asked the Israelites, "Why is this burden placed upon you every day?"
36. They told him about their suffering and the decrees Pharaoh had placed upon them before his birth.
37. They also revealed Balaam's counsel against them and how he had plotted to kill Moses for taking the crown.
38. Hearing this, Moses grew angry with Balaam and plotted to kill him, lying in wait for him each day.
39. Fearing for his life, Balaam fled Egypt with his two sons and escaped to the land of Cush, seeking refuge with King Kikianus.
40. Meanwhile, Moses continued to live in Pharaoh's house, going out and coming in as he pleased.
41. The LORD granted Moses favor in the sight of Pharaoh, his servants, and all the people of Egypt, who loved him deeply.
42. One day, Moses went to Goshen to see his people and was grieved to see them under such heavy burdens.
43. Returning to Pharaoh, Moses bowed before him and said, "My lord, I have a small request; do not turn me away empty-handed."
44. Pharaoh replied, "Speak."
45. Moses requested, "Allow your servants, the children of Israel in Goshen, one day of rest each week from their labors."
46. Pharaoh agreed and issued a proclamation throughout Egypt and Goshen.
47. The proclamation stated, "For six days, the sons of Israel shall work, but on the seventh day they shall rest."
48. Moses rejoiced at Pharaoh's decree, and the Israelites followed his command.
49. This decree was from the LORD, for He had begun to remember the children of Israel and sought to deliver them for their ancestors' sake.
50. The LORD was with Moses, and his fame spread throughout Egypt.
51. Moses grew in the esteem of both the Egyptians and the Israelites for his care for his people and his words of peace to Pharaoh.

CHAPTER 71

1. When Moses turned eighteen, he longed to see his parents and went to Goshen. There, he saw an Egyptian beating one of his Hebrew brothers.
2. The beaten man saw Moses and ran to him for help, for Moses was highly respected in Pharaoh's household. He cried, "My lord, save me! This Egyptian attacked me in my home and threatened my life."
3. Angered by this injustice, Moses looked around and, seeing no one else nearby, struck the Egyptian and hid him in the sand, saving the Hebrew.
4. The Hebrew man returned home, while Moses went back to Pharaoh's palace.
5. Upon returning, the Hebrew man considered divorcing his wife, as it was deemed improper in Israel for a man to stay with a defiled wife.
6. The woman told her brothers, who sought to kill the Egyptian attacker. The man fled and escaped their wrath.
7. The next day, Moses went out and saw two Hebrews fighting. He asked the wrongdoer, "Why are you striking your neighbor?"
8. The man replied, "Who made you a prince and judge over us? Do you intend to kill me as you killed the Egyptian?" Moses grew afraid, realizing his deed was known.
9. Pharaoh soon learned of the matter and ordered Moses to be killed. But the LORD's messenger appeared in the likeness of a guard captain, standing before Pharaoh.
10. The messenger took the sword from the guard's hand and beheaded him, causing him to resemble Moses.
11. Taking hold of Moses' hand, the LORD's messenger led him out of Egypt to a place forty days' journey from the borders of Egypt.
12. Only Aaron remained in Egypt, prophesying to the Israelites.
13. Aaron said, "Thus says the LORD God of your fathers: Put away the idols of Egypt and purify yourselves."
14. But the people of Israel resisted Aaron's words, unwilling to listen.
15. The LORD thought to destroy them but remembered His covenant with Abraham, Isaac, and Jacob.
16. During this time, Pharaoh's oppression of Israel increased, crushing them until the day God sent His word and took notice of them.

CHAPTER 72

1. Around this time, a great war erupted between Cush and the eastern tribes of Aram, who had rebelled against their king.

2. Kikianus, king of Cush, led a vast army against Aram and the eastern tribes to subdue them.
3. Before departing, he left Balaam and his two sons to guard the city along with the common people.
4. Kikianus fought Aram and struck down many of their people, capturing prisoners and enforcing tribute.
5. He camped on their land, demanding tribute as usual.
6. Balaam, meanwhile, incited the people of Cush to rebel against Kikianus, planning to prevent his return.
7. The people of Cush agreed, swearing loyalty to Balaam and making him king with his sons as captains.
8. They reinforced the city walls, fortifying it to prepare for Kikianus' return.
9. They dug numerous ditches between the city and the surrounding river, causing the waters to flood.
10. They gathered serpents through enchantments, further securing the city, allowing no one to enter or leave.
11. Kikianus successfully subdued Aram and exacted tribute, then returned to his land.
12. Approaching the city, Kikianus and his captains saw the fortified walls and were astonished.
13. They said, "The people must have feared our delay and fortified the walls against potential attackers."
14. The king and troops advanced to the city gate, calling for entry.
15. But the guards, following Balaam's orders, refused to open the gates.
16. Kikianus' forces attacked the gate, losing one hundred and thirty men.
17. The next day, they tried to cross the river, but many were lost in the pits.
18. Kikianus ordered rafts built to cross, but two hundred men drowned in the swirling waters.
19. On the third day, they approached the serpents' corner, but one hundred and seventy men perished.
20. Seeing no progress, Kikianus besieged the city for nine years.
21. During the siege, Moses fled Egypt to escape Pharaoh's wrath.
22. Moses, then eighteen, arrived at Kikianus' camp, which still surrounded Cush.
23. Moses spent nine years with Kikianus' army, gaining favor for his strength, wisdom, and courage.
24. The king and captains admired Moses, valuing his counsel.
25. After nine years, Kikianus fell ill and died on the seventh day.
26. His servants embalmed him, burying him at the city gate.
27. A grand structure was built over his grave, with inscriptions of his deeds.
28. These inscriptions remain to this day.
29. After Kikianus' death, his army mourned deeply.

30. They debated their next move, fearing the siege or a hostile attack.
31. They considered retreat, fearing they might perish without leadership.
32. They feared that without a king, their enemies might attack and leave no survivors.
33. They decided to choose a king to lead them, continuing the siege.
34. Searching among Kikianus' army, they found none as fit as Moses to lead them.
35. They cast their garments before him, declaring him their new king.
36. Trumpets were blown, and they shouted, "Long live the king!"
37. Moses was given Adoniah, Kikianus' widow, as a wife, and he became king of Cush.
38. The people decreed each man to give Moses a gift from his possessions.
39. They spread a sheet on the ground, and the people contributed gold, coins, and jewels.
40. Onyx stones, pearls, silver, and gold filled the heap.
41. Moses took the treasures, adding them to his own.
42. Thus, Moses reigned over Cush in Kikianus' place.

CHAPTER 73

1. In the fifty-fifth year of Pharaoh's reign over Egypt, which marked the one hundred and fifty-seventh year since the Israelites came into Egypt, Moses reigned over Cush.
2. Moses was twenty-seven years old when he began his reign over Cush, and he ruled for forty years.
3. The LORD granted Moses favor and grace in the eyes of the people of Cush, and they loved him exceedingly. Thus, Moses was blessed by both God and man.
4. On the seventh day of his reign, all the people of Cush assembled, came before Moses, and bowed to him on the ground.
5. They spoke together in the king's presence, saying, "Advise us on what should be done to take the city."
6. "It has been nine years that we have besieged this city without seeing our wives and children."
7. The king replied, "If you will heed my commands, the LORD will deliver the city into our hands, and we will take it."
8. "If we fight them as before, many will be wounded or die, as happened before the death of Kikianus."
9. "Here is counsel for you: if you follow my advice, the city will be delivered into our hands."
10. The people answered the king, "We will do all that our lord commands."
11. Moses then said, "Proclaim throughout the camp that the king commands each man to go to the forest and bring back a young stork in his hand."
12. "Anyone disobeying the king's command shall die, and his possessions will be taken by the king."
13. "When you have brought them, you shall care for them, rear them to maturity, and teach them to swoop like hawks."

14. All the people of Cush heard Moses' words and caused a proclamation to go forth throughout the camp.
15. The proclamation stated, "All the children of Cush must go to the forest together and catch the young storks, each bringing one in his hand."
16. "Anyone violating the king's order shall die, and his possessions shall be taken by the king."
17. The people obeyed, went to the forest, climbed fir trees, and each brought back a young stork.
18. They took them to the desert and reared them, teaching them to swoop like hawks.
19. When the storks were fully grown, the king commanded them to starve the birds for three days, and the people obeyed.
20. On the third day, Moses instructed them, "Strengthen yourselves, gird on your armor, mount your horses, and each man take his stork in hand."
21. "We shall go to the place where the serpents are and fight against the city." The people did as Moses commanded.
22. Each man took his stork in hand, and they went to the place of the serpents. Moses instructed, "Release your storks upon the serpents."
23. The storks attacked the serpents, devouring and destroying them all.
24. When the people saw that the serpents were eliminated, they raised a great shout.
25. They advanced, fought against the city, and captured it, subduing all within.
26. On that day, one thousand one hundred men of the city's inhabitants died, but not a single man of the besieging army was lost.
27. The people of Cush returned to their homes, to their wives, children, and belongings.
28. When Balaam, the magician, saw the city taken, he opened the gates and fled with his sons and eight brothers back to Egypt, to Pharaoh.
29. These are the sorcerers and magicians later mentioned in the Law, who opposed Moses during the plagues of Egypt.
30. By his wisdom, Moses took the city, and the people of Cush placed him on the throne as king in place of Kikianus.
31. They set the royal crown on Moses' head and gave him Adoniah, the Cushite queen, as his wife.
32. However, Moses feared the LORD and did not approach her nor turn his eyes toward her.
33. Moses remembered Abraham's oath to his servant Eliezer, that he would not take a Canaanite wife for Isaac.
34. He also recalled how Isaac commanded Jacob not to marry a Canaanite or make alliances with Ham's children.
35. For the LORD gave Ham and his descendants as servants to Shem and Japheth's children.
36. Moses refrained from Adoniah all the days of his reign in Cush.

37. Moses feared the LORD his entire life, walking in truth and with his whole heart and soul, never turning from the righteous path.
38. He strengthened his rule over Cush, guiding them with wisdom, and prospered in his kingdom.
39. During this time, Aram and the children of the east heard of Kikianus' death and rebelled against Cush.
40. Moses gathered a mighty force of thirty thousand men of Cush and went to battle against Aram and the eastern tribes.
41. First, they engaged the children of the east, who met them in battle.
42. The war was fierce, but the LORD delivered the eastern tribes into Moses' hand, with three hundred men falling slain.
43. The eastern tribes retreated, and Moses and his army pursued and subdued them, imposing tribute as was customary.
44. They then turned toward Aram for battle.
45. The people of Aram met them in battle, and the LORD delivered them into Moses' hands, with many men of Aram falling wounded.
46. Aram, too, was subdued by Moses and the people of Cush, and they paid tribute as usual.
47. Moses brought both Aram and the eastern tribes under Cush's authority and returned to Cush.
48. Moses strengthened his rule over Cush, with the LORD supporting him, and all the people of Cush feared him.

CHAPTER 74

1. In the final years of Saul, king of Edom, he died, and Ba'al Chanan, son of Achbor, reigned in his place.
2. In the sixteenth year of Moses' reign over Cush, Ba'al Chanan reigned over Edom for thirty-eight years.
3. During his reign, Moab rebelled against Edom, having been under Edom's rule since Hadad, son of Bedad, subdued both Moab and Midian.
4. When Ba'al Chanan became king of Edom, all the children of Moab withdrew their allegiance.
5. Angeas, king of Africa, also died around this time, and his son Azdrubal reigned in his place.
6. In those days, Janeas, king of the children of Chittim, died and was buried in the temple he had built in Canopia. Latinus succeeded him as king.
7. In the twenty-second year of Moses' reign over Cush, Latinus began his forty-five-year reign over Chittim.
8. Latinus built a large and fortified tower as his residence, establishing it as his seat of government.

9. In the third year of his reign, he called upon skilled craftsmen to construct numerous ships for him.
10. Latinus assembled all his forces, boarded the ships, and set sail to wage war against Azdrubal, king of Africa.
11. Arriving in Africa, Latinus engaged Azdrubal's forces in battle and overpowered him, taking control of an aqueduct that Azdrubal's father had obtained through marriage.
12. Latinus destroyed the aqueduct bridge and inflicted a severe defeat on Azdrubal's army.
13. Azdrubal's remaining warriors, filled with envy and courage, resumed the battle with Latinus, seeking death over surrender.
14. The battle was fierce, and many Africans fell before Latinus and his troops. Azdrubal, too, perished in the conflict.
15. Azdrubal had a beautiful daughter named Ushpezena, whose likeness was embroidered on the garments of African soldiers as a mark of admiration.
16. The men of Latinus saw Ushpezena and praised her beauty to Latinus, who ordered her to be brought to him as a wife.
17. Latinus took Ushpezena as his wife and then returned to Chittim with her.
18. After Azdrubal's death, the people of Africa appointed Anibal, the younger brother of Azdrubal, as king.
19. Anibal, determined to avenge his brother and people, gathered an army and prepared to attack Chittim.
20. Anibal launched an assault on Chittim, leading his forces with great vigor, and struck the people of Chittim with heavy casualties.
21. For eighteen years, Anibal continued to wage war against Chittim, occupying their land and maintaining a stronghold there.
22. Anibal severely weakened Chittim, killing many of its leaders and people, and returned to Africa victorious after long years of conflict.
23. Anibal reigned peacefully in Africa, taking the throne in place of his brother Azdrubal.

CHAPTER 75

1. In the one hundred and eightieth year since the Israelites entered Egypt, thirty thousand warriors from the tribe of Joseph left Egypt.
2. These men believed that the time appointed by the LORD to deliver Israel, as foretold to Abraham, had arrived.
3. Each warrior girded his sword and armor, relying on his strength, and set out from Egypt with confidence.
4. They brought silver and gold but no provisions, assuming they could purchase food from the Philistines or take it by force if necessary.
5. These men were mighty warriors, each capable of defeating a thousand enemies, confident in their strength as they set forth.

6. Their journey took them toward the land of Gath, where they encountered shepherds tending the flocks of Gath.
7. They said to the shepherds, "Give us sheep for food, for we are hungry and have eaten nothing today."
8. The shepherds replied, "These are not our sheep to give, even for payment." The children of Ephraim then tried to seize the flocks by force.
9. The shepherds cried out, alerting the people of Gath, who gathered to confront the Ephraimites.
10. When the men of Gath saw the children of Ephraim attempting to take the sheep, they armed themselves and prepared for battle.
11. The battle took place in the Valley of Gath, with both sides suffering heavy casualties.
12. On the second day, the people of Gath sent messengers to the cities of the Philistines, asking for reinforcements.
13. They requested, "Come help us repel the Ephraimites, who have come from Egypt to steal our cattle and wage war against us."
14. Exhausted from hunger and thirst after three days without food, the children of Ephraim faced an overwhelming force of forty thousand Philistines.
15. The Philistines engaged the Ephraimites in battle, and the LORD delivered the Ephraimites into their hands.
16. The Philistines killed all the Ephraimites who had left Egypt, sparing only ten men who escaped the slaughter.
17. This disaster befell the Ephraimites because they had disregarded the LORD's command, leaving Egypt before the appointed time.
18. The Philistines also suffered casualties, with twenty thousand men killed. The bodies of the fallen were carried back to their cities for burial.
19. The slain Ephraimites were left unburied in the Valley of Gath for many years, leaving the valley littered with bones.
20. The few survivors returned to Egypt and informed the Israelites of all that had happened.
21. Ephraim, the father of the slain men, mourned deeply, and his brothers came to console him.
22. Ephraim went to his wife, who bore a son named Beriah, as she had experienced great sorrow in their household.

CHAPTER 76

1. Moses, son of Amram, continued to reign over Cush and governed with justice, righteousness, and integrity.
2. All the people of Cush loved Moses,
3. And the entire land revered him throughout his reign.
4. In the fortieth year of Moses' reign,
5. He sat on the throne with Adoniah, the queen, and all the nobles before him.

6. Adoniah said, "Why have you, the people of Cush, allowed this man to rule for so long?"
7. "You know that during his forty-year reign,
8. He has neither approached me nor worshiped the gods of Cush."
9. "Now, hear me, children of Cush: let this man no longer rule over you, for he is not one of us."
10. "My son Menacrus has come of age; let him reign over you, for it is better to serve your own than a foreigner, a former slave of Egypt's king."
11. The people and nobles of Cush listened to Adoniah's words.
12. They waited until evening
13. Then rose early the next morning to make Menacrus, son of Kikianus, their king.
14. Out of fear of the LORD, they did not harm Moses
15. Remembering their oath to him.
16. The people of Cush gave Moses many gifts and sent him away with great honor.
17. Moses departed from Cush, relinquishing his reign at sixty-six years of age, as the LORD had ordained.
18. Moses journeyed to Midian, avoiding Egypt out of fear of Pharaoh
19. And rested by a well.
20. The seven daughters of Reuel, a Midianite, came to the well to water their father's flocks.
21. They drew water for the flocks, but shepherds of Midian arrived and drove them away.
22. Moses stood up, assisted the daughters, and watered the flock.
23. The daughters returned to Reuel
24. And recounted Moses' help in defending them.
25. They said, "An Egyptian man rescued us from the shepherds and watered our flocks."
26. Reuel asked, "Where is he? Why did you leave him?"
27. Reuel sent for Moses, brought him home, and offered him bread.
28. Moses told Reuel he had fled from Egypt
29. And ruled over Cush for forty years before being honorably dismissed.
30. Reuel, hearing Moses' story, thought to imprison him to gain favor with Cush.
31. Moses was placed in prison for ten years
32. During which Zipporah, Reuel's daughter, secretly provided him with food and water.
33. Meanwhile, Israel remained in Egypt, suffering under harsh labor and oppression.
34. The LORD struck Pharaoh with leprosy as a punishment for his cruelty to Israel.
35. The LORD heard Israel's cry and remembered their suffering
36. But Pharaoh's heart remained hardened.
37. Pharaoh's condition worsened
38. And his magicians suggested he apply the blood of children to his sores for healing.
39. Pharaoh sent his ministers to seize Israelite infants
40. Slaughtering one daily to use their blood for his healing.
41. Pharaoh's cruelty led to the death of three hundred and seventy-five children.
42. However, the LORD did not permit Pharaoh's sores to heal

43. And his illness grew worse.
44. Pharaoh suffered with the affliction for ten years, but his heart remained hardened against Israel.
45. At the end of ten years, the LORD intensified Pharaoh's affliction, causing tumors and boils.
46. Two of Pharaoh's ministers reported that Israel was neglecting their work due to his illness.
47. Angered, Pharaoh decided to visit Goshen himself to confront Israel
48. Though he could barely ride due to his suffering.
49. Upon reaching a narrow road near a vineyard, his chariot overturned, and he fell, breaking his bones.
50. Realizing his death was imminent, he was carried back to Egypt.
51. Pharaoh's wife and nobles wept for him
52. And they urged him to appoint a successor.
53. Pharaoh had three sons, Othri, Adikam, and Morion, and two daughters, Bathia and Acuzi.
54. Othri, the eldest, was inept
55. While Adikam was wise but short-statured.
56. Pharaoh chose Adikam to succeed him.
57. Adikam, married to Gedudah, had four sons
58. And later took three more wives, fathering eight more children.
59. Pharaoh's illness worsened
60. And his body became putrid, so they buried him hastily.
61. This was a punishment from the LORD for Pharaoh's cruelty to Israel.
62. Pharaoh died in shame, and his son Adikam reigned in his place.

CHAPTER 77

1. Adikam was twenty years old when he began to reign over Egypt, and he reigned for four years.
2. In the two hundred and sixth year of Israel's time in Egypt, Adikam ascended the throne, but his reign was shorter than those of his predecessors.
3. His father Melol reigned ninety-four years in Egypt, but he suffered illness for ten years and died, for he had been wicked before the LORD.
4. As was customary, the Egyptians called Adikam "Pharaoh," following the tradition of naming their kings.
5. The wise men in Pharaoh's court referred to Adikam as "Ahuz," which was a shortened version of his name in the Egyptian language.
6. Adikam was exceedingly unattractive; he stood at a cubit and a span in height and had a beard that reached the soles of his feet.

7. Adikam sat on his father's throne to rule over Egypt and exercised his governance with wisdom.
8. During his reign, he surpassed his father and all previous kings in wickedness, intensifying the yoke over the children of Israel.
9. Adikam went with his servants to Goshen to visit the children of Israel and commanded them to complete their daily tasks without fail, warning them against any slackness.
10. He appointed officers from among the Israelites to oversee the labor, with Egyptian taskmasters placed above them.
11. Each day, the taskmasters demanded a specific number of bricks from the Israelites, as directed by Adikam, and then returned to Egypt.
12. The taskmasters enforced Pharaoh's command, instructing the Israelite officers to meet the daily requirement without any reduction.
13. Pharaoh declared, "If you are deficient in your daily bricks, I will place your young children in their stead."
14. The taskmasters strictly followed these orders, ensuring that the Israelites fulfilled their quotas.
15. Whenever there was a shortfall, the taskmasters would seize Israelite infants to replace the missing bricks, taking them from their mothers' laps.
16. Fathers and mothers wept as they heard their children crying from within the walls, their infants entombed in the construction bricks.
17. The taskmasters forced the Israelites to place their children in the walls, compelling them to cover their own offspring with mortar as their eyes wept.
18. This brutality continued for many days, with no one showing mercy to the suffering families of Israel.
19. In total, two hundred and seventy children were either walled in or pulled from the construction, sacrificed to meet the labor demands.
20. The Israelites' labor under Adikam was far more severe and oppressive than during his father's reign.
21. Each day, the people of Israel sighed under the weight of their burdens, longing for deliverance.
22. They had once believed that Adikam's reign would bring them relief, but now their suffering was even greater.
23. Their sighs and cries rose up to God as they struggled under the increased labor.
24. In those days, God heard the cries of the Israelites and remembered His covenant with Abraham, Isaac, and Jacob.
25. Seeing their affliction, God resolved to deliver His people.
26. Moses, the son of Amram, was still confined in the dungeon of Reuel the Midianite, but Reuel's daughter Zipporah secretly supported him with food.
27. Moses had been imprisoned in the dungeon for ten years.

28. At the end of this time, which was the first year of Pharaoh's reign, Zipporah spoke to her father about Moses.
29. She asked, "No one has inquired after the Hebrew man you confined for ten years. Should we not see whether he lives?"
30. Reuel replied, "How could anyone survive in prison for ten years without food?"
31. Zipporah, who had secretly sustained Moses, answered, "The God of the Hebrews is mighty and does wonders for His people."
32. She reminded her father of stories of God's deliverance, such as His saving of Abraham, Isaac, and Jacob.
33. Zipporah explained how God had rescued Moses from various dangers in Egypt and beyond.
34. Reuel, persuaded by her words, agreed to send someone to check on Moses in the dungeon.
35. When they found him, Moses was alive, standing and praising God.
36. Reuel ordered Moses to be released, and they shaved and clothed him.
37. Moses then went into Reuel's garden to pray, giving thanks to God for his survival.
38. While praying in the garden, Moses noticed a stick planted in the ground with the Name of the LORD inscribed upon it.
39. He read the inscription, took hold of the stick, and pulled it from the earth.
40. This was the very stick used in God's works since the creation of the world.
41. Adam had taken this stick when he left Eden, and it had passed down through Noah, Shem, and Abraham.
42. The stick traveled from Isaac to Jacob, who took it to Egypt, and from Joseph to Reuel in Midian.
43. Many men in Midian had tried to pull it from the ground but were unsuccessful.
44. When Reuel saw the stick in Moses' hand, he marveled and gave him his daughter Zipporah in marriage.
45. Moses took Zipporah as his wife and lived with Reuel, his father-in-law.
46. God blessed Moses and gave him favor in the sight of Reuel and the people of Midian.
47. The LORD prepared Moses for the mission he would soon undertake to deliver the Israelites from Egypt.
48. Moses grew in strength, wisdom, and favor with both God and man.
49. Reuel was pleased with Moses and honored him for his righteousness.
50. Moses began to fulfill his purpose under God's guidance, awaiting the appointed time for his calling.
51. And thus, God was with Moses, preparing him for the task that lay ahead in delivering His people.

CHAPTER 78

1. Ba'al Channan, son of Achbor, king of Edom, passed away, and he was buried in his home in the land of Edom.
2. Following his death, the children of Esau traveled to Edom and selected a man from among them named Hadad, appointing him as king in Ba'al Channan's place.
3. Hadad reigned over the people of Edom for forty-eight years.
4. When he became king, Hadad set his sights on waging war against the children of Moab, intending to bring them back under the authority of Edom.
5. However, the children of Moab learned of Hadad's intentions and quickly gathered a great assembly to strengthen their defenses.
6. Moab called upon their allies, the children of Ammon, to join them in standing against Hadad, king of Edom.
7. Hadad, upon hearing of Moab's preparations and their alliance with Ammon, grew fearful and abandoned his plan to attack.
8. During this period, Moses, the son of Amram, married Zipporah, the daughter of Reuel, the Midianite, while residing in Midian.
9. Zipporah, like the matriarchs Sarah, Rebekah, Rachel, and Leah, was upright in her character and walked in the ways of Jacob's daughters.
10. Zipporah bore Moses a son, and he named him Gershom, saying, "I have been a stranger in a foreign land."
11. However, Moses did not circumcise Gershom, as Reuel had instructed him not to do so.
12. Zipporah later bore another son, and this time she circumcised him, and Moses named him Eliezer, declaring, "The God of my fathers was my help, delivering me from Pharaoh's sword."
13. Meanwhile, Pharaoh, king of Egypt, continued to oppress the Israelites, increasing the difficulty of their labor.
14. Pharaoh issued a decree in Egypt, proclaiming that no more straw would be given to the Israelites for making bricks.
15. They were commanded to gather straw on their own, yet still expected to meet their daily brick quota without reduction.
16. The children of Israel, heavily burdened by this decree, cried out to the LORD in their anguish. The LORD heard their cries and saw their suffering, remembering His covenant with Abraham, Isaac, and Jacob.

CHAPTER 79

1. Moses was tending the flock of Reuel, his father-in-law, the Midianite, beyond the wilderness of Sin, carrying the staff he had taken from Reuel.
2. One day, a kid from the flock wandered, and Moses followed it, reaching the mountain of God, Horeb.
3. At Horeb, the LORD appeared to him in a burning bush, which was not consumed by the fire.

4. Astonished, Moses drew closer to observe, and the LORD called to him from the fire, commanding him to go to Pharaoh and bring the Israelites out of Egypt.
5. The LORD instructed Moses to return to Egypt, saying, "All those who sought your life are now dead."
6. The LORD commanded him to perform signs and wonders in Egypt so that Pharaoh and his people might believe he was sent by God.
7. Moses obeyed and returned to his father-in-law Reuel, telling him all that the LORD had commanded, and Reuel said, "Go in peace."
8. Moses set out for Egypt, taking his wife and sons with him; at an inn along the way, a messenger of the LORD sought an occasion against him.
9. The messenger intended to kill Moses because he had not circumcised his firstborn son, violating the covenant established with Abraham.
10. Moses had followed his father-in-law's words and did not circumcise his son Gershom.
11. Seeing the danger, Zipporah took a sharp stone and circumcised her son, thus delivering Moses from the hand of the messenger.
12. Aaron, Moses' brother, was in Egypt by the riverside when the LORD appeared to him, instructing him to go meet Moses in the wilderness.
13. Aaron obeyed and met Moses at the mountain of God, embracing him warmly.
14. Aaron saw Moses' wife and children and asked, "Who are these to you?"
15. Moses replied, "They are my wife and sons, whom God gave me in Midian," which grieved Aaron on account of their presence.
16. Aaron urged Moses, "Send them back to her father's house," and Moses agreed, sending Zipporah and her sons back to Reuel.
17. Zipporah and her children stayed with Reuel until the LORD delivered the Israelites from Egypt.
18. Moses and Aaron went to the Israelites in Egypt, relaying all the words of the LORD, and the people rejoiced greatly.
19. The next morning, Moses and Aaron went to Pharaoh's palace, carrying the staff of God.
20. At the king's gate, they encountered two lions bound with iron; no one entered unless the magicians subdued the lions with their spells.
21. Moses raised his staff, releasing the lions, who followed him and Aaron joyfully into the palace, like a dog to its master.
22. Seeing this, Pharaoh was astonished and greatly afraid, perceiving them as children of God.
23. Pharaoh asked, "What do you seek?" and they answered, "The LORD God of the Hebrews has sent us to demand the release of His people."
24. Pharaoh, terrified, said, "Return tomorrow," and Moses and Aaron left as he commanded.
25. That evening, Pharaoh summoned Balaam, Jannes, and Jambres, along with his magicians and counselors, to discuss Moses and Aaron's demand.

26. Pharaoh recounted the lions' release, and the magicians questioned how this was possible without enchantments.
27. Pharaoh explained that Moses raised his staff and the lions followed them as loyal pets.
28. Balaam responded, "They are mere magicians like ourselves."
29. Pharaoh agreed, saying, "Bring them tomorrow so we may test them," and ordered their return.
30. The next day, Moses and Aaron again presented themselves before Pharaoh, holding the staff of God, and repeated their demand.
31. Pharaoh challenged them, saying, "Prove that you are sent by God."
32. Aaron threw down his staff, and it transformed into a serpent before Pharaoh and his servants.
33. The magicians threw their own staffs, and each turned into a serpent.
34. However, Aaron's serpent lifted its head and swallowed the serpents of the magicians.
35. Balaam observed and said, "This is merely a serpent devouring another; it proves nothing."
36. He suggested they each retrieve their rods, which returned to their original form.
37. When Aaron's staff swallowed the others, Pharaoh ordered the scrolls recording the gods of Egypt to be brought, seeking the name of the LORD among them.
38. Failing to find the Name, Pharaoh declared, "I do not know this LORD of whom you speak."
39. His counselors advised, "The God of the Hebrews is merely a wise son of ancient kings."
40. Pharaoh dismissed Moses and Aaron, saying, "I do not know your God, nor will I release His people."
41. Moses and Aaron replied, "The LORD God of gods has sent us, commanding, 'Let My people go to worship Me.'"
42. They warned that if Pharaoh refused, God would strike Egypt with plagues or the sword.
43. Pharaoh replied, "Show me His power, for I created my own river."
44. Angered by their words, Pharaoh dismissed them and ordered harsher labor upon the Israelites.
45. Moses, seeing the Israelites' suffering, returned to the LORD, asking, "Why have You sent me, only to increase their burden?"
46. The LORD reassured Moses, saying, "Soon you will witness Pharaoh releasing My people by My mighty hand."
47. Moses and Aaron remained with the Israelites, who continued to endure severe oppression by the Egyptians.
48. Pharaoh then summoned his magicians again and discussed the signs Moses performed, but they still doubted his divine power.
49. Balaam advised Pharaoh to increase the burdens on the Israelites, thinking this would suppress any hope of deliverance.

50. Pharaoh ordered that no straw be provided to the Israelites, making their labor even harder.
51. The Israelites groaned under the weight of this new demand, and their cries grew louder.
52. Many began to lose faith, questioning Moses and Aaron's promises of deliverance.
53. Moses again sought the LORD, who assured him that Pharaoh's heart would harden before God's wonders were displayed.
54. The LORD instructed Moses to remain faithful, promising that His hand would be strong against Egypt.
55. Aaron comforted the Israelites, reminding them of God's covenant and the promises given to Abraham, Isaac, and Jacob.
56. The Israelites, though weary, took hope in Aaron's words, trusting that God would indeed rescue them from bondage.
57. Thus, Moses and Aaron prepared to reveal God's wonders before Pharaoh, waiting for the LORD's timing to fulfill His mighty plan.

CHAPTER 80

1. At the end of two years, the LORD sent Moses to Pharaoh again to bring out the sons of Israel and lead them from the land of Egypt.
2. Moses went to Pharaoh's house and spoke the words of the LORD, but Pharaoh would not listen, and God stirred His might against Pharaoh and his people, striking them with severe plagues.
3. The LORD sent Aaron, and all the waters of Egypt, their streams and rivers, were turned to blood.
4. When an Egyptian came to drink or draw water, he found his pitcher filled with blood, and even the water in his cup became blood.
5. When a woman kneaded her dough and prepared food, it too took on the appearance of blood.
6. The LORD sent another plague, filling Egypt with frogs, which entered every Egyptian's house.
7. As they drank, their bellies were filled with frogs, which danced inside them as if in the river.
8. All the drinking and cooking water turned to frogs; even in bed, the Egyptians found their sweat breeding frogs.
9. Yet, the LORD's anger did not subside, and His hand remained stretched out over Egypt to strike them with severe plagues.
10. He struck their dust, turning it into lice, which spread across Egypt to the height of two cubits on the ground.
11. Lice covered man and beast, even the king and queen, filling all of Egypt with misery.
12. Still, the LORD's anger did not turn away, and His hand was yet stretched out over Egypt.

13. The LORD sent all kinds of wild animals into Egypt, destroying the land, harming people, animals, trees, and all that was in Egypt.
14. Fiery serpents, scorpions, mice, weasels, toads, and other crawling creatures invaded the land.
15. Flies, hornets, fleas, bugs, and gnats, each swarm according to its kind, came upon Egypt.
16. Reptiles and winged animals overran the Egyptians, grieving them exceedingly.
17. Flies and fleas crawled into their eyes and ears.
18. The hornets attacked them, driving them to hide in their homes, but still pursued them inside.
19. When the Egyptians locked themselves away from the swarming creatures, God summoned the Sulanuth from the sea to invade Egypt.
20. Sulanuth, with arms ten cubits long, climbed the roofs, tearing down rafters and floors to enter homes.
21. She reached inside houses, removing locks and bolts, allowing other animals to invade.
22. The swarming creatures entered every home, bringing destruction and intense suffering upon the Egyptians.
23. Yet, the LORD's anger did not turn away, and His hand remained stretched over Egypt.
24. God sent a pestilence upon Egypt, afflicting horses, donkeys, camels, herds of oxen, sheep, and people.
25. Each morning, Egyptians found their cattle dead, with only one in ten surviving, while in Goshen, none of Israel's cattle perished.
26. A burning inflammation afflicted the Egyptians, bursting their skin into sores, causing intense itching from their feet to their heads.
27. Boils covered them, causing their flesh to waste away and turn putrid.
28. Yet, the LORD's anger did not turn away, and His hand continued to be stretched over Egypt.
29. The LORD sent heavy hail, shattering their vines and fruit trees, drying them up and causing them to fall.
30. Every green herb withered, as mingled fire descended with the hail, consuming all.
31. Men and beasts caught outside perished in the flames of hail and fire; even young lions were exhausted.
32. The LORD sent a plague of locusts—the Chasel, Salom, Chargol, and Chagole—devouring what the hail had left.
33. Although the locusts consumed the crops, the Egyptians rejoiced, capturing and salting them as food.
34. But the LORD brought a strong sea wind, carrying away all the locusts, including the salted ones, casting them into the Red Sea; none remained in Egypt.
35. God sent darkness over Egypt, blanketing the land of Egypt and Pathros in thick darkness for three days.
36. So dense was the darkness that no one could see their own hand lifted to their mouth.

37. During this time, many rebellious Israelites who had rejected Moses and Aaron's guidance died.
38. These people had refused to believe, saying, "We will not leave Egypt lest we starve in the wilderness."
39. The LORD plagued these rebellious ones during the three days of darkness, and the Israelites buried them in secret so the Egyptians would not know or rejoice.
40. The darkness over Egypt lasted three days, immobilizing all Egyptians, each person frozen where they were when darkness struck.
41. Once the darkness lifted, the LORD instructed Moses and Aaron to tell the Israelites to prepare for the Passover.
42. He said, "I will pass through Egypt at midnight, striking all their firstborn, both human and animal, but when I see the Passover sign, I will pass over you."
43. The Israelites did as the LORD commanded Moses and Aaron, preparing themselves that night.
44. In the middle of the night, the LORD struck down all the firstborn in Egypt, from the firstborn of men to that of animals.
45. Pharaoh awoke in the night, along with his servants and all Egyptians, and there was great mourning throughout Egypt, for every household had lost someone.
46. Even the images of the firstborn, carved on the walls of Egyptian homes, fell and broke apart.
47. The bones of Egypt's previously deceased firstborn, buried in their houses, were unearthed by dogs and scattered before their families.
48. Every Egyptian family mourned that night, each grieving for a lost son or daughter, filling the land with sorrowful cries.
49. Bathia, Pharaoh's daughter, accompanied the king that night to seek Moses and Aaron among the Israelites.
50. She found them celebrating with the Israelites, eating and drinking joyfully.
51. Bathia confronted Moses, saying, "Is this your reward for my kindness to you, who raised and nurtured you, now bringing calamity upon me and my father's house?"
52. Moses replied, "The LORD brought ten plagues upon Egypt. Did any of them harm you?"
53. Bathia answered, "No, they did not."
54. Moses reassured her, "Though you are your mother's firstborn, you shall not die; no harm will befall you in Egypt."
55. She responded, "But what comfort is this when my brother, the king, and all his household suffer so greatly?"
56. Moses answered, "Your brother and his household would not heed the LORD's words, hence this calamity."
57. Pharaoh approached Moses, pleading, "Rise, take your people, along with their flocks and herds, and leave nothing behind. Only pray to the LORD for me."

58. Moses assured Pharaoh, "You will live, though you are your mother's firstborn, for the LORD has commanded that you should see His might and power."
59. Pharaoh ordered the Israelites to be released, and the Egyptians urged them to leave, saying, "We are all perishing."
60. The Egyptians sent Israel out with riches—sheep, oxen, and precious items—as per the LORD's oath to Abraham.
61. The Israelites refused to depart at night, saying, "Are we thieves to leave in darkness?"
62. The Israelites requested silver, gold, and garments from the Egyptians, taking them as the LORD had commanded.
63. Moses rose early, going to the Nile, where he retrieved Joseph's coffin, bringing it with him.

CHAPTER 81

1. The sons of Israel journeyed from Rameses to Succoth, about six hundred thousand men on foot, besides the little ones and their wives.
2. A mixed multitude went up with them, along with flocks, herds, and many cattle.
3. The sons of Israel had sojourned in Egypt, enduring hardship, for two hundred and ten years.
4. At the end of these two hundred and ten years, the LORD brought Israel out of Egypt with a strong hand.
5. The sons of Israel departed from Egypt, leaving Goshen and Rameses, and encamped in Succoth on the fifteenth day of the first month.
6. Meanwhile, the Egyptians buried all their firstborn, whom the LORD had struck down, and mourned for three days.
7. The Israelites traveled from Succoth and encamped at Etham, at the edge of the wilderness.
8. Three days after the Egyptians had buried their firstborn, many of them regretted letting the Israelites go and set out after them to bring them back to Egypt.
9. One Egyptian said to his neighbor, "Did not Moses and Aaron tell Pharaoh that they would go a three-day journey to worship their God?"
10. They decided, "Let us rise early, capture them, and bring them back. If they come willingly, we will know they are loyal; if not, we will fight them and force their return."
11. Pharaoh's nobles and about seven hundred thousand men rose early and pursued Israel, reaching the place where Israel was encamped.
12. The Egyptians saw Moses, Aaron, and all Israel sitting by Pi-Hahiroth, celebrating the feast to the LORD.
13. The Egyptians questioned them, saying, "Did you not say you would journey three days to worship? It is now five days since you left; why have you not returned?"

14. Moses and Aaron replied, "The LORD our God has commanded us never to return to Egypt, but to journey to the land flowing with milk and honey, as promised to our ancestors."
15. Seeing that Israel would not return, the Egyptians prepared to fight them.
16. But the LORD strengthened the hearts of the Israelites, and they fought back with courage, inflicting a severe blow on the Egyptians.
17. The Egyptians fled, and many of them perished by Israel's hand, while the rest returned to Pharaoh to report the situation.
18. Pharaoh and his people's hearts were hardened, and they regretted sending Israel away.
19. Pharaoh's advisors urged him to pursue Israel and bring them back to serve as slaves once more.
20. Each Egyptian said to his neighbor, "What have we done, releasing Israel from our servitude?"
21. The LORD hardened the Egyptians' hearts to pursue Israel, intending to defeat them in the Red Sea.
22. Pharaoh rose and harnessed his chariot, ordering all Egypt's warriors to assemble; none stayed behind except the women and children.
23. A massive camp of Egyptians set out with Pharaoh, one million men strong, to pursue Israel, who were encamped by the Red Sea.
24. The Israelites looked up and saw the Egyptians approaching, and fear filled their hearts, prompting them to cry out to the LORD.
25. Dividing into four groups, Israel had differing ideas on how to respond to the Egyptians. Moses addressed each group.
26. The first group, from Reuben, Simeon, and Issachar, wanted to throw themselves into the sea, fearing the Egyptians' wrath.
27. Moses told them, "Do not fear; stand firm and witness the LORD's salvation today."
28. The second group, from Zebulun, Benjamin, and Naphtali, suggested returning to Egypt with the Egyptians.
29. Moses replied, "Do not fear; as you see the Egyptians today, so you will never see them again."
30. The third group, from Judah and Joseph, wanted to confront the Egyptians in battle.
31. Moses urged them, "Hold your positions, for the LORD will fight for you; you only need to be silent."
32. The fourth group, from Levi, Gad, and Asher, resolved to enter the Egyptians' camp to cause confusion.
33. Moses instructed them to stay put and cry out to the LORD for deliverance.
34. After this, Moses left the people and prayed to the LORD, saying,
35. "O LORD, God of all the earth, save Your people, whom You brought out of Egypt; do not let the Egyptians boast of their strength."

36. The LORD answered Moses, "Why do you cry to Me? Speak to the Israelites and tell them to advance, and stretch out your rod over the sea to divide it, allowing them to pass through."
37. Moses did as instructed, lifting his rod over the sea, which divided into twelve parts for each tribe to cross on dry ground.
38. The LORD performed wonders before Israel in Egypt and at the sea through Moses and Aaron.
39. As Israel entered the sea, the Egyptians followed, but the waters returned and engulfed them, leaving none alive except Pharaoh, who acknowledged the LORD's might and believed.
40. The LORD sent an angel to rescue Pharaoh, who washed ashore and eventually went on to rule over Nineveh for many years.
41. On that day, the LORD saved Israel from Egypt's hand, and Israel saw the Egyptians' destruction, witnessing the LORD's mighty power.
42. Then Moses and Israel sang a song to the LORD, celebrating His triumph over the Egyptians.
43. They sang in unison, "I will sing to the LORD, for He is highly exalted; the horse and its rider He has thrown into the sea," as recorded in the Scroll of the Law.
44. After this, Israel journeyed to Marah, where the LORD provided them with statutes and judgments, instructing them to walk in His ways.
45. From Marah, they moved to Elim, where they found twelve springs and seventy palm trees, camping by the waters.
46. They traveled from Elim to the wilderness of Sin on the fifteenth day of the second month after their departure from Egypt.
47. At that time, the LORD provided Israel with manna, raining down food from heaven daily for them to eat.
48. Israel ate manna for forty years while in the wilderness until they reached the land of Canaan.
49. From the wilderness of Sin, they camped at Alush.
50. From Alush, they journeyed to Rephidim, where Amalek, Esau's grandson, came to battle Israel.
51. Amalek brought with him a vast army, including magicians and warriors, to confront Israel at Rephidim.
52. The battle between Amalek and Israel was fierce, but the LORD delivered Amalek into Moses and Joshua's hands.
53. Israel struck down Amalek and his people with the sword, though the struggle was difficult.
54. The LORD instructed Moses, "Write this as a memorial in a scroll and place it in Joshua's hand, commanding Israel to blot out Amalek's memory from under heaven."

55. Moses obeyed, recording the LORD's command to Israel concerning Amalek's destruction.
56. Moses wrote, "Remember what Amalek did to you on the way out of Egypt,
57. attacking those who lagged behind when you were weary and faint."
58. Therefore, when the LORD your God has given you rest from all your surrounding enemies in the land that He is giving you as an inheritance, you shall blot out the memory of Amalek from under heaven. Do not forget this command."
59. "Any king who shows mercy to Amalek or preserves his memory or his descendants shall be held accountable by Me, and I will cut him off from among his people," says the LORD.
60. Moses wrote all these things in the scroll, recording the LORD's instructions to the people of Israel regarding Amalek.
61. The LORD's command was clear: "Do not let the memory of Amalek remain, for he rose up against you without cause."
62. Moses emphasized to the people, "Remember this command from the LORD, that you may be vigilant in obedience, for His word shall stand."

CHAPTER 82

1. The sons of Israel departed from Rephidim and camped in the wilderness of Sinai in the third month after their exodus from Egypt.
2. At that time, Reuel the Midianite, Moses' father-in-law, arrived with Zipporah, Moses' wife, and her two sons, having heard of the LORD's wonders for Israel in delivering them from Egypt.
3. Reuel came to Moses in the wilderness, where Israel was camped near the mountain of God.
4. Moses, accompanied by all Israel, went out to meet his father-in-law with great respect and honor.
5. Reuel and his children stayed among the Israelites for many days, and from that time onward, Reuel came to know the LORD.
6. In the third month after Israel's departure from Egypt, on the sixth day, the LORD gave Israel the Ten Commandments on Mount Sinai.
7. All Israel heard these commandments and rejoiced exceedingly in the LORD that day.
8. The glory of the LORD settled on Mount Sinai, and He called Moses, who ascended the mountain and entered the midst of a cloud.
9. Moses remained on the mountain for forty days and forty nights, consuming no bread or water, as the LORD instructed him in statutes and judgments to teach Israel.
10. The LORD inscribed the Ten Commandments on two stone tablets, which He gave to Moses to deliver to Israel.
11. After forty days and forty nights, when the LORD had finished speaking to Moses on Mount Sinai, He gave him the tablets, inscribed by the finger of God.

12. Meanwhile, the Israelites, seeing that Moses delayed in returning, gathered around Aaron and said, "As for this Moses who led us from Egypt, we do not know what has happened to him.
13. Rise up, make for us a god to lead us, so that we will not die."
14. Aaron, fearing the people, ordered them to bring him their gold, which he fashioned into a molten calf.
15. The LORD spoke to Moses before he descended, saying, "Go down, for your people, whom you led out of Egypt, have corrupted themselves.
16. They have made a molten calf and are bowing to it. Now, leave Me to consume them, for they are a stiff-necked people."
17. Moses pleaded with the LORD on behalf of the people for their sin with the calf, and afterward, he descended from the mountain carrying the two stone tablets.
18. When Moses neared the camp and saw the calf, his anger burned, and he shattered the tablets at the base of the mountain.
19. He entered the camp, seized the calf, burned it, ground it into fine dust, and scattered it on the water, making the Israelites drink it.
20. About three thousand men who had worshiped the calf perished by the sword that day.
21. The following day, Moses addressed the people, "I will go to the LORD; perhaps I can make atonement for your sin."
22. Moses ascended to the LORD and remained there forty days and nights, interceding for Israel.
23. During those forty days, the LORD listened to Moses' prayer and was moved by his intercession for Israel.
24. Then the LORD instructed Moses to chisel two new stone tablets, and the LORD would inscribe on them the Ten Commandments once more.
25. Moses obeyed, carved two tablets, and ascended Mount Sinai, where the LORD wrote the commandments anew.
26. Moses stayed another forty days and nights with the LORD, learning further statutes and judgments for Israel.
27. The LORD also instructed Moses about constructing a sanctuary where His Name would dwell, showing him its design and all its furnishings.
28. After forty days, Moses descended from the mountain with the two tablets in hand.
29. Moses assembled Israel and shared all the LORD's words, teaching them the laws, statutes, and judgments given to him.
30. He also conveyed the LORD's command to construct a sanctuary for His presence among Israel.
31. The people rejoiced at the LORD's promises and said, "We will do all that the LORD has spoken."
32. United, the people brought generous offerings for the sanctuary's construction, each one giving willingly for the LORD's work.

33. Each man contributed from what he had—gold, silver, brass, and all suitable materials for the sanctuary's construction.
34. Skilled artisans among Israel came together to make the sanctuary and its furnishings according to the LORD's instructions to Moses.
35. In five months, the sanctuary and all its furnishings were completed, just as the LORD had commanded Moses.
36. They presented the sanctuary and its items to Moses, precisely as the LORD had shown him.
37. Moses inspected the work and saw that it was done according to the LORD's command, and he blessed the people.

CHAPTER 83

1. In the twelfth month, on the twenty-third day, Moses took Aaron and his sons, dressed them in their garments, anointed them, and performed all that the LORD had commanded him regarding their consecration.
2. Moses instructed Aaron and his sons, "For seven days, you will remain at the door of the Dwelling Place, for this is the LORD's command."
3. Aaron and his sons did as the LORD had commanded through Moses, remaining at the door of the Dwelling Place for seven days.
4. On the eighth day, which was the first day of the first month in the second year since the Israelites left Egypt, Moses erected the sanctuary and arranged all the furniture within it.
5. Moses called Aaron and his sons to offer the burnt offering and the sin offering for themselves and the Israelites, as the LORD had instructed.
6. On that day, Nadab and Abihu, the sons of Aaron, brought strange fire before the LORD, which He had not commanded, and a fire went out from the LORD and consumed them, and they died.
7. After the sanctuary was erected, the princes of the tribes of Israel began presenting offerings for the dedication of the altar.
8. Each prince brought offerings over the span of twelve days, with one prince offering each day.
9. Each offering included one silver charger weighing one hundred thirty shekels, one silver bowl weighing seventy shekels, filled with fine flour mixed with oil for a grain offering,
10. one golden spoon weighing ten shekels filled with incense,
11. one young bull, one ram, and one lamb of the first year for a burnt offering,
12. and one goat for a sin offering.
13. For the peace offering, each prince brought two oxen, five rams, five male goats, and five yearling lambs.
14. Thus, each of the twelve princes of Israel brought their offerings on their respective days.
15. Afterward, on the thirteenth day of the month, Moses commanded the Israelites to observe the Passover.

16. The Israelites kept the Passover on the fourteenth day of the month as the LORD had commanded Moses.
17. On the first day of the second month, the LORD spoke to Moses, instructing him to count all the men of Israel twenty years old and older, alongside Aaron and the twelve tribal princes.
18. Moses obeyed, and Aaron, along with the twelve tribal princes, numbered the Israelites in the wilderness of Sinai.
19. The total number of men aged twenty and up by their father's houses was six hundred three thousand five hundred fifty.
20. However, the Levites were not counted among their fellow Israelites.
21. The number of all males from one month old and older among the Israelites was twenty-two thousand two hundred seventy-three.
22. The number of Levite males from one month old and above was twenty-two thousand.
23. Moses assigned the priests and Levites their specific duties and responsibilities in serving the sanctuary, as the LORD had commanded him.
24. On the twentieth day of the month, the cloud lifted from above the Dwelling Place of Testimony.
25. The Israelites set out from the wilderness of Sinai, journeying for three days, and the cloud rested in the wilderness of Paran.
26. There, the anger of the LORD was kindled against the Israelites for their complaints and demands for meat.
27. The LORD listened to their cries and provided them with meat, which they consumed for an entire month.
28. However, after this, the LORD's anger burned against them, and He struck them with a severe plague, burying many there.
29. The place was named Kibroth Hattaavah, as there they buried the people who craved flesh.
30. The Israelites moved on from Kibroth Hattaavah to camp at Hazeroth in the wilderness of Paran.
31. During their time in Hazeroth, the LORD's anger turned against Miriam due to her words against Moses, causing her to become leprous, white as snow.
32. She was confined outside the camp for seven days until her leprosy was healed and she was allowed back into the camp.
33. Afterward, the Israelites departed from Hazeroth and camped at the edge of the wilderness of Paran.
34. At that time, the LORD instructed Moses to send twelve men from the tribes of Israel to explore the land of Canaan.
35. Moses sent these twelve men, who explored Canaan from the wilderness of Zin to Rehob near Hamath.

36. After forty days, they returned to Moses and Aaron and reported what was in their hearts, with ten men bringing a discouraging report about the land.
37. The ten men claimed, "It is better for us to return to Egypt than to enter this land, for it consumes its inhabitants."
38. However, Joshua son of Nun and Caleb son of Jephunneh, who were among those who explored the land, declared, "The land is exceedingly good.
39. If the LORD is pleased with us, He will bring us into this land, flowing with milk and honey."
40. Yet, the Israelites listened to the words of the ten men, disregarding the encouragement from Joshua and Caleb.
41. The LORD heard the murmurings of Israel and swore in His anger, "Not one man of this wicked generation will see the land, except Caleb and Joshua."
42. He decreed that this generation would perish in the wilderness, and only their children would inherit the land.
43. Thus, the LORD's anger was kindled against Israel, and He caused them to wander in the wilderness for forty years until that generation passed away.

CHAPTER 84

1. At that time, Korah, the son of Izhar, the son of Kohath, the son of Levi, gathered many men from among the Israelites, and they rose up in rebellion against Moses, Aaron, and the entire congregation.
2. The LORD's anger was kindled against them, and the earth opened its mouth and swallowed them, their households, and all their belongings, along with the men associated with Korah.
3. Following this, God caused the Israelites to journey around the area of Mount Seir for an extended period.
4. During that time, the LORD said to Moses, "Do not provoke war with the descendants of Esau, for I will not give you any part of their land, not even as much as a footstep, for I have given Mount Seir to Esau as his inheritance."
5. The descendants of Esau had fought against the inhabitants of Seir in the past, and the LORD had delivered the people of Seir into Esau's hands, allowing the descendants of Esau to dwell in their land, where they remain to this day.
6. Therefore, the LORD said to the Israelites, "Do not engage in battle with your brothers, the descendants of Esau, for nothing in their land is yours; you may only purchase food and water from them."
7. The Israelites followed the LORD's instruction and passed peacefully by the land of Esau without provoking a fight, traveling in that district for nineteen years.
8. In the meantime, Latinus, king of the Chittim, died in the forty-fifth year of his reign, which was the fourteenth year since Israel's departure from Egypt.

9. Latinus was buried in the place he had built for himself in the land of Chittim, and Abimnas reigned in his place for thirty-eight years.
10. After nineteen years of wandering, the Israelites moved past the borders of Edom, following the wilderness road around Moab.
11. The LORD commanded Moses, "Do not lay siege to Moab or engage in war, for I will not give you any of their land."
12. So the Israelites traveled along the wilderness road of Moab for nineteen years without engaging in battle against them.
13. In the thirty-sixth year after Israel's departure from Egypt, the LORD hardened the heart of Sihon, king of the Amorites, who declared war and went to battle against Moab.
14. Sihon sent messengers to Beor, the son of Janeas, the son of Balaam, an advisor to the king of Egypt, and to his son Balaam, asking them to curse Moab to aid him in his conquest.
15. The messengers brought Beor and his son Balaam from Pethor in Mesopotamia, and they arrived in Sihon's city, where they cursed Moab in Sihon's presence.
16. Strengthened by this, Sihon led his entire army against Moab, defeating them and capturing all their cities, including Heshbon, which was Moab's city.
17. Sihon settled his princes and nobles in Heshbon, establishing his rule there.
18. Consequently, the poets Beor and Balaam spoke, saying, "Come to Heshbon, the city of Sihon, which will be built and established.
19. Woe to Moab! You are vanquished, O people of Chemosh! This is recorded in the Scroll of the Law of God."
20. After conquering Moab, Sihon stationed guards in the captured cities, and many Moabite people, including their king, fell in battle.
21. Sihon returned to his land with a large group of captives, including sons and daughters of Moab, as well as valuable spoils.
22. Sihon gave substantial gifts of silver and gold to Beor and his son Balaam and dismissed them, allowing them to return to Mesopotamia.
23. Meanwhile, the Israelites traveled around Moab and moved toward the wilderness of Edom.
24. The entire congregation camped in the wilderness of Zin at the beginning of the first month in the fortieth year since their departure from Egypt, and Miriam passed away there and was buried.
25. At that time, Moses sent messengers to Hadad, king of Edom, with a message
26. "Thus says your brother Israel: Permit us to pass through your land; we will not tread through fields or vineyards, nor drink from any wells. We will follow the king's highway."
27. However, Edom responded, "You may not pass through my territory," and they mobilized a large force to meet the Israelites.

28. The descendants of Esau, therefore, denied passage to Israel, and Israel respected the LORD's command not to engage them in battle, withdrawing peacefully.
29. Israel then departed from Kadesh and journeyed to Mount Hor.
30. At this time, the LORD spoke to Moses, saying, "Tell Aaron that he will pass away on Mount Hor, for he will not enter the land I have promised the Israelites."
31. Aaron ascended Mount Hor at the LORD's command on the first day of the fifth month in the fortieth year since the Israelites left Egypt.
32. Aaron was one hundred and twenty-three years old at the time of his death on Mount Hor.

CHAPTER 85

1. And King Arad the Canaanite, who dwelt in the south, heard that the Israelites had come by the way of the spies, and he arranged his forces to fight against the Israelites.
2. The sons of Israel were greatly afraid of him, for he had a large and formidable army, so they resolved to return to Egypt.
3. The sons of Israel turned back about a three days' journey to Maserath Beni Jaakon, as they were very afraid of King Arad.
4. The sons of Israel could not make up their minds to return, so they stayed in Beni Jaakon for thirty days.
5. When the children of Levi saw that the Israelites would not turn back, they were zealous for the LORD's sake
6. And they rose up and fought against their brothers, the Israelites, slaying a great number of them and forcing them to return to Mount Hor.
7. When they returned, King Arad was still preparing his host for battle against the Israelites.
8. Israel made a vow, saying, "If You will deliver this people into my hand, I will completely destroy their cities."
9. The LORD listened to Israel's voice and delivered the Canaanites into their hand, and Israel utterly destroyed them and their cities, naming the place Hormah.
10. The sons of Israel journeyed from Mount Hor and pitched their tents in Oboth, then moved from Oboth and pitched at Ije-abarim, on the border of Moab.
11. The sons of Israel sent to Moab, saying, "Let us pass through your land into our place,"
12. But Moab would not permit them, fearing Israel might do to them as Sihon, king of the Amorites, had done.
13. Thus, Moab would not allow Israel to pass, and the LORD commanded Israel not to fight Moab, so they moved away from Moab.
14. Israel journeyed from Moab's border to the other side of Arnon, the boundary between Moab and the Amorites,
15. And camped at the edge of Sihon's territory in the wilderness of Kedemoth.
16. Israel sent messengers to Sihon, king of the Amorites, saying,

17. "Let us pass through your land; we will not enter fields or vineyards but will travel along the king's highway until we pass your borders."
18. However, Sihon would not allow them to pass, gathering all his people and marching to the wilderness to fight Israel at Jahaz.
19. The LORD delivered Sihon, king of the Amorites, into Israel's hand, and Israel defeated him and his people with the sword, avenging Moab.
20. Israel took possession of Sihon's land, from Aram to Jabuk, up to the border of the Ammonites, seizing all the cities and spoils.
21. Israel settled in all the cities of the Amorites.
22. All Israel resolved to fight against the Ammonites to take their land as well.
23. But the LORD said to Israel, "Do not besiege the Ammonites or engage them in battle, for I will not give you any of their land," so Israel obeyed.
24. Israel then turned and went by way of Bashan, where they encountered Og, king of Bashan, who prepared for battle with his large army.
25. Og, a powerful man, was accompanied by his son Naaron, who was even mightier.
26. Og thought, "Since Israel's camp covers seven miles, I will strike them all at once."
27. He climbed Mount Jahaz, picked up a stone seven miles in length, placed it on his head, and prepared to hurl it on Israel's camp.
28. But the Messenger of the LORD pierced the stone on Og's head, causing it to fall on his neck and bring him down due to its weight.
29. The LORD told Israel, "Do not fear him, for I have given him, his people, and his land into your hand, and you will do to him as you did to Sihon."
30. Moses then led a small group of Israelites to Og, and Moses struck Og's ankles with a staff, killing him.
31. Israel pursued Og's people and defeated them until there was no survivor.
32. Moses sent scouts to Jaazer, a renowned city, to explore it.
33. The scouts went, relying on the LORD, fought Jaazer's men, and took the city and its villages.
34. The LORD delivered Jaazer into their hands, and they expelled the Amorites there.
35. Israel took the land of the two Amorite kings, sixty cities on the other side of the Jordan, from Arnon to Mount Hermon.
36. Israel then camped in the plains of Moab, across the Jordan from Jericho.
37. Moab heard of the destruction Israel had brought upon Sihon and Og and became greatly afraid.
38. Moab's elders said, "The two Amorite kings, Sihon and Og, who were mightier than all kings, could not withstand Israel; how can we?"
39. They reasoned, "Israel asked to pass peacefully, and we refused. Now they may turn on us and destroy us with their swords."
40. In fear, Moab appointed Balak, son of Zippor, a wise man, as their king.

41. The elders of Moab also sought peace with Midian, as they had been enemies since Hadad, king of Edom, had defeated Midian in Moab's fields.
42. Moab sent to Midian, made peace, and consulted with them to plan against Israel.
43. Moab feared Israel's strength, saying, "They devour all around them like oxen consuming grass."
44. Midian responded, "When Sihon fought Moab, he summoned Balaam, who cursed Moab, enabling Sihon's victory."
45. Moab's elders agreed to send for Balaam, Beor's son, to curse Israel.
46. They sent messengers to Balaam, saying,
47. "Behold, a people from Egypt now cover the land and dwell near us.
48. Come, curse them, for they are too strong for us
49. Perhaps I may then prevail to fight and expel them, for I know whom you bless is blessed, and whom you curse is cursed."
50. Balak's messengers brought Balaam, hoping he would curse Israel to fight Moab.
51. Balaam came, but the LORD told him, "Do not curse this people, for they are blessed."
52. Though Balak daily urged Balaam to curse Israel, Balaam refused, honoring the LORD's command.
53. Balak, seeing Balaam's refusal, returned home, and Balaam went to Midian.
54. Israel journeyed from the plains of Moab and camped by the Jordan, from Beth-Jesimoth to Abel-Shittim in Moab's plains.
55. While in Shittim, Israel committed whoredom with Moab's daughters.
56. Moab, fearing Israel, set their beautiful daughters and wives at their tents' doors, adorned with fine attire, to entice Israel.
57. Moab's men encouraged Israel, saying, "We are brothers, descendants of Lot and Abraham; join us in peace and eat of our sacrifices."
58. Moab overwhelmed Israel with flattery, leading them to feast with them and commit idolatry.
59. Israel turned to Moab's daughters and fell into sin.
60. When a Hebrew approached a Moabite woman, he was enticed with wine, leading to intimacy in their drunkenness.
61. The LORD's anger was kindled, and He sent a pestilence among Israel, killing twenty-four thousand.
62. A Simeonite man, Zimri, openly sinned with Cosbi, a Midianite princess, in Israel's sight.
63. Phinehas, Eleazar's son, saw this, took a spear, pursued, and pierced them both, ceasing the pestilence among Israel.

CHAPTER 86

1. At that time, after the plague had ceased, the LORD spoke to Moses and Eleazar, the son of Aaron the priest, saying,

2. "Take a census of the entire congregation of the sons of Israel, from twenty years old and above, all who are able to go out to war in Israel."
3. Moses and Eleazar obeyed, and they took the census of the sons of Israel according to their families.
4. The total number of the men of Israel came to seven hundred thousand, seven hundred and thirty.
5. Among the children of Levi, from one month old and up, there were twenty-three thousand males.
6. Not a single man was left from those counted by Moses and Aaron at Sinai because the LORD had declared they would die in the wilderness.
7. All the men of that generation died, as the LORD had spoken, except Caleb, the son of Jephunneh, and Joshua, the son of Nun.
8. Afterward, the LORD spoke to Moses, saying, "Avenge the sons of Israel on the Midianites for the cause of Israel."
9. Moses obeyed, choosing twelve thousand men, one thousand from each tribe, to go to war against Midian.
10. The sons of Israel fought against Midian, and they killed every male, including the five princes of Midian and Balaam, the son of Beor, with the sword.
11. Israel captured the women, children, livestock, and all the spoils of Midian.
12. They brought the spoils and captives to Moses, Eleazar, and the congregation in the plains of Moab, where Moses and Eleazar met them with joy.

CHAPTER 87

1. At that time, the LORD said to Moses, "Behold, your days are drawing to a close. Take Joshua, the son of Nun, your servant, and bring him into the Tent of Meeting, for I will give him a charge."
2. Moses did as the LORD commanded, bringing Joshua to the Tent, and the LORD appeared in a pillar of cloud at the entrance.
3. The LORD instructed Joshua, saying, "Be strong and courageous, for you will lead the sons of Israel into the land that I promised them, and I will be with you."
4. Moses encouraged Joshua before all Israel, saying, "Be strong and courageous, for you will bring the sons of Israel into the promised land. The LORD will be with you, and He will not leave or forsake you."
5. Moses gathered all Israel and reminded them of all the good the LORD had done for them in the wilderness.
6. He instructed them to observe all the commands of the LORD, walking in His ways without turning aside.
7. Moses taught them statutes, judgments, and laws as the LORD had commanded him, writing them in the Book of the Law.

8. When Moses had completed his instructions, the LORD spoke to him, saying, "Go up to Mount Abarim, for there you will die and be gathered to your people as Aaron was."
9. Moses ascended the mountain as the LORD commanded, and he died there in Moab, in the fortieth year after the Israelites left Egypt.
10. The sons of Israel mourned Moses in the plains of Moab for thirty days, and the days of weeping and mourning for Moses were fulfilled.
11. Joshua, the son of Nun, was filled with the spirit of wisdom, for Moses had laid his hands upon him, and the sons of Israel listened to him and did as the LORD had commanded Moses.

CHAPTER 88

1. And it was after the death of Moses that the LORD spoke to Joshua the son of Nun, saying,
2. "Rise up and pass over the Jordan to the land which I have given to the sons of Israel, and you will cause the sons of Israel to inherit it.
3. Every place where the sole of your foot will tread will be yours, from the wilderness of Lebanon to the great river, the Euphrates; this will be your boundary.
4. No one will be able to stand against you all the days of your life; as I was with Moses, so I will be with you.
5. Be strong and of good courage to observe the Law that Moses commanded you.
6. Do not turn from it, either to the right or to the left, so that you may prosper in all that you do."
7. And Joshua commanded the officers of Israel, saying, "Pass through the camp and instruct the people, saying,
8. 'Prepare provisions for yourselves, for in three days you will cross the Jordan to take possession of the land.'"
9. And the officers of the sons of Israel did as Joshua commanded, and they instructed the people.
10. Joshua sent two men to spy out the land of Jericho, and they went and spied on Jericho.
11. After seven days, the men returned to Joshua and said, "The LORD has given the land into our hands, and the people are melting in fear before us."
12. Joshua rose early in the morning, and he and all Israel set out from Shittim, and they crossed the Jordan
13. Joshua was eighty-two years old at that time.
14. The people camped at Gilgal on the eastern edge of Jericho on the tenth day of the first month.
15. The sons of Israel kept the Passover in Gilgal on the fourteenth day of the month, as it is written in the Law of Moses.
16. The manna ceased on the day after the Passover, and they ate the produce of the land of Canaan from that time onward.

17. Jericho was entirely closed to the sons of Israel; no one went in or out.
18. In the second month, on the first day, the LORD said to Joshua,
19. "Rise up, for I have given Jericho into your hand, with all its people."
20. "Your warriors will circle the city once each day for six days."
21. "The priests will blow on trumpets, and when you hear the trumpet sound, all the people will shout, and the walls of the city will fall down
22. Every man will go straight up to take the city."
23. Joshua did all that the LORD commanded him.
24. On the seventh day, they circled the city seven times, and the priests blew on the trumpets.
25. At the seventh round, Joshua said to the people, "Shout, for the LORD has given you the city."
26. "Only keep yourselves from the accursed things, lest you bring trouble upon Israel."
27. "All silver, gold, and vessels of brass and iron are consecrated to the LORD; they will be placed in the LORD's treasury."
28. The people shouted and blew trumpets, and the walls of Jericho fell down. They captured the city and utterly destroyed everything within.
29. They burned the entire city with fire, but placed the silver, gold, brass, and iron vessels into the treasury of the LORD.
30. Joshua declared, "Cursed is the man who rebuilds Jericho; he will lay its foundation at the cost of his firstborn, and set up its gates at the cost of his youngest son."
31. Achan, son of Carmi, son of Zabdi, of the tribe of Judah, took some of the accursed things, and the LORD's anger burned against Israel.
32. After burning Jericho, Joshua sent men to spy out Ai, saying, "Go and assess the city."
33. The men returned, saying, "Do not send all the people; about three thousand will be sufficient to strike Ai, as the men are few."
34. Joshua sent about three thousand men, but the men of Ai struck down thirty-six Israelites, and Israel fled from Ai.
35. Joshua tore his garments and fell face down before the LORD, along with the elders of Israel, and they put dust on their heads.
36. Joshua said, "Why, O LORD, did You bring us across the Jordan only to let us be defeated? Now all the Canaanites will hear and surround us, cutting off our name."
37. The LORD said, "Rise up! Israel has sinned and taken from the accursed things; I will not be with you unless the accursed things are destroyed."
38. Joshua assembled the people, and the tribe of Judah was taken, and then Achan was taken.
39. Joshua said, "Tell me, my son, what have you done?" Achan replied, "I saw a beautiful garment, silver, and a wedge of gold; I coveted them and hid them in my tent."
40. Joshua sent men who brought back the stolen items from Achan's tent.

41. Joshua took Achan, along with the stolen items, and all that belonged to him, and brought them to the Valley of Achor.
42. They stoned Achan and his family, burned them, and raised a heap of stones over them.
43. Afterward, the LORD's anger was appeased, and Joshua then led Israel to fight against Ai.
44. The LORD instructed Joshua, "Do not fear; I have given Ai into your hand, and you will do to Ai as you did to Jericho."
45. Joshua followed the LORD's command, setting an ambush for the city.
46. Joshua pretended to be retreating, and the men of Ai pursued Israel, leaving their city unguarded.
47. The men in ambush seized the city and set it on fire.
48. The men of Ai saw the smoke and had no escape; they were surrounded by Israel on both sides.
49. Israel took the king of Ai alive, and Joshua hanged him.
50. Israel returned to the city and destroyed its inhabitants, sparing only the cattle and spoils as the LORD commanded.
51. The men of Ai, numbering twelve thousand, were defeated, and the city was burned.
52. News of Israel's victories spread throughout Canaan, and the kings gathered to fight against Israel.
53. However, the inhabitants of Gibeon sought to make peace, deceiving Israel by pretending to be from a distant land.
54. The sons of Israel made a covenant with Gibeon, but later learned they were neighbors.
55. Israel spared Gibeon due to the oath, and they became servants to Israel.
56. Joshua questioned them, and they admitted their deception out of fear for their lives.
57. They were made hewers of wood and drawers of water.
58. When Adonizedek king of Jerusalem heard of this, he called other kings to join him in battle.
59. The kings gathered with numerous armies, as the sands of the seashore, to fight against Israel and Gibeon.
60. Gibeon requested help from Joshua, and he led a sudden attack.
61. The LORD confused the enemies, and Israel struck them down.
62. The LORD sent hailstones that killed more than the sword.
63. As they fought, Joshua prayed for the sun and moon to stand still, and they did so for a whole day.
64. The LORD listened to Joshua
65. And there was no day like it before or after.

CHAPTER 89

1. Then Joshua spoke this song on the day the LORD delivered the Amorites into the hand of Israel, saying in the sight of all Israel,

2. "You have done mighty things, O LORD, || You have performed great deeds; Who is like You? My lips will sing to Your Name.
3. My goodness and my fortress, my high tower, || I will sing a new song to You, || I will sing to You with thanksgiving; You are the strength of my salvation.
4. All the kings of the earth will praise You, || The princes of the world will sing to You, || The sons of Israel will rejoice in Your salvation, || They will sing and praise Your power.
5. To You, O LORD, we confided; We said, 'You are our God,' || For You were our shelter and strong tower against our enemies.
6. To You we cried and were not ashamed; In You we trusted and were delivered; When we cried to You, You heard our voice, || You delivered our souls from the sword, || You showed Your grace to us, || You gave Your salvation to us, || You made our hearts rejoice with Your strength.
7. You went out for our salvation, || With Your arm You redeemed Your people; You answered us from the heavens of Your holiness, || You saved us from tens of thousands of people.
8. The sun and moon stood still in [the] heavens, || And You stood in Your wrath against our oppressors || And commanded Your judgments over them.
9. All the princes of the earth stood up, || The kings of the nations gathered themselves together; They were not moved at Your presence, || They desired Your battles.
10. You rose against them in Your anger || And brought down Your wrath on them; You destroyed them in Your anger || And cut them off in Your heart.
11. Nations have been consumed with Your fury, || Kingdoms have declined because of Your wrath, || You wounded kings in the day of Your anger.
12. You poured out Your fury on them—Your wrathful anger took hold of them; You turned their iniquity on them || And cut them off in their wickedness.
13. They spread a trap, they fell therein, || In the net they hid, their foot was caught.
14. Your hand was ready for all Your enemies who said, 'Through their sword they possessed the land, || Through their arm they dwelt in the city.'
15. You filled their faces with shame, || You brought their horns down to the ground, || You terrified them in Your wrath, || And destroyed them in Your anger.
16. The earth trembled and shook at the sound of Your storm over them, || You did not withhold their souls from death, || And brought down their lives to the grave.
17. You pursued them in Your storm, || You consumed them in Your whirlwind, || You turned their rain into hail; They fell into deep pits so that they could not rise.
18. Their carcasses were like rubbish cast out in the middle of the streets.
19. They were consumed and destroyed in Your anger, || You saved Your people with Your might.
20. Therefore our hearts rejoice in You, || Our souls exalt in Your salvation.
21. Our tongues will relate Your might, || We will sing and praise Your wondrous works.

22. For You saved us from our enemies, || You delivered us from those who rose up against us, || You destroyed them from before us || And brought them beneath our feet.
23. Thus all Your enemies will perish, O LORD, || And the wicked will be like chaff driven by the wind, || And Your beloved will be like trees planted by the waters."
24. So Joshua and all Israel with him returned to the camp in Gilgal after having struck down all the kings so that no remnant was left of them.
25. The five kings fled on foot and hid themselves in a cave, and Joshua sought them on the battlefield but did not find them.
26. It was later told to Joshua, saying, "The kings have been found hidden in a cave."
27. Joshua said, "Appoint men to guard the mouth of the cave, lest they escape," and Israel did so.
28. Joshua called to all Israel, saying to the officers of war, "Place your feet on the necks of these kings," and Joshua said, "So the LORD will do to all your enemies."
29. Joshua commanded that the kings be slain and thrown into the cave, with large stones placed over the cave's mouth.
30. Joshua then led Israel to Makkedah and struck it with the sword, destroying all within.
31. He passed from Makkedah to Libnah, and the LORD delivered it into his hand, and he did to Libnah as he had done to Jericho.
32. Joshua proceeded from Libnah to Lachish, and Horam king of Gaza came to help Lachish, but Joshua struck him and his people until none remained.
33. Joshua took Lachish and all within it, doing to it as he had done to Libnah.
34. He passed from Lachish to Eglon, struck it, and utterly destroyed it with all its people.
35. Joshua went from Eglon to Hebron, capturing it and striking all within with the sword.
36. From Hebron, he moved to Debir, fought against it, and destroyed every soul within, leaving none.
37. Joshua struck all the kings from Kadesh-Barnea to Azah, taking their land, as the LORD fought for Israel.
38. Joshua returned to Gilgal with all Israel after these conquests.
39. When Jabin king of Chazor heard of Joshua's victories, he sent messages to neighboring kings for assistance.
40. Seventeen kings and their armies, as numerous as sand on the seashore, gathered to fight against Israel at the waters of Merom.
41. The LORD told Joshua, "Do not fear them; tomorrow, I will deliver them all slain before you. You will hamstring their horses and burn their chariots."
42. Joshua came upon them suddenly, and they fell into Israel's hands, as the LORD had promised.
43. The Israelites pursued them and struck them down until none were left.
44. Joshua returned to Chazor, struck it with the sword, and destroyed all within it, burning the city.
45. He passed from Chazor to Shimron and did likewise, destroying it.

46. He went to Achshaph and did as he had done to Shimron.
47. Joshua continued to Adulam, striking all people within, as he had done to Shimron and Achshaph.
48. He struck all the cities of the conquered kings, leaving no soul alive.
49. The Israelites kept only the cattle and spoils, in accordance with the LORD's command.
50. As the LORD had instructed Moses, so Joshua and Israel obeyed fully in all matters.
51. Joshua struck all the land of Canaan, conquering all thirty-one kings and their territories.
52. Moses had given the lands of Sihon and Og to the tribes of Reuben, Gad, and half the tribe of Manasseh.
53. Joshua gave the remaining conquered lands to the nine and a half tribes west of the Jordan.
54. For five years, Joshua waged war with these kings, and Israel took their cities, leading to peace from battle throughout Canaan.

CHAPTER 90

1. In the fifth year after the Israelites crossed the Jordan, after they had rested from their battles with the Canaanites, a fierce conflict arose between Edom and the people of Chittim, with Chittim advancing against Edom.
2. That year, Abianus, king of Chittim, in the thirty-first year of his reign, led a vast force of Chittim's mighty men to Seir to engage the children of Esau.
3. Hadad, the king of Edom, heard of their approach, and he mobilized a large army to confront them in the plains of Edom.
4. The forces of Chittim overpowered Esau's descendants, slaying twenty-two thousand of them, and the people of Edom fled in defeat.
5. Chittim's army pursued them, capturing Hadad, the king of Edom, and presenting him to Abianus.
6. Abianus ordered his execution, and Hadad was slain in the forty-eighth year of his reign.
7. Chittim continued its pursuit of Edom, inflicting severe losses, eventually subjugating Edom under their rule.
8. Thus, Edom came under Chittim's control, merging with their kingdom from that time forward.
9. Edom could no longer rise up against them, and their kingdom was united with Chittim's.
10. Abianus appointed officers in Edom, rendering the people of Edom subjects and tributaries to him, before he returned to Chittim.
11. Upon his return, Abianus fortified his rule, constructing a spacious royal residence and reigning securely over both Chittim and Edom.

12. Meanwhile, after Israel had driven out the Canaanites and Amorites, Joshua grew old.
13. The LORD said to Joshua, "You are advanced in years, yet much of the land remains to be possessed.
14. Now divide this land among the nine tribes and the half-tribe of Manasseh," and Joshua obeyed the LORD's command.
15. He apportioned the land as an inheritance for the tribes of Israel, in line with their divisions.
16. To the tribe of Levi, however, he gave no territory, as the offerings of the LORD were deemed their inheritance.
17. Joshua awarded Mount Hebron to Caleb, the son of Jephunneh, in fulfillment of the LORD's promise through Moses.
18. To this day, Hebron remains an inheritance for Caleb and his descendants.
19. Joshua allocated all the land by lots to Israel, fulfilling the LORD's command.
20. The Israelites granted the Levites cities from their own inheritances, along with pastures for livestock and possessions, as Moses had commanded.
21. Each tribe took possession of its allotted territory, while Israel gave Joshua his own inheritance among them.
22. As per the LORD's word, they granted him Timnath-Serah in Mount Ephraim, where Joshua built a city and resided.
23. These are the territories assigned by Eleazar the priest, Joshua, and the leaders of the tribes, distributed by lot in Shiloh before the LORD, marking the end of their land divisions.
24. The LORD delivered the land to Israel, and they took possession of it, fulfilling the LORD's oath to their ancestors.
25. The LORD granted them rest from their enemies, with no one able to stand against them, as He delivered all their foes into their hands, completing all He had promised to Israel.
26. Joshua gathered Israel, blessing and urging them to serve the LORD, before dismissing each tribe to its allotted city and inheritance.
27. Israel continued to serve the LORD during Joshua's lifetime, enjoying peace and security in their towns.
28. Abianus, king of Chittim, died in the thirty-eighth year of his reign, which was the seventh year of his rule over Edom; they buried him in the tomb he had prepared, and Latinus reigned in his place for fifty years.
29. During his reign, Latinus led an army against Britannia and Kernania, descendants of Elishah, son of Javan, conquering them and imposing tribute.
30. Learning of Edom's revolt, he subdued them, restoring Edom under Chittim's control, making them one kingdom once more.
31. For many years, Edom had no king, governed instead by Chittim's rulers.
32. In the twenty-sixth year after Israel crossed the Jordan, sixty-six years after they left Egypt, Joshua reached the age of one hundred and eight.

33. Summoning Israel's elders, judges, and officers, Joshua spoke to them after the LORD had given Israel rest from their enemies, saying, "I am old, advanced in years, and you have witnessed all that the LORD has done, for it is He who has fought for you.
34. Be strong, therefore, in keeping the law of Moses, neither veering right nor left, nor mingling with the remaining nations or mentioning their gods; remain steadfast to the LORD as you have done."
35. Joshua encouraged Israel to serve the LORD with dedication, reminding them of their covenant.
36. In response, Israel affirmed, "We will serve the LORD our God throughout our generations."
37. Joshua made a covenant with the people that day, dismissing them to their cities and lands.
38. During Israel's peace, they interred their ancestors' coffins from Egypt in the land of their inheritance, burying each of Jacob's sons in their respective territories.
39. Reuben and Gad were buried on the Jordan's east side in Romia, assigned to their descendants by Moses.
40. Simeon and Levi were laid to rest in Mauda, Simeon's city, with Levi's suburbs nearby.
41. Judah was buried near Bethlehem in Benjamin's territory.
42. Issachar and Zebulun were laid to rest in Zidon, in their descendants' portion.
43. Dan was interred in Eshtaol, among his children.
44. Naphtali and Asher were buried in Kadesh-Naphtali, each in his designated land.
45. Joseph's bones were laid in Shechem, in the field Jacob had purchased from Hamor.
46. Benjamin was buried in Jerusalem near the Jebusite's land.
47. After two years, Joshua, aged one hundred and ten, passed away; he had served Israel as judge for twenty-eight years.
48. His battles and commands, as well as the cities conquered under his leadership, are recorded in the book of the Wars of the LORD.
49. Israel buried Joshua in his inheritance at Timnath-Serah in Mount Ephraim.
50. Eleazar, son of Aaron, also passed, and was buried in a hill owned by his son Phinehas in Mount Ephraim.

CHAPTER 91

1. After Joshua's death, Israel remained among the Canaanites and resolved to drive them out.
2. Israel asked the LORD, "Who will go up first against the Canaanites?" and the LORD answered, "Judah will go."
3. The tribe of Judah invited Simeon to join them in battle against the Canaanites, promising to return the favor, and Simeon agreed.

4. Together, they went up and the LORD delivered the Canaanites into Judah's hands, where they struck down ten thousand men at Bezek.
5. They defeated Adoni-Bezek, who fled but was captured, and they cut off his thumbs and big toes.
6. Adoni-Bezek acknowledged, "Seventy kings with thumbs and big toes cut off once gathered crumbs under my table; as I have done, so has God repaid me." He later died in Jerusalem.
7. The people of Judah, with Simeon, attacked the Canaanites, defeating them with the sword.
8. The LORD was with Judah, enabling them to conquer the mountains, while Joseph's descendants went up to Bethel and the LORD supported them.
9. The people of Joseph found a man leaving Bethel and offered to spare him if he showed them the city's entrance.
10. The man led them to Bethel's entrance, and Joseph's descendants took the city by the sword.
11. They spared the man and his family, and he moved to the Hittites, founding a city named Luz.
12. Israel resided in their cities, serving the LORD during the lifetimes of Joshua and the elders who outlived him, having witnessed the LORD's great works.
13. The elders ruled Israel for seventeen years after Joshua's death.
14. These leaders fought against the Canaanites, with the LORD driving them out to establish Israel's inheritance.
15. The LORD faithfully kept His covenant with Abraham, Isaac, and Jacob, granting their descendants rest and secure dwelling in the land.
16. Blessed be the LORD forever—amen and amen!
17. Let all who trust in the LORD be strengthened and take heart.

Book of Jubilees

The *Book of Jubilees*, also known as *Lesser Genesis* or *Leptogenesis*, is a significant ancient Jewish religious text composed of 50 chapters. It holds canonical status within the Ethiopian Orthodox Church and the Beta Israel community (Ethiopian Jews), where it is referred to as the *Book of Division*. However, in other branches of Christianity, including Protestant, Roman Catholic, and Eastern Orthodox traditions, *Jubilees* is categorized among the pseudepigrapha and not considered part of the canonical scriptures. Similarly, within mainstream Judaism, it is generally not regarded as canonical outside the Beta Israel community.

Scholars typically date *The Book of Jubilees* to the 2nd century BCE, suggesting that one of its primary purposes was to promote a unique 364-day calendar, structured into 52 weeks of seven days each. This calendar, without any system of intercalation, would gradually misalign with the solar year and seasonal cycles over time. Additionally, the book provides a retelling and reimagining of events from the *Book of Genesis*, introducing distinctive interpretations, including the concept of certain sins as unatonable—a notion not found in traditional Judeo-Christian teachings.

"THIS IS THE ACCOUNT OF THE DIVISION OF THE DAYS OF THE LAW AND THE TESTIMONY, THE EVENTS OF EACH YEAR, AND THEIR CYCLES OF SEVEN AND JUBILEES, ACROSS THE ENTIRE SPAN OF THE WORLD'S HISTORY. IT IS AS THE LORD SPOKE TO MOSES ON MOUNT SINAI WHEN HE ASCENDED TO RECEIVE THE TABLETS OF THE LAW AND COMMANDMENTS, IN ACCORDANCE WITH THE VOICE OF GOD, WHO INSTRUCTED HIM, 'GO UP TO THE TOP OF THE MOUNTAIN.'"

Chapter 1

1. In the first year of Israel's exodus from Egypt, on the sixteenth day of the third month, God spoke to Moses, saying, "Come up to Me on the mountain. I will give you two tablets of stone, containing the Law and commandments I have written, so that you may teach them."
2. Moses ascended Mount Sinai, and the glory of the Lord rested upon it. A cloud covered the mountain for six days.
3. On the seventh day, God called Moses from the midst of the cloud, and His glory appeared like a flame on the mountain's peak.
4. Moses remained on the mountain for forty days and forty nights, during which time God revealed the history of the divisions of the days, the Law, and the Testimony.
5. God said, "Focus your heart on every word I speak on this mountain. Write them in a scroll so that future generations may understand how I have not forsaken them, despite their transgressions against the covenant I establish with you here today on Mount Sinai."

6. "When all these events unfold, they will see that I have been just in all My judgments and actions, and they will recognize My constant presence with them."
7. "Write down all the words I tell you today, for I know their rebellion and stubbornness even before I lead them into the land I promised to their ancestors—Abraham, Isaac, and Jacob—a land rich with milk and honey."
8. "They will eat and be satisfied, but they will turn to foreign gods, which cannot save them in their distress; this will stand as a witness against them."
9. "They will forget My commands, and instead follow the ways of other nations and their idols, bringing upon themselves shame, tribulation, and entrapment."
10. "Many will perish, and they will be taken captive, falling into the hands of their enemies because they have abandoned My commandments, My festivals, My Sabbaths, My holy place, and My dwelling, which I consecrated in their midst to bear My name."
11. "They will build high places and worship carved images, following the error of their hearts, even sacrificing their children to demons."
12. "I will send witnesses to testify against them, but they will not listen; they will even kill these witnesses and persecute those who seek the Law, distorting everything to act wickedly before Me."
13. "I will hide My face from them, allowing them to be taken captive and scattered among the nations as prey, away from the land I gave them."
14. "They will forget My laws, commands, judgments, and will abandon the observance of new moons, Sabbaths, festivals, jubilees, and all ordinances."
15. "In time, they will return to Me from among the nations with all their heart, soul, and strength. I will gather them and reveal Myself to them when they sincerely seek Me."
16. "I will grant them abundant peace and righteousness, and they will be a blessing and not a curse, becoming the head and not the tail."
17. "I will establish My sanctuary among them, dwell with them, and be their God, while they will be My people in truth and righteousness."
18. "I will never forsake or fail them, for I am the Lord, their God."
19. Moses then bowed in prayer, saying, "O Lord my God, do not abandon Your people to wander in error, nor deliver them to the nations who will lead them into sin."
20. "Let Your mercy be upon Your people, creating in them an upright spirit. Do not let the spirit of wickedness accuse or ensnare them, lest they perish before You."
21. "They are Your people and inheritance, whom You delivered from Egypt with great power. Create in them a clean heart and holy spirit so that they may not be entrapped by sin."
22. The Lord replied to Moses, "I know their rebellious nature and stubborn thoughts. They will not obey until they confess their sins and the sins of their ancestors."
23. "After this, they will return to Me sincerely, and I will transform their hearts, cleansing them so that they will not turn away from Me."

24. "Their souls will cling to Me, fulfilling My commands. I will be their Father, and they will be My children."
25. "All will know that they are My children and that I am their righteous Father who loves them."
26. "Record all these words, both the first and the last, which will come to pass across the divisions of days, the Law, the Testimony, and the jubilee periods until I come to dwell with them forever."
27. Then God instructed the Angel of the Presence, saying, "Record the history from the beginning of creation until My sanctuary is established among them for all time."
28. "The Lord will appear for all to see, and all will know that I am the God of Israel, Father to the children of Jacob, reigning on Mount Zion for all eternity. Zion and Jerusalem will be holy."
29. The Angel of the Presence took the tablets of the years—from the creation onward—recording the Law, the Testimony, the cycles of seven, and the jubilees according to each year and generation, until the day when the heavens and earth will be renewed and God's sanctuary will be established on Mount Zion for blessing, healing, and peace for all the chosen of Israel, as it shall remain forever.

Chapter 2

1. The Angel of the Presence spoke to Moses, following the word of the Lord: "Record the full account of creation, how in six days, the Lord completed all His works and rested on the seventh day, consecrating it for all time as a sign for all creation."
2. "On the first day, He created the heavens above, the earth, the waters, and all the spirits that serve before Him—spirits of the presence, of sanctification, of fire, of the winds, of clouds, and of the elements like darkness, snow, hail, frost, voices, thunder, lightning, cold, heat, winter, spring, autumn, summer, and all other spirits that dwell in heaven and on earth. He also formed the abysses, darkness, evening, dawn, and day, all according to His divine wisdom."
3. We, as His creation, witnessed His works and praised Him for all He made, acknowledging that seven great works were completed on the first day.
4. On the second day, God formed the expanse within the waters, separating them. Half of the waters rose above the expanse, while the other half remained below, over the face of the earth. This was the only work He created on the second day.
5. On the third day, He commanded the waters to gather in one place, revealing dry land.
6. The waters obeyed, moving off the face of the earth into their designated space, and the dry land appeared.
7. That same day, He created all the seas, rivers, water sources in the mountains, lakes, dew, seeds, plants, fruit-bearing trees, forest trees, and the Garden of Eden. These four works were completed on the third day.

8. On the fourth day, God created the sun, moon, and stars, placing them in the heavens to provide light on earth, rule over day and night, and separate light from darkness.
9. He designated the sun as a sign for the earth to mark days, Sabbaths, months, festivals, years, Sabbath years, jubilees, and all seasons. It separates light from darkness, fostering growth and prosperity on earth.
10. Three types of heavenly bodies were created on the fourth day to serve this purpose.
11. On the fifth day, God created the great sea creatures in the depths, marking the first living flesh He made, along with fish, all creatures in the waters, and birds in the sky.
12. The sun shone upon them to bring prosperity, nourishing all that grew and thrived on earth. Three categories of creatures were created on the fifth day.
13. On the sixth day, He created all land animals, cattle, and all creatures that move upon the earth.
14. Afterward, He created humankind, both male and female, granting them dominion over all creatures in the sea, sky, and land. These four types of creation were completed on the sixth day.
15. In total, He made twenty-two kinds of creations across the six days.
16. On the sixth day, He completed all His works in the heavens, earth, seas, abysses, and all realms of light and darkness.
17. God then provided a great sign—the Sabbath day—declaring that work shall be done for six days, while the seventh day shall be set apart as a day of rest.
18. All the angels of presence and sanctification were instructed to observe the Sabbath with Him in both heaven and on earth.
19. God proclaimed, "I will select a people from all nations to keep the Sabbath day. I will set them apart as My own and bless them, as I have sanctified the Sabbath day for Myself. In the same way, I will bless them to be My people, and I will be their God."
20. "I have chosen the descendants of Jacob from all that I have seen and declared them My firstborn. They are consecrated to Me forever, and I will teach them to observe the Sabbath and refrain from all work on that day."
21. "This will serve as a sign, allowing them to observe the Sabbath with us on the seventh day, enjoying food, drink, and blessings, just as I have sanctified and blessed them as a chosen people above all others."
22. He commanded His words to ascend as a sweet aroma acceptable to Him at all times.
23. There were twenty-two patriarchs from Adam to Jacob, and twenty-two kinds of works were completed by the seventh day; this number is blessed and holy, standing in sanctification.
24. It was given to Jacob's descendants to remain forever the blessed and holy people, holding to the first testimony and the Law, even as He sanctified the Sabbath day.
25. Having completed all creation in six days, God made the seventh day sacred. He commanded that whoever works on this day should be put to death, and whoever defiles it shall surely die.

26. Therefore, instruct the children of Israel to observe this day, keeping it holy by not working or defiling it, for it is holier than all other days.
27. Anyone who desecrates it or works on it shall be condemned, so the children of Israel may keep this day for all generations, never losing their place in the land, for it is a holy and blessed day.
28. Whoever observes the Sabbath from all his work will be blessed and holy for all days, like us.
29. Declare to the children of Israel the law of the Sabbath, so they may keep it without straying, avoiding unseemly actions, and refraining from preparing food or drink, drawing water, or moving goods through the gates on the Sabbath. They must prepare everything they need on the sixth day.
30. They should not bring or take anything from house to house, for this day is more sacred than any jubilee day in all cycles; in heaven, we kept the Sabbath before it was known to humanity.
31. The Creator blessed this day, but He did not sanctify it for all peoples and nations, only for Israel. Israel alone is allowed to eat, drink, and keep the Sabbath on earth.
32. The Creator blessed this day as a time of blessing, sanctification, and glory above all days.
33. This law and testimony was given to the children of Israel as an eternal covenant for all their generations.

Chapter 3

1. During the six days of the second week, by God's command, we brought all creatures to Adam—the beasts, cattle, birds, and everything that moves on land and in the water, each according to its kind. The animals were brought on specific days: beasts on the first day, cattle on the second, birds on the third, land creatures on the fourth, and water creatures on the fifth.
2. Adam named each one, and the name he gave them became their name.
3. Over those five days, Adam observed all these creatures, each with its male and female, yet he himself was alone and found no suitable companion.
4. The Lord said, "It is not good for man to be alone; let us make a helper for him."
5. So God caused Adam to fall into a deep sleep, took one of his ribs, and created the woman from it, filling in the flesh in place of the rib.
6. When Adam awoke on the sixth day, God presented the woman to him. He recognized her, saying, "This is bone of my bones and flesh of my flesh; she shall be called Woman, for she was taken from Man."
7. Thus, man and woman shall be united as one, with a man leaving his father and mother to cleave to his wife, becoming one flesh.

8. Adam was created in the first week, and his wife, from his rib, in the second week. Because of this, a law was established concerning purification: a male child requires seven days of purification, while a female requires double, or fourteen days.
9. After Adam had spent forty days in the place of his creation, we brought him to the Garden of Eden to work and care for it. His wife joined him on the eightieth day, and she too entered the Garden.
10. For this reason, the command regarding purification is written on heavenly tablets: if a woman bears a male child, she remains in her impurity for seven days, followed by thirty-three days for purification, refraining from sacred things and the sanctuary during this time.
11. However, if she bears a female, she must remain in impurity for fourteen days, followed by sixty-six days of purification, totaling eighty days.
12. After completing these eighty days, she may enter the Garden of Eden, as it is a place holier than all others, where every tree is sacred.
13. This law for women who bear children is to be observed, with the days of purification completed before approaching anything holy or entering the sanctuary.
14. This law and testimony were established for Israel, that they may observe it continually.
15. During the first week of the first jubilee, Adam and his wife were in the Garden of Eden for seven years, tending and caring for it. They were taught all the tasks suitable for its upkeep.
16. They worked in the garden, unaware of their nakedness, and felt no shame. Adam guarded the garden from animals and birds, gathered fruit, ate, and stored what was needed for himself and his wife.
17. At the end of seven years, on the seventeenth day of the second month, the serpent approached the woman and questioned her, "Did God indeed command you not to eat from every tree in the garden?"
18. She replied, "God told us we may eat the fruit of the trees, but not from the tree in the center of the garden, for if we eat or touch it, we will die."
19. The serpent responded, "You will not surely die. God knows that on the day you eat it, your eyes will be opened, and you will be like gods, knowing good and evil."
20. Seeing that the tree was appealing, the woman took and ate its fruit. She covered herself with fig leaves and gave some to Adam, who also ate.
21. Their eyes were opened, and they realized their nakedness.
22. Adam sewed fig leaves together to cover himself.
23. God was angry with the serpent and cursed it for eternity.
24. He was also displeased with the woman for listening to the serpent. He said, "I will greatly increase your pain in childbirth; you will bear children in sorrow, and your desire will be for your husband, who will rule over you."

25. To Adam, He said, "Because you listened to your wife and ate from the tree, the ground is now cursed. It will bring forth thorns and thistles, and you will toil for your food by the sweat of your brow until you return to the earth, for from it you were taken."
26. God made garments of skins to clothe Adam and his wife and sent them out from the Garden of Eden.
27. On the day Adam left the garden, he offered a sacrifice, including frankincense, galbanum, stacte, and spices at sunrise, as a symbol of covering his shame.
28. On that day, the mouths of all beasts, birds, and other creatures were closed, so they could no longer speak as they once had, in a shared language with humankind.
29. God sent all creatures out of the Garden of Eden, each to its designated place in the world, by kind and species.
30. Only humans were given the ability to cover their shame among all creatures.
31. Therefore, it is recorded on the heavenly tablets that those who know the law should cover their bodies and not expose themselves as the nations do.
32. On the new moon of the fourth month, Adam and his wife departed from the Garden of Eden and settled in the land of 'Elda, where they were originally created.
33. Adam named his wife Eve, and they did not have a son until after the first jubilee.
34. Following that, Adam knew his wife
35. And he continued to work the land as he had been instructed in the Garden of Eden.

Chapter 4

1. In the third week of the second jubilee, Eve bore Cain; in the fourth week, she bore Abel; and in the fifth week, she gave birth to her daughter, Awan.
2. During the first year of the third jubilee, Cain killed Abel because God accepted Abel's offering but rejected Cain's.
3. Cain killed Abel in a field, and Abel's blood cried out from the ground to Heaven, protesting his murder.
4. The Lord condemned Cain for Abel's death, making him a fugitive on the earth and cursing him because of his brother's blood.
5. Because of this, it is written on the heavenly tablets: "Cursed is anyone who treacherously strikes his neighbor; let all who witness this declare it. And those who witness and do not report it will also be cursed."
6. For this reason, whenever we stand before the Lord, we declare all sin committed in Heaven, on earth, in light, in darkness—wherever it may be.
7. Adam and Eve mourned for Abel for four years. In the fourth year of the fifth week, they found joy again, and Adam had relations with his wife, who bore a son named Seth. Adam said, "God has granted us another child in place of Abel, whom Cain killed."
8. In the sixth week, Eve bore a daughter named Azura.

9. Cain married his sister Awan, and she bore him Enoch at the end of the fourth jubilee. In the first year of the first week of the fifth jubilee, people began building houses, and Cain established a city, naming it after his son, Enoch.
10. Adam knew his wife Eve again, and she bore nine more sons.
11. During the fifth week of the fifth jubilee, Seth married his sister Azura, and in the fourth year of the sixth week, she bore him Enos.
12. Enos was the first to call upon the Name of the Lord on earth.
13. In the seventh jubilee, during the third week, Enos took his sister Noam as his wife, and she bore him a son named Kenan in the third year of the fifth week.
14. At the end of the eighth jubilee, Kenan married his sister Mualeleth, and she bore him a son named Mahalalel in the ninth jubilee, during the first week in the third year.
15. During the second week of the tenth jubilee, Mahalalel married Dinah, daughter of Barakiel, his father's brother's daughter. She bore him a son in the third week of the sixth year, and he named him Jared. In Jared's time, the Watchers—angels of the Lord—descended to earth to instruct humanity in justice and righteousness.
16. In the eleventh jubilee, Jared married Baraka, daughter of Rasujal, his father's brother's daughter. In the fourth week of that jubilee, she bore him a son named Enoch.
17. Enoch was the first human on earth to learn writing, knowledge, and wisdom. He recorded the signs of the heavens according to their months in a scroll, so people could understand the seasons and the yearly cycles.
18. Enoch was the first to create a written testimony, explaining the jubilee cycles and making known the days of the years, setting the months and recounting the Sabbath years as we revealed to him.
19. In a vision, he saw and understood the events that would unfold for humanity up to the Day of Judgment. He documented all he saw as a witness for future generations.
20. During the twelfth jubilee, in the seventh week, Enoch married Edni, daughter of Danel, his father's brother's daughter. In the sixth year of that week, she bore him a son, and he named him Methuselah.
21. Enoch spent six jubilees with the angels of God, who showed him all things on earth and in the heavens, including the order of the sun, which he recorded.
22. He testified against the Watchers who had sinned by mingling with the daughters of men and warned them of their defilement.
23. Enoch was taken from among humankind, and we brought him to the Garden of Eden, where he wrote down judgments against the world and humanity's wickedness.
24. Because of this, God brought the Flood upon the earth, using Enoch as a sign and a witness against all people, recounting their deeds until the day of condemnation.
25. Enoch burned incense in the sanctuary, offering fragrant spices on the mountain.
26. The Lord designated four holy places on earth: the Garden of Eden, the Mountain of the East, Mount Sinai (where you stand today), and Mount Zion, which will be consecrated

in the new creation as a source of sanctification for the earth, purifying it from guilt and uncleanness for all generations.
27. In the fourteenth jubilee, Methuselah married Edna, daughter of Azriel, his father's brother's daughter. In the third week, in the first year of that week, she bore him a son named Lamech.
28. In the fifteenth jubilee, during the third week, Lamech married Betenos, daughter of Barakiel, his father's brother's daughter. She bore him a son named Noah, saying, "He will bring comfort for our toil and labor over the cursed ground."
29. At the end of the nineteenth jubilee, in the seventh week and the sixth year, Adam died, and his sons buried him in the land where he was created, making him the first person buried in the earth.
30. Adam's life lacked seventy years from reaching a thousand years, for as it is written in the heavenly testimony, "A thousand years is as one day." Because he ate from the Tree of Knowledge, he did not complete a full day of years, dying within it.
31. At the close of this jubilee, Cain also died in the same year when his house collapsed upon him, killing him with stones. This was fitting, for with a stone he had killed Abel, and by a stone, he was justly punished.
32. This event established a rule on the heavenly tablets: "Whoever kills another with an instrument shall be killed with the same, receiving the same measure of judgment."
33. In the twenty-fifth jubilee, Noah married Emzara, daughter of Rakeel, his father's brother's daughter, in the first year of the fifth week. In the third year, she bore Shem; in the fifth year, she bore Ham; and in the first year of the sixth week, she bore Japheth.

Chapter 5

1. As humanity multiplied on earth, daughters were born to them. In a specific year of that jubilee, the angels of God noticed that these daughters were beautiful, and they took wives from among them. The offspring of these unions were giants.
2. Lawlessness began to increase on the earth, with all flesh—humans, animals, birds, and everything else—corrupting its ways. They began to devour one another, and the earth was filled with violence and wickedness, with every thought of humanity being evil continuously.
3. God observed the earth and saw its corruption; all flesh had deviated from its proper order, and evil filled the earth before His eyes.
4. The Lord decided to destroy humankind and all living beings on earth, which He had created.
5. However, Noah found favor in the eyes of the Lord.
6. God was exceedingly angry with the angels He had sent to earth. He commanded that they be stripped of their authority and bound in the depths of the earth, where they remain separated.

7. A command was also given for their offspring, the giants, to be struck down by the sword, removing them from under heaven.
8. God declared, "My Spirit will not remain with humanity forever, as they are flesh. Their lifespan will be one hundred and twenty years."
9. He sent a sword among them, causing them to turn against one another, killing each other until they were wiped out.
10. Their fathers witnessed this destruction. Afterward, the angels were bound in the depths of the earth until the day of judgment, when all who have corrupted their ways will face divine judgment.
11. God destroyed all beings from their places, leaving none unjudged according to their wickedness.
12. He then created a new nature for all His works, establishing righteousness so that no creature would sin in its essence, but would remain just according to its kind.
13. Judgment for all creatures and every type of being is inscribed on the heavenly tablets, recorded in righteousness for those who stray from the path ordained for them.
14. Nothing, whether in heaven or earth, in light or darkness, in the depths of Sheol or in hidden places, escapes judgment, for every act is inscribed and decreed.
15. All are judged, the great by their greatness, the small by their smallness, each according to their deeds.
16. God does not show partiality nor accepts bribes. If He declares judgment upon anyone, no offering on earth can sway Him, as He is a righteous judge.
17. For the children of Israel, it is written that if they turn to God in righteousness, He will forgive their transgressions and pardon their sins.
18. It is inscribed and ordained that He will show mercy each year to those who turn from their guilt.
19. As for those who corrupted their ways before the flood, none were shown favor except Noah. Noah's righteousness saved him and his family from the waters of the flood, as he adhered to everything commanded of him.
20. The Lord declared His intention to destroy all life on earth, including humans, animals, birds, and all that moves on the ground.
21. He commanded Noah to build an ark to save himself from the floodwaters.
22. Noah built the ark exactly as instructed during the twenty-seventh jubilee, in the fifth week, in the fifth year, on the first month's new moon.
23. He entered the ark in the sixth year, during the second month, between the new moon and the sixteenth day. Everything that was brought to him entered the ark, and the Lord closed it from the outside on the evening of the seventeenth.
24. The Lord opened the seven floodgates of heaven and the seven fountains of the great deep.
25. For forty days and forty nights, rain poured from heaven, and the fountains of the deep released waters until the earth was entirely submerged.

26. The waters rose until they covered the highest mountains by fifteen cubits, lifting the ark above the earth, where it floated on the water's surface.
27. The waters prevailed over the earth for five months, totaling one hundred and fifty days.
28. Finally, the ark came to rest on Mount Lubar, one of the mountains of Ararat.
29. On the fourth month's new moon, the fountains of the great deep were closed, and the floodgates of heaven were restrained. On the seventh month's new moon, the mouths of the earth's abysses opened, and the water began to recede.
30. On the tenth month's new moon, the mountain tops became visible, and by the first month's new moon, the earth's surface appeared.
31. The waters completely disappeared from the earth by the fifth week of the seventh year, and on the seventeenth day of the second month, the earth was dry.
32. On the twenty-seventh day of the second month, Noah opened the ark and released all the animals—beasts, cattle, birds, and every creature that moved—to repopulate the earth.

Chapter 6

1. On the new moon of the third month, Noah left the ark and built an altar on the mountain.
2. He offered a sacrifice to atone for the earth, using the blood of a young goat to cleanse the land, as everything had been destroyed except those saved in the ark with him.
3. Placing the fat of the offering on the altar, he added an ox, a goat, a sheep, kids, salt, a turtledove, and a young dove. He burned these offerings and poured oil, wine, and scattered frankincense over them, creating a pleasing aroma for the Lord.
4. The Lord, pleased by the aroma, made a covenant with Noah, promising that He would never again destroy the earth by flood. He declared that the cycles of seedtime and harvest, cold and heat, summer and winter, day and night would remain in their proper order.
5. He blessed Noah and his sons, saying, "Be fruitful, multiply, and fill the earth. I will place a fear and dread of you in every creature on land and sea.
6. "I have given you all animals, birds, and fish for food, just as I gave you green plants."
7. "But do not eat meat with its lifeblood still in it, for life is in the blood, and I will hold you accountable for it. The blood of each person and animal will be required as well.
8. "Whoever sheds another's blood will have his own blood shed, for humankind was created in God's image."
9. The Lord continued, "Be fruitful and multiply on the earth."
10. Noah and his sons vowed never to eat blood in any flesh, making a lasting covenant with the Lord for all generations.
11. Because of this, God commanded Moses to establish a covenant with Israel on the mountain, sealed with blood, as a reminder of the Lord's eternal covenant.
12. This commandment is a testimony for all generations, so that no one will eat the blood of animals, birds, or livestock for as long as the earth endures. Those who do so will be cut off from the land.

13. Command the people of Israel not to consume blood, so their names and descendants may continue in the Lord's sight.
14. This law is everlasting, and they must observe it throughout their generations, offering sacrifices daily at morning and evening for forgiveness.
15. As a sign to Noah and his sons, God promised never to flood the entire earth again.
16. He set a rainbow in the clouds as a sign of His eternal covenant that a flood would never again destroy the earth.
17. It is written on the heavenly tablets that the Festival of Weeks shall be celebrated annually in this month to renew the covenant.
18. This festival has been observed in heaven from creation until Noah's time—twenty-six jubilees and five weeks of years. Noah and his sons continued the observance for seven jubilees and one week of years, until Noah's death. After his death, his descendants neglected it until the time of Abraham, and they began eating blood.
19. However, Abraham, Isaac, and Jacob observed it, as did their children, until the time of Moses, when the Israelites resumed the celebration on the mountain.
20. The Lord commanded Israel to observe this festival for all generations, celebrating it on one day each year in this month.
21. This festival is known as the Festival of Weeks or the Festival of First Fruits, having a dual significance as recorded and engraved on the tablets.
22. The Lord wrote in the first law for Israel to observe it in its season, once a year, explaining the sacrifices they should offer, so that the people would remember and observe this festival each year.
23. Additionally, four new moons—of the first, fourth, seventh, and tenth months—are designated as days of remembrance, marking the year's four divisions. These are written as a testimony forever.
24. Noah established these feasts for future generations as a lasting memorial.
25. On the new moon of the first month, God instructed him to build an ark; on this day, the land dried, and Noah opened the ark to view the earth.
26. On the new moon of the fourth month, the depths of the abysses closed.
27. On the new moon of the seventh month, the abysses of the earth opened, allowing the waters to recede.
28. On the new moon of the tenth month, the mountain tops were visible, bringing joy to Noah.
29. Because of these events, Noah established these as commemorative feasts forever.
30. These were recorded on the heavenly tablets, with each quarter year having thirteen weeks, providing continuity from season to season and keeping the full year intact.
31. This calendar is written on the heavenly tablets and is to be observed each year without alteration.
32. Instruct the people of Israel to observe the years by this count—364 days—to maintain accuracy in timing and festival observance.

33. If they do not keep to this command, they will disrupt their seasons, neglect their festivals, and fall out of alignment with God's appointed times.
34. All of Israel will lose the path of the years, forgetting the new moons, seasons, and Sabbaths, and will stray from the intended yearly order.
35. This warning was given to prevent them from following the lunar calendar of the nations, which brings disorder, leading them to miss the appointed feasts due to ignorance.
36. Observing the moon's cycles disrupts the seasons by approximately ten days each year.
37. As a result, they will eventually hold impure days as holy, confusing the sacred with the profane, neglecting the true holy days.
38. Therefore, this testimony is commanded to remind them of the correct observance, so that after Moses' death, the people do not deviate from the year's 364-day cycle. By failing to keep this, they will lose alignment with new moons, seasons, Sabbaths, and festivals and will begin consuming blood unlawfully.

Chapter 7

1. In the seventh week of the first year of that jubilee, Noah planted a vineyard on Mount Lubar, where the ark had come to rest, one of the mountains of Ararat. The vines bore fruit in the fourth year, and Noah gathered the harvest in the seventh month.
2. Noah made wine from the grapes, stored it in a vessel, and kept it until the fifth year, on the new moon of the first month.
3. On this day of celebration, he joyfully offered a burnt sacrifice to the Lord—a young ox, a ram, seven yearling sheep, and a young goat as atonement for himself and his sons.
4. He prepared the young goat first, placing some of its blood on the flesh of the altar he had made, then placed the fat on the altar with the ox, ram, and sheep.
5. He mingled the offerings with oil, then sprinkled wine on the fire on the altar, adding incense, which created a pleasing aroma before the Lord.
6. Noah rejoiced and drank some of the wine with his sons in celebration.
7. In the evening, he went to his tent, lay down, and, being intoxicated, fell asleep uncovered.
8. Ham saw his father's nakedness and went outside to inform his two brothers.
9. Shem and Japheth, respectfully, took a garment, placed it on their shoulders, walked backward into the tent, and covered their father without looking at him.
10. When Noah awoke, he realized what his youngest son had done, and he declared, "Cursed be Canaan; he will be a servant to his brothers."
11. Noah then blessed Shem, saying, "Blessed be the Lord, the God of Shem; Canaan shall serve him."
12. He added, "May God expand Japheth's territory; may he live in harmony with Shem, and Canaan shall be his servant."
13. Ham realized that Noah had cursed his youngest son, Canaan, and he was displeased. He departed from his father, taking his sons Cush, Mizraim, Put, and Canaan with him.

14. Ham built a city and named it after his wife, Ne'elatama'uk.
15. Japheth saw this and, feeling envious, built a city named after his wife, 'Adataneses.
16. Shem remained with Noah, building a city near his father's on the mountain, naming it after his wife, Sedeketelbab.
17. These three cities are located near Mount Lubar: Sedeketelbab to the east, Ne'elatama'uk to the south, and 'Adataneses to the west.
18. The sons of Shem were Elam, Asshur, Arphaxad (who was born two years after the flood), Lud, and Aram.
19. The sons of Japheth were Gomer, Magog, Madai, Javan, Tubal, Meshech, and Tiras. These were the descendants of Noah.
20. In the twenty-eighth jubilee, Noah instructed his grandsons in the commandments, ordinances, and judgments he knew. He encouraged them to live righteously, honor their Creator, respect parents, love their neighbors, and protect themselves from sin and all forms of immorality.
21. He reminded them that the flood came because of three sins: the Watchers taking human wives and engaging in unlawful unions, beginning the cycle of impurity.
22. Their offspring, the Nephilim, were distinct in nature and eventually turned on one another. The giants killed the Nephilim, the Nephilim killed the Eljo, the Eljo killed humans, and men fought among themselves.
23. Humanity descended into lawlessness, selling themselves to wickedness and shedding much blood, filling the earth with violence.
24. They also sinned against the animals, birds, and all creatures, shedding blood and constantly imagining evil.
25. Because of their deeds and the bloodshed in the earth, the Lord destroyed everything.
26. Noah said to his sons, "We alone remain, along with all that entered the ark. But I see that you are not living in harmony, that jealousy and discord are growing among you, which leads to destruction."
27. He warned them, "I see that demons have begun to tempt you and your children. I fear that after my death, you will shed innocent blood and face destruction as those before the flood."
28. He continued, "Anyone who sheds human blood or consumes blood will be destroyed from the earth, without leaving any descendants under heaven; they will be taken to Sheol and cast into condemnation's darkness, where violent death awaits."
29. Noah instructed them not to let any blood remain visible on the earth after slaughtering animals or birds but to cover it as an act of righteousness.
30. "Do not be like those who consume blood. Guard yourselves so that no one eats blood in your presence. Cover it, as I have been commanded to teach you and all living beings."
31. "Let no soul be consumed with the flesh, so that the blood, which is life, is not held against you."

32. "Only through the blood of the one who shed it can the earth be cleansed from spilled blood."
33. Noah urged his children, "Pursue justice and righteousness so you may be firmly planted on the earth. Let your glory be lifted before God, who saved me from the floodwaters."
34. He added, "You will build cities and plant every type of fruit-bearing tree.
35. "For three years, the fruit of all edible trees is not to be gathered. In the fourth year, the fruit is consecrated as holy to the Most High God, creator of all things."
36. "Offer the first of your wine and oil as first fruits on the altar of the Lord, who will accept it, and allow His servants to partake of what remains before His altar."
37. "In the fifth year, release all the produce in righteousness, so that you may be blessed and all that you plant may prosper."
38. "This was the command given by Enoch to his son Methuselah, who passed it to Lamech, and he entrusted it to me, as each father instructed his sons."
39. Noah concluded, "Now I entrust these teachings to you as Enoch commanded, and I testify to you and your descendants, even as Enoch did, until the day of his death."

Chapter 8

1. In the twenty-ninth jubilee, at the beginning of the first week, Arphaxad married Râsû'ĕjâ, daughter of Sûsân and granddaughter of Elam. In the third year of that week, they had a son, whom he named Kâinâm.
2. As Kâinâm grew, his father taught him to write. Eventually, Kâinâm set out to find a place to establish a city.
3. During his search, he discovered an ancient inscription on a rock left by earlier generations. Upon reading it, he transcribed its contents, which included knowledge from the Watchers regarding omens and the movements of the sun, moon, and stars. This led him into error.
4. Fearing Noah's displeasure, Kâinâm kept silent about his discovery.
5. In the thirtieth jubilee, during the second week's first year, he married Mêlkâ, daughter of Madai, son of Japheth. In the fourth year, they had a son named Shelah, signifying, "Truly I have been sent."
6. Shelah grew up and married Mû'ak, daughter of his uncle Kêsêd, during the thirty-first jubilee's fifth week in the first year.
7. In the fifth year of that week, Mû'ak bore a son named Eber. He married 'Azûrâd, daughter of Nêbrôd, in the thirty-second jubilee's seventh week in the third year.
8. In the sixth year, they had a son named Peleg, so named because, during his lifetime, Noah's descendants began to divide the earth among themselves.
9. The family kept this division secret, only informing Noah.
10. At the start of the thirty-third jubilee, Noah's descendants divided the earth into three parts, one for each son—Shem, Ham, and Japheth—under the supervision of a heavenly messenger.

11. Noah gathered his sons and their families and allocated the land, allowing each son to take their inheritance from his hands.
12. Shem's portion included the central part of the earth, extending from the middle of Mount Râfâ to the waters of the River Tînâ. His territory stretched westward through the river to the abysses, where the river empties into the sea Mê'at, eventually reaching the Great Sea. The land north of this was given to Japheth, while Shem's territory lay to the south.
13. Shem's land extended to Kârâsô in the south and stretched along the Great Sea in a straight line to the westernmost part of the Egyptian Sea.
14. From there, it curved southward to the mouth of the Great Sea, reaching the area known as 'Afrâ, and continued to the waters of the River Gihon, down to its southern banks.
15. The boundary reached eastward, encompassing the Garden of Eden to the south, turning east
16. And extending to the mountain Râfâ, finally descending to the River Tînâ's mouth.
17. This land was assigned to Shem and his descendants as an eternal inheritance.
18. Noah was joyful that Shem received this blessed portion, recalling the prophecy he had spoken: "Blessed is the Lord, the God of Shem; may the Lord dwell in Shem's land."
19. Noah recognized that the Garden of Eden was the Holy of Holies, the dwelling place of the Lord, with Mount Sinai at the heart of the desert and Mount Zion at the earth's center, all three created as holy sites.
20. Noah blessed God, who placed these words of prophecy in his mouth, praising Him eternally.
21. He understood that a special blessing had been given to Shem and his descendants, covering Eden, the Red Sea, the eastern lands, and regions like India, Bashan, Lebanon, Kaftûr, Sanîr, Amana, Asshur, and the area surrounding Mount Ararat and beyond.
22. Ham's portion extended south of the Gihon River, encompassing land to the right of the Garden and reaching south to the mountains of fire.
23. It spread westward to the Sea of 'Atêl and west to the Sea of Mâ'ûk, where all that is indestructible descends.
24. Ham's territory extended north to Gâdîr's limits, continuing along the Great Sea's coast to the River Gihon, skirting the edge of Eden.
25. This land was designated for Ham and his descendants as their eternal inheritance.
26. Japheth's territory lay beyond the River Tînâ to the north, stretching northeast to the lands of Gog and its eastern borders.
27. His land extended northward, covering the Qêlt Mountains, reaching the Sea of Mâ'ûk and extending to the east of Gâdîr.
28. It stretched west to Fârâ, then returned to 'Afêrâg, extending eastward to the waters of the Sea of Mê'at, reaching the River Tînâ's boundary near Mount Râfâ, then veering north.
29. This land became Japheth's eternal inheritance, including five major islands and a vast northern land.

30. Japheth's region was colder, while Ham's was hot. Shem's land had a temperate blend of cold and heat.

Chapter 9

1. Ham divided his land among his sons: Cush received the eastern part, Mizraim to the west, Put further west, and Canaan by the sea.
2. Shem also divided his land. Elam's portion extended east from the Tigris to India, the Red Sea coast, Dêdân's waters, Mebrî and Êlâ's mountains, Sûsân, and the region bordering the Red Sea to the River Tînâ.
3. Asshur received all the land of Asshur, including Nineveh, Shinar, and extending to India's border.
4. Arphaxad's portion included the Chaldean region east of the Euphrates, the Red Sea coast, Lebanon, Sanîr, Amana, and the area bordering the Euphrates.
5. Aram's territory spanned Mesopotamia between the Tigris and Euphrates, reaching the northern Chaldean border and Asshur's mountains.
6. Lud received the Asshur mountains extending to the Great Sea, to the east of Asshur's land.
7. Japheth divided his land among his sons.
8. Gomer's portion stretched east from the north side to the River Tînâ. Magog's land covered the northern regions up to the Sea of Mê'at.
9. Madai's portion included territories westward to various islands.
10. Javan received all the islands near Lud's land.
11. Tubal's portion spanned from the area near Lud's boundary toward the second and third tongues of land.
12. Meshech received the region beyond the third tongue extending east to Gâdîr.
13. Tiras's portion included four large islands in the sea, bordering Ham's territory, while Kamâtûrî's islands were designated for Arphaxad's descendants.
14. Thus, the sons of Noah divided the lands in Noah's presence, swearing an oath and invoking a curse on anyone who seized land outside their assigned portion.
15. They declared, "So be it," binding themselves and their descendants until the Day of Judgment, when the Lord will judge all who filled the earth with transgressions, uncleanness, and sin.

Chapter 10

1. During the third week of this jubilee, unclean demons began leading the children of Noah's descendants astray, causing them to stumble and face destruction.
2. Noah's sons approached him, describing how the demons were misleading, blinding, and even killing their descendants.

3. Noah prayed to the Lord, saying, "God of all spirits, You have shown mercy to me and saved me and my sons from the flood. You did not let me perish as the wicked did, showing great grace and mercy to my soul. Lift up Your grace upon my sons and prevent these evil spirits from ruling over them, lest they destroy them from the earth.
4. Bless me and my sons, allowing us to grow, multiply, and fill the earth.
5. You know the actions of the Watchers, the fathers of these spirits, in my day. Bind and imprison these evil spirits, preventing them from harming the descendants of Your servant, for they were created only to destroy.
6. Do not let them dominate the spirits of the living, for You alone have authority over them. Do not grant them power over the righteous, now or forevermore."
7. The Lord commanded His angels to bind these spirits.
8. Mastêmâ, the chief of the spirits, came and said, "Lord, Creator, allow some of them to remain with me, to follow my commands, so that I may carry out my purposes upon the sons of men. Without them, I cannot fulfill my intentions, for they are needed to corrupt and mislead before my judgment, as humanity's wickedness is great."
9. The Lord replied, "Let one-tenth remain with you, but send the other nine-tenths into the place of condemnation."
10. He instructed one of His angels to teach Noah remedies and medicines for all ailments, knowing that people would stray from righteousness.
11. The angels carried out His instructions, binding the malevolent spirits and leaving a tenth of them under Satan's authority on earth.
12. They revealed to Noah the cures for diseases and explained the deceptions of these spirits, so Noah could heal with the herbs of the earth.
13. Noah wrote down all their teachings in a scroll as he was instructed, ensuring that the evil spirits could no longer harm his descendants.
14. He entrusted this knowledge to Shem, his eldest son, whom he loved deeply.
15. Eventually, Noah passed away and was buried on Mount Lubar in the land of Ararat.
16. He lived nine hundred and fifty years—a span of nineteen jubilees, two weeks, and five years.
17. Noah excelled in righteousness among humanity, surpassed only by Enoch, who was dedicated to testifying about each generation's deeds until the Day of Judgment.
18. In the thirty-third jubilee, during the first year of the second week, Peleg took a wife named Lômnâ, daughter of Sînâ'ar. In the fourth year of that week, they had a son named Reu. Peleg named him this because he observed that humanity was becoming wicked, gathering to build a city and a tower in the land of Shinar.
19. They left the land of Ararat, migrating eastward to Shinar, where they resolved to build a city and a tower, saying, "Let us ascend to the heavens."
20. Construction began, and by the fourth week, they made bricks from fire, using them in place of stone, binding them with asphalt obtained from the sea and water sources in Shinar.

21. They continued building for forty-three years, with the tower's base measuring two hundred and three bricks wide and each brick a third of a cubit in height. The tower's height eventually reached five thousand four hundred and thirty-three cubits and two palms. One wall extended thirteen stadia, with the other reaching thirty stadia.
22. The Lord observed their unity and ambition, saying, "They are one people with a single purpose, and nothing will be withheld from them. Let us go down and confuse their language, so they cannot understand each other and will disperse into different cities and nations."
23. The Lord descended with His angels to see the city and the tower that humanity was building.
24. He confounded their language, and as a result, they could no longer understand one another, causing them to abandon the project.
25. The area became known as Babel, for it was there that the Lord confused their language. From Babel, humanity dispersed into various cities, each with its own language and nation.
26. The Lord sent a strong wind against the tower, toppling it to the ground. Its remains lay between Asshur and Babylon in the land of Shinar, and it was named "Overthrow."
27. In the first year of the thirty-fourth jubilee, during the fourth week, humanity was scattered from Shinar.
28. Ham and his sons settled in the land designated as their inheritance in the southern regions.
29. Canaan, however, noticed the fertile land of Lebanon extending to the river of Egypt. Instead of going to his assigned inheritance to the west, he chose to settle in Lebanon, spanning from east to west, near the Jordan River and the sea.
30. Ham, along with Cush and Mizraim, confronted Canaan, saying, "You have settled in land that does not belong to you, land that was not given to us by lot. If you remain here, you and your descendants will fall under a curse for taking land by rebellion, and by rebellion, you will fall, being uprooted forever.
31. This land was given to Shem and his descendants; you must not dwell in Shem's inheritance.
32. You are cursed beyond all the sons of Noah by the oath we swore before the Holy Judge and in the presence of our father Noah."
33. Despite their warnings, Canaan ignored them and continued to dwell in Lebanon, from Hamath to the border of Egypt, along with his descendants.
34. For this reason, the land became known as Canaan.
35. Japheth and his sons settled by the sea in the land of their inheritance, but Madai was dissatisfied with the coastal land. He requested a portion from his wife's brothers, Elam, Asshur, and Arphaxad.
36. Madai then settled in Media, near his wife's brothers, and named his dwelling place, as well as his sons', Media after himself, Madai.

Chapter 11

1. During the thirty-fifth jubilee, in the third week, Reu married a woman named 'Ôrâ, daughter of 'Ûr, son of Kêsêd. She gave birth to a son, whom they named Sêrôḫ in the seventh year of that week.
2. As the sons of Noah multiplied, conflicts arose, and they began to wage war against each other. They captured one another, spilled blood, consumed blood, constructed fortified cities with walls and towers, and some began exalting themselves, establishing the early foundations of kingdoms. Cities clashed, nations battled, and individuals indulged in wickedness, building arsenals and teaching their sons the art of war. They captured cities and began the practice of enslaving people.
3. 'Ûr, the son of Kêsêd, established the city of 'Arâ of the Chaldees, naming it after himself and his father.
4. They crafted idols and molten images, worshipping these false gods. They carved graven images and erected unclean statues, and malevolent spirits influenced them, leading them to transgress and act with impurity.
5. Mastêmâ, the prince of wickedness, spurred these actions, sending other spirits under his command to spread sin, violence, and bloodshed on the earth.
6. Consequently, Sêrôḫ was named Serug, for in his time, people turned increasingly to sin and wickedness.
7. Serug grew up in Ur of the Chaldees, near his wife's family. He practiced idol worship and, in the thirty-sixth jubilee, he married Mêlkâ, daughter of Kâbêr, his cousin.
8. Mêlkâ bore him a son, Nahor, in the first year of the week. Nahor was taught the arts of divination and interpreting signs in the heavens.
9. In the thirty-seventh jubilee, during the sixth week, Nahor married 'Îjâskâ, the daughter of Nêstâg of the Chaldees.
10. She bore him a son, Terah, in the seventh year of this week.
11. Mastêmâ, the prince of evil, sent ravens and birds to ruin the fields, consuming seeds before they could take root, devastating the land and leaving people destitute.
12. Terah's name reflects this hardship, as the ravens' attacks left people impoverished.
13. The land experienced a period of barrenness, with birds devouring the fruit from the trees, so that only minimal yields were saved.
14. In the thirty-ninth jubilee, during the second week, Terah married 'Êdnâ, the daughter of 'Abrâm.
15. In the seventh year of this week, she bore him a son, Abram, named after her father, who had passed before Abram's birth.
16. Abram, growing up, began to recognize the misguided ways of his time. He saw people following idols and impurity. Terah taught him to write, and by age fourteen, Abram distanced himself from idol worship, refusing to partake in his father's practices.
17. Abram prayed earnestly to the Creator, asking to be shielded from the corrupt ways of humanity, desiring not to be tainted by their sins.

18. When it was time to sow seeds, everyone went out to guard the fields from the ravens. Abram, a young man of fourteen, joined them.
19. As a swarm of ravens descended, Abram ran toward them, commanding them not to land. Miraculously, they obeyed, returning from where they came.
20. Abram repelled the ravens seventy times that day, preventing a single one from settling in the fields.
21. Witnesses across the land observed Abram's actions, recognizing him as a remarkable figure in the land of the Chaldees.
22. That year, many came to him seeking guidance for sowing, and he assisted them until planting was complete. Their crops thrived, and they enjoyed a bountiful harvest.
23. The following year, Abram introduced a wooden apparatus for the plow, allowing seeds to fall directly into the furrow, concealing them from the ravens.
24. This innovation, adopted by many, allowed them to sow their fields without fear of the birds, as Abram had shown them.

Chapter 12

1. In the sixth week, during the seventh year, Abram spoke to his father Terah, saying, "Father!"
2. Terah responded, "Here I am, my son."
3. Abram questioned, "What benefit is there in worshiping these idols before which you bow? They have no spirit and are but lifeless forms, misleading hearts. Do not worship them.
4. Instead, worship the God of Heaven, who brings rain and dew upon the earth, oversees all creation, and sustains life by His will.
5. Why honor what has no life? These idols are made by human hands and must be carried on shoulders. They bring shame to those who create and worship them."
6. Terah replied, "I know this, my son, but what can I do? The people compel me to serve these idols.
7. If I speak the truth, they will kill me, for they are devoted to these images. Be silent, my son, lest they harm you too."
8. Abram shared these thoughts with his brothers, angering them, so he chose to remain silent.
9. In the fortieth jubilee, during the second week, Abram married Sarai, his half-sister, and she became his wife.
10. His brother Haran married in the third year of the third week and had a son named Lot in the seventh year.
11. Nahor, Abram's other brother, also married.
12. When Abram was sixty, in the fourth week of the fourth year, he rose in the night and burned the house of idols, destroying everything within, without anyone's knowledge.
13. During the night, the family attempted to save their gods from the fire.

14. Haran tried to rescue them, but the flames overwhelmed him, and he perished in Ur of the Chaldees. His family buried him there.
15. Afterward, Terah and his sons left Ur of the Chaldees, journeying toward the lands of Lebanon and Canaan. They eventually settled in Haran, where Abram remained with Terah for fourteen years.
16. In the sixth week, during the fifth year, Abram stayed up all night on the new moon of the seventh month, observing the stars to predict the year's rainfall.
17. He pondered, "All celestial signs, whether from stars, moon, or sun, are controlled by the Lord. Why do I seek them out?
18. If God wills it, He brings rain; if not, He withholds it. Everything is under His authority."
19. That night, Abram prayed, "My God, the Most High, You alone are my chosen God. You created all things, the works of Your hands. Deliver me from the sway of evil spirits that mislead humanity and keep me steadfast in Your ways.
20. Let my descendants and I follow You without straying, now and forever."
21. Abram then asked, "Should I return to Ur of the Chaldees, where they seek me, or stay here? Guide me on the right path, that I may follow Your will without succumbing to my own desires, O my God."
22. As he finished his prayer, the Lord's message came to him, instructing, "Leave your country, your family, and your father's house for a land I will show you.
23. I will make you a great nation, bless you, and make your name renowned. You will be a blessing to all families of the earth.
24. I will bless those who bless you and curse those who curse you. I will be God to you and your descendants, so do not fear. From now on and for all generations, I am your God."
25. The Lord instructed His angel to open Abram's mouth, allowing him to speak the Hebrew language, which had been lost since Babel's fall.
26. Abram then began speaking and writing in Hebrew. He took his ancestors' scrolls, written in this language, and diligently studied them.
27. For six months of the rainy season, Abram immersed himself in these studies, guided by divine insight.
28. In the seventh year of the sixth week, Abram informed Terah of his intention to travel to Canaan to explore it and then return.
29. Terah blessed him, saying, "Go in peace. May God make your journey successful, protect you from harm, and grant you favor.
30. If you find a place that pleases you, take me with you, along with Lot, Haran's son, whom I entrust to you. May the Lord be with you."
31. "Leave Nahor with me," Terah continued, "until you return in peace, and then we shall all join you together."

Chapter 13

1. Abram set out from Haran with his wife, Sarai, and his nephew, Lot, the son of his late brother Haran, traveling to the land of Canaan. He journeyed through Asshur and reached Shechem, where he camped near a prominent oak tree.
2. As he surveyed the land, he saw that it was fruitful and beautiful, stretching from Hamath to the towering oak.
3. The Lord spoke to Abram, saying, "I will give this land to you and to your descendants."
4. Abram then built an altar and offered a sacrifice to the Lord, who had revealed Himself to him.
5. From there, he traveled to a mountain with Bethel on the west and Ai on the east, setting up his tent in that location.
6. He observed the land, finding it broad, fertile, and filled with diverse trees—vines, figs, pomegranates, oaks, holm trees, terebinths, olive trees, cedars, cypresses, date palms, and other trees. Water was abundant on the mountains.
7. He blessed the Lord, who had led him out of Ur of the Chaldees and brought him to this land.
8. In the first year of the seventh week, on the new moon of the first month, Abram built an altar on this mountain and called on the name of the Lord, declaring, "You, the eternal God, are my God."
9. Abram offered a burnt sacrifice, praying that the Lord would be with him always.
10. From there, he continued his journey southward, reaching Hebron, which was already established at that time. He stayed there for two years and later traveled further south to Bealoth. However, a famine struck the land.
11. In the third year of that week, Abram went to Egypt, residing there for five years until a conflict arose concerning Sarai.
12. At that time, the city of Tanis (Zoan) in Egypt had been established—seven years after Hebron.
13. When Pharaoh seized Sarai, the Lord sent severe plagues upon Pharaoh's household because of her.
14. Abram prospered in Egypt, amassing great wealth in livestock, servants, and abundant silver and gold. Lot, his nephew, also became wealthy.
15. Pharaoh ultimately released Sarai and sent Abram away. Abram returned to the land where he had first camped, between Ai and Bethel, where he had previously built an altar, and there he offered thanks to the Lord for bringing him back safely.
16. In the forty-first jubilee, during the third year of the first week, Abram returned to this spot and offered a burnt sacrifice, calling upon the Lord, acknowledging Him as "the Most High God, forever."
17. In the fourth year of that week, Lot parted ways with Abram, choosing to dwell in Sodom, though the people of Sodom were notorious for their wickedness.
18. Abram was saddened by Lot's departure, as he had no children of his own.

19. That year, after Lot was taken captive, the Lord spoke to Abram, saying, "Lift up your eyes and look in every direction—north, south, east, and west.
20. All the land you see I will give to you and your descendants forever. Your descendants will be as numerous as the sands of the sea; though one may attempt to count the dust of the earth, your offspring shall be beyond measure."
21. The Lord instructed Abram to explore the land's length and breadth, for it was destined for his descendants. Abram then went to Hebron and settled there.
22. In that same year, Chedorlaomer, king of Elam; Amraphel, king of Shinar; Arioch, king of Ellasar; and Tidal, king of the nations, waged war, defeating the king of Gomorrah. The king of Sodom fled, and many died in the Valley of Siddim near the Salt Sea.
23. These kings captured Sodom, Adam, and Zeboim, taking Lot and his possessions with them as they marched toward Dan.
24. A survivor informed Abram of Lot's capture. Abram gathered his trained servants and set out to rescue Lot.
25. Abram committed a tenth of all first-fruits to the Lord as a lasting ordinance for his descendants to offer to the priests who serve God, to be observed forever.
26. This law, without expiration, ordained that a tenth of everything—grains, wine, oil, cattle, and sheep—be given to the Lord.
27. This portion was designated for the priests to consume with joy before God.
28. When the king of Sodom came to Abram, he bowed and requested the return of the people Abram had rescued, offering him the spoils.
29. Abram replied, "I have raised my hand to the Most High God, and I will not take anything from you—not even a thread or a shoe strap—lest you claim, 'I have made Abram rich.' Only the food that my men have eaten and the share due to Aner, Eschol, and Mamre, who fought alongside me, will be kept."

Chapter 14

1. After these events, in the fourth year of the week, on the new moon of the third month, the word of the Lord came to Abram in a vision, reassuring him, "Fear not, Abram; I am your shield, and your reward will be exceedingly great."
2. Abram responded, "Lord God, what will You give me since I remain childless? My heir is Eliezer of Damascus, the son of Mâsêq, born to my servant."
3. The Lord answered, "This man will not be your heir. Instead, a son from your own body shall be your heir."
4. The Lord led Abram outside and instructed him, "Look toward the heavens and count the stars, if you are able."
5. As Abram gazed at the countless stars, the Lord declared, "So shall your descendants be."
6. Abram believed the Lord's promise, and it was credited to him as righteousness.

7. The Lord said, "I am the Lord who brought you out of Ur of the Chaldees to give you this land of the Canaanites as an everlasting possession. I will be God to you and your descendants."
8. Abram asked, "Lord God, how shall I know that I will inherit it?"
9. The Lord instructed, "Bring me a heifer, a goat, a ram—all three years old—a turtledove, and a young pigeon."
10. Abram gathered these animals in the middle of the month and went to the oak of Mamre near Hebron.
11. He built an altar, sacrificed the animals, and poured their blood upon the altar. He divided the animals but left the birds whole.
12. As birds descended upon the sacrifice, Abram drove them away.
13. At sunset, Abram fell into a deep trance, and a profound darkness overwhelmed him. The Lord spoke, "Know for certain that your descendants will be strangers in a land not their own, enslaved and oppressed for four hundred years.
14. But I will judge the nation that enslaves them, and afterward, they will emerge with great wealth.
15. You will go to your ancestors in peace and be buried at a ripe old age.
16. Your descendants will return here in the fourth generation, for the iniquity of the Amorites is not yet complete."
17. Abram awoke to find the sun setting and a smoking furnace and a blazing torch passing between the pieces of his sacrifice.
18. On that day, the Lord made a covenant with Abram, promising, "To your descendants, I give this land, from the river of Egypt to the great River Euphrates—the lands of the Kenites, Kenizzites, Kadmonites, Perizzites, Rephaim, Phakorites, Hivites, Amorites, Canaanites, Girgashites, and Jebusites."
19. The day concluded as Abram offered the sacrificial animals along with fruit and drink offerings, which were consumed by the fire.
20. On this day, the Lord renewed His covenant with Abram, similar to the covenant made with Noah.
21. Abram joyfully shared these promises with Sarai, holding faith that they would have offspring, although she remained barren.
22. Sarai proposed that Abram marry her Egyptian maidservant, Hagar, in hopes of having children through her.
23. Abram agreed, and Sarai gave Hagar to him as a wife.
24. Abram went to Hagar, who conceived and bore him a son, named Ishmael, in the fifth year of this week. Abram was eighty-six years old at the time.

Chapter 15

1. In the fifth year of the fourth week of this jubilee, during the third month and in the middle of the month, Abram observed the Festival of the First-Fruits of the grain harvest.

2. He offered new sacrifices on the altar, presenting the first-fruits of his crops to the Lord: a heifer, a goat, and a sheep as burnt offerings. He also brought fruit offerings and drink offerings with frankincense on the altar.
3. The Lord appeared to Abram, saying, "I am God Almighty; walk before Me faithfully and be blameless.
4. I will establish My covenant between Me and you, and I will greatly increase your descendants."
5. Abram fell on his face, and God spoke to him, saying,
6. "My covenant is with you, and you will become the father of many nations.
7. Your name will no longer be Abram, but Abraham, for I have made you the father of many nations.
8. I will make you exceedingly fruitful; nations and kings will come from you.
9. I will establish My covenant as an everlasting covenant between Me and you and your descendants after you, to be your God and the God of your descendants.
10. I will give to you and your descendants the land where you are a foreigner, the land of Canaan, as an everlasting possession, and I will be their God."
11. Then the Lord said to Abraham, "As for you, keep My covenant, you and your descendants after you. Every male among you must be circumcised as a sign of this covenant.
12. On the eighth day, every male, whether born in your household or bought with money from a foreigner, must be circumcised.
13. This sign in your flesh is to be a lasting sign of My covenant.
14. Any uncircumcised male who is not circumcised on the eighth day will be cut off from his people, as he has broken My covenant."
15. God also told Abraham, "Your wife's name will no longer be Sarai; her name will be Sarah.
16. I will bless her and give you a son by her. She will be blessed, and nations and kings of peoples will come from her."
17. Abraham bowed, filled with joy, and said to himself, "Can a child be born to a man who is a hundred years old, or to Sarah, who is ninety?"
18. He then said to God, "If only Ishmael might live under Your blessing."
19. God replied, "Yes, but Sarah will bear you a son, and you will call him Isaac. I will establish My covenant with him as an everlasting covenant for his descendants after him.
20. As for Ishmael, I have heard you; I will bless him and make him fruitful. He will be the father of twelve princes and will become a great nation.
21. But My covenant I will establish with Isaac, whom Sarah will bear to you by this time next year."
22. When God had finished speaking, He departed from Abraham.
23. Abraham obeyed God's command, circumcising his son Ishmael, all the males born in his household, and those he had bought.

24. On that same day, Abraham and all the males in his household, including those he had purchased, were circumcised.
25. This law is for all generations, and the command to circumcise on the eighth day must never be neglected, for it is an eternal ordinance recorded on the heavenly tablets.
26. Anyone not circumcised on the eighth day does not belong to the people of the covenant and is considered separated from God's chosen people.
27. All the messengers of God's presence and sanctification were created in this covenant, and God set Israel apart to be with Him.
28. Command the children of Israel to observe this sign for all generations, so they are not cut off from the land.
29. The covenant is everlasting, binding Israel to this observance for all time.
30. Though Ishmael and Esau are also descendants of Abraham, God did not choose them, for He reserved Israel to be His people.
31. Many nations and peoples exist, yet God alone is the ruler of Israel, with no appointed spirit to govern them.
32. God announced that while Israel will stray from this command, they will return to it in time.
33. However, the sons of Belial will lead some astray, neglecting this practice and abandoning God's command.
34. Because of this disregard for the covenant, Israel will face great anger from God, who will remove them from the land and bring judgment upon them for their continuous neglect of this command.

Chapter 16

1. On the new moon of the fourth month, messengers appeared to Abraham at the oak of Mamre, informing him that Sarah would bear him a son.
2. Sarah overheard and laughed, doubting the message. She was then admonished and became fearful, denying her laughter.
3. The messengers revealed the child's name, Isaac, as it was written in the heavenly tablets.
4. They promised to return, and by that time, Sarah would have conceived.
5. In that same month, God's judgment came upon Sodom, Gomorrah, Zeboim, and the entire Jordan region, consuming them with fire and brimstone due to their wickedness.
6. God declared that similar judgment would fall upon any place that replicated the sinfulness of Sodom.
7. Lot, however, was saved as God remembered Abraham's faithfulness, delivering him from the destruction.
8. Lot and his daughters sinned afterward in a way unlike anything seen since Adam, as he lay with his daughters.
9. Due to this act, a command was engraved on the heavenly tablets to remove Lot's descendants from the earth on the day of judgment.

10. Following these events, Abraham moved from Hebron, settling between Kadesh and Shur in the Gerar mountains.
11. Midway through the fifth month, he relocated to the Well of the Oath.
12. In the sixth month, the Lord visited Sarah, fulfilling His promise, and she conceived.
13. She gave birth to a son in the third month, during the first-fruits festival, and he was named Isaac.
14. Abraham circumcised Isaac on the eighth day, marking the first circumcision under the eternal covenant.
15. In the sixth year of the fourth week, messengers returned to Abraham at the Well of the Oath, confirming that Isaac's line would carry Abraham's name and promise.
16. They blessed him, ensuring his survival to see many more sons, though only Isaac's line would be set apart as God's holy seed.
17. While nations would arise from his other sons, only Isaac's descendants would be God's chosen people.
18. Isaac's line would be God's possession, a kingdom and a priestly nation, set apart from all other nations.
19. Abraham and Sarah rejoiced at the news, celebrating God's blessings.
20. Abraham built an altar to the Lord, celebrating a festival of joy for seven days at the Well of the Oath.
21. He constructed shelters for himself and his household, marking the first celebration of the Festival of Shelters on earth.
22. Each day, he offered sacrifices, atoning for himself and his lineage.
23. As a thank-offering, he presented numerous animals, ensuring each offering was accompanied by drink and fruit offerings, sending up a pleasing aroma to the Lord.
24. He burned incense every morning and evening—frankincense, galbanum, stacte, nard, myrrh, spice, and costus—all pure and in equal parts.
25. For seven days, he celebrated joyfully with his household, excluding any uncircumcised or foreign person.
26. He blessed his Creator, who had set him apart, foreseeing that from Abraham would arise a lineage of righteousness.
27. Abraham named this festival the Festival of the Lord, a joyful time of worship to the Most High.
28. God blessed him and his descendants, establishing this celebration as a yearly observance for Israel.
29. It was ordained on the heavenly tablets that Israel would keep this festival with joy each year, throughout all generations.
30. This command is eternal, requiring Israel to observe it by dwelling in shelters, adorning themselves with wreaths, and using leafy branches and willows.
31. Abraham took branches of palm trees and other beautiful trees, circling the altar each morning seven times in thanksgiving and praise to God.

Chapter 17

1. In the first year of the fifth week, Isaac was weaned during this jubilee, and Abraham held a great feast in the third month to celebrate the occasion.
2. Ishmael, Hagar's son, was also there, and Abraham was filled with joy, blessing God for the children he had been given, knowing he would not pass away without heirs.
3. He recalled God's promises to him when Lot departed and praised the Creator with all his heart, feeling blessed to have a family that would inherit the land.
4. Sarah saw Ishmael playing and dancing, and Abraham joining in the celebration, which sparked jealousy in her. She said to Abraham, "Send away this bondwoman and her son, for he will not share in Isaac's inheritance."
5. Abraham was troubled at the thought of casting out Hagar and Ishmael.
6. But God said to Abraham, "Do not be distressed about the child or the bondwoman. Do as Sarah has asked, for it is through Isaac that your name will be carried forward.
7. Yet, I will also make Ishmael a great nation, for he too is your seed."
8. Early the next morning, Abraham took bread and water, gave them to Hagar and Ishmael, and sent them away.
9. They wandered in the wilderness of Beersheba until the water was gone, and the child grew weak with thirst.
10. In despair, Hagar placed Ishmael under an olive tree, sitting at a distance so she wouldn't witness his suffering. She wept in sorrow.
11. Then, a divine messenger appeared to her, saying, "Why are you weeping, Hagar? Arise, hold the child, for God has heard your voice and seen the boy."
12. Her eyes were opened, and she saw a well. She filled her water bottle and gave Ishmael a drink, and they continued their journey toward the wilderness of Paran.
13. Ishmael grew up to become an archer, and God was with him. His mother later arranged a marriage for him with a woman from Egypt.
14. They had a son, whom he named Nebaioth, acknowledging, "The Lord was with me when I called upon Him."
15. During the first year of the seventh week, on the twelfth day of the first month, there were voices in Heaven honoring Abraham for his faithfulness to God.
16. Mastêmâ, the adversary, challenged God, saying, "Abraham treasures Isaac above all else. Command him to offer Isaac as a burnt offering, and You will see if he remains faithful."
17. But God already knew Abraham's steadfastness, as He had tested him through his homeland, the famine, the kings' wealth, the separation from Sarah, circumcision, and the departure of Hagar and Ishmael.
18. Abraham had proven faithful and unwavering through all trials, always acting promptly and out of love for the Lord.

Chapter 18

1. God called to Abraham, who answered, "Here I am."
2. He instructed Abraham, "Take your beloved son, Isaac, and go to the mountains. There, I will show you where to offer him as a burnt sacrifice."
3. Rising early, Abraham saddled his donkey, took two servants and Isaac, split the wood for the offering, and journeyed. On the third day, he saw the designated mountain.
4. Near a well, he told the servants, "Stay here with the donkey. The boy and I will go to worship, then return to you."
5. Abraham placed the wood on Isaac and took the fire and knife himself. Together, they walked to the appointed place.
6. Isaac asked, "Father, we have the fire and wood, but where is the lamb for the offering?"
7. Abraham answered, "God will provide a lamb for the offering, my son." They continued toward the mount of God.
8. Upon arrival, Abraham built an altar, arranged the wood, bound Isaac, and laid him upon it. He raised the knife to slay his son.
9. But a divine messenger intervened, stopping Abraham, saying, "Do not harm the boy, for now I see that you fear God, as you did not withhold your son."
10. Calling out from Heaven, the messenger repeated, "Abraham, Abraham!" Abraham responded, trembling, "Here I am."
11. The messenger affirmed, "Do not harm the child. You have shown your fear of God and your unwavering faith by not withholding your son."
12. Mastêmâ, the adversary, was shamed. Abraham looked up to see a ram caught by its horns. He offered the ram in place of Isaac.
13. Abraham named the site "The Lord has provided," which became known as Mount Zion.
14. God called Abraham again, through the heavenly messenger, speaking blessings over him.
15. "By Myself, I swear that because you did not withhold your beloved son,
16. I will multiply your descendants as the stars and the sand on the shore. They will possess the gates of their enemies, and through your seed, all nations will be blessed because you obeyed My voice."
17. Abraham returned to the servants, and they journeyed to Beersheba, where Abraham made his home.
18. He celebrated a festival in honor of the Lord, observing it every year for seven days with joy.
19. This festival became an ordinance for Israel, observed for seven days with gladness each year.

Chapter 19

1. In the first year of the first week of the forty-second jubilee, Abraham returned to Hebron, residing near Kirjath-Arba for fourteen years.
2. During the first year of the third week, Sarah passed away in Hebron.

3. Abraham mourned her, and though tested by grief, he remained patient and calm in his words.
4. He spoke humbly with the sons of Heth, requesting a place to bury his wife.
5. The Lord granted him favor in the eyes of those around him, and they offered him land for burial.
6. Although they offered it freely, Abraham insisted on paying the full price of four hundred silver pieces and purchased the Cave of Machpelah.
7. Sarah's life had spanned one hundred and twenty-seven years—two jubilees, four weeks, and one year.
8. This was the tenth test of Abraham, and he remained faithful, even amid sorrow.
9. He did not question God's promise of the land, choosing to pay for a burial place for Sarah. He was recorded on the heavenly tablets as a friend of God.
10. In the fourth year, Abraham arranged a marriage for Isaac with Rebekah, daughter of Bethuel, the son of Abraham's brother Nahor.
11. Later, Abraham married Keturah, a woman from his household servants, for Hagar had passed.
12. Keturah bore him six sons: Zimram, Jokshan, Medan, Midian, Ishbak, and Shuah.
13. In the sixth week of the second year, Rebekah bore Isaac twin sons, Jacob and Esau. Jacob was peaceful and thoughtful, while Esau was wild and aggressive.
14. Jacob remained at home, while Esau pursued hunting and warfare.
15. Abraham loved Jacob deeply, recognizing in him the future of his lineage, though Isaac favored Esau.
16. Observing Esau's nature, Abraham called Rebekah, entrusting her with Jacob's care, as she loved him dearly.
17. "Watch over Jacob," he urged, "for he will carry forward our blessing and will be a light among humanity and a glory to Shem's lineage.
18. I see that the Lord will set Jacob apart as His chosen people among all the earth."
19. Abraham knew that Isaac's heart inclined toward Esau, while Rebekah cherished Jacob.
20. He blessed her to remain vigilant over Jacob, for in him, the promises of God would be fulfilled.
21. "Let your hands be strong, and rejoice in Jacob, for he will fill the earth with blessing
22. And descendants, uncountable as the sands of the earth.
23. The Lord's blessing upon me and my offspring will be inherited by Jacob's lineage.
24. In him, my name, and the names of my ancestors—Shem, Noah, Enoch, Mahalalel, Enos, Seth, and Adam—will be blessed.
25. Jacob will carry forward the purpose of Heaven and establish foundations on earth."
26. Calling Jacob before him, with Rebekah present, Abraham blessed him, saying,
27. "Beloved Jacob, may God's blessings flow upon you, as He blessed Adam, Enoch, Noah, and Shem.
28. May the promises spoken to me be realized through you and your seed forever.

29. May the spirits of Mastêmâ never have sway over you or your descendants, for the Lord is your God eternally.
30. Go forth in peace, my son." And with that, they left Abraham's presence.
31. Rebekah continued to love Jacob deeply, far more than Esau, while Isaac's affection remained with Esau.

Chapter 20

1. In the forty-second jubilee, during the first year of the seventh week, Abraham gathered his family, including Ishmael and his twelve sons, Isaac and his two sons, the six sons of Keturah, and their sons.
2. He instructed them to follow the ways of the Lord, urging them to live righteously, love one another, and practice justice and kindness toward everyone on earth.
3. He reminded them of their covenant with God, specifically the practice of circumcision, warning them to stay true to God's commandments and avoid straying from His path.
4. "If any among you commits immorality, she is to be punished, and avoid intermarrying with the daughters of Canaan, for their seed will not be preserved."
5. Abraham recounted the downfall of the giants and the judgment on the people of Sodom, who perished due to their wickedness, immorality, and corruption.
6. "Guard yourselves from immorality and wrongdoing to avoid disgrace upon our family, lest we become cursed like Sodom and our remnant like the sons of Gomorrah."
7. He implored his sons to love the God of Heaven, reject idolatry, and avoid impurity.
8. "Do not create idols, for they are worthless creations of men's hands. Those who trust in them trust in nothing."
9. Instead, Abraham instructed them to serve the Most High God with hope and integrity, promising that by doing so, God would bless their endeavors, provide for their needs, and ensure prosperity.
10. "You will be a blessing on earth, and nations will desire your favor, blessing your sons as I have been blessed."
11. Abraham gave gifts to Ishmael, his sons, and Keturah's sons before sending them eastward. To Isaac, he entrusted all his possessions.
12. Ishmael and Keturah's sons settled in the lands stretching from Paran to the borders of Babylon.
13. These families mingled, and collectively, they became known as the Arabs and Ishmaelites.

Chapter 21

1. In the sixth year of the seventh week, sensing the end of his life, Abraham called his son Isaac.

2. "I am one hundred and seventy-five years old," Abraham said, "and have spent my days devoted to the Lord, striving to walk in His ways."
3. "My heart has despised idols, and I have wholeheartedly sought the will of Him who created me."
4. He reminded Isaac of God's righteousness, explaining that He judges all justly, showing no favoritism.
5. "Keep His commands and avoid the detestable practices of idols and graven images."
6. Abraham advised Isaac to refrain from consuming blood of any kind, emphasizing the significance of respecting life.
7. He outlined the proper method for offering sacrifices, instructing Isaac to pour out the blood on the altar and place the fat and fine flour offerings upon it.
8. The fat from various parts of the animal was to be burned, creating an offering pleasing to God.
9. Isaac was to consume the sacrificial meat within two days, ensuring that nothing remained beyond the second day to avoid sin.
10. Abraham reminded him of ancient instructions found in the writings of his ancestors, including Enoch and Noah.
11. Every offering was to be seasoned with salt, as commanded by God.
12. Only certain woods, such as cypress, cedar, and pine, were permitted for burning on the altar.
13. Abraham instructed Isaac to avoid using old or split wood, which lacks fragrance, and to ensure that his offerings remained pure.
14. Only woods with a pleasing aroma were suitable for the altar.
15. "Follow these commands faithfully, my son, so that you may live in righteousness."
16. Cleanliness was paramount; Isaac was to wash before offering sacrifices and again afterward.
17. "Guard against bloodstains, and cover any spilled blood with dust."
18. Abraham repeated the prohibition against consuming blood, as it represents life itself.
19. He urged Isaac to avoid accepting gifts in exchange for bloodshed, as it pollutes the earth and cannot be cleansed except by the one who shed it.
20. God is the defender of the righteous, and He would protect Isaac from evil.
21. "Beware of following the ways of the unrighteous, lest God turn His face from you."
22. Isaac was to avoid the paths of sinners, upholding God's ordinances to be blessed.
23. "The Lord will raise a righteous lineage through you, and my name, along with yours, will be remembered forever."
24. Abraham blessed Isaac, saying, "May the Most High guide you, and may you be a blessing on earth."
25. Abraham's final words to his son were filled with encouragement and blessings
26. And Isaac left rejoicing.

Chapter 22

1. In the forty-fourth jubilee, during the second year of the first week—the year of Abraham's death—Isaac and Ishmael visited Abraham to celebrate the Festival of Weeks, the festival of the first-fruits.
2. Isaac, who owned much land in Beersheba, visited his father regularly.
3. Ishmael, too, came to see Abraham, and the two sons offered sacrifices together on Abraham's altar in Hebron.
4. Rebekah baked fresh bread from the new grain and sent it with Jacob to give to Abraham, along with a thank-offering from Isaac.
5. Abraham blessed the Most High God, who created heaven and earth and provided abundantly for mankind.
6. "I am grateful, my God, that You have allowed me to see this day. I am now an old man, content with the peaceful life You have granted me."
7. He prayed for God's mercy and peace to be with his descendants forever.
8. Abraham called Jacob, blessing him with a special prayer for strength and righteousness, asking God to choose him and his descendants as His people.
9. He embraced Jacob, declaring blessings upon him, saying, "May nations bow before your descendants, and may they become a holy people."
10. "Be strong, my son, and may you and your descendants lead with righteousness."
11. "The blessings given to me, to Noah, and to Adam will rest upon you and your lineage eternally."
12. Abraham prayed that Jacob would be cleansed from all wrongdoing and would inherit the earth.
13. He urged Jacob to remain distinct from the other nations, warning him of the impurities of their practices.
14. "They worship idols and feast among graves, practices that bring no understanding or benefit."
15. Abraham warned him against taking a wife from the daughters of Canaan, as their line was cursed.
16. "All idol worshipers will face judgment, just as Sodom did."
17. "But fear not, my son. God will preserve you from destruction and guide you on the right path."
18. Abraham promised that his legacy and name would continue through Jacob and that his household would remain sacred.
19. He blessed Jacob with the protection and grace of the Most High.
20. Abraham and Jacob lay together that night, and Jacob slept peacefully in his grandfather's embrace.
21. Abraham rejoiced over him and said, "Blessed is the God of all who brought me to this land, and who will make of Jacob a holy lineage."
22. He blessed Jacob once more, asking God to uphold His covenant with Jacob's descendants.

23. "May Your presence be with him always, and may Your covenant endure with him and his offspring throughout the generations of the earth."
24. With these words, Abraham's blessings were complete, and he rested in peace.
25. Abraham completed his words of guidance and blessing.
26. Together, he and Jacob lay down on the same bed, and Jacob rested in the arms of his grandfather, Abraham. Abraham embraced him with warmth, kissing him seven times, and his heart was filled with joy and affection.
27. With great love, Abraham spoke blessings over Jacob with all his heart, saying, "The Most High God, Creator of all things, who brought me out from Ur of the Chaldees to grant me this land as an everlasting inheritance, and to establish a holy lineage through me—blessed be the Most High forever."
28. Turning his blessing toward God, Abraham continued, "This son of mine, in whom I find boundless joy and affection, may Your grace and mercy forever rest upon him and his descendants.
29. Do not abandon him, but watch over him through the ages. May Your gaze be always upon him and his lineage, to protect, bless, and consecrate them as Your chosen people and treasured inheritance.
30. Bestow upon him all Your blessings for now and for all eternity, renewing Your covenant and grace with him and his descendants according to Your perfect will, throughout all generations on earth."

Chapter 23

1. Abraham placed Jacob's hands on his eyes as he offered a final blessing to the Almighty. He then covered his face, stretched out his legs, and passed into eternal rest, joining his ancestors.
2. Unaware of his grandfather's passing, Jacob lay peacefully in Abraham's embrace.
3. When Jacob awoke, he found Abraham's body cold and lifeless. In alarm, he called, "Father! Father!" But there was no answer, and he realized Abraham had died.
4. Jacob hurried to tell his mother, Rebekah, who then informed Isaac. They went together with Jacob, carrying a lamp, and found Abraham lying peacefully in death.
5. Isaac fell upon his father and wept, kissing him tenderly.
6. The sorrowful sounds of mourning echoed through the house. Ishmael arrived, joining Isaac and the rest of Abraham's household in mourning.
7. Isaac and Ishmael buried Abraham in the double cave next to Sarah, his beloved wife. They mourned for him deeply, along with all of Abraham's family and servants, for a period of forty days.
8. Abraham lived 175 years, spanning three jubilees and four weeks. He lived a life of righteousness, full of years and blessed by God.

9. His life marked a diminishing of human lifespans after the flood, and his years exceeded most of his descendants who would live less than two jubilees, as righteousness and peace became increasingly rare.
10. Unlike many, Abraham's life was full of goodness, as he had been righteous in all his ways, pleasing God throughout his life.
11. From Abraham's time onward, lifespans would continue to decrease, and people would live with little knowledge as their days shortened.
12. A life that reached a jubilee and a half would be deemed long, yet marked by sorrow, tribulation, and little peace.
13. Misery would follow such lives: sickness, conflict, and suffering would afflict future generations.
14. This fate would befall an evil generation that indulges in uncleanness, corruption, and wickedness.
15. They would look back on the long, peaceful lives of their ancestors and lament their own troubled days, which, even if extended to eighty years, would be filled with hardship.
16. In that generation, sons would confront fathers and elders for their sins and disregard for the covenant with the LORD.
17. All of their works would become filled with iniquity, pollution, and destruction.
18. Because of their wickedness, the earth itself would face devastation, and no vine, oil, or harvest would remain.
19. Strife would fill the land: young against old, poor against rich, commoner against ruler, all abandoning the covenant and commands of God.
20. There would be endless bloodshed and conflict until the ways of righteousness were utterly forgotten.
21. Those who escaped would persist in their wickedness, exalting deceit and wealth above all else, even invoking God's name falsely to corrupt the holy places.
22. For these sins, a great punishment would descend from God, leading them to captivity, judgment, and devastation.
23. God would raise enemies who knew neither mercy nor compassion, who would respect neither age nor status, and who would bring great suffering upon Israel and the descendants of Jacob.
24. In those days, the people would cry out to God for deliverance, but none would answer.
25. Children would appear aged and frail, wearied by unceasing afflictions and the weight of their burdens.
26. Then, some would begin to study the laws again, seeking righteousness and the path of truth.
27. Their lives would start to lengthen once more, approaching the lifespans of earlier generations.
28. None would feel unfulfilled, as all would live joyfully and in peace.

29. The LORD would bring healing and drive out all adversity, so that His people could live in eternal joy.
30. The righteous would witness the fulfillment of God's judgment, rejoicing in His justice.
31. Their spirits would rest, knowing that God had shown mercy to those who love Him.
32. And the LORD instructed Moses to write these words as a lasting testament for all generations.

Chapter 24

1 After the death of Abraham, the Lord blessed Isaac, who then left Hebron and settled at the Well of the Vision for seven years, beginning in the first year of the third week of that jubilee.
2 During the first year of the fourth week, a famine struck the land, similar to the one that had occurred in Abraham's time.
3 On one such day, Jacob was cooking a lentil stew when Esau returned from the field, famished. Esau asked Jacob for some of the stew.
4 Jacob, however, proposed an exchange: "Sell me your birthright, and I'll give you bread and some of this lentil stew."
5 Esau, dismissive of the value of his birthright, replied, "I am close to death; what good is a birthright to me?" He agreed to Jacob's terms.
6 Jacob insisted that Esau swear an oath, which he did. In exchange, Jacob provided Esau with bread and stew, and Esau ate and was satisfied. Esau's careless attitude toward his birthright led to his nickname, *Edom*, signifying the red stew.
7 Thus, Jacob assumed the role of the elder, while Esau's dignity was diminished.

8 When the famine spread, Isaac decided to journey toward Egypt. In the second year of the week, he visited King Abimelech of the Philistines in Gerar.
9 There, the Lord appeared to Isaac, instructing him, "Do not go down into Egypt; stay in the land I will show you, and I will be with you and bless you.
10 For I will give all this land to you and your descendants, fulfilling the oath I swore to your father, Abraham. I will make your descendants as numerous as the stars in the heavens, and through them, all the nations of the earth will be blessed,
11 because your father obeyed My voice, keeping My commands, laws, and covenant. Now, obey My voice and stay in this land."
12 Isaac remained in Gerar for many years.

13 King Abimelech issued a command for the safety of Isaac and his household, declaring, "Anyone who harms Isaac or anything that belongs to him will surely die."
14 Over time, Isaac's wealth increased greatly among the Philistines, as he acquired numerous possessions, including oxen, sheep, camels, donkeys, and a large household.
15 Isaac sowed crops in the land of the Philistines and reaped a hundredfold. His success stirred jealousy among the Philistines,

16 who subsequently blocked all the wells Abraham's servants had dug by filling them with earth.

17 Abimelech then said to Isaac, "Leave us, for you have become far mightier than we are." Thus, Isaac departed, and in the first year of the seventh week, he moved to the valleys near Gerar,
18 where he reopened the wells that had been stopped up after Abraham's death. He named them as his father had done.
19 Isaac's servants dug a new well and found living water, but the shepherds of Gerar quarreled with Isaac's men, claiming ownership of the water. Isaac named the well "Perversity" due to the opposition he faced.
20 Isaac's servants dug another well, which also led to disputes, so he named it "Enmity." Moving on, they dug a third well, for which there was no contention, and he called it "Room." Isaac proclaimed, "Now the Lord has made room for us, and we have flourished in this land."

21 Isaac then went to the Well of the Oath in the first year of the forty-fourth jubilee.
22 That night, on the new moon of the first month, the Lord appeared to him, saying, "I am the God of your father, Abraham. Do not fear, for I am with you and will bless and multiply your descendants as the sand on the seashore, all for the sake of My servant Abraham."
23 At this location, Isaac built an altar, following in his father Abraham's footsteps, and called upon the name of the Lord, offering sacrifices.
24 His servants dug another well and found living water. However, when they dug an additional well and found none, they reported it to Isaac, who declared, "I have made an oath this day with the Philistines."

25 Isaac named the place "Well of the Oath" because of the agreement he made with Abimelech, along with Ahuzzath, his friend, and Phicol, the commander of Abimelech's army.
26 It was then that Isaac realized he had reluctantly sworn to maintain peace with the Philistines.
27 That day, Isaac invoked a curse upon the Philistines, proclaiming, "Cursed are the Philistines until the day of wrath and judgment, marked for scorn, and destined to endure God's indignation at the hands of sinful nations, including the Kittim.
28 Let those who evade the enemy's sword and the Kittim's wrath be judged and rooted out by a righteous nation, as they will be adversaries to my descendants for generations."

29 Isaac continued, "There will be no remnant or survivor on the day of divine wrath for the Philistines, as their entire lineage will be uprooted and expelled from the earth.
30 They will vanish without name or lineage, leaving no memory among the Caphtorim.
31 Though they rise to Heaven, they will be brought down; though they gain strength on earth, they will be cast out; though they hide among the nations, they will be discovered and uprooted.
32 And if they descend into Sheol, they will find no peace, but only condemnation. Even if they

go into captivity, they will be slain along the way by those seeking their lives, leaving neither name nor legacy on the earth."

33 This curse, along with the decree to root out the Philistines from the earth, is written and recorded on the heavenly tablets, destined to be fulfilled on the Day of Judgment.

Chapter 25

1. Rebekah advised Jacob, warning him against taking a wife from the Canaanites as Esau had done, whose wives troubled her deeply.
2. She expressed her love and blessing for Jacob
3. Urging him to seek a wife from her own family
4. Promising God's blessing upon him and his children if he did so.
5. Jacob responded by assuring his mother that he would honor her request
6. Recalling his grandfather Abraham's command to avoid Canaanite wives.
7. He assured Rebekah that he had kept himself pure
8. And would not follow Esau's example.
9. Rebekah, overjoyed, praised the Most High for granting her such a righteous son.
10. She placed her hands on Jacob's head, blessing him with a prayer for prosperity and righteousness.
11. Rebekah asked that Jacob's descendants be numerous and strong, blessed as Abraham's heirs in the land promised by God.
12. She prayed that Jacob's name and lineage would flourish, rejoicing in God's love and grace.
13. Rebekah ended her blessing, expressing her deep love for Jacob and her hope for God's enduring presence with him and his descendants.
14. Rebekah continued, "My son, your heart has always sought righteousness, and your path has been one of purity and integrity. May the LORD protect you and guide you in the ways of truth, for your life will be filled with blessings if you keep to His ways."
15. Then she called upon the LORD, saying, "Blessed be You, O God of all creation, who has granted me this son. May You keep him in Your care, guard him in Your love, and grant him favor all his days."
16. Filled with joy, Rebekah placed her hands on Jacob's head, speaking from her heart, "May your days be many, my son, and may your children fill the earth with righteousness and goodness."
17. She continued, "May you prosper in all that you do, and may your seed grow in strength, reflecting the blessings of our fathers.
18. May you always walk in the path of our God, and may His covenant be a shield over you and your descendants."
19. As she ended her blessing, Jacob embraced his mother with gratitude and reassurance, vowing to uphold her teachings and continue in the faith of Abraham and Isaac.

20. Rebekah held him close, offering one last prayer, "May all who bless you be blessed, and may all who seek to harm you be kept far away by the hand of the LORD.
21. May your name endure for generations, and may your descendants be a people set apart, shining with the light of our God."
22. Rebekah then kissed Jacob and, with great emotion, released him, confident that he would follow her guidance and fulfill his purpose.
23. And thus, Rebekah concluded her blessings, and Jacob departed, carrying her words and blessings with him, deeply rooted in his heart, ready to face the future as the chosen heir to the promises given by God to Abraham.

Chapter 26

1 In the seventh year of this week, Isaac called his elder son, Esau, and said, "I am old, my son, and my sight is failing. I do not know the day of my death.
2 So now, take your hunting gear—your quiver and bow—and go out to the field to hunt game for me. Prepare the kind of savory meat that I love and bring it to me, so that I may eat and bless you before I die."
3 Rebekah overheard Isaac speaking to Esau.

4 As Esau went out to hunt,

5. Rebekah called her son Jacob and said, "I heard your father speaking to Esau, saying, 'Hunt for me and prepare savory meat that I may eat and bless you in the presence of the Lord before I die.'
6. Now, my son, listen to me and do as I instruct. Go to the flock and bring me two good young goats. I will prepare them as savory meat, the way your father loves,
6 and you shall bring it to him to eat so that he may bless you before the Lord."
7 Jacob replied, "Mother, I fear that he will recognize my voice and want to touch me.
8 You know that I am smooth-skinned, while Esau is hairy. I will appear as a deceiver in his eyes, and he will curse me instead of blessing me."
9 Rebekah assured him, "Let any curse fall on me, my son; just do as I say."
10 Jacob obeyed, fetching the two young goats, which Rebekah prepared into a savory dish as Isaac liked.

11 Rebekah took Esau's best clothes, which were in the house, and dressed Jacob in them. She covered his hands and neck with the goatskins,
12 then handed him the prepared food and bread to give to his father.
13 Jacob went to Isaac and said, "I am your son; I have done as you asked. Rise, sit, and eat of my catch so that you may bless me."
14 Isaac asked, "How did you find the game so quickly, my son?" Jacob replied, "Because the Lord your God granted me success."
15 Isaac then asked him to come closer so he could feel him, to verify if he was truly Esau.

16 Jacob approached, and Isaac touched him, saying, "The voice is Jacob's, but the hands are Esau's."

17. Because it was meant to be, Isaac's senses were clouded, and he did not recognize Jacob.
17. Isaac asked again, "Are you really my son, Esau?" Jacob replied, "I am."
19. Isaac then asked for the meal, saying, "Bring it near so I may eat of your catch, that I may bless you." Jacob brought it, and Isaac ate, then drank the wine Jacob gave him.
20. Isaac asked Jacob to come near and kiss him. When Jacob did, Isaac smelled his clothes and blessed him, saying, "The smell of my son is like a field blessed by the Lord.
21. May God give you the dew of heaven, the richness of the earth, and abundant grain and wine.
22. Let nations serve you and people bow before you. Be lord over your brothers, and may the sons of your mother bow to you. May those who curse you be cursed, and those who bless you be blessed."

23. Just after Isaac finished blessing Jacob, Esau returned from his hunt.
24. He also prepared a meal and brought it to his father, saying,

25. "Rise, Father, and eat of my game so that you may bless me."
26. Isaac, surprised, asked, "Who are you?" Esau replied, "I am your firstborn, Esau."
27. Trembling greatly, Isaac said, "Who then brought me the meal I just ate? I blessed him, and he shall remain blessed."
28. On hearing this, Esau cried out bitterly, "Bless me too, Father!"
29. Isaac replied, "Your brother came deceitfully and took your blessing." Esau lamented, "Is he not rightly named Jacob? He has supplanted me twice—first my birthright, and now my blessing."
30. He asked his father if he had reserved any blessing for him.

31. Isaac responded, "I have made him lord over you and given him all his brothers as servants, along with plenty of grain and wine. What can I possibly do for you, my son?"
32. Esau pleaded, "Do you have only one blessing, Father? Bless me too!" And he wept aloud.
33. Isaac answered, "You shall live far from the richness of the earth and the dew of heaven.

34. You will live by your sword and serve your brother. Yet, when you grow restless, you shall break free from his yoke."
35. From that day, Esau harbored anger toward Jacob, saying, "Let the days of mourning for my father be soon, so that I may kill my brother Jacob."

Chapter 27

1. Rebekah learned in a dream of Esau's intentions and called Jacob, saying, "Your brother Esau plans to take vengeance on you and kill you.
2. Now, my son, listen to me: flee to my brother Laban in Haran,

3. And stay with him for a while until your brother's anger subsides and he forgets what you have done. Then I will send for you."
4. Jacob responded, "If he seeks to kill me, I will defend myself.
5. Rebekah pleaded, "Let me not lose both my sons on one day." Jacob then added, "If my father sends me, I will go."
6. Rebekah went to Isaac and expressed her distress over Esau's wives, saying, "If Jacob takes a wife from the daughters of this land, my life will be meaningless."
7. Isaac called Jacob and blessed him, instructing, "Do not take a wife from the daughters of Canaan.
8. Go to Mesopotamia, to the house of your grandfather Bethuel, and take a wife from among Laban's daughters.
9. May God Almighty bless and increase you so that you become a community of nations,
10. And may He grant you the blessing of Abraham, so that you may inherit the land of your sojourning, which God gave to Abraham."
11. Isaac sent Jacob to Mesopotamia to find a wife.
12. After he left, Rebekah mourned deeply. Isaac comforted her, saying, "Do not weep for Jacob; he goes in peace and will return safely.
13. The Most High God will protect him, for I know his ways will be blessed until he returns to us in peace."
14. Isaac reassured her, "Do not fear, for he is on the righteous path."
15. Jacob journeyed from Beersheba and reached Luz, also known as Bethel, on the new moon of the first month of the week.
16. As the sun set, he rested, placing a stone under his head.
17. He dreamed of a ladder reaching from earth to heaven, with angels ascending and descending.
18. The Lord stood above it, saying, "I am the Lord, the God of your father Abraham and Isaac. The land where you lie, I will give to you and your descendants.
19. Your descendants shall be as numerous as the dust of the earth and spread in all directions. Through you, all the families of the earth shall be blessed.
20. I am with you, and I will watch over you wherever you go and bring you back to this land."
21. Jacob awoke, saying, "Surely this is the house of God, though I did not realize it."
22. In awe, he declared, "This place is sacred; it is none other than the house of God, the gate of heaven."
23. Jacob rose early, set the stone as a pillar, and poured oil on it, naming the place Bethel.
24. He vowed, "If the Lord is with me and provides for me on this journey, then the Lord shall be my God. This stone will be a sign of His house, and I will give Him a tenth of all He gives me."
25. And Jacob made his vow to the Lord, saying, "If You will be with me and keep me safe on this journey that I undertake, and give me food to eat and clothing to wear,

26. So that I return to my father's house in peace, then You, O Lord, shall be my God.
27. This stone that I have set up as a pillar will be a place to honor You, and of all that You give me, I will dedicate a tenth back to You."
28. With his vow made, Jacob continued on his journey with renewed faith and trust in God, confident that the Lord would fulfill His promises and watch over him as he traveled to his mother's family and sought a wife from among his kin.

Chapter 28

1. And Jacob went on his journey and came to the land of the east, to Laban, the brother of Rebekah. He stayed with him and served him for his daughter Rachel for seven years.
2. And in the first year of the third week, Jacob said to Laban, "Give me my wife, for whom I have served you these seven years." And Laban said, "I will give her to you."
3. Laban then made a feast and took his elder daughter, Leah, and gave her to Jacob as his wife, along with her handmaid, Zilpah. Jacob did not realize the deception, thinking she was Rachel.
4. When Jacob discovered that he was with Leah, he was angered and said to Laban, "Why have you deceived me? Did I not serve you for Rachel, not for Leah? Why have you wronged me in this way? Take your daughter back, and I will go, for you have done evil to me."
5. Jacob loved Rachel more than Leah, for Leah's eyes were weak, though she had an attractive form, while Rachel had beautiful eyes and was also of lovely form.
6. Laban replied, "In our country, it is not our custom to give the younger before the elder. Such an act is also written on the heavenly tablets: no one should give his younger daughter in marriage before the elder, for this is evil before the Lord."
7. Laban continued, "Let the seven days of the celebration for Leah pass, and I will also give you Rachel, provided you serve me another seven years as you did before."
8. So, after the seven days of Leah's celebration had ended, Laban gave Rachel to Jacob as his wife, with her handmaid, Bilhah, as a servant.
9. And Jacob served Laban for another seven years for Rachel, as Leah had been given to him without his desire.
10. The Lord saw that Leah was unloved, and He opened her womb, allowing her to conceive and bear Jacob a son, whom she named Reuben, on the fourteenth day of the ninth month, in the first year of the third week.
11. But Rachel's womb remained closed, as the Lord had seen Leah's affliction and that she was not loved.
12. Leah conceived again and bore Jacob a second son, whom she named Simeon, on the twenty-first day of the tenth month, in the third year of this week.
13. Leah conceived once more and bore Jacob a third son, Levi, on the new moon of the first month, in the sixth year of this week.

14. Leah bore yet another son and named him Judah on the fifteenth day of the third month, in the first year of the fourth week.
15. Rachel, seeing that Leah had borne four sons to Jacob—Reuben, Simeon, Levi, and Judah—envied her and said to Jacob, "Give me children." Jacob replied, "Am I in the place of God, who has withheld from you the fruit of your womb?"
16. When Rachel saw her own barrenness, she said to Jacob, "Take my maid Bilhah; she will conceive and bear a child on my behalf."
17. Jacob agreed, and Bilhah bore him a son, whom Rachel named Dan, on the ninth day of the sixth month, in the sixth year of the third week.
18. Bilhah conceived again and bore Jacob a second son, whom Rachel named Naphtali, on the fifth day of the seventh month, in the second year of the fourth week.
19. When Leah saw that she had ceased bearing, she envied Rachel and gave her maid Zilpah to Jacob as a wife. Zilpah conceived and bore a son, whom Leah named Gad, on the twelfth day of the eighth month, in the third year of the fourth week.
20. Zilpah conceived again and bore Jacob a second son, whom Leah named Asher, on the second day of the eleventh month, in the fifth year of the fourth week.
21. Leah conceived once more and bore a son, whom she named Issachar, on the fourth day of the fifth month, in the fourth year of the fourth week, and she gave him to a nurse.
22. Leah bore two more children, a son whom she named Zebulun and a daughter named Dinah, on the seventh day of the seventh month, in the sixth year of the fourth week.
23. The Lord remembered Rachel, opened her womb, and she conceived and bore a son, whom she named Joseph, on the new moon of the fourth month, in the sixth year of this fourth week.
24. After Joseph's birth, Jacob said to Laban, "Give me my wives and my children and let me go back to my father Isaac, for I have fulfilled my years of service for your daughters. Let me now go to my own household."
25. But Laban said to Jacob, "Stay with me for your wages, and continue to pasture my flock for me."
26. They agreed that Jacob's wages would consist of all the lambs and kids born that were black, spotted, or white.
27. Those would belong to Jacob, while the others would remain Laban's.
28. And all the sheep gave birth to spotted, speckled, and black lambs, and all that were marked this way were Jacob's, while the rest were Laban's.
29. Jacob's possessions grew greatly, and he acquired many oxen, sheep, donkeys, camels, menservants, and maidservants.
30. But Laban and his sons became envious of Jacob, and Laban took back some of his sheep from him and began watching Jacob with ill intent.

Chapter 29

1. After Rachel had borne Joseph, Laban went out to shear his sheep, traveling three days away from where Jacob was.
2. Seeing this, Jacob spoke kindly to Leah and Rachel, asking them to join him in returning to the land of Canaan. He shared with them the vision he had seen in a dream, in which God instructed him to go back to his father's house.
3. Leah and Rachel agreed, saying, "Wherever you go, we will go with you."
4. Jacob blessed the God of his father Isaac, and the God of Abraham, his grandfather. He gathered his wives, children, and possessions, crossed the river, and entered the land of Gilead, keeping his plans hidden from Laban.
5. In the seventh year of the fourth week, Jacob set his face toward Gilead in the first month, on the twenty-first day. But Laban pursued him, overtaking Jacob in the mountains of Gilead in the third month, on the thirteenth day.
6. However, the Lord appeared to Laban in a dream, restraining him from harming Jacob. The two spoke, and on the fifteenth of those days, Jacob prepared a feast for Laban and all those with him.
7. Jacob swore to Laban that day, and Laban swore to Jacob as well, that neither of them would cross the mountains of Gilead to harm the other.
8. They built a stone heap as a witness to their agreement, naming the place "The Heap of Witness."
9. Before this, the land was known as Gilead, the land of the Rephaim, where giants had once lived, with heights ranging from ten to seven cubits.
10. The Rephaim's domain stretched from the land of the Ammonites to Mount Hermon, with their kingdom seated in cities like Karnaim, Ashtaroth, Edrei, Misur, and Beon.
11. The Lord had destroyed the Rephaim due to their malevolence, and the Amorites, a wicked people, replaced them.
12. There remains no other people who have sinned to the extent of these Amorites.
13. After this encounter, Jacob sent Laban away, and Laban returned to Mesopotamia, the land of the east, while Jacob continued his journey into the land of Gilead.
14. Jacob then crossed the Jabbok River in the ninth month, on the eleventh day. On that day, his brother Esau came to him, and they reconciled before Esau returned to his land in Seir, while Jacob dwelt in tents.
15. In the first year of the fifth week, Jacob crossed the Jordan River and settled beyond it. He pastured his sheep from the sea near Bethshan to Dothan, and even to the Akrabbim forest.
16. Jacob sent gifts of food, drink, and clothing to his father Isaac, and to his mother Rebekah, four times a year: between planting and harvest, before the rains, during winter, and in spring, sending these to the tower of Abraham.
17. Isaac had left the Well of the Oath and moved to Abraham's tower, separating himself from Esau after Jacob had gone to Mesopotamia.

18. While Jacob was in Mesopotamia, Esau had married Mahalath, the daughter of Ishmael, and taken all his father's flocks and his wives, settling on Mount Seir, leaving Isaac alone at the Well of the Oath.
19. Isaac then moved from the Well of the Oath to his father Abraham's tower in the hills of Hebron.
20. Jacob continued to send all that his father and mother required, blessing them with all his heart and soul.

Chapter 30

1. In the first year of the sixth week, Jacob went up to Salem, east of Shechem, in peace, during the fourth month.
2. During that time, Dinah, Jacob's daughter, was taken by Shechem, son of Hamor the Hivite, a prince in the land. He defiled her; she was only a child of twelve.
3. Shechem sought his father's and her brothers' permission to marry her. However, Jacob and his sons were angry at the people of Shechem for what they had done to Dinah, and they spoke to them with deceitful intent.
4. Then Simeon and Levi secretly entered Shechem, enacting judgment on all the men there; they killed every man in the city, inflicting suffering upon them because of the dishonor they had brought upon Dinah.
5. This was ordained in Heaven as a judgment against those who would defile a daughter of Israel, ensuring the Shechemites would face destruction by the sword for their shameful actions against Israel.
6. The LORD delivered the Shechemites into the hands of Jacob's sons, so they could execute judgment and prevent such acts of defilement from happening again to Israel's daughters.
7. Any man in Israel who would give his daughter or sister to a man from the nations would surely die by stoning for bringing shame upon Israel. The woman, too, would be burned for disgracing her family.
8. Adulterers and all unclean behavior must not be found in Israel, for Israel is holy to the LORD, and anyone who defiles it shall die by stoning.
9. This decree, inscribed on the heavenly tablets, applies to all of Israel's descendants: no one who defiles Israel shall be spared, for they have committed a grievous sin.
10. There is no limitation to this law, no forgiveness or atonement for those who defile their daughters or give their seed to Moloch.
11. Moses was commanded to warn Israel against marrying into the nations, as it is detestable to the LORD.

12. Therefore, the Law records the deeds of the Shechemites against Dinah, along with Jacob's sons' declaration that they would not allow their sister to marry an uncircumcised man, for it would disgrace them.
13. It is a reproach for Israel to give or take daughters to or from the nations, for this is unclean and offensive to Israel.
14. Israel will remain unclean if it marries outside, bringing upon itself various curses and punishments.
15. The nation will be judged collectively for any unclean actions, with no offerings accepted on behalf of those who defile the sanctuary.
16. For this reason, Israel was warned, learning from the Shechemites' fate, which the two sons of Jacob justly enforced.
17. Levi was chosen for the priesthood, his descendants blessed, because he acted with zeal to execute justice and righteousness on behalf of Israel.
18. His actions are recorded as righteous, his blessings established on the heavenly tablets, and he is remembered for a thousand generations.
19. Thus, Moses was instructed to remind Israel to follow God's commandments and avoid any sin or transgression.
20. However, should they break these laws, they will be recorded as adversaries and removed from the Scroll of Life, destined for destruction.
21. When the sons of Jacob executed judgment on Shechem, Heaven recorded their actions as righteous, and their deeds as blessings.
22. They rescued Dinah, bringing her out of Shechem's house
23. Seizing all the wealth, livestock, and flocks from the city, and brought them to Jacob.
24. Jacob rebuked them for their actions, fearing retaliation from the Canaanites and Perizzites in the land.
25. Yet the LORD placed a great fear on the cities surrounding Shechem,
26. And they did not dare pursue the sons of Jacob, for terror had gripped them.

Chapter 31

1. On the new moon of the seventh month, Jacob spoke to his household, saying, "Purify yourselves and change your garments, for we are going up to Bethel. There, I made a vow to God on the day I fled from my brother Esau. He has been with me and has brought me back safely to this land. Now put away the strange gods among you."
2. The people handed over the foreign gods they had, including the earrings and ornaments from their necks. Rachel also gave up the idols she had taken from her father Laban. Jacob took these and destroyed them, burying them under an oak tree near Shechem.
3. On the new moon of the seventh month, Jacob went up to Bethel, where he built an altar at the place he had once slept. He sent word to his father Isaac and mother Rebekah to come to the sacrifice he would make.
4. Isaac replied, "Let my son Jacob come to me, that I may see him before I die."

5. So Jacob went to his father Isaac and mother Rebekah, taking two of his sons, Levi and Judah, with him to the house of his father Abraham.
6. Rebekah came out from the tower, embracing and kissing Jacob, for her spirit was revived when she heard that Jacob had returned.
7. She saw his two sons and asked, "Are these your sons, my son?" Embracing and blessing them, she said, "In you, the seed of Abraham will be renowned, and you will be a blessing upon the earth."
8. Jacob then went in to see Isaac, and he brought his sons with him. Jacob took his father's hand, kissed him, and Isaac held him close, weeping.
9. Isaac's eyesight had grown dim, but now he looked upon Levi and Judah and said, "Are these truly your sons, Jacob?"
10. Jacob confirmed, "Yes, father, these are my sons."
11. Isaac embraced his grandsons, and the spirit of prophecy filled him. He took Levi by the right hand and Judah by the left.
12. Turning first to Levi, he blessed him, saying, "May the God of all ages bless you and your descendants forever.
13. May the LORD grant you greatness and honor, setting you and your seed apart to serve in His sanctuary as holy messengers.
14. Like the angels of Heaven, may your descendants be revered, and may they serve as judges and teachers of Israel.
15. Let the word of the LORD be spoken through them, and may they lead Israel with righteousness.
16. Your mother named you Levi, meaning 'joined,' for you are bound to the LORD, and your place is at His table. May it be filled for you and your descendants for all generations.
17. Let those who oppose you fall before you, and may your enemies be removed from the earth. Blessed is the one who blesses you, and cursed is every nation that curses you."
18. Isaac then turned to Judah and blessed him, saying, "May the LORD give you strength and victory over those who hate you.
19. You will be a prince among your brothers, and your name will travel across all lands.
20. Nations will tremble before you, and in you will Jacob find help, and Israel will find salvation.
21. When you sit upon the throne of righteousness, there will be peace for the descendants of the beloved. Blessed is the one who blesses you, and cursed is the one who opposes you."
22. Isaac embraced and kissed Judah, rejoicing to see the sons of his son Jacob, in whom he found great joy and hope.
23. Jacob and his father Isaac spent the night together, and they ate and drank with gladness.
24. That night, Isaac laid Levi on his right side and Judah on his left, a symbolic gesture counted to him as righteousness.

25. Through the night, Jacob recounted to his father how the LORD had blessed him, preserved him from harm, and guided him on his journey.
26. Isaac praised God, the God of Abraham, who had shown His mercy and righteousness to Isaac's descendants.
27. In the morning, Jacob shared with Isaac the vow he had made to the LORD and the vision he had seen, explaining that he had prepared an altar and was ready to fulfill his vow before the LORD.
28. Isaac responded, "I cannot go with you, my son, for I am old and cannot bear the journey. Go in peace, for I am now one hundred and sixty-five years old and no longer able to travel.
29. But may the day be blessed, for you have come to see me while I still live, and I have seen you, my son. May you prosper and fulfill your vow, and may the Creator, to whom you have vowed, accept your offering."
30. Isaac turned to Rebekah and said, "Go with Jacob, my sister." So Rebekah and her maid Deborah went with Jacob to Bethel.
31. Jacob remembered his father's blessing over him and his sons, Levi and Judah, and he rejoiced, praising the God of Abraham and Isaac.
32. He declared, "Now I know that I have a lasting hope, and my sons too, before the God of all." Thus, it was recorded as an eternal testimony for Levi and Judah on the heavenly tablets, showing how Isaac had blessed them.

Chapter 32

1. That night, Jacob stayed at Bethel, and Levi dreamed that he was appointed as a priest of the Most High God, along with his descendants forever. Levi awoke and blessed the Lord.
2. Early in the morning, on the fourteenth day of the month, Jacob rose and offered a tithe of everything he possessed: people, cattle, gold, vessels, and garments—giving a tenth of all.
3. During that time, Rachel became pregnant with Benjamin. Jacob counted his sons, and Levi was chosen as the Lord's portion. Jacob then dressed Levi in priestly garments and entrusted him with sacred duties.
4. On the fifteenth of the month, Jacob brought to the altar fourteen oxen, twenty-eight rams, forty-nine sheep, seven lambs, and twenty-one kids as burnt offerings, each presented as a sweet aroma pleasing to God.
5. This offering was given as part of his vow, which he had pledged to fulfill by offering a tenth of his possessions, along with grain and drink offerings.
6. Once the fire had consumed the offerings, he burned incense and presented a thank offering, consisting of two oxen, four rams, four sheep, four goats, two lambs, and two more kids. Jacob did this for seven consecutive days.

7. During these days, he, along with his sons and men, joyfully feasted and praised the Lord, who had delivered him from his troubles and allowed him to fulfill his vow.
8. Jacob offered a tithe of all clean animals as burnt sacrifices but kept the unclean animals aside. He also entrusted the lives of all menservants to Levi.
9. Levi served as priest at Bethel, performing duties before Jacob and receiving favor over his ten brothers. Jacob fulfilled his vow by giving a second tithe to the Lord and consecrating it as holy.
10. This practice of a second tithe, designated for consumption in the presence of the Lord annually at His chosen dwelling place, was ordained as a perpetual law on the heavenly tablets.
11. This commandment was to be observed yearly, with the tithe eaten before the Lord and nothing from it remaining until the following year.
12. The produce of each year was to be consumed within its season, be it grain, wine, or oil
13. And anything remaining from the previous year would be deemed unclean and was to be burned.
14. Thus, everything was to be consumed within the sanctuary and not left to become spoiled.
15. All tithes from livestock were consecrated to the Lord and designated for His priests, who would consume them annually in His presence, in accordance with what was inscribed on the heavenly tablets.
16. On the night of the twenty-second day of that month, Jacob resolved to build a permanent sanctuary there, surrounding it with a wall and dedicating it for his descendants.
17. That night, the Lord appeared to Jacob and blessed him, saying, "Your name will no longer be Jacob; it will now be Israel."
18. He continued, "I am the Lord who created the heavens and the earth, and I will make you exceedingly fruitful. Kings shall arise from you and rule wherever mankind has set foot.
19. I will grant your descendants the entire earth beneath the heavens, and they shall judge the nations as they choose. Eventually, they will inherit the whole earth forever."
20. After speaking, the Lord ascended, and Jacob watched as He rose into the heavens.
21. That night, Jacob saw a vision: an angel descended from heaven carrying seven tablets. He handed them to Jacob, who read them and understood all that was written, revealing what would happen to him and his descendants through the ages.
22. The angel explained, "Do not build this place into a permanent sanctuary. Do not dwell here, for this is not the chosen place. Return to your father Isaac's house and remain with him until his death.
23. You will die peacefully in Egypt, but you will be buried with honor in this land, alongside your fathers, Abraham and Isaac.
24. Do not fear, for what you have read will indeed come to pass. Record everything you have seen and read."

25. Jacob asked, "Lord, how can I remember all I've read and seen?" The Lord replied, "I will help you remember."
26. The angel then departed, and Jacob awoke, recalling all he had read and seen. He wrote down every word from his vision.
27. Jacob then observed one more day of offerings, just as he had done before, and he named it "Addition," as it was added to the prior days of feasting.
28. This event was inscribed on the heavenly tablets, signifying its addition to the annual feast days.
29. Its name, "Addition," was given because it was added to the days of celebration in the calendar year.
30. On the night of the twenty-third day of that month, Rebekah's nurse, Deborah, passed away. They buried her by the river beneath the city, naming the place "The River of Deborah" and the oak "The Oak of Mourning for Deborah."
31. Rebekah then returned to Isaac's household, carrying gifts from Jacob, including rams, sheep, and goats, for Isaac's enjoyment.
32. Jacob accompanied his mother as far as the land of Kabrâtân, where he then settled.
33. During the night, Rachel gave birth to a son. Overwhelmed by her labor pains, she named him "Son of My Sorrow," but Jacob named him Benjamin. The birth took place on the eleventh of the eighth month, in the first year of the sixth week of that jubilee.
34. Rachel passed away and was buried in Ephrath, known as Bethlehem. Jacob placed a pillar on her grave along the road, marking her final resting place.

Chapter 33

1. Jacob then traveled and settled south of Magdalâdrâ'êf. He later visited his father Isaac, along with his wife Leah, on the new moon of the tenth month.
2. During this time, Reuben saw Bilhah, Rachel's maid and his father's concubine, bathing in a hidden place. He felt a desire for her.
3. Reuben hid himself and, under the cover of night, entered Bilhah's dwelling where he found her asleep.
4. Reuben lay beside her, and when she awoke, she realized Reuben was there with her.
5. She felt deep shame because of him, released him, and he fled from her presence.
6. Bilhah lamented what had happened and did not reveal it to anyone.
7. When Jacob returned and sought her company, she confessed, saying, "I am not clean for you; I have been defiled. Reuben lay with me while I was asleep, and I did not know until he uncovered my covering and lay with me."
8. Upon hearing this, Jacob was enraged with Reuben, for he had dishonored his father by lying with his concubine.
9. Because of this defilement, Jacob never went to her again. For a man who uncovers his father's skirt commits a grave sin before the Lord.

10. It was decreed and recorded on the heavenly tablets that no man should lie with his father's wife or uncover his father's covering, as this act is unclean. Both the man and the woman involved would face death as punishment, for they have committed a serious transgression on the earth.
11. In the nation chosen by God, there shall be no impurity.
12. The tablets also record, "Cursed is he who lies with his father's wife, for he has uncovered his father's shame," and all of God's holy ones said, "So be it; so be it."
13. Moses was commanded to teach the sons of Israel to observe this decree, for such a sin warrants death. It is considered unclean, and there can be no atonement; the one guilty of this act must be executed and removed from the people of God.
14. No one in Israel who commits such a sin should be permitted to live, for it is an abomination.
15. They must not think, "Life and forgiveness were granted to Reuben after he lay with his father's concubine, even though her husband, Jacob, was still alive."
16. At that time, this commandment and law were not yet fully revealed. However, in Moses' days, this law was established as an eternal ordinance, binding upon all generations.
17. For this law, there is no end of days and no atonement. Both parties involved in the act must be cut off from the nation; they are to be executed on the very day they committed the sin.
18. Moses was instructed to record this law for Israel so that they might obey it and avoid the sin that leads to death. The Lord is a judge who shows no favoritism and accepts no bribes.
19. Moses was to proclaim these words of the covenant to Israel so they would listen, obey, and be cautious, thus avoiding destruction and banishment from the land. Those who commit these acts bring defilement, abomination, and impurity before God.
20. There is no greater sin than the fornication they commit on earth. Israel is a holy nation chosen by the Lord, a nation of inheritance, and a royal priesthood. Such defilement should not exist among the holy people.
21. In the third year of this sixth week, Jacob and all his sons went to dwell with Abraham's household, near Isaac and Rebekah.
22. The names of Jacob's sons were: Reuben, Simeon, Levi, Judah, Issachar, and Zebulun, sons of Leah; Joseph and Benjamin, sons of Rachel; Dan and Naphtali, sons of Bilhah; and Gad and Asher, sons of Zilpah. Jacob's only daughter was Dinah, Leah's child.
23. They gathered and bowed before Isaac and Rebekah, who blessed Jacob and all his sons. Isaac was overjoyed to see the sons of his younger son Jacob and blessed them all.

Chapter 34

1. In the sixth year of this week, during the forty-fourth jubilee, Jacob sent his sons, along with his servants, to graze their sheep in the pastures of Shechem.

2. Meanwhile, seven kings of the Amorites gathered together, intending to ambush and kill them, hiding among the trees and planning to seize their livestock as plunder.
3. Jacob, along with Levi, Judah, and Joseph, stayed at home with their father Isaac, who was sorrowful in spirit, making them unwilling to leave his side. Benjamin, the youngest, also remained with his father.
4. Soon, the kings of Tâphû, 'Arêsa, Sêragân, Sêlô, Gâ'as, Bêthôrôn, Ma'anîsâkîr, and other inhabitants of the mountains and forests in Canaan gathered against them.
5. Messengers came to Jacob, saying, "The Amorite kings have surrounded your sons and plundered their herds."
6. Jacob immediately gathered his sons and servants, and, along with six thousand armed men, went to confront the attackers.
7. In the pastures of Shechem, he struck down the Amorite kings—'Arêsa, Tâphû, Sêragân, Sêlô, Ma'anîsâkîr, and Gâ'as—and reclaimed his herds.
8. Jacob prevailed, imposing tribute on these kings, requiring them to pay him five of their land's fruits. He also established the cities of Rôbêl and Tamnâtârês, then returned peacefully and made an agreement with them; they became his subjects until he and his sons eventually moved to Egypt.
9. In the seventh year of this week, Jacob sent his son Joseph to Shechem to check on the welfare of his brothers, finding them in Dothan.
10. Joseph's brothers betrayed him, initially planning to kill him, but changed their minds and sold him to Ishmaelite merchants, who took him to Egypt and sold him to Potiphar, an official of Pharaoh and priest in the city of 'Êlêw.
11. To cover up their actions, Joseph's brothers slaughtered a young goat and dipped Joseph's coat in its blood, sending it to Jacob on the tenth of the seventh month.
12. Jacob mourned deeply throughout the night, for he believed a wild animal had devoured Joseph, and all his household joined in his grief.
13. Despite his family's efforts to comfort him, Jacob refused to be consoled.
14. On that day, upon hearing of Joseph's supposed death, Bilhah passed away, mourning for him, and Dinah, Jacob's daughter, also died shortly afterward.
15. Within one month, Jacob faced the loss of Bilhah, Dinah, and his son Joseph.
16. Bilhah was buried near Rachel's tomb, and Dinah was laid to rest beside her.
17. Jacob mourned for Joseph for an entire year, refusing to be comforted, saying, "I will go down to the grave mourning for my son."
18. For this reason, it was ordained that the sons of Israel should afflict themselves on the tenth of the seventh month, the same day Jacob received the sorrowful news, as a day of atonement. Each year on this day, they would sacrifice a young goat to seek forgiveness for their sins, having grieved their father regarding Joseph.
19. This day was thus established as a time for them to lament their sins, transgressions, and errors, allowing them to cleanse themselves annually.

20. After Joseph's presumed death, Jacob's sons began to take wives: Reuben married 'Adâ; Simeon took 'Adîbâ'a, a Canaanite; Levi married Mêlkâ, a descendant of Terah from the line of Aram; Judah married Bêtasû'êl, also a Canaanite; Issachar wed Hêzaqâ; Zebulun took Nî'îmân; Dan married 'Êglâ; Naphtali wed Rasû'û of Mesopotamia; Gad took Mâka; Asher wed 'Îjônâ; Joseph's wife was Asenath, an Egyptian; and Benjamin's wife was 'Îjasaka.
21. Later, Simeon repented and took a second wife from Mesopotamia, following the example of his brothers.

Chapter 35

1. In the first year of the first week of the forty-fifth jubilee, Rebekah called her son Jacob and instructed him to honor his father and his brother all his days.
2. Jacob replied, "I will do everything as you have commanded, for honoring them will bring me greatness and righteousness before the Lord."
3. He continued, "You know, mother, that from the day I was born until now, my thoughts and actions have always been good toward others.
4. Why would I not fulfill this request to honor my father and brother? Show me any fault in me, and I will turn from it to seek mercy."
5. Rebekah answered, "My son, I have seen no fault in you, only uprightness. Yet I must tell you: I have seen in a dream that this will be my final year, that I will not live beyond one hundred fifty-five years. My days are complete."
6. Jacob laughed gently, saying, "Mother, you are still strong and full of life. How can you speak of death?"
7. Rebekah, still robust, could walk freely, with strong eyesight and teeth, untroubled by ailments throughout her life.
8. Jacob said, "Blessed am I if my life is as long and full of strength as yours. Surely, you jest about your death."
9. Rebekah then went to Isaac, saying, "Grant me one request: have Esau swear not to harm Jacob or harbor hatred against him. You know Esau's temper; since his youth, he has harbored ill will, desiring to kill his brother after your passing."
10. She reminded him, "Consider all Esau has done since Jacob went to Haran—how he abandoned us, taking your flocks and possessions.
11. When we sought mercy from him, he showed only reluctant pity. He is bitter because you blessed Jacob, your honest and upright son."
12. She added, "Since Jacob's return from Haran, he has faithfully provided for us and rejoices in every season when we receive from him. He has never left us, always honoring us."
13. Isaac replied, "I, too, see Jacob's goodness and how he honors us with all his heart. Although I once favored Esau as the firstborn, I now love Jacob more, for Esau has done much wrong, with no righteousness in him.

14. My heart is troubled over Esau's deeds. Neither he nor his descendants will be saved, for they have forsaken the God of Abraham, turning to unclean ways with his wives."
15. Isaac continued, "You ask me to have him swear not to harm Jacob. Even if he swears, I doubt he will uphold his oath, for he desires only evil.
16. But if he attempts to harm Jacob, the Lord will protect Jacob, and Esau will not prevail."
17. He comforted her, saying, "Do not fear for Jacob, for his guardian is greater and more honored than Esau's."
18. Rebekah then called Esau, who came to her, and she said, "I have a request, my son. Will you fulfill it?"
19. Esau replied, "I will do anything you ask."
20. She said, "When I die, I ask that you bury me near Sarah, your father's mother. Also, promise to love Jacob and desire no harm for him, so you both may prosper in the land, honored and beloved."
21. Esau agreed, saying, "I will bury you as you wish, near Sarah, so that your bones may rest together.
22. I will love Jacob above all others, for he is my only brother, and we shared the same womb. How could I not love him?"
23. He asked her to encourage Jacob to have goodwill toward him and his children, acknowledging, "I know Jacob will rule over me and my sons, for on the day of blessing, our father made him greater and me lesser."
24. Esau swore to love Jacob and not seek harm against him, pledging only goodwill.
25. Then Rebekah called Jacob in Esau's presence and repeated her words to him.
26. Jacob assured her, "I will do as you wish. No harm will come from me or my sons toward Esau. I will be first in love alone."
27. That night, they shared a meal together, and Rebekah passed away, aged three jubilees, one week, and one year. Her sons, Esau and Jacob, buried her in the cave alongside Sarah, their grandmother.

Chapter 36

1. In the sixth year of this week, Isaac called his sons, Esau and Jacob, and they came to him. He said, "My sons, I am nearing the end of my life and going to join my ancestors.
2. When I pass, bury me near my father, Abraham, in the cave in the field of Ephron the Hittite, the tomb that Abraham purchased and where I have prepared a place for myself.
3. I ask you, my sons, to live with righteousness on the earth so that the Lord may fulfill all the promises He made to Abraham and his descendants.
4. Love one another, as a man loves his own soul, and seek ways to benefit each other. Live and act together in peace and love as if you were one soul."
5. Isaac continued, "I also command you to reject and hate idols, for they deceive those who worship and bow to them.

6. Remember the Lord God of your father, Abraham, and how I too have worshiped and served Him in joy and righteousness, so that He might multiply you and establish your descendants as an enduring plant of righteousness on the earth.
7. Now I ask you to take a great oath by the glorious, splendid, and powerful Name—the Name that created the heavens, the earth, and all things—that you will fear Him, worship Him,
8. and love each other with righteousness. May you never wish harm upon your brother, so that you may prosper in all your ways and not come to destruction."
9. He warned them, "If either of you schemes against his brother, know that all who plot harm will fall into the hand of the one they sought to harm, and their offspring will be cut off from the land of the living.
10. On the day of wrath and fury, their land and city will be burned like Sodom, and they will be erased from the record of the righteous, entering instead the record of those marked for destruction, to be condemned in torment, wrath, plagues, and disease forever.
11. I say and testify this to you, my sons, according to the judgment for anyone who desires harm upon his brother."
12. On that day, Isaac divided all his possessions between Esau and Jacob
13. Giving the larger portion to the firstborn, along with the tower and all Abraham's property at the Well of the Oath.
14. Esau said, "I have sold my birthright to Jacob. Let it belong to him; I have no claim on it."
15. Isaac blessed them, saying, "May a blessing rest upon you and your descendants for bringing me peace and avoiding conflict over the birthright.
16. May the Most High God bless the man who acts righteously—him and his descendants forever."
17. With that, Isaac finished blessing his sons, and they shared a meal, rejoicing together. They rested and slept peacefully that night.
18. Isaac, at peace, lay in his bed and passed away in his sleep at the age of one hundred and eighty years. He completed twenty-five weeks and five years of life, and his sons, Esau and Jacob, buried him.
19. Afterward, Esau moved to the land of Edom, settling in the mountains of Seir,
20. while Jacob remained in Hebron in the land where his father, Abraham, had sojourned. There he worshiped the Lord with all his heart, keeping the commands as given to his generation.
21. In the fourth year of the second week of the forty-fifth jubilee, Leah, Jacob's wife, passed away, and he buried her in the double cave near his mother, Rebekah, to the left of Sarah's grave.
22. All of Leah's sons and Jacob's sons gathered to mourn with him and to offer comfort, as he deeply grieved her loss.

23. After Rachel's passing, Jacob loved Leah dearly, for she was upright, gentle, and honorable. Throughout her life, she never spoke a harsh word, always bringing peace and kindness.
24. Remembering her deeds, Jacob mourned her greatly, for he had loved her with all his heart and soul.

Chapter 37

1. On the day Isaac, father of Jacob and Esau, died, the sons of Esau heard that Isaac had given the elder's portion to Jacob. Angered,
2. they argued with Esau, saying, "Why has our father passed over you, his eldest, in favor of Jacob, the younger?"
3. Esau responded, "Because I sold my birthright to Jacob for a simple meal. Then, on the day my father sent me to hunt for food to receive his blessing, Jacob came deceitfully, bringing food to my father, who then blessed him and put me under Jacob's authority.
4. Furthermore, our father made us swear not to harm each other, to live in peace, and to love one another."
5. But they replied, "We won't listen to you. We are stronger than Jacob and his sons. Let us attack them, and if you don't join us, we will harm you as well.
6. Let us gather warriors from Aram, Philistia, Moab, and Ammon to fight against Jacob before he grows stronger."
7. Esau advised them not to go to war, warning that they might fall in battle.
8. But they ignored him, accusing him of always surrendering to Jacob's authority.
9. They sent for one thousand warriors from Aram and other allies, including Moab, Ammon, Philistia, Edom, and the Horites.
10. Altogether, they amassed four thousand skilled fighters, including mighty warriors from the Kittim
11. And insisted Esau lead them, threatening him if he refused.
12. Angered, Esau initially resisted, recalling his oath to his parents not to harm Jacob.
13. ,But, remembering his hidden resentment, he decided to lead the forces against his brother.
14. Meanwhile, Jacob remained unaware of the impending attack, as he mourned for his wife Leah.
15. When Esau's forces neared the tower where Jacob resided, the people of Hebron warned Jacob, telling him that Esau had brought four thousand armed men.
16. They loved Jacob, who was more kind-hearted and generous than Esau.
17. Initially, Jacob did not believe the report until he saw the approaching army.

18. He secured the tower gates, climbed the battlements, and called out to Esau, saying, "Is this how you come to comfort me in my time of mourning? Have you broken the oath sworn to our father and mother?"
19. Esau replied, "Oaths are meaningless to both men and beasts, for everyone seeks to overcome their adversaries.
20. You have hated me and my children from the start, and I have no ties of brotherhood with you.
21. Listen to me: if a boar's skin softens like wool, or it grows horns like a stag, then I will honor our bond.
22. If wolves make peace with lambs, if lions become friends with oxen and plow together, then I will make peace with you.
23. And if ravens turn white, then I will show love and peace toward you. But until then, know that I am your enemy, and there will be no peace between us."
24. Seeing Esau's unwavering hostility, Jacob prepared his family and servants to defend themselves.

Chapter 38

1. Judah spoke to Jacob, saying, "Father, draw your bow and strike down the enemy, but do not harm your brother. Show him mercy, for he is still your kin."
2. Jacob aimed his bow, releasing an arrow that struck Esau in the chest, killing him.
3. He then sent another arrow, hitting Adoram the Aramean, who fell backward and died.
4. Jacob's sons, along with their servants, divided into four groups and defended the tower from all sides.
5. Judah led the southern front, joined by Naphtali, Gad, and fifty servants, defeating every foe before them.
6. Levi, Dan, and Asher guarded the eastern side with fifty men, routing the Moabites and Ammonites.
7. Reuben, Issachar, and Zebulun defended the northern side, striking down the Philistine forces.
8. Simeon, Benjamin, and Enoch, Reuben's son, took the western side, defeating four hundred warriors from Edom and the Horites. Six hundred enemies managed to flee, including four of Esau's sons, leaving Esau slain on a hill at Aduram.
9. Jacob's sons pursued the fleeing enemies to the mountains of Seir. Jacob buried Esau on the hill at Aduram before returning home.
10. His sons subdued the people of Seir, who became servants to Jacob's descendants.
11. They sought their father's counsel, asking if they should continue to fight or make peace with the survivors.
12. Jacob instructed them to make peace, establishing a servitude arrangement
13. Where the people of Edom would pay tribute to Jacob's family.
14. The Edomites paid tribute to Jacob until the day he went down to Egypt

15. And they have borne this yoke of servitude ever since.
16. The kings who ruled Edom before Israel had a king were:
17. Balak, son of Beor, who ruled in the city of Danaba;
18. Upon his death, Jobab, son of Zerah from Bosera, reigned.
19. After Jobab's passing, Asam from the land of Teman took the throne,
20. followed by Adath, son of Barad, who conquered Midian in the field of Moab, ruling from Avith.
21. Salman from Amaseqa succeeded Adath,
22. Followed by Saul of Raeboth by the river,
23. then Baalunan, son of Achbor, and finally Adath, whose wife was Maetabith, daughter of Matrat, granddaughter of Mezahab.
24. These were the kings who reigned over Edom.

Chapter 39

1. Jacob settled in the land of Canaan, where his father had sojourned.
2. At seventeen, Joseph was taken down to Egypt, where he was purchased by Potiphar, an official of Pharaoh, the chief cook.
3. Potiphar placed Joseph in charge of his household, and the LORD blessed the Egyptian's home on Joseph's account, bringing prosperity to all he did.
4. Observing that the LORD was with Joseph, Potiphar entrusted everything he owned to him.
5. Joseph was handsome and well-favored, which caught the attention of Potiphar's wife. She desired him and repeatedly asked him to lie with her, but Joseph refused.
6. He remembered the teachings of his father, who had recited the words of Abraham about avoiding adultery, a sin punishable by death in the heavens and recorded against a man's soul before the LORD.
7. These teachings restrained him, and he consistently denied her advances for a full year.
8. One day, she grasped Joseph in an attempt to force him, closing the doors to prevent his escape.
9. Joseph, however, left his garment in her hands, broke through the door, and fled outside.
10. Angered by his rejection, she falsely accused him before Potiphar, claiming, "Your Hebrew servant attempted to force me, but when I cried out, he fled, leaving his garment."
11. Seeing the torn door and hearing his wife's accusations, Potiphar had Joseph imprisoned in the place designated for the king's detainees.
12. In prison, the LORD granted Joseph favor with the chief prison guard, who observed the LORD's blessings upon him.
13. Entrusting all responsibilities to Joseph, the chief guard was unconcerned with anything under Joseph's care, as everything prospered under his hand.

14. Joseph remained in prison for two years. During this time, Pharaoh became displeased with his chief butler and chief baker, imprisoning them alongside Joseph.
15. The chief guard appointed Joseph to serve these two men, who each dreamed significant dreams.
16. Joseph interpreted their dreams accurately: the chief butler would be restored to his position, while the chief baker would be executed, fulfilling Joseph's predictions.
17. Although Joseph had asked the butler to remember him before Pharaoh
18. The butler forgot about him after his release.

Chapter 40

1. In those days, Pharaoh dreamed two dreams in a single night, foreshadowing a great famine that would strike the land.
2. Disturbed, he summoned all the magicians and dream interpreters of Egypt, yet none could explain his dreams.
3. At that moment, the chief butler recalled Joseph and informed Pharaoh, who had Joseph brought from prison.
4. Pharaoh shared his dreams with Joseph, who interpreted them as foretelling seven years of abundant harvests followed by seven years of severe famine.
5. Joseph advised Pharaoh to appoint overseers throughout Egypt to store food during the plentiful years, ensuring a reserve for the lean years to prevent devastation.
6. Impressed by Joseph's wisdom and discernment, Pharaoh declared, "Where can we find such a man, endowed with the Spirit of the LORD?"
7. Pharaoh appointed Joseph as the second in command over Egypt, giving him authority throughout the land. He placed Joseph in his second chariot, arrayed him in fine linen, placed a golden chain around his neck, and put a ring on his hand.
8. Pharaoh exalted Joseph above all, saying, "Only on the throne will I be greater than you."
9. Joseph ruled justly, without pride or partiality, judging all people fairly and refusing gifts. His wise governance brought peace to the land.
10. Pharaoh named him Zaphenath-Paneah and gave him Asenath, daughter of Potiphera, the priest of Heliopolis, as his wife.
11. Joseph was thirty years old when he took his position in Egypt, the same year Isaac passed away.
12. As Joseph had predicted, the land of Egypt enjoyed seven years of great abundance, with each measure yielding eighteen hundredfold.

13. Joseph stored grain in every city, eventually amassing so much that it could no longer be counted or measured due to its vastness.

Chapter 41

1. In the forty-fifth jubilee, during the second week and in its second year, Judah chose a wife named Tamar from the daughters of Aram for his firstborn son, Er.
2. Er, however, despised Tamar and refused to be with her. His heart leaned toward the daughters of Canaan, like his mother, and he desired a wife from among them. Yet, his father Judah did not permit it.
3. Er, Judah's firstborn, acted wickedly, and because of this, the Lord took his life.
4. Judah then instructed his next son, Onan, saying, "Fulfill your duty to your brother's wife. Marry her and raise descendants for your brother."
5. Onan, knowing the offspring would not be counted as his own but his brother's, went to his brother's wife but spilled his seed on the ground. This act displeased the Lord, and He took Onan's life as well.
6. Judah then told Tamar, "Return to your father's house and remain as a widow until my son Shelah grows up. Then, I will give him to you in marriage."
7. However, Bêdsû'êl, Judah's wife, did not allow Shelah to marry Tamar. Later, Bêdsû'êl died in the fifth year of this week.
8. In the sixth year, Judah went to Timnah to shear his sheep. Tamar was informed, "Your father-in-law is on his way to Timnah for the shearing."
9. Tamar removed her widow's garments, veiled herself, adorned herself, and waited by the roadside at the entrance to Timnah.
10. As Judah passed by, he noticed her and mistook her for a harlot. He approached her, saying, "Let me come in to you," to which she agreed.
11. She then asked for payment. Judah, having nothing with him, offered his ring, necklace, and staff as a pledge until he could send her a young goat as payment.
12. He left these items with her, lay with her, and she conceived.
13. Afterward, Judah returned to his flock, while Tamar went back to her father's house.
14. Judah sent a young goat through his shepherd, an Adullamite, to reclaim his pledge, but the shepherd could not find her.
15. When he asked the locals about the harlot, they replied, "There is no harlot here." The shepherd returned to Judah, relaying what he had learned. Judah then remarked, "Let her keep the pledge, lest we become a laughingstock."
16. Three months later, word reached Judah that Tamar was pregnant by whoredom.

17. Enraged, Judah went to her father's house, demanding her execution by fire for her transgression.
18. As she was brought out, Tamar sent Judah the ring, necklace, and staff, with a message: "Discern whose items these are. I am pregnant by the man to whom these belong."
19. Judah recognized them and admitted, "Tamar is more righteous than I. Therefore, let her not be harmed."
20. Consequently, she was not given to Shelah, and Judah did not approach her again.
21. Later, Tamar bore twin sons, Perez and Zerah, during the seventh year of this second week.
22. Shortly thereafter, the seven years of plenty that Joseph had foretold to Pharaoh came to completion.
23. Reflecting on his actions, Judah acknowledged the wrong he had done by lying with his daughter-in-law and viewed it with disdain.
24. He earnestly repented, supplicating before the Lord, who forgave him through a dream due to Judah's genuine remorse and commitment not to repeat the act.
25. Judah's repentance and humility led to his forgiveness, as he turned away from his sin. This served as a commandment: any man lying with his mother-in-law would be punished by fire to cleanse the land of impurity.
26. The command was extended to Israel to maintain purity: anyone lying with a daughter-in-law or mother-in-law had to be punished by fire, both man and woman, to turn away wrath from Israel.
27. The Lord assured Judah that neither of his two sons had sinned in this way, so his lineage was preserved for future generations.
28. In his righteousness, Judah sought punishment for Tamar in line with the judgment given by Abraham to his sons, intending to burn her. However, through repentance and God's mercy, his family line was continued.

Chapter 42

1. In the first year of the third week of the forty-fifth jubilee, a great famine struck the land, and the rain ceased entirely, leaving the earth barren.
2. However, in Egypt, there was food because Joseph had stored up grain during the seven years of abundance.
3. The people of Egypt came to Joseph for food, and he opened the storehouses, selling grain to the people in exchange for gold.
4. Meanwhile, the famine in Canaan grew severe, and Jacob heard there was food in Egypt. So he sent his ten sons to procure grain, though he kept Benjamin behind.
5. When they arrived in Egypt, Joseph recognized his brothers, but they did not recognize him. Speaking to them harshly, he accused them of being spies seeking to scout the land's weak points and detained them.

6. After some time, he released them but kept Simeon in custody, sending the remaining nine brothers back to Canaan.
7. Joseph filled their sacks with grain and secretly returned their gold into each sack without their knowledge.
8. He instructed them to bring their youngest brother back with them, as they had mentioned both their father and younger brother were alive.
9. The brothers returned to Canaan and reported to Jacob all that had happened, including the demand to bring Benjamin and the detainment of Simeon.
10. Jacob was distressed, exclaiming, "You have taken my children from me! Joseph is gone, Simeon is now gone, and now you wish to take Benjamin. This is too much grief to bear."
11. He resisted letting Benjamin go, fearing he might fall ill or suffer misfortune on the journey, which would bring him down in sorrow to his grave.
12. Jacob's hesitation grew as he noticed their returned gold in each sack, increasing his fear of sending Benjamin with them.
13. As the famine intensified throughout the region, only Egypt had food
14. And even the Egyptians had been wise to store provisions under Joseph's guidance.
15. When Israel realized that no other option remained, he told his sons, "Return to Egypt and bring food, or we will perish."
16. The brothers replied, "We cannot go unless Benjamin goes with us; otherwise, we cannot appear before the lord of the land."
17. Seeing no alternative, Israel reluctantly agreed, understanding that their survival depended on this journey.
18. Reuben, trying to reassure his father, said, "Entrust him to my care. If I do not bring him back, you may take the lives of my two sons." But Jacob refused his offer.
19. Judah then stepped forward, saying, "Send Benjamin with me, and if I fail to return him safely, I will bear the blame for the rest of my life."
20. On the first day of the month, in the second year of this week, Jacob sent Benjamin along with the brothers to Egypt.
21. They carried gifts of stacte, almonds, terebinth nuts, and pure honey to present to the Egyptian ruler.
22. When they stood before Joseph, he immediately recognized Benjamin and asked, "Is this your youngest brother?" They confirmed, "Yes, it is he." Joseph then blessed him, saying, "May the LORD be gracious to you, my son!"
23. Joseph invited them into his house, released Simeon to join them, and prepared a feast. They presented their gifts to him, and as they ate, he served each brother a portion, though Benjamin's was seven times larger than the others.
24. They ate and drank heartily, then rested with their donkeys.

25. Joseph devised a plan to test their intentions and sincerity. He instructed his steward, "Fill their sacks with food, return their money into their vessels, and place my silver cup in the sack of the youngest. Then send them on their way."

Chapter 43

1. Joseph instructed his steward to fill his brothers' sacks with food, place their money in each sack, and secretly put his silver cup in Benjamin's sack.
2. Early the next morning, the brothers departed, but after they had left, Joseph commanded his steward to chase after them and accuse them of repaying his kindness with theft by taking the silver cup used by his lord. He also asked for the youngest brother to be brought back swiftly.
3. The steward caught up with them and repeated Joseph's accusations.
4. The brothers protested, "God forbid we would do such a thing! We even returned the money we found in our sacks from the first time.
5. How could we steal any of your lord's possessions? Search our sacks, and if the cup is found with any of us, let him die, and the rest of us will become your lord's servants."
6. The steward replied, "Only the one with whom the cup is found will become a servant, and the rest may return in peace."
7. The steward began his search, starting with the eldest and finishing with the youngest. When the cup was found in Benjamin's sack
8. The brothers tore their garments in distress, loaded their donkeys, and returned to the city.
9. Upon arrival at Joseph's house, they all bowed before him, and Joseph confronted them, saying, "You have done an evil thing." The brothers responded, "What can we say? You have uncovered our fault. We are now your servants, along with our donkeys."
10. Joseph replied, "I fear the LORD. The rest of you may return home, but your youngest brother will remain here as my servant, for he has done wrong. Do you not know the value a man places on his own cup? Yet you have taken it from me."
11. Judah stepped forward and pleaded, "My lord, allow me to speak. Our father had two sons from the same mother, but one went missing long ago. This younger son is all that remains to him, and our father's life is bound up with his.
12. If we return without him, our father will surely die from sorrow, and we will bring his gray hairs down to the grave in grief."
13. Judah then offered, "Let me stay as a servant in place of the boy, for I promised our father that I would be responsible for his safe return. If I fail to bring him back, I will bear the blame forever."
14. Seeing their genuine concern and unity, Joseph could no longer restrain himself. He revealed his identity, saying, "I am Joseph."
15. Speaking to them in Hebrew, he embraced them, weeping. Though initially they did not recognize him, they too began to weep as realization dawned.

16. Joseph reassured them, saying, "Do not weep. Hurry and bring our father here. You see that it is truly I, Joseph, and Benjamin can see my face.
17. This is only the second year of the famine, and five more years remain with no harvest.
18. Bring your families down quickly to avoid perishing from the famine. Do not worry about your possessions, for the LORD sent me ahead to save many lives."
19. Joseph continued, "Tell my father that I am alive and that the LORD has made me a father to Pharaoh, ruling over his house and all Egypt. Describe to him all the honor and wealth the LORD has given me."
20. By Pharaoh's order, Joseph provided his brothers with chariots, provisions for the journey, colorful clothing, and silver.
21. He also sent gifts of clothing, silver, and ten donkeys loaded with grain for their father, then sent them on their way.
22. When they arrived, they told their father that Joseph was alive, ruling over Egypt, and distributing grain to all the nations.
23. At first, Jacob could not believe them and was overwhelmed, but when he saw the wagons Joseph had sent, his spirit revived.
24. Jacob said, "It is enough for me that Joseph lives. I will go and see him before I die."

Chapter 44

1. Israel set out from his home in Haran on the new moon of the third month, journeying along the path to the Well of the Oath. On the seventh day of this month, he offered a sacrifice to the God of his father, Isaac.
2. As Jacob recalled the dream he had seen at Bethel, he felt apprehensive about traveling down to Egypt.
3. Thinking he might send for Joseph instead of going himself, he stayed at the Well of the Oath for seven days, hoping for a vision to guide his decision.
4. During this time, he celebrated the festival of the first-fruits with old grain, as the famine had left the land of Canaan barren, affecting animals, birds, and people alike.
5. On the sixteenth day, the Lord appeared to Jacob, calling, "Jacob, Jacob." Jacob responded, "Here I am." The Lord reassured him, saying, "I am the God of your fathers, the God of Abraham and Isaac. Do not fear going down to Egypt, for there I will make you a great nation.
6. I will go with you, and I will bring you back again, and you shall be buried in this land. Joseph will be with you in your final moments. Do not be afraid; go down to Egypt."
7. Jacob's sons and grandsons prepared for the journey, placing him and all their belongings on wagons.
8. On the sixteenth day of the third month, Israel departed from the Well of the Oath and traveled toward Egypt.
9. Israel sent Judah ahead to Joseph to prepare for their arrival in the land of Goshen
10. Where Joseph had advised his family to settle close to him.

11. The sons of Jacob who traveled with him to Egypt included:
12. **Reuben**, Israel's firstborn, with his sons Enoch, Pallu, Hezron, and Carmi—five in total.
13. **Simeon** and his sons Jemuel, Jamin, Ohad, Jachin, Zohar, and Shaul, son of the Zephathite woman—seven in all.
14. **Levi** and his sons Gershon, Kohath, and Merari—four in total.
15. **Judah** and his sons Shela, Perez, and Zerah—four in total.
16. **Issachar** and his sons Tola, Pua, Jashub, and Shimron—five in total.
17. **Zebulun** and his sons Sered, Elon, and Jahleel—four in total.
18. These were the sons of Jacob by Leah, who bore them in Mesopotamia, along with their sister Dinah. Including Jacob, the total number of Leah's descendants who entered Egypt was thirty.
19. The descendants of **Zilpah**, Leah's handmaid, were as follows:
20. **Gad** and his sons Ziphion, Haggi, Shuni, Ezbon, Eri, Areli, and Arodi—eight in all.
21. **Asher** and his sons Imnah, Ishvah, Ishvi, Beriah, and their sister Serah—six in total.
22. Together, Zilpah's descendants numbered fourteen, making Leah's family's total count forty-four.
23. The descendants of **Rachel**, Jacob's wife, included:
24. **Joseph**, to whom were born Manasseh and Ephraim in Egypt by Asenath, the daughter of Potiphar, priest of Heliopolis—three in total.
25. **Benjamin** and his sons Bela, Becher, Ashbel, Gera, Naaman, Ehi, Rosh, Muppim, Huppim, and Ard—eleven in all.
26. Altogether, Rachel's descendants numbered fourteen.
27. The descendants of **Bilhah**, Rachel's handmaid, included:
28. **Dan** and his sons Hushim, Shimon, Asudi, Ijaka, and Salomon—six in total
29. Although only Hushim survived the year of their arrival in Egypt.
30. **Naphtali** and his sons Jahziel, Guni, Jezer, and Shallum.
31. Another son, Iv, born after the famine, also died in Egypt.
32. With these, Bilhah's descendants totaled twenty-six.
33. In all, the total number of Jacob's family who went down to Egypt was seventy. This included his children and grandchildren, though five of his descendants died in Egypt before Joseph and left no children.
34. In Canaan, two of Judah's sons, Er and Onan, also died without leaving descendants, and those who had perished were counted among the seventy nations.

Chapter 45

1. Israel entered Egypt, arriving in the land of Goshen on the new moon of the fourth month, in the second year of the third week of the forty-fifth jubilee.
2. Joseph went to meet his father Jacob in Goshen, and as they embraced, Joseph wept on his father's neck.
3. Israel said to Joseph, "Now I am ready to die, for I have seen your face. May the LORD, the God of Israel, be blessed—the God of Abraham and Isaac—who has shown me mercy and grace."
4. He continued, "It is enough that I have seen you while I am still alive; the vision I saw at Bethel is true. Blessed be the LORD my God forever, and blessed is His Name."
5. Joseph and his brothers shared a meal with their father, eating bread and drinking wine together. Jacob rejoiced greatly to see Joseph with his brothers, and he praised the Creator who had preserved him and his twelve sons.
6. Joseph granted his father and brothers the right to settle in the land of Goshen, as well as in Rameses and the surrounding regions under his rule, given by Pharaoh. So Israel and his family lived in the best part of Egypt. Israel was 130 years old when he arrived in Egypt.
7. Joseph provided for his father, his brothers, and all their families with the bread they needed throughout the seven years of famine.
8. The famine brought hardship across Egypt, and Joseph acquired all the land for Pharaoh in exchange for food, including the people's livestock and other possessions.
9. When the years of famine ended, Joseph distributed seed and food to the people for planting in the eighth year, as the river had begun to overflow across Egypt once more.
10. During the famine, the river had not overflowed except along a few spots near its banks. But in this new year, it irrigated the land, allowing the Egyptians to plant, and their crops yielded abundantly.
11. This marked the first year of the fourth week of the forty-fifth jubilee.
12. Joseph established a rule for Egypt, taking a fifth of the harvest for Pharaoh and leaving the remaining four parts to the people for food and seed. This decree remained in effect for Egypt to this day.
13. Israel lived in Egypt for seventeen years, and his total lifespan was three jubilees, amounting to 147 years. He passed away in the fourth year of the fifth week of the forty-fifth jubilee.
14. Before his death, Israel blessed his sons, foretelling what would happen to them in Egypt and in the last days. He gave Joseph a double portion in the land as a blessing.
15. Israel then rested with his ancestors and was buried in the double cave in Canaan, near his father Abraham, in the grave he had prepared in Hebron.
16. He entrusted all his scrolls, along with those of his fathers, to his son Levi, to be preserved and renewed for future generations.

Chapter 46

1. After Jacob's death, the descendants of Israel flourished in Egypt, growing into a strong and united nation. They supported one another, and each brother loved his fellow, leading to significant growth and prosperity throughout the ten weeks of years that marked Joseph's lifetime.
2. During Joseph's life, no adversary arose against them, and no evil befell them, for all the Egyptians held the sons of Israel in high esteem while Joseph lived.
3. Joseph lived to be 110 years old. He spent 17 years in Canaan, served for 10 years, endured 3 years in prison, and ruled under the king for 80 years over all the land of Egypt.
4. When he died, all his brothers and their generation also passed.
5. Before his death, Joseph made the sons of Israel promise to carry his bones with them when they eventually left Egypt.
6. He knew that the Egyptians would not allow his burial in Canaan, for during the reign of Mâkamârôn, the king of Canaan, a battle had taken place between him and the king of Egypt. Mâkamârôn had defeated the Egyptian king in the valley and pursued him to the gates of 'Êrmôn.
7. However, he could not enter Egypt, for a new, stronger king had taken the throne. Mâkamârôn returned to Canaan, and the borders of Egypt were closed, preventing anyone from entering or leaving.
8. Joseph passed away during the forty-sixth jubilee, in the sixth week, in the second year, and was buried in Egypt. His brothers died afterward.
9. Later, in the forty-seventh jubilee, in the second week, in the second year, the king of Egypt waged war with the king of Canaan. The sons of Israel took all the bones of Jacob's children, except Joseph's, and buried them in the field of the double cave in the mountain.
10. Most of them returned to Egypt, though a few stayed in the hills of Hebron, including your father, Amram.
11. The king of Canaan prevailed over the king of Egypt and sealed Egypt's borders.
12. He then devised a cruel plan to oppress the Israelites, saying to the Egyptians,
13. "Look, the people of Israel have grown more numerous and powerful than us. Let us act shrewdly and enslave them before they become too great and join our enemies in battle, forcing us out of our own land. Their hearts and gaze remain fixed on Canaan."
14. Taskmasters were appointed to oppress them with hard labor, compelling them to build fortified cities for Pharaoh, including Pithom and Raamses, as well as repairing the walls and fortifications throughout Egypt.
15. The Egyptians forced them into harsh servitude, but the more they were oppressed, the more the Israelites multiplied and strengthened.
16. This led the people of Egypt to despise the sons of Israel.

Chapter 47

1. In the seventh week, during the seventh year of the forty-seventh jubilee, your father left Canaan, and you were born in the sixth year of the fourth week of the forty-eighth jubilee, a time of hardship for the people of Israel.
2. Pharaoh, the king of Egypt, issued a decree that all newborn Hebrew boys should be cast into the river.
3. For seven months, male infants were cast into the river until the day of your birth. Your mother hid you for three months, but eventually, news reached the Egyptians.
4. She crafted a small ark, sealed it with pitch and asphalt, and placed it among the reeds on the riverbank, hiding you inside. For seven days, your mother visited at night to nurse you, while your sister Miriam kept watch during the day to protect you from the birds.
5. One day, Tharmuth, Pharaoh's daughter, came to bathe in the river. Hearing your cries, she instructed her maidens to retrieve you.
6. When she saw you, she was filled with compassion.
7. Your sister approached and asked, "Shall I find a Hebrew woman to nurse the child for you?" Tharmuth agreed, saying, "Go."
8. Miriam fetched your mother, Jochebed, who was then paid to nurse and care for you.
9. When you were older, they brought you to Pharaoh's daughter, and she adopted you as her son. Your father, Amram, taught you to read and write, and after completing three weeks of years, you were brought into the royal court.
10. You spent three more weeks of years at court until the day you witnessed an Egyptian beating a fellow Israelite, and in defense, you struck down the Egyptian and buried him in the sand.
11. The following day, you encountered two Israelites arguing. Addressing the one at fault, you asked, "Why do you strike your fellow Hebrew?"
12. The man responded angrily, saying, "Who made you a prince and judge over us? Will you kill me as you did the Egyptian yesterday?" Fearing these words, you fled.

Chapter 48

1. In the sixth year of the third week of the forty-ninth jubilee, you left Egypt and stayed in the land of Midian for five weeks and one year. You returned to Egypt during the second week of the second year of the fiftieth jubilee.
2. You remember what was revealed to you on Mount Sinai and how prince Mastêmâ sought to harm you as you journeyed back to Egypt, encountering him at the lodging-place.
3. With all his might, Mastêmâ attempted to kill you, hoping to prevent the liberation of the Egyptians from your judgment when he saw you were sent to deliver justice upon them.
4. But I rescued you from his hands, and you performed the signs and wonders you were commanded to do in Egypt against Pharaoh, his household, his officials, and his people.

5. The LORD executed severe judgment on the Egyptians for Israel's sake, striking them with blood, frogs, lice, biting flies, and painful boils. Their cattle perished, hailstones destroyed their crops, locusts devoured what the hail left, darkness covered the land, and the firstborn of men and animals perished. Even their idols were destroyed by fire as the LORD took vengeance.
6. All these events happened through you; you announced each judgment before it came to pass, speaking before the king of Egypt, his officials, and his people.
7. Everything unfolded according to your words, as ten mighty and dreadful plagues struck Egypt to bring justice for Israel.
8. The LORD carried out these acts on behalf of Israel, fulfilling the covenant He made with Abraham to take vengeance on those who had enslaved them.
9. During this time, prince Mastêmâ opposed you, attempting to hand you over to Pharaoh's control. He supported the Egyptian sorcerers, who rose up to challenge you.
10. We allowed them to perform their acts of evil, but prevented them from bringing any remedy or relief.
11. The LORD afflicted them with painful ulcers, leaving them unable to stand or perform any further signs.
12. Despite these signs and wonders, prince Mastêmâ refused to be humbled and encouraged the Egyptians to pursue you, bringing all of Egypt's chariots, horses, and soldiers against you.
13. But I stood between the Egyptians and Israel, delivering Israel from Mastêmâ's hand and leading them safely through the sea on dry ground.
14. The LORD cast all the pursuing Egyptians into the depths of the sea, as they had once cast Israel's children into the river. God's vengeance struck down a million Egyptians, with a thousand strong men destroyed for each Hebrew child they had drowned.
15. On the fourteenth, fifteenth, sixteenth, seventeenth, and eighteenth days, Mastêmâ was bound and prevented from accusing Israel.
16. On the nineteenth day, he was released, aiding the Egyptians as they chased after Israel.
17. The LORD hardened the Egyptians' hearts and devised this plan to bring them to ruin in the sea.
18. On the fourteenth day, Mastêmâ was bound to prevent him from accusing Israel as they asked the Egyptians for silver, gold, and bronze vessels and garments, despoiling them as compensation for their years of bondage.
19. The LORD did not allow Israel to leave Egypt empty-handed.

Chapter 49

1. Remember the command of the LORD regarding the Passover: it is to be celebrated each year on the fourteenth day of the first month. The lamb should be sacrificed before evening, and the meal eaten at night, beginning on the evening of the fifteenth, as the sun sets.

2. On this night—marked as the start of the festival and the beginning of joy—Israel celebrated the Passover in Egypt while the forces of Mastêmâ were unleashed to strike down the firstborn across Egypt, from Pharaoh's household to the lowliest servant and their cattle.
3. The LORD gave a sign: any house marked with the blood of a lamb on its doorposts would be passed over, sparing those within, as the blood served as a protective sign.
4. The LORD's forces obeyed this command, passing by all the homes of the Israelites so that no harm came to any soul, whether human or animal, within those houses.
5. The plague was severe in Egypt, and there was weeping and mourning in every Egyptian household, with no family untouched by loss.
6. Meanwhile, Israel ate the Passover lamb, drank wine, praised, and thanked the LORD, ready to leave the yoke of Egypt and its oppressive bondage.
7. Remember this day for all your life, and observe it each year on its designated date, without delaying or shifting it from day to day or month to month.
8. This is a lasting ordinance, recorded on the heavenly tablets, that all Israel shall keep every year, without end, throughout their generations.
9. Anyone who is free from uncleanness and is nearby, yet fails to observe the Passover, to bring an offering, and to eat and drink before the LORD on this appointed day, will be cut off. Such a person must bear the guilt of neglecting the LORD's offering.
10. Let Israel celebrate the Passover at its fixed time on the fourteenth day of the first month, between the evening portions of the day—from the third part of the day until the third part of the night
11. For two parts are given to daylight and one part to evening.
12. It must not be sacrificed during the daytime but rather in the evening, and it should be eaten until the third part of the night. Any remaining meat after this time should be burned.
13. They must not cook the lamb with water or eat it raw; it must be roasted over the fire and eaten with care, including its head, organs, and feet. No bones are to be broken, as this symbolizes the unbroken unity of Israel.
14. For this reason, the LORD commanded that no bone be broken during Passover, emphasizing the fixed day of this festival, with no shifting from its appointed time.
15. Command Israel to observe Passover throughout all generations, every year, on its designated day, as a lasting memorial before the LORD, ensuring no plague strikes those who celebrate it faithfully.
16. Passover is not to be observed outside the sanctuary of the LORD.
17. All Israel must gather at the sanctuary on its appointed day.
18. When Israel enters the land of Canaan and establishes the LORD's Dwelling Place within one of their tribes, they shall celebrate Passover there until the LORD's sanctuary is built in the land.

19. Once the house of the LORD is established in their inheritance, Israel willgo there and sacrifice the Passover lamb at sunset, at the third part of the day.
20. They shall offer its blood at the altar's threshold and place its fat upon the altar fire, eating the roasted lamb within the sacred court.
21. Passover is not to be celebrated within city gates or in any location except at the Dwelling Place of the LORD, where His Name resides, ensuring Israel remains faithful to Him.
22. Moses, command Israel to keep the Passover laws as they were given, instructing them each year regarding its date and the Feast of Unleavened Bread. For seven days, they shall eat unleavened bread, observing the festival and bringing daily offerings of joy before the LORD on His altar.
23. Israel celebrated this festival upon leaving Egypt and continued to observe it until they reached the wilderness of Shur, completing the observance on the seashore.

Chapter 50

1. After giving this law, I revealed to you the days of the Sabbaths while you were in the wilderness of Zin, situated between Elim and Sinai.
2. I explained the Sabbaths of the land on Mount Sinai and introduced the jubilee years, which are marked by Sabbaths of years, but I did not reveal the exact year until you enter the land that you are to possess.
3. While you dwell in the land, it will also observe its Sabbaths, and you will recognize the jubilee years.
4. For this reason, I established for you cycles of years, week-years, and jubilees. There have been forty-nine jubilees from the days of Adam until now, plus one week and two years. Another forty years remain for you to learn the commandments of the LORD before crossing the Jordan to enter Canaan from the west.
5. These jubilees will continue until Israel is fully cleansed from all guilt, impurity, sin, and error, and they will dwell securely in the land. From that time forward, there will be no adversary or evil presence, and the land will remain pure forever.
6. I have recorded the command regarding the Sabbaths for you, along with all the judgments and laws related to it.
7. You will work for six days, but the seventh day is a Sabbath dedicated to the LORD your God. On that day, you are to do no work, nor are your sons, servants, animals, or any foreigners among you.
8. Anyone who docs work on the Sabbath will face death. This includes those who desecrate the day by engaging in activities such as lying with a spouse, embarking on a journey, buying or selling, drawing water that wasn't prepared on the sixth day, or carrying burdens from their tent or house.
9. The only permissible activity on the Sabbath is to consume what has been prepared on the sixth day, to eat, drink, rest, and honor the LORD for this festival day, a holy day for Israel among their days forever.

10. Great is the honor the LORD has bestowed upon Israel, allowing them to eat, drink, and rest on this holy day, free from the labor of mankind, except for the burning of incense and the bringing of offerings and sacrifices before the LORD on appointed days and Sabbaths.
11. Only this work may be done in the LORD's sanctuary on the Sabbath, to offer atonement for Israel through sacrifice, as a continual memorial that is pleasing to the LORD, as commanded.
12. Anyone who works on the Sabbath, goes on a journey, tills the soil, lights a fire, rides an animal, travels by sea, strikes or kills anything, slaughters a creature, catches animals, birds, or fish, fasts, or wages war on the Sabbath:
13. Whoever does any of these things on the Sabbath will face death. This is to ensure that the sons of Israel observe the Sabbaths in accordance with the commandments related to the land's Sabbaths, as it is written in the tablets given to Me, so I might record the laws governing the seasons and their designated days. The account of the division of days is now complete.